THE CORRESPONDENCE OF

W. E. B. DU BOIS

VOLUME II   SELECTIONS, 1934–1944

THE CORRESPONDENCE OF

W. E. B. DU BOIS

VOLUME II SELECTIONS, 1934–1944

EDITED BY HERBERT APTHEKER

UNIVERSITY OF MASSACHUSETTS PRESS—Amherst

Copyright © 1976 by
The University of Massachusetts Press
Paperback edition with corrections, 1997
All rights reserved
Printed in the United States of America
LC 72-90496
ISBN 0-87023-132-4 (cloth); ISBN 1-55849-104-X

Library of Congress Cataloging in Publication Data

Du Bois, William Edward Burghardt, 1868–1963.
  The correspondence of W. E. B. Du Bois.

  Includes bibliographical references.
  CONTENTS: v. 1. Selections, 1877–1934.—v. 2. Selections, 1934–1944.
—v. 3. Selections, 1944–1963.
  1. Du Bois, William Edward Burghardt, 1868–1963. 2. Afro-Americans—
Correspondence. 3. Intellectuals—United States—Correspondence. I. Aptheker,
Herbert, 1915–   ed,
E185.97.D73A4   1973   301.24'2'0924 [B]   72-90496

British Library Cataloguing in Publication data are available.

∞ The paper used in this publication meets the minimum requirements of the
American National Standard for Information Sciences—Permanence of Paper for
Printed Library Materials, ANSI Z39.48-1984.

GRATEFUL ACKNOWLEDGMENT is extended to the following for permission to print their letters: Sadie T. M. Alexander; Alexander Alland; Andrew J. Allison; Charles Angoff; Roger N. Baldwin; Theodore M. Berry; Joseph A. Brandt; Sherman Briscoe; Gordon Carroll; Cyril Clemens; Merle Curti; Thomas E. Drake; Shirley Graham Du Bois; John Farrar; Ruth Anna Fisher; John Hope Franklin; Ralph Friedman; Ann Fagan Ginger; Marshall Gray; Archie Casely-Hayford; Augustus M. Kelley; Frank W. Klingberg; Metz T. P. Lochard; Rayford W. Logan; Benjamin E. Mays; Margaret Mead; Broadus Mitchell; Gunnar Myrdal; Kenneth Wiggins Porter; A. Philip Randolph; Wilson Record; Anne Cooke Reid; Sherman D. Scruggs; Joseph Semper; William Sloane; Hugh H. Smythe; Irving Stone; J. W. Studebaker; Frank E. Taylor; Robert C. Weaver; Edward Weeks; Donald West; Roy Wilkins.

Grateful acknowledgment for permission to publish is also extended to: Mrs. Frederick Lewis Allen for the letter of Frederick Lewis Allen; Franziska Boas for the letters of Franz Boas; Mrs. Malcolm Bryan for the letter of Malcolm Bryan; Edward Tatnall Canby for the letter of Henry Seidel Canby; Mrs. Rufus E. Clement for the letters of Rufus E. Clement; Maurice C. Clifford for the letter of Carrie W. Clifford; Charlotte Crawford Watkins for the letter of George W. Crawford; Adelaide Hill Gulliver for the letter of Otelia Cromwell; Mrs. Countee Cullen for the letters of Countee Cullen; Catherine Embree Harris for the letters of Edwin R. Embree; Mrs. E. Franklin for the letters of E. Franklin Frazier; Ida Repole for the letters of Amy Jacques Garvey; Mrs. Gordon B. Hancock for the letter of Gordon B. Hancock; Harcourt Brace Jovanovich, Inc., for the letters of Alfred Harcourt; *Harper's Magazine* for the letter of the editors; John Hope II for the letter of John Hope; Harold Ober Associates for the letters of Langston Hughes; Dorothy K. Hunton for the letters of Addie W. Hunton; David L. Jones for the letters of Thomas E. Jones; Carnegie Corporation of New York for the letters of F. P. Keppel; W. M. Laski for the letter of Harold J. Laski; Mercantile-Safe Deposit and Trust Company for the letter of H. L. Mencken; Peter Smith for the letter of Howard W. Odum; Theodore O. Kingsbury for the letter of Mary White Ovington; William Pickens III for the letters of William Pickens; Sylvester Hall for the letter of A. S. Pinkett; Fred D. Banks for the letters of H. J. Pinkett; Harvard Law School Library for the letter of Roscoe Pound; I. M. Sedgwick for the letter of Ellery Sedgwick; Marjorie A. Shepard for the letters of James E. Shepard; Helen H. Shotwell for the letters of James T. Shotwell; Edna May Stevenson for the letter of R. J. Simmons; Paula Snelling for the letters of Lillian Smith; H. H. Zand for the letters of Arthur B. Spingarn; The Papers of Henry L. Stimson, Yale University Library, for the letter of Henry L. Stimson; Anson Phelps

Stokes, Jr., for the letters of Anson Phelps Stokes; Albert G. Redpath for the letters of Frank Tannenbaum; Michael Lewis for the letter of Dorothy Thompson; Mabel V. Johnson for the letters of Robert L. Vann; Mrs. Karl R. Wallace for the letters of Karl R. Wallace; Gordon H. Ward for the letter of Harry F. Ward; Poppy Cannon White for the letters of Walter White.

CONTENTS

1935

1937

1938

1939

1942

1944

Contents   [xvii]

INTRODUCTION

Editorial principles affirmed in the introduction to the first volume of the
correspondence of W. E. B. Du Bois have guided the work on this second volume.
Again, purely personal letters have been excluded and, in presenting those having
larger historical consequence, an effort was made to choose representative examples
and so avoid repetition. As was true in the first volume, correspondents or their heirs
were almost always generous in granting permission for the publishing of letters;
again, as then, only one person chose not to give permission.

While the correspondence is very voluminous and space was a major consideration,
the letters published are given, in every case, in full. Obvious typographical slips are
corrected, usually silently, though in a few special instances attention is called to the
change.

Occasionally, those kind enough to comment on the first volume expressed
disappointment that the work represented selections; no one has been more
disappointed than I that it has not yet been possible to obtain the resources to do
more. As it is, I stated in the introduction to the first volume that two volumes were
contemplated; I am happy to be able to write now that a third volume, which will deal
with the years from 1945 until Du Bois's death in the summer of 1963, is being
prepared.

The decade in this volume forms a unit in Du Bois's life, since throughout it he was
a teacher at Atlanta University; the ten-year period may be characterized as a kind of
return by Du Bois to his first love—scholarship and education. Having left Atlanta
University in 1910 to help found and then lead the NAACP, in this decade he left the
NAACP and returned to Atlanta. The unity of the period is retained through Du Bois's
having learned at the end of 1944, in his seventy-sixth year, of his dismissal from the
university, and through his subsequent return to the NAACP. Considering the
interrelatedness of Du Bois's activities during the decade, it seemed logical to organize
the volume simply according to the years of its span.

Of course, with Du Bois, the activities of any ten-year period were as extensive as
those marking the full lifetime of most people. During this time he was the author of
three volumes, one of which was the monumental *Black Reconstruction* (1935), another
a survey of the entire Black historical experience, *Black Folk Then and Now* (1939), and
the third his first autobiography, *Dusk of Dawn* (1940). He contributed a weekly
column to the *Pittsburgh Courier* from February 1936 through January 1938 and one to
the *Amsterdam News* from October 1939 through October 1944.

Du Bois also was engaged for endless hours in supervising the preparation of what
amounted to an outline for an Encyclopedia of the Negro (1945), of which

tremendous project he was the chief editor. Further, he founded in 1940 the quarterly magazine *Phylon*, issued at his university, and edited it until 1944.

In addition, Du Bois contributed reviews and essays to such periodicals as the *New York Herald-Tribune, Yale Review, Current History, Journal of Negro Education, American Scholar, New Republic* and the *American Journal of Sociology*. His travels were especially extensive, including not only his annual lecture tours taking him through much of the United States, but also rather lengthy visits to Germany, the Soviet Union, China, Japan, and Haiti. And all the time, he taught several classes and headed the sociology department at his university—and found the energy to conduct a correspondence with hundreds of people throughout the world, a selection of which is before the reader.

The decade is that of the Great Depression, Hitlerism, the aggressions against China and Ethiopia, the counterrevolution in Spain, the strengthening of the U.S.S.R., and the coming of World War II. In the United States these events had enormous impact, of course; the decade saw also the New Deal, the rise of the CIO, and significant developments in the Black liberation movement. Du Bois was an actor in all these events and, in turn, they reacted upon him. Especially notable in this period was Du Bois's great emphasis upon economic problems and questions of Black survival and organization, and his mounting sympathy towards Marxism.

I acknowledge with deep appreciation the assistance given me by many institutions and people. Some are identified within the text, but I wish here to thank the following for courtesy and help: Ann Fagan Ginger of Berkeley, California; Michael Yellin, on the staff of the *Michigan Daily* at the University of Michigan in Ann Arbor; Alice E. Station of the Omaha Public Library in Nebraska; Professor Raymond Wolters of the University of Delaware; Professor John Hope Franklin of the University of Chicago; Professor Kenneth W. Porter of the University of Oregon. At various times, I have had the help of several younger people, including Judith N. Kerr, Anthony Flood, Hilmar Jensen and, especially, Hugh T. Murray, Jr.

With this volume, as with the first, I was able to lean upon the knowledge of Professor Sidney Kaplan of the University of Massachusetts and of Ernest Kaiser of the Schomburg Collection, New York Public Library. Both read the entire manuscript with diligence and both caught serious mistakes and made invaluable suggestions. Of course, responsibility for all shortcomings that may still mar this volume, all judgments in editing and selecting, belong to the editor; all errors that may remain are my fault alone.

One of the great pleasures in this work has been the association with the staff of the Press producing it. Its director, Leone Stein, has continued as a source of encouragement; its editors, Malcolm Call and Janis Bolster, have gone far beyond normal duties in helping make this work possible.

Dr. Du Bois's widow, Shirley Graham Du Bois, has helped sustain this project from the beginning and her faith in it is deeply appreciated.

In the entire effort—beginning back in 1946—my wife, Fay P. Aptheker, has been collaborator, corrector, adviser and indispensable partner.

Herbert Aptheker

THE CORRESPONDENCE OF

W. E. B. DU BOIS

VOLUME II   SELECTIONS, 1934–1944

*Footnotes to letters are keyed numerically,
beginning with 1 each new letter.
Footnotes to headnotes are keyed
symbolically,* * † ‡

1934

Since pre-world *War I days, a comrade in struggle with Du Bois was Carrie W. Clifford (Mrs. W. H. Clifford), of Ohio and Washington, D.C. She was part of the Niagara Movement, one of the founders of the* naacp, *and a president of the National Association of Colored Women. After months of rumors, Du Bois's decision to sever all connection with the* naacp *and the* Crisis *became final with his letter of resignation, dated 26 June 1934 and published in the August issue of the* Crisis *(41: 245–46). Mrs. Clifford wrote to him an undated letter.*

Highland Beach, Md.

Dr. W. E. B. Du Bois,
My very dear friend:

I am profoundly saddened! Your letter of resignation or rather your explanatory letter has torn my heart.

Our beautiful n.a.a.c.p. which you built up and developed so painfully through 25 years and more!

How could you leave us? And yet, I see it caused you pain. Did it have to be? At the end of my life I am saying "All is vanity."

All the wonderful dreams of accomplishment and achievement—all gone.

Poor Race, what now?

We have followed you, we have worked, we have tried. And the little house of cards is wrecked!

I cannot express myself.

With faith as ever,

Sincerely yours,
Carrie W. Clifford

p. s. Am here in the country without ink, pen or energy.

Reflective of the many letters Du Bois received following the announcement of his resignation from the naacp *was one sent by Lady Kathleen (Harvey) Simon. She was the author of* Slavery, *published in London in 1929 and reviewed, somewhat critically, by Du Bois in the* Crisis *38 (April 1930): 129. This led to a correspondence (see volume one of this work, pp. 422–23) and later to a meeting, when Lady Kathleen visited the United States in 1930. She was the wife of Sir John Simon, whose distinguished public career included service as attorney general during World War I and as chancellor of the exchequer in the 1930s.*

Lady Kathleen's letter was addressed to Du Bois at the New York City office of the Crisis, *and forwarded to him at Atlanta University, where he was by then serving as professor and head of the sociology department.*

London, 3rd September 1934.

Dear Mr. Du Bois,

I am on the eve of leaving for Brazil as I have been very ill and the sea voyage is supposed to set me up. I cannot leave England without writing to you on what I read in the last number of the Crisis, and to express my intense regret that you have severed your connection with the National Association for the Advancement of Colored People. It owes its life to you and we of another race, who take an interest in your race, have felt that you were the great inspiration for the betterment of your people. I do not know what you are doing now, but would you write and tell me if you believe that the segregation of your people to build up their strength by themselves is what was the trouble? I may be wrong in thinking this was the reason, but I do believe you are right. You have all suffered so much at the hands of other races, that, being a very independent spirited Irish woman, I do not feel that you would ever rise to the heights to which you are able if you try either to assimilate or work with the rest, especially in America which despises you. *Do* write to me and tell me.

I shall carry with me all my life a remembrance of that interview I had when I was in America some years ago—a happy memory of meeting a great man. You always knew how much I admired your book "Dark Water" and "Souls of Black Folk," and I do not wish, as far as I am concerned, for you to pass out of my life because you have merely severed your connection with the N.A.A.C.P.

My kind regards to Walter White.

Yours very sincerely,
(Lady) Kathleen Simon

Atlanta, Georgia, October 1, 1934

Lady Kathleen Simon,
My dear Madam:

I appreciate your kind note of September 3 and regret to hear of your illness. I hope by the time this reaches you you will be restored to good health.

I leave *The Crisis* with great regret but I am more and more sure it was the best thing to do. There is a splendid work to be done here at Atlanta University, and I hope that some day if you are near here with any of your friends, you will look in upon us. Today, the first slum clearance project in the United States was begun by the Secretary of Interior just off the campus. It involves replacing miserable dwellings with a Two Million Dollar re-building project.[1]

Very sincerely yours,
W. E. B. Du Bois.

1. The ground-breaking ceremonies for the housing projects—there were two, one for Black families near the university and another for white families, known as the Techwood Drive

In addition to letters from individuals following news of his resignation, Du Bois received letters from several branches of the NAACP commending his services. An example is one from the Duluth, Minnesota, branch, signed by its president, the Reverend Robert Jackson Simmons (1877–1957).

Duluth, Minn., September 27th, 1934

Dear Sir:–

By this note the Duluth Branch N.A.A.C.P. wishes to express to you its hearty commendation for the fine work you have done for the advancement of the race since your early public activities. We have observed the same with great interest.

As a teacher and journalist you have been a fearless champion of our cause politically, economically and socially.

We remember with much pleasure your visit to Duluth some years ago. Both races profited by that visit. The leading white citizens here still speak of your scholarly attainments and ability as a leader—not only for our race, but for any people.

The information that you have severed your connection with the N.A.A.C.P. was a severe shock to us, as we already are missing your inspiring articles in the Crisis. We now feel that the race and all others who read the Crisis will be much poorer from a literary standpoint, also from the point of race understanding by the absence of your monthly message.

Frankly, we feel that your loss to the cause is next to irreparable, and wish you would reconsider and return.

We have followed with interest, the various discussions on segregation, and have tried, along with the rest to arrive at a safe interpretation of proper attitude and procedure. Certainly, it is a difficult proposition to solve, and, from our viewpoint, will be for many years. But at present, we believe you have hit upon the sanest and most practical course for a peaceable and permanent solution of our case, viz, work out our salvation behind the barriers of prejudice which all the efforts of previous years have failed to break down.

With every good wish for your success and hoping to hear from you at convenience,

Yours very truly,
R. J. Simmons
President.

In 1931, the Du Bois Literary Prize was announced in the Crisis *38 (April):137–38. Each subsequent year a sum of one thousand dollars was to be given for the best work by a Black writer*

project—were actually held, with Secretary of the Interior Harold Ickes officiating, on 29 September 1934. Their combined cost was over four million dollars. There is an unsigned account of "The Atlanta Housing Project"—surely written by Du Bois—in the *Crisis* 41 (June 1934):174–75, and full accounts of the ceremonies in the *New York Times*, 30 September 1934, and the *New York Amsterdam News*, 6 October 1934.

in fiction, nonfiction, and poetry—in that rotation. This prize was endowed by Mrs. Edward Roscoe Mathews (nee Loulie Shaw Albee), a white woman originally from Massachusetts whose family had an abolitionist and literary background.

The secretary of the awards committee was William Stanley Braithwaite (1878–1962), a professor at Atlanta University and a widely known poet and anthologist, who in 1918 had been the Spingarn Medalist. From his summer home, he wrote Du Bois in connection with his committee duties.

Arlington Heights, Mass.,
August 15th, 1934

My dear Dr. Du Bois:—

It is imperative that the Candidates for the 1934 Award of the Du Bois Literary Prize, for the best book of poetry by a Negro poet, be submitted by the Nominating Committee.

The following five books are available for consideration, and it is hoped that the committee has made acquaintance with them; if not, the secretary upon request, will submit a copy of such titles the Members have not seen:[1]

Trumpet in the New Moon, by Welborn Victor Jenkins

Southern Road, by Sterling Brown

Black, by Benjamin Gardner

Dundo, by Cleveland Negro Youth

Desert Sands, by Henry B. Wilkinson

May I urge the Members of the Committee to submit their nominations at the earliest possible date?

It is herewith suggested that the Members also when submitting their candidates, name their selections of the three judges to be invited to serve in making the decision of the book to be given the Award. In accordance with the custom each Member will submit three names.

In behalf of the Committee may I urge the immediate attention of the Members to the performance of this service for the distinguished ideals and purposes of the Du Bois Literary Prize Awards?

Very sincerely yours,
William Stanley Braithwaite

1. The books were: Welborn V. Jenkins, *Trumpet in the New Moon, and Other Poems,* foreword by E. H. Webster (Boston: The Peabody Press, 1934), 62 pp.

Sterling A. Brown, *Southern Road,* with drawings by E. Simms Campbell (New York: Harcourt, Brace and Co., 1932), 135 pp.

Benjamin F. Gardner, *Black* (Caldwell, Idaho: The Caxton Printers, 1933), 79 pp.

Clarence F. Dryson and James H. Robinson, eds., *Dundo: Anthology of Poetry by Cleveland Negro Youth* (Cleveland: The January Club, 1931), 76 pp.

Henry B. Wilkinson, *Desert Sands: A Volume of Verse Touching Various Topics* (London: A. H. Stockwell, 1933), 108 pp.

In addition to Braithwaite and Du Bois, the committee members were Oliver La Farge, Lewis Gannett, and James Weldon Johnson. The book by Sterling Brown received the award.

Braithwaite, not having received a response from Du Bois, wrote again on 29 September 1934 urging a reply, which came as follows.

Atlanta, Ga., November 2, 1934

My dear Mr. Braithwaite:

I am very apologetic for not having answered your letters concerning the Du Bois Prize for poetry. To tell the truth, I think that the output for last year has been very small and unimportant and only Sterling Brown's poems ought in my opinion to be considered. Please count on me as voting for any Board of Judges which the majority of the others agree to.

With best regards

Very sincerely yours,
W. E. B. Du Bois

The National Negro Congress was an organization of significance in the late 1930s; an early suggestion for this kind of organization came in 1934 from Harrison S. Jackson (1903–63), an attorney in New York City. Jackson, born in Charleston, West Virginia, graduated from Howard University in 1926, receiving a law degree from Fordham three years later and a doctorate in juridical science from New York University in 1931. He was to be an attorney for Representative Adam Clayton Powell and at the time of his death was a civil court judge in New York City.

New York City, August 18, 1934.

Dr. W. E. B. Du Bois

My Dear Sir:

Recently I gave to the Negro press a plan termed *National Negro Congress* which I believe would promulgate racial solidarity and strength along our political, social, religious and economical lines.

This plan was published in many of our foremost newspapers and in some instances it received favorable editorials.

Briefly, the plan is this:

1. To have colored representation from each State in the Union, to meet each year in a Congress and pass upon any and all problems confronting the Negro Race.

2. To make Rules and Regulations (which could not legally but morally be enforced) affecting and guiding the best and most advantageous course for our group to follow.

As to how the group would be elected: I propose the following:

(a) Cities, towns, villages and hamlets comprising state delegate districts would vote for and elect a state delegate from each district to the state convention, to be held annually or biennially.

(b) The state delegates in the convention assembled would in turn elect its national

Congressmen or Congresswomen. The number of representatives from each state can easily be worked out.

When all of these representatives have assembled in a National Negro Congress, and measures, edicts, rules and laws passed, and the positions voted upon and assumed as regards to various racial problems, then, all of this, will in my judgment mean collective leadership, and I do believe, that because of the various and diversified individual opinions as to "Where Shall We Go," there is only one way out, because of the lack of cooperation and racial consciousness, and that is, Collective Leadership, brought about by the proposed National Negro Congress. It is my firm belief, that if the colored people of a state vote for its favorite son or daughter, then, by moral suasion they will support and abide by the edicts, rules and positions assumed by their Congressmen.[1]

To me, this is a big step and I would not wish to enter into this gigantic task without the aid of seasoned and informed opinions and cooperation. Would you be so kind as to write me your frank opinion of this plan as to its feasibility and any criticisms of the approach by details of this plan. I shall appreciate an early reply from you.

> Yours very sincerely,
> Harrison S. Jackson

P. S. May I give excerpts from your remarks to the press?

> New York City, August 22, 1934

Mr. Harrison S. Jackson
My dear Sir:

The matter of a National Negro Congress has been discussed dozens of times during the last fifty years. I do not think that the time has yet come when such a movement is practical or advisable.

> Very sincerely yours,
> W. E. B. Du Bois

Du Bois's resignation from the NAACP *reflected dissatisfaction with traditional forms of Black protest and struggle; such dissatisfaction, a marked feature of the depression decade, is suggested by the letter from attorney Jackson. Still another facet of that dissatisfaction, applying especially to youth, is indicated in a letter from a young Black dentist, Dr. Phillips Brooks, practicing in Brooklyn, New York.**

1. The plan is strikingly similar to the government of Black people in the United States in Sutton Griggs's *Imperium in Imperio*, published by the author in 1899 and reissued, with a preface by Hugh M. Gloster, in 1969 by Arno Press–The New York Times. Gloster remarks that Sutton's novel was "probably more widely circulated among Negroes than the works of Charles W. Chesnutt and Paul Laurence Dunbar." Griggs's work was known by Du Bois.

* This letter is to be seen in the context of a National Conference of [Black] Students held in Chicago 1–5 August 1934. The conference was called by the National Student Club of Chicago,

Brooklyn, N.Y., August 18, 1934

Dear Sir:

A small group here in New York City, in which I am included, has undertaken the task of launching a Negro Youth Movement.

Our vision is not fully formed but we at least realize the need for economic and social development among our people and intend to direct our energies toward achieving this. We consider that your recent stand on the race question is most sound if we correctly interpret your statements on the subject to mean that the race must expect development from within rather than from without its environs. We consider this intra-racial development the only logical and sure means of achieving full blown growth socially, economically or any other way.

Our group has great admiration for you sir, and hold you in high esteem because we are not unmindful of the tedious labyrinths through which you have journeyed for so long a time in quest of equality for our people. Equality comparable to that of any other group of human beings in the world who are free and unfettered.

We intend to adapt your race philosophy and Mr. J. A. Rogers' anthropologic data and psychology expressed in his noble work "From Superman to Man"[1] as a composite nucleus for our organization's intellectual growth.

We ask the privilege of acquainting you with our progress from time to time and we make a unanimous bid for your moral support.

I trust that you are enjoying the best of health and happiness in this the mellow afternoon of your life and remain,

Yours very truly,
Phillips Brooks[2]

New York City, August 25, 1934

Dr. Phillips Brooks
My dear Sir:

I am interested in all efforts of Negro youth to realize their opportunities and take active part in the development of the Negro race. I should be glad to know of anything that your group does from time to time.

Very sincerely yours,
W. E. B. Du Bois

which had two hundred Black college student and graduate members; its president was Ulysses Keys. The presiding officer of the conference was Harriet Glover, a Chicago public school teacher. See the article on this conference by Ulysses Keys in the *Crisis* 41 (September 1934): 266, 275.

1. Joel A. Rogers, *From "Superman" to Man* (Chicago: J. A. Rogers, 1917; 4th ed., New York: Lenox Publishing Co.; 5th ed., New York: J. A. Rogers Publications, 1941).

2. The *Brooklyn Daily Eagle,* 10 February 1953, noted that "Dr. Phillips Brooks, Negro civic leader," would participate in a Negro History Week celebration to be held in Brooklyn; no more recent references to Brooks have been found.

Mrs. L.D. Shivery, a teacher at the Booker Washington High School in Atlanta, was at this time a graduate student under Du Bois. Du Bois had known the Shivery family for years and was godfather to a daughter, Henrietta, whom he assisted in the summer of 1934 in gaining a position as a teacher in the public school system in Meridian, Mississippi.

Certain exchanges of letters between Du Bois and the young Henrietta illuminate aspects of his nature and some of his ideas concerning the duties and role of a teacher. They tell something, too, of the problems facing the young lady in her first employment in Mississippi. The exchange begins with a letter from Du Bois, written from his summer residence in New York City to Miss Shivery in Atlanta, just before she was to leave for Meridian.

New York City, September 7, 1934

My dear Henrietta:

I am writing this while I think of it because it is important advice.

When a person goes to work and for the first time earns money, he feels tremendously rich. So that he ought to take certain precautions in order not to overspend. You did not tell me what your salary is. Suppose it is $800 for an eight-months' year. The first thing you must do is to divide the $800 by 12 and not by 8. Then calculate that you are really earning $66 a month and not $100 a month. Then, you must carefully calculate your expenses, especially travel from Meridian home and back, as many times as you may have to go. Then from the remainder, subtract the amount that you must spend for board and lodging. After you have reduced your income by these subtractions, you will know how much you can afford to spend for clothes. You must get in the habit each month of saving something, no matter how little it is, and do not run bills at stores. Pay cash.

You won't follow this advice but you ought to.

With best love

W. E. B. Du Bois

Meridian, Miss., Oct. 11, 1934

Dear D. D.:

I haven't forgotten how to write. I just haven't felt like doing any thing. My foot is just about well and I am able to navigate from my house to the school by walking very slow.

I must say something about this school to some body. *System* there is none. Principal quite backward. Believe it or not you can count the degrees in this school on one hand. The people here are all quite backward and dumb. Sometimes I feel like dying.

Lets forget all of that shop. What have you been doing this fall. Please write me something encouraging. I've actually taken your advice about the money. Kiss yourself for me.

Lovingly,
Henrietta

Atlanta, Ga., October 16, 1934

My dear Dimples:

I am glad to hear from you and hope that your foot is really all right. Be careful of it and do not neglect it or overuse it.

You must view your school with charity. Remember that Mississippi in practically all respects is the most backward state in the nation, and that the colored people there have had wretchedly little opportunity for advancement. Remember that the principal of a school like that is between two fires; he must satisfy the white folks first of all, or lose his job. He must satisfy the colored folks, and he must satisfy his own con-science, if he has one. Under the present circumstances, it's a pretty hard job: and he can use a good deal more sympathy than he gets. Try, therefore, to be charitable. Your real duty is, of course, to the children, and they are entirely deserving. You ought to put your whole life and energy in stirring them out of their lethargy and carelessness and make them get off to school and continue their education.

Remember that the person who does a good job in Meridian will have all the better chance to do it in a bigger place. At any rate, feeling like dying isn't going to help things a bit. It certainly isn't going to help the school, and I doubt if it does you any good.

Buck up and get hold of some enthusiasm and use it. At least you are making your own way and giving your mother a fighting chance to do something beside pay debts. That's a good debt,[1] isn't it?

Thank you for taking my advice. That's of course an invitation to send more. With much love.

W. E. B. Du Bois

Meridian, Miss., Nov. 8, 1934

Dear Dr. Du Bois:

I know you think that I have been negligent about writing, but I havent. I have been waiting to write you a letter with out a mistake[2] so that you could see what I have been doing with my spare time. It seems that I will never reach that stage so I am taking a chance on sending you this one.

I have quit grumbling and am quite satisfied with lot. I am quite willing to agree that it could be much worse. Last week I had quite an accident in my room. While I was out a small boy took my water jar and split his class-mates head open. I am told that that is a common occurence around here. If they dont have a fight a day isnt complete. I know that a common [comma] should be here some where but I dont know where it is found on this blooming unlettered machine. If my teacher should see me writing this letter she would tell me to wait until I shouldnt make mistakes. That will be to long.

---

1. As in the original; probably "deal" is meant.
2. This is the first typed letter and, as the reader will see, the errors recur.

And I [how] has my Godfather been geting along. It seems ages since I have seen you. How is Mamma she dosent write often. It seems that all of our bad luck is coming at onee, also all of my mistakes. Have you seen any good football games this year. Down here in this wilderness we dont know what they are. I have seen some very good pictures, The Barrets of Wimpole Street, Mrs. Wiggs of the Cabbage Patch, and Belle of the Ninties.

Other than going to pictures I have been in my little cubby hole. I may come home for the holidays, I mean Thanksgiving if we have long enough. Over-look all mistakes please. Remember always that I love you evan though my letters dont come often. Many kisses for you.

> Affectionately yours,
> Dimples

Atlanta, Ga., November 19, 1934

My dear Dimples:

I am very glad to know that you are reasonably satisfied. The matter of disciplining children and especially growing youth is no easy thing. When you are dealing with grownups you can withdraw in yourself and impelled by curiosity they will usually come across and draw you out. With children that simply won't do. When you take refuge in your own soul you lose them entirely. They do not see you and you do not see them. On the other hand, they are singularly sensitive to a frank and honest camaraderie. A little friendly smile or pat will do wonders with even recalcitrant youth. At any rate, you've got to build a bridge and a strong one between yourself and the pupils and then with a firm hand you must rule them. It isn't an easy job but it can and must be done and it spells for the young teacher success or failure.

I hope your wounds are quite all right and if not, you are not neglecting them. I am going to be away Thanksgiving unfortunately so I shall not see you. I had hoped to drive to Meridian but it's a terrible distance from Atlanta and I may not be able to, but I shall see you some of these days.

With best love

> Very sincerely yours
> W. E. B. Du Bois

George W. Crawford was—along with Du Bois and William Monroe Trotter—one of the handful of founders of the modern civil rights movement. He was born in Alabama in 1877, moved to New Haven, Connecticut, in 1900, and graduated from the Yale Law School three years later. He practiced law in that city until his death at the age of 94 in 1972, and held various public offices in New Haven. He was one of the founders of the Niagara Movement in 1905 and of the NAACP and was a member of the NAACP board until 1933. The two men were friends in good times and bad for some sixty years.

Atlanta, Ga., September 20, 1934

My dear Crawford:

I am kicking myself for not having seen you this summer. I was persuaded again to stay for summer school in order to help out the demand for graduate teaching. We had about 100 graduate students. I did not get to New York until late in July, and then hung around close to the city waiting for proof of my book to come. It did not, as a matter of fact, begin to come in until August 20, and then.I was working night and day to finish it, always promising myself a trip to New Haven, but it didn't come off. Meantime, how are you and how's the good health and the family? My best regards.

The work here is going well, or starting well. My book on Reconstruction is in print, and will come out, I trust, sometime in November. Please begin to save money for it. It will be over 500 pages and cost a small fortune.[1] It will be a lovely Christmas present for a number of your friends.

With best regards

Very sincerely yours
W. E. B. Du Bois

New Haven, Conn., October 1st, 1934

Dear Du Bois:

I am glad to have your recent note. You will not expect me to accept at its face value that old bromide about planning to run up to New Haven and being prevented by unexpected contingencies, etc. etc.

Really, I am glad that you are going to continue at Atlanta. You ought to welcome the opportunity to follow pursuits more in keeping with your tastes and to be comfortable in them. Having been in the thick of controversy and the fighting out of race issues for the last thirty years, you deserve an opportunity for rest and repose which you should embrace.

We will be glad to see the new book, especially to note what you have been able to do with certain pet theories of Mr. James Truslow Adams.[2]

The family all join me in sending their regards.

Sincerely yours,
George W. Crawford

1. The reference is to Du Bois's *Black Reconstruction: An Essay toward a History of the Part Which Black Folk Played in the Attempt to Reconstruct Democracy in America, 1860–1880* (New York: Harcourt, Brace and Co.). The 746-page book appeared in 1935.

2. The reference is almost certainly to James Truslow Adams's *America's Tragedy* (New York: Scribner's Sons, 1934), a study of the Reconstruction era in the tradition of Dunning-Fleming and as popularized in the late 1920s by Claude Bowers's *The Tragic Era*. A similar pro-Bourbon, racist bias—which even approved of the KKK—was revealed in volume two of Adams's *March of Democracy*, subtitled *From Civil War to World Power*, also published by Scribner's Sons in New York City in 1933—see its chapter 4. There is a scathing review of *America's Tragedy* by Du Bois's good friend Martha Gruening in the *New Republic* 84 (6 November 1935): 369–70.

One of the outstanding Black women activists of the early twentieth century was Addie W.
Hunton (1870–1943). Educated in the public schools of Boston and at City College in New York,
she served as a teacher in Alabama, a field organizer for the NAACP, *a leader in the Women's*
International League for Peace and Freedom, a fighter in the battle to end United States
occupation of Haiti, and a participant in the Pan-African movement. Her husband, mentioned
in the correspondence below, was William Alphaeus Hunton, a leading figure in YMCA *work.*
The question raised in Mrs. Hunton's two letters and the answer supplied by Du Bois are of
great interest.

New York City, Sept. 25, 1934

My dear Dr. Du Bois:

Will you be kind enough to give me the names of ten or fifteen white friends—men
or women—who you feel have been *most* outstanding in helping the progress of
colored people since Emancipation. This help may have been rendered either
financially or in some other positive way.

I shall be very grateful for this information and thank you in advance for the same.
With best wishes, I am

Very faithfully,
Addie W. Hunton

New York City [undated]

My Dear Dr. Du Bois:

Quite a long time ago, I requested your permission to use [as] the title of Mr.
Hunton's biography a name you had once given him—"Pioneer Prophet."[1] You very
kindly consented. It has been so long that I want to ask you again now that I am ready
to use it and assure you that I shall be happy to give you due credit.

Not so long ago I wrote you, enclosing self-addressed envelope, asking, if you
would kindly give me the names of a dozen or more men, who, in your opinion, have
been our greatest benefactors since the Civil War. I have wondered if my letter
reached you?

With deep respect and very sincere good wishes, I am

Faithfully,
A. W. Hunton

Atlanta, Ga., October 18, 1934

My dear Mrs. Hunton:

Answering your two letters of September 25 and the last one without date, I am
enclosing the names of ten persons who have in my opinion been of the greatest help
to the colored people since Emancipation.

1. Shortly after Hunton's death in 1916, Du Bois wrote a tribute to him in which this phrase
·occurred: *Crisis* 13 (January 1917): 119. Mrs. Hunton's biography of her husband was indeed
entitled *William Alphaeus Hunton: A Pioneer Prophet of Young Men* (New York: Association Press,
1938).

I shall be only too glad for you to use the term "Pioneer Prophet" in connection with your husband's biography.

With best regards

Very sincerely yours,
W. E. B. Du Bois

P. S. Tomorrow, if asked, I shall probably make quite a different list.
Enclosure 1.

Thaddeus Stevens
Charles Sumner
Erastus M. Cravath
[Edmund] Asa Ware
John Eaton
O. O. Howard
Thomas W. Higginson
Samuel C. Armstrong
Julius Rosenwald
Wendell Phillips[1]

Throughout his life, whenever he visited or lived in the South, Du Bois tried to avoid public transportation with its savage jim-crowism. Before World War I, he used a horse and carriage,

1. Stevens (1792–1868) and Sumner (1811–74) were leaders of Radical Reconstruction in the House and Senate, respectively; both men, in their personal and public lives, were principled foes of racism. Erastus Cravath (1833–1900), as a field secretary of the American Missionary Association, helped establish both Atlanta and Fisk Universities; he was the first president (1875) of Fisk and served there until his death, including the period when Du Bois was a student at Fisk. Edmund Asa Ware (1837–85) was a founder and first president of Atlanta University (1869–85). John Eaton (1829–1906), a brigadier general in the Civil War, actively assisted the so-called "contrabands" during that war and was an anti-racist superintendent of schools in Tennessee (1867–69) and an effective United States commissioner of education (1870–86). He later served as president of Marietta College and at the end of his life was inspector of education in Puerto Rico. Oliver Otis Howard (1830–1909), a major general in the Civil War, served for some time as chief commissioner of the Freedmen's Bureau; he was a founder of Howard University and its first president (1869–73). Thomas Wentworth Higginson (1823–1911), a Unitarian minister, was a militant abolitionist and friend of John Brown; during the Civil War he served as colonel of the First South Carolina Volunteers, made up of Black volunteers. His writings were widely read. Samuel C. Armstrong (1839–93) was a major general in the Civil War and the chief founder (in 1868) of Hampton Institute, which he headed until his death. He had decisive influence upon Booker T. Washington. Julius Rosenwald (1862–1932), head of Sears Roebuck, was responsible for the fund named for him, which contributed millions of dollars towards erecting schools and YMCA and YWCA buildings for Black youngsters in the South and in Northern ghettoes. Wendell Phillips (1811–84), a leading abolitionist, friend of John Brown, president of the American Abolitionist Society after the Civil War until the enactment of the Fifteenth Amendment, remained generally radical until his death. Du Bois's high school valedictorian speech was devoted to the life of Phillips, who had then recently died.

and thereafter an automobile—always providing himself with coveralls and tools in case of a breakdown south of the Mason-Dixon Line.* While teaching at Fisk and later at Atlanta University he walked to work and to stores, rather than using buses. But, of course, there were occasions when he had to use the railroads; the result would be the kind of letter given below.

Atlanta, Ga., November 17, 1934

Mr. E. E. Barry
Southern Railway System
My dear Sir:

I should be glad if you could secure me pullman accommodations from here to Washington, leaving on the 5:25 P.M. train, Wednesday, November 21.

I am a colored teacher at Atlanta University.

Very sincerely yours
W.E.B. Du Bois

Walter Francis White (1893–1955) was, of course, an outstanding leader of the NAACP, *serving as assistant secretary under James Weldon Johnson and succeeding him, in 1931, as secretary, a position White held until his death. To say that he and Du Bois did not get along well would be an understatement; indeed, of all Du Bois's personal relationships, that with White was probably most hostile. In public, however, and particularly in any action relevant to the movement against discrimination, their conduct always was "correct." The letter White sent to Du Bois in connection with the impending appearance of* Black Reconstruction *is exemplary. If Du Bois replied, no copy seems to have survived.*

New York City, October 5th, 1934
(Dictated October 4th)

My dear Dr. Du Bois:

I enclose self-explanatory copy of letter which I wrote Alfred Harcourt offering our aid in pushing Black Reconstruction. Miss Helen K. Taylor of Harcourt, Brace writes this morning saying that as soon as the definite date of publication, which they expect will be around the middle of November, is settled upon, they will get in touch with us to work out details of cooperation.

I send this to you so that if you have any additional suggestions of ways in which we can help you can let us know and we will be glad to do what we can. I am sure the book is going to have a great effect and we want to do everything we can to bring it to the attention of as many readers—and especially buyers—as possible.

Ever sincerely,
Walter White
Secretary.

---

* From 1900 to 1905 Du Bois was engaged in litigation against the Southern Railway on the basis of its jim-crow transportation; he was not successful—see volume one of the present work, pp. 46–47.

September 22nd, 1934 (Dictated September 20th)

[Enclosure]

Mr dear Mr. Harcourt:

I am writing to inform you that we will be very glad to do whatever we can to publicize Dr. Du Bois's *Black Reconstruction* which Harcourt, Brace is publishing this fall. Please let me know the date of publication as we can help through our press service through a review by Miss Ovington which we supply through this press service to some 225 colored newspapers as well as to a large list of individuals, and also through a review in the *Crisis*. I also may personally do a review of the book.[1]

Ever sincerely,
Walter White
Secretary

Though Harcourt, Brace announced Black Reconstruction *as among its publications for the fall of 1934, Du Bois was making changes in the page proofs as late as October and November 1934. The last of these was sent to Harcourt, Brace from Atlanta, Georgia, on 9 November 1934. Here are examples of letters he wrote to his editor, Charles Pearce, in New York City.* *

Atlanta, Ga., October 26, 1934

My dear Mr. Pearce:

Enclosed are the first 160 pages of corrected page proof. You will notice that there are comparatively few changes.

However, in the 10, 11, and 14 chapters there are certain changes which I should like to make. They are not so much corrections as differences of phraseology. I think that if you will let me have set up at my own expense the enclosed seven pages as an extra galley, that then without loss of time I can insert this matter in the paged proof of these chapters and save piecemeal correction.

1. The book was announced in the Harcourt, Brace catalogue of fall 1934 publications, but for reasons indicated in ensuing letters it did not appear until May 1935. The book was noticed in the July 1935 *Crisis* (p. 218), and a striking photograph of Du Bois was published. A review was promised for the August issue, but none appeared until November 1935(42:245–46); it was written by James O. Hopson, who concluded by calling *Black Reconstruction* "a most significant contribution to American historical studies."

In volume one of this work (pp. 442–43) will be found a brief account of Alfred Harcourt and the history of his long association with Du Bois. Also noted there are the beginnings, in 1931, of Harcourt's interest in publishing Du Bois's work on Reconstruction, for which he had that summer received a grant from the Rosenwald Fund.

* Charles A. Pearce (1906–70) began editorial work in 1927 with D. Appleton and Co.; from 1929 to 1939 he was an editor with Harcourt, Brace. In the latter year he was a founder of the publishing firm Duell, Sloan and Pearce, of which he was chief editor until 1961.

I hope this can be done.

Very sincerely yours,
W.E.B. Du Bois

Atlanta, Ga., November 5, 1934

My dear Mr. Pearce:

I am sending herewith the last of the paged proofs. I have made a minimum of corrections and I think I have only made real trouble in Chapters 13 and 14. There, on account of the intricacy of the subject, that is, the end of Reconstruction in Louisiana, and the attitude of the North, I have been compelled to insert some matter which is not as much new matter as it is a more careful re-statement of what was there. It seemed easier to me to insert this as new matter rather than to try to correct that which was there. I hope this will not cause you too great delay. For the purposes of the index, I would rather like to see a revise of these two chapters.

The index will be mailed this week.

Very sincerely yours,
W.E.B. Du Bois

In addition to corrections on page proof, Du Bois was having difficulty getting permissions for various quotations. All this was seriously delaying and possibly even threatening actual publication. As a result, Alfred Harcourt wrote Du Bois.

New York City, November 8, 1934

Dear Dr. Du Bois:

I have a serious situation to report to you in connection with the proofreading of Black Reconstruction, and particularly your changes in page proof. As a preface, I must quote the clause from our agreement covering these matters:

> "IV. For alterations which the author makes in proof after the type has been set up in conformity with the manuscript, he shall pay all charges in excess of twenty-five per cent of the cost of the type-setting from the original manuscript; and he shall pay in full for any corrections in the plates which he requires, or which are necessary for the correction of actual errors, after the plates have been made in conformity with the last page proof as corrected by the author. At any rate, after proofreading begins, in case the publishers find the rate of alterations in proof materially above the allowance, the author shall, on demand, deposit on account of them such a reasonable amount as the publishers may ask for."

You, of course, have done enough editing to realize that a change in page proof is more expensive than a change in galleys, and there is the added expense, when an insertion in page proof is made, of resetting all the matter from there to the end of the chapter, or at least transferring lines of type from one page to the next, as the number of lines on any one page is fixed. The regular charge of the printers for corrections, which is fixed by their rates for union labor, is 12¢ a line for all the lines they have to touch in page proofs. I have not had a careful estimate made, but the cost of your changes in the page proofs will run into hundreds of dollars—$600 or $700, I should guess.

Beyond this, we find on careful examination that your reading of the galleys was careless and skipped a great many errors which cannot be passed either for your sake or for our own. For instance, you uniformly spell Robert Owen's name with a final "s" and George Holyoake's name without the "a." These are samples of a multitude of errors which we are catching in the page proofs.

It is now so late in the year that your page corrections and the corrections of the most obvious of the errors will entail enough delay so that the book cannot be published this year.

The expense of the corrections will run into so considerable a sum that before we proceed further with the book we must ask you to put in our hands a sum sufficient to reimburse us for this extra outlay, in accordance with the provision in the contract quoted above.

You can't imagine how distressed I am to have to write you this letter. I hope you can secure funds perhaps from the Carnegie people or from some foundation to take care of this expense.

We, too, have a couple of thousand dollars tied up in the composition and plates, to say nothing of the advance on account of royalties, and we just cannot stand this further investment in the enterprise. To attempt to make a joke about so serious a matter is ill-timed, but I must say that I wish you had had your afterthoughts first.

> Sincerely yours,
> Alfred Harcourt[1]

Faced with the crisis represented by the above letter, Du Bois acted quickly and decisively, as he characteristically did when under pressure. The letters that follow are self-explanatory.

Atlanta, Ga., November 12, 1934

My dear Mr. Harcourt:

I cannot quite make out from your letter of November 28 [obviously a slip for November 8] just what my financial responsibility is going to be for corrections on the proof and whether with my limited resources I can even attempt to meet it. However, I venture to enclose my check for ($250.00), Two Hundred and Fifty Dollars.

> Very sincerely yours,
> W.E.B. DuBois

New York, N.Y., November 14, 1934

Dear Dr. Du Bois:

Thank you for your note of November 12th with check for $250. I am afraid it is

---

1. Publication of this letter from Alfred Harcourt to W.E.B. Du Bois has been granted by Harcourt Brace Jovanovich, Inc.; copyright © 1976 by Harcourt Brace Jovanovich, Inc.

going to take at least $600 to cover the cost of the corrections in Black Reconstruction for which you are responsible.

May I suggest that you apply to Mr. [F. P.] Keppel [President] of the Carnegie Corporation for $500 so as to be sure that this is covered? I met Keppel at dinner the other night and told him that I thought you might need a little more help on this book, and he said he thought he might be able to "steal" a moderate sum from some of his contingent resources.

Of course, another thing that would help would be to cut down the number of corrections in the page proofs, particularly those that upset the pagination. You see, when a paragraph is inserted on one page, it means that the material has to be repaged from there to the end of the chapter, where there is usually some extra space. For the time being, I am holding your check for $250 until I hear what you think of my suggestions of applying to Keppel and my further suggestion that we return the page proofs to you to see if you can cut down the number of corrections.

Sincerely yours,
Alfred Harcourt[1]

Atlanta, Ga., November 17, 1934

My dear Mr. Harcourt:

The money, of course, for the balance necessary must be found. I could probably borrow it but I hate to do it because I do not know how I can pay it back. Certainly, not from any returns that could be expected from a book of this sort.

I do not want to omit any of the corrections. My method of writing is a method of "after-thoughts." I mean that after all the details of commas, periods, spelling and commas, there comes the final and to me the most important work of polishing and re-setting and even re-stating. This is the crowning of my creative process.

Of course, in this case, what I ought to have done, was to have made a second set of corrections on the revised galley proofs, but the galley proof came late, near the middle of August instead of the 1st of July, and I let myself be hurried by the wish to get the book out before Christmas, which was, of course, a mistake.

I am writing to Mr. Keppel, although I hate to do this, and will let you know after I hear from him. If I do not hear from him, I will attempt to borrow, and at any rate, before December 15, I shall let you know just exactly what I can or cannot do.

Very sincerely yours,
W.E.B. Du Bois

P.S. In the meantime, if you will return the paged proof, I will go over it carefully and see if any of the proposed corrections can be omitted.

---

1. Publication of this letter from Alfred Harcourt to W.E.B. Du Bois has been granted by Harcourt Brace Jovanovich, Inc.; copyright © 1976 by Harcourt Brace Jovanovich, Inc.

Atlanta, Ga., November 17, 1934

My dear Mr. Keppel:

Mr. Harcourt suggests that I write you again. I am loathe to do this because the difficulty that my book is up against now is partly my fault. When I applied before to the Carnegie Fund it was to help me in the matter of citations.[1] I had used hundreds of books and pamphlets over a stretch of four years, and the exact citations were lost, twisted and distorted in all sorts of ways, and I had to spend a great deal of time and money to get them straight. They are now satisfactory.

Meantime, I had saved out of your appropriation about $300 to pay for corrections in the proof. I knew that these would come because of my method of writing. I compose with after-thoughts and corrections, continual readjustment and polishing, to get the great impression and setting. It is always necessary on account of time to send out my work before the final polishing, but the last efforts are really of the greatest importance.

On the galley proof, I made a large number of corrections, but necessarily on the galleys my thought was directed to details, words, sentences, figures. On the other hand, on the paged proofs, I was thinking of the general story, and made a large number of corrections. Each one of which, to my mind is much more important than even spelling and punctuation. The cost, however, has been enormous. I had ex-pected it to be large but with the allowance of 25% of the setting costs and the $300, I thought I was more than safe. I have sent Mr. Harcourt $250 but he tells me that I will need $400 or $500 more. I do not like to ask for this because I know the position in which all benevolent agencies are at this time. I might borrow the money but I do not like to do this. I am, therefore, putting the situation before you.

I think I have a book of unusual importance. Of course, it will not sell widely; it will not pay, but in the long run, it can never be ignored. I shall be glad to know if you think anything can be done? Perhaps you would like to look at a set of proofs. They are rather formidable, nearly 750 pages, but if you would care to see them, I will get them to you.

Very sincerely yours,
W. E. B. Du Bois

New York, N.Y., November 28, 1934

Dear Dr. Du Bois:

We have your letter of the 17th. Unfortunately, the cupboard is pretty bare, but if a supplementary grant of $250 would see the job through, I can find that amount. Just call on us if and when you need it.

Sincerely yours,
F. P. Keppel

1. In 1933, the Carnegie Corporation had made a grant of one thousand dollars to Dr. Du Bois for the purposes indicated.

Atlanta, Ga., December 3, 1934

My dear Mr. Keppel:

I thank you very much for your kind offer of November 28. I am writing Mr. Harcourt and sincerely hope that the sum which you offer will see us through. I will write you again as soon as I hear from him.

Very sincerely yours,
W. E. B. Du Bois

Atlanta, Ga., December 3, 1934

My dear Mr. Harcourt:

I have a letter from Mr. Keppel, a copy of which I enclose, and my answer. Meantime, I am working on the proof.

Very sincerely yours,
W. E. B. Du Bois

New York City, December 6, 1934

Dear Dr. Du Bois:

Thank you for your letter of December third. Mr. Keppel's $250 together with your $250 will see us through on the following condition: I have had a careful estimate made by the printers of the cost of author's alterations, and they think $500 will cover the excess charges for which you are responsible, provided the new material you have added does not cause run-overs at the end of chapters which would require repaging from that point on to the end of the book. With the proofs in your hands, I think you can watch for this either by cutting down the additional material or cutting out a sufficient number of lines to accommodate it in each chapter. On this understanding, you can tell Mr. Keppel that we'll go ahead. We are now depositing your check. If you will send us Mr. Keppel's check when it comes, we'll deposit that. Then as soon as the proofs arrive, we will proceed as rapidly as the manufacturing problems warrant.

Sincerely yours,
Alfred Harcourt[1]

Atlanta, Ga., December 10, 1934

My dear Mr. Keppel:

I have a letter from Mr. Harcourt in which he says: "I have had a careful estimate made by the printers of the cost of author's alterations, and they think $500 will cover the excess charges for which you are responsible." I have paid him $250 myself, which with the $250 which you kindly promised, will see the book through. I shall be glad to have the check, therefore, at your convenience.

I am deeply grateful for your interest.

Very sincerely yours
W. E. B. Du Bois

1. Publication of this letter from Alfred Harcourt to W.E.B. Du Bois has been granted by Harcourt Brace Jovanovich, Inc.; copyright © 1976 by Harcourt Brace Jovanovich, Inc.

Atlanta, Ga., December 10, 1934

My dear Mr. Harcourt:

I have gone carefully through the manuscript on the assumption that my changes would amount to $700. On that basis, I have cut down the changes I think about one-third. If, therefore, the changes after all would not have amounted to more than $500 as your last letter intimates, then the final changes will not amount, I think, to more than $350 or $400. In no case does the insertion of new matter involve running over the chapter end so as to require re-paging, and I have reduced the new matter inserted to a minimum. Also, I have nearly finished the index and will send the proof and the index before Christmas.

I have written Mr. Keppel for the $250 check and will forward that to you as soon as I hear from him.

Very sincerely yours
W. E. B. Du Bois

New York City, December 13, 1934

Dear Dr. Du Bois:

I have your letter of December tenth. I am gratified to know that you have been able to cut down your changes in page proofs about one-third. Of course, this will reduce the cost of changes for which you are responsible, and it will give us a little leeway to take care of other necessary changes in verifying the spelling of proper names and references and such matters as I mentioned to you in my letter of November eighth. If the cost of the changes for which you are responsible does not amount to $500, we shall be unusually glad to return any unexpended part of that sum.

Sincerely yours,
Alfred Harcourt[1]

Atlanta, Ga., January 3, 1935

My dear Mr. Harcourt:

Enclosed please find my check for ($250.00) Two Hundred and Fifty Dollars, which represents the additional amount contributed by the Carnegie Fund to pay the expenses of corrections in the proof of "Black Reconstruction." This, with the $250.00 already sent you, makes a total sum of $500, which according to your estimate will cover the cost.

The proof is all ready to be returned to you, and also I have finished the index. I am having the index, however, carefully checked for a third time so as to avoid any necessity of corrections on that proof. I shall mail the corrected galley proof and the manuscript of the index next week.

As soon as you have decided, I should like to know when you plan for the book to appear, as I am having several inquiries.

Very sincerely yours,
W. E. B. Du Bois

1. Publication of this letter from Alfred Harcourt to W.E.B. Du Bois has been granted by Harcourt Brace Jovanovich, Inc.; copyright © 1976 by Harcourt Brace Jovanovich, Inc.

Du Bois had a high regard for the writings of Sterling A. Brown (b. 1901), in the thirties a young professor of English at Howard University and a poet and essayist of distinction. Du Bois was the kind of writer who made it a practice to seek out the opinion of those he respected concerning his own work in progress. Sometime in 1934 he had asked Brown to read the galleys of Black Reconstruction *and the latter had undertaken this task. Precise dates are not known, for much of this correspondence seems not to have survived; but a fairly long handwritten letter from Brown, evaluating the book, does exist.*

Washington, D. C., January 29, 1935
My. dear Dr. Du Bois,

I have just got through an examination siege. I wanted to get this letter written earlier, but the pressure of a speed-up and stretch-out to complete the semester, and the racking worry incidental to college dramatics and avalanches of freshman themes would not permit it.

When the manuscript got to me (much later than your note predicted) I was myself in the act of getting a rather tardy manuscript in shape. I could steal time only now and again for the type of proofreading that I knew was expected, and was due a work so important. I went over the manuscript twice. I ran down many errors, some of punctuation, but more of spelling (I am afraid I attended Webster more closely than Woolley in my elementary schooling). I wrote these in the margins, with other corrections or queries. Your letter states that there was no word of criticism, and asks if I found anything wrong. I did find many things wrong in the proof; I hope that the pencilled corrections were not overlooked.

I should have been better able to give criticism of the book if I had not considered myself primarily proof-reader. I do think, however, from the two readings I gave it, that *Black Reconstruction* is a first rate piece of work that has for a long time needed doing. I have read quite a few of the histories of Reconstruction: Dunning, Fleming, Bowers, the revisionists on Johnson—Stryker, Winston—and popularized things of Thompson and Don Seitz[1]—I am therefore glad that you wrote the last chapter as you did, although condemnation of the lost cause school of historians is implicit throughout your book—in the point of view, and in the evidence you advance which

1. Brown's references are probably to the following: Edwin C. Woolley, *Handbook of Composition: A Compendium of Rules Regarding Good English . . . and Letter Writing* (Boston: D.C. Heath, 1907); William A. Dunning, *Reconstruction: Political and Economic, 1865–1877* (New York: Harper and Bros., 1907); Walter L. Fleming, *Civil War and Reconstruction in Alabama* (New York: Columbia University Press, 1905), and *The Sequel of Appomattox: A Chronicle of the Reunion of the States* (New Haven: Yale University Press, 1921); Clara M. Thompson, *Reconstruction in Georgia: Economic, Social, Political, 1865–1872* (New York: Columbia University Press, 1915); Lloyd Paul Stryker, *Andrew Johnson: A Study in Courage* (New York: Macmillan Co., 1930); Robert W. Winston, *Andrew Johnson: Plebeian and Patriot* (New York: Henry Holt and Co., 1928); Don C. Seitz, *The James Gordon Bennetts, Father and Son: Proprietors of the "New York Herald"* (Indianapolis: Bobbs-Merrill Co., 1928); Claude G. Bowers, *The Tragic Era* (Boston: Houghton Mifflin Co., 1929).

they consider inadmissible—or never went to the pains to hunt up. The book seemed original in the best sense. the tying-up with American labor history will stand it in good stead, I believe. I think it important to point out as you have done here—and in some essays in *Souls of Black Folk* the true tragedies of Reconstruction—and the real lost cause—which wasn't that of planters but of the people, poor people whether black or white—Walter Hines Page's two "forgotten men."[2] I am glad that you point out—if my memory serves me—that it wasn't the "radicalism" of Stevens, et al. that was to blame for the prostrate South—but the fact that "radicalism" in its best and contemporary sense was not given a chance.

I think your book will be attacked by the vested Southern—and perhaps Northern—interests, but that is a mark of its distinction. It is certainly no piece of bloody-shirt waving—though some fire-eater may call it so. I thought it tempered, and restrained—although it has its own pungency. I could see the large amount of work necessary for its documentation. In some cases I could not see that you had given the reader fullest points of reference for checking. I did not always think that the poetry quoted was fortunate as some of the prose it followed, but that is a matter of taste.

I think you have done a much needed job, excellently. I realize my limitations as a student of history, and that partly accounts for my not writing this commentary earlier. As I promised this summer, I was more than ready to help with the proof. But as for rushing as critic into this field—I was hesitant.

If I had the book before me my comments could be more specific. But the general impressions, after a period of many interventions, are as I have told you. I think *Black Reconstruction* belongs with the best historical interpretations I have read. I think it belongs with the best of your writings; I surely do not need to tell you that I believe that best to be very high.

> Sincerely yours,
> Sterling A. Brown

Among the Du Bois papers is a one-page, handwritten sheet, without date, headed Black Reconstruction *and signed by Benjamin Brawley. It comments upon the book itself and probably was written soon after its appearance in mid-June 1935. Benjamin G. Brawley (1882–1939) was educated at Morehouse, the University of Chicago, and Harvard. He taught at Morehouse from 1912 to 1932, becoming in 1933 professor of English literature at Howard. He published several books in Afro-American history and biography, as well as others on English drama and religious music.*

2. Walter Hines Page did not make reference to two forgotten men. In his speech "The Forgotten Man," delivered in 1897 at the State Normal and Industrial School of Women at Greensboro, North Carolina, he argued against aristocratic education and for the education of all men *and* women, but he referred only to those who were white. The speech was published as a chapter in Page's book *The School That Built A Town* (New York: Doubleday, Page and Co., 1902; reprint ed., New York: Harper, and Bros., 1952).

Howard University, Washington, D. C.
Black Reconstruction

   The book gives a thorough study of the literature of Reconstruction, bringing to
light many documents that have not been used before. At the same time the most
notable feature is the author's brisk writing in the last forty pages. In these he exposes
the bias and errors in many well known works dealing with the Reconstruction era,
especially the fallaciousness of such studies as those conducted at Columbia and Johns
Hopkins. If honesty and truth means anything in scholarship, this book should go far
in revising the traditional view of one of the most critical periods in our history.

Benjamin Brawley

*Considerable interest attaches to a letter from Emmett J. Scott (1873–1957) to Du Bois concern-
ing* Black Reconstruction. *From 1897 until Booker T. Washington's death in 1915, Scott was
private secretary to the "Wizard of Tuskegee"; during the First World War he served as an
assistant on Negro affairs to the secretary of war. In both capacities Scott's relationship with Du
Bois was far from cordial. Indeed, in 1919 there was a fierce exchange between the two men in
connection with Du Bois's exposure of the brutality practiced upon Afro-American soldiers
during the war. Scott moved on to become secretary of Howard University, from where he wrote
to Du Bois.*

Washington, D. C., June 27, 1935
Dear Dr. Du Bois:
   The Negro people of the United States—in fact, the colored peoples of the world,
owe you a sincere debt of gratitude for your monumental work, "Black Reconstruction." We have long needed a virile pen such as yours to set forth the true facts of
Reconstruction. It must be most gratifying to you to read the approving criticisms
which are appearing in the Metropolitan newspapers.[1] It will not be easy in the future
for so-called historians to smear the Negroes' part in that lamentable period.

Sincerely yours,
Emmett J. Scott

*The very month of the book's appearance, Du Bois received a glowing letter from his dear friend
and co-worker of nearly four decades, James Weldon Johnson; it was addressed from the summer
home of the Johnsons—and Du Bois's birthplace.*

---

   1. The book received immediate, extensive, and generally very positive reviews in the *Literary
Digest*, 15 June 1935 (unsigned); the *New York Times*, 13 June 1935 (by John Chamberlain); the
New York Post, 14 June 1935 (by Herschel Brickell); the *New York Herald-Tribune*, 13 June 1935
(by Lewis Gannett); the *New York World-Telegram*, 13 June 1935 (by Harry Hansen); and a notice
of over a full page in the book review section of the Sunday *New York Times*, 16 June 1935 (by
William MacDonald).

Great Barrington, Mass., June 25, 1935

Dear Du Bois:

You have done a grand piece of work in Black Reconstruction—and no one else could have done it. You have done it with facts (the amount of research is stupendous) with logic and with biting eloquence—and, where the subject called for it, with impassioned poetry. I believe the book will clear away a lot of false history, and serve as a sword for truth on a field where Truth has been practically vanquished.

I wish for the book the widest distribution possible.

Sincerely yours
Johnson

Two additional letters received by Du Bois in the year of Black Reconstruction's *publication surely gave him special satisfaction. One was from Walter White; the other from Mary White Ovington, whose correspondence with Du Bois began in 1904.**

New York City, September 13, 1935
(Dictated September 12)

Dear Dr. Du Bois:

I recently sent Mrs. Roosevelt a copy of *Black Reconstruction* as I wanted her to get this more accurate picture of the Reconstruction period so that she would understand more clearly the southern scene as it is today. This morning she acknowledges receipt of the book and says: "I will get 'Black Reconstruction' and read it as soon as I can, and I will also try to get the President to read it."

Ever sincerely,
Walter White

New York, New York, September 16, 1935

My dear Mr. White:

I thank you very much for calling the attention of Mrs. Roosevelt to my recent book.

Very sincerely yours,
W. E. B. Du Bois

New York City, Nov. 7, 1935

My dear Dr. Du Bois:

I made a long summer in the Berkshires and the Green river was never more lovely or my friends kindlier, but the summer will always stand for me as the time I read "Black Reconstruction."

I knew it was going to be a fine piece of work, but I did not realize the immensity of the material and the very interesting way it would be presented. I've felt for many

* See volume one of this work.

years that Reconstruction offered the country a great experiment in democracy and
that the country failed; but to have it all told so clearly and dramatically, to see race
consciousness used to kill class consciousness (Hitler could read and get points), to
have an American history at last told from the standpoint of the workers, that has
been a unique experience.

It's great American history and one's next thought is that it will be in the libraries of
the country and hereafter students will have something to read besides sloppy senti-
mentalism and race prejudice.

I hope you are finding something of satisfaction in the student world again, and that
you may find some student to carry on the work if you won't want to do it yourself.
The next story would be of populism, and its failure—And I wonder, what after that?

Yours sincerely,

Mary W. Ovington

*Du Bois's intense interest in and activity on behalf of Africa are well known; in particular, he
evinced the greatest possible concern about Liberia's reputation and sovereignty. As President
Coolidge's special representative—with ambassadorial rank—at the inauguration of President
King of Liberia early in 1924, Du Bois had learned firsthand something of the realities of
Liberia's precarious position; thereafter he kept close contact with United States officials in
Liberia and with Liberian leaders and frequently wrote on the subject, not only in the* Crisis
but also in such magazines as the New Republic *(18 November 1925) and* Foreign Affairs
(April 1925, July 1933).

*Loans from United States banks, with governmental approval, and conflicts among British,
French, and United States rubber interests (in the latter case, especially Firestone), together
with the financial stringency of the Great Depression, produced by the early 1930s a situation
where Liberia's existence as an even nominally independent state was in question. This crisis was
reflected in various proposals by the United States and other powers to "save" Liberia and
produced significant debates in the League of Nations.*

*For a time in 1934, the Liberian government—and Du Bois—seriously considered having Du
Bois speak for Liberia in the League; proposals also were brought forward for a book by Du Bois
in response to pro-Firestone propaganda just then appearing. These circumstances surround the
correspondence among Du Bois, Anna Melissa Graves, a Baltimore friend very active in anti-
imperialist struggles, Dorothy Detzer, executive secretary of the Women's International League
for Peace and Freedom (1925–46), and L. A. Grimes, a member of Liberia's Supreme Court and
a representative of Liberia at the League of Nations. These letters were exchanged just at the
moment when Great Britain had suggested that the United States compel Liberia to accept a
League of Nations settlement of its finances, when powerful French newspapers were alluding to
the possibility of armed intervention, and when —on 22 June 1934—the bishops of the African
Methodist Episcopal Church had called on the Christian world and especially the colored peoples
of the world to come to Liberia's defense since, said the bishops, it was "in serious danger of being
mandated by some European Power." Settlement, with United States backing, was forthcoming*

through loans that Liberia did agree to accept and under terms where its sovereignty was not further vitiated. Hence, the book Du Bois suggested never was prepared.

Miss Graves was then in Bahia, Brazil; it was to that city that Du Bois wrote.

Atlanta, Georgia, November 17, 1934

My dear Miss Graves:

I am answering your letter of October 16. I have heard nothing of the meeting of the League nor have I heard from Miss Detzer for sometime. Several letters passed between her and myself and one or two from Liberia concerning the possibility of my representing Liberia in the League but nothing came of it. So far as I know, the Liberian matter was not taken up by the League at all. I think Miss Detzer is not at all deceived by the State Department and that she has been doing whatever she could. The situation is difficult. There is nothing that I could do. I was unable to influence the N.A.A.C.P. Walter White, the Secretary, is definitely under the influence of George Schuyler.

George Schuyler was sent out by an American newspaper in 1930 to get a sensational story about Liberian slavery. He got it and published articles and a book unfairly attacking Liberia. More recently, Schuyler has been hired indirectly by White to attack me in various ways and consequently White feels under obligations to him. I had to sever all connections with the N.A.A.C.P. because they had no economic program. They will have nothing to do with Africa or the Negroes outside the United States, and I could not agree with them. Recently, the Firestone Company has published a propaganda book on Liberia which ought to be answered.

I have written Miss Detzer concerning the possibility of using some of my articles and supplementing them for a book, [replying to] "Liberia Re-Discovered" by James C. Young, but have not heard from her as she is absent in the West. I am also writing Grimes on the subject.[1]

I am always glad to co-operate in any way for the saving of Liberia.

Very sincerely yours,

W. E. B. Du Bois

Atlanta, Ga., November 19, 1934

My dear Mr. Grimes:

You of course know of the recent publication of the book "Liberia Re-Discovered"

1. Schuyler's book was *Slaves Today* (New York: Brewer, Warren and Putnam, 1931); it was sharply criticized by Du Bois in the *Crisis* 39 (February 1932): 67–69. Young's book was *Liberia Rediscovered* (Garden City, New York: Doubleday, Doran and Co., 1934). Its frontispiece was a photograph of Harvey S. Firestone, and stated themes were that Liberia's "continued existence remains an issue yet to be determined" (p.vi) and that Firestone's plans offered a way out for the republic. James C. Young (1892–1945) was a Georgia-born newspaper man. In addition to the Liberia book he published an attack on F. D. Roosevelt and a biography of Robert E. Lee called *Marse Robert:Knight of the Confederacy*. At his death he was public relations consultant to Firestone Tire and Rubber Company and the Ford Motor Company.

by James C. Young. As I have just written Miss Graves, this book ought to be answered and it ought to be done immediately. I think my two articles in *Foreign Affairs*, and some things which I have published in *The Crisis*, would furnish the basis of such a book which I should like to prepare and get published. Of course, this would cost something as no publisher would issue a book of the sort without being reimbursed at least in part for the cost of manufacture, since I cannot hope to recoup his expenditure by sales. Of course, Young's book, without doubt, has been paid for by Firestone.

I am writing to ask if Liberia could and would finance a book of this sort? As soon as I hear from you, I shall be glad to get figures on the matter from responsible publishers. Off-hand, I should imagine that a publication of this sort would cost about $2,000 or $2,500.

I shall be glad to hear from you at your convenience.

Very sincerely yours,
W. E. B. Du Bois

Monrovia, Liberia, December 12, 1934

My dear Dr. Du Bois:

Your letter of November 19th reached me Sunday afternoon the 9th inst.

I myself had felt that the book of Young's should be promptly answered, but with the new duties that presently devolve upon me, the tardiness of my restoration to health, and consequent delay in re-assorting my papers after my several trips, I had hesitated to undertake it.

Your offer, therefore, received my warmest support, and, having submitted same to His Excellency the President, I am pleased to be able to inform you that I have been advised: "that the Government of Liberia would be interested in and would pay for the cost of such a publication; but, before committing itself, should like to know the exact figure the Publishers would charge for the work."

This limitation is due to your not having approached any publishers before writing, and the necessity of leaving a margin in the budget now under consideration to cover. Nevertheless I have every reason to believe that upon the receipt of your next, all the necessary arrangements will be promptly completed.

With that pleasurable anticipation I desire to add that if you need for the work any data I can supply either from my notes, reports, contacts in Europe or otherwise you have but to indicate your needs and I shall spare no pains to collect and forward same so far as is within my power on receipt of your request.

Thanking you for the offer and with my kindest regards,

Believe me, dear Dr. Du Bois,

Yours sincerely,
L. A. Grimes

Atlanta, Ga., December 4, 1934

My dear Mr. Grimes;

Since writing my last letter, I have finally gotten in touch with Dorothy Detzer.[1] She agrees with me that a book of the sort that I propose is very necessary but suggests the thought that had not occurred to me: "I am wondering whether it would be wise or well for the Liberian government to finance" it.

This does bring up a question, if it wouldn't be best not to have the government finance it directly, but to have it done through some organizations here to which Liberia might make an indirect contribution.

I will co-operate with Miss Detzer and see if any organizations are willing to do this. In the meantime, I should be very glad to have your reaction.

Very Sincerely yours,
W. E. B. Du Bois

There is a fairly extensive correspondence between Du Bois and a mysterious George S. Oettlé, about whom the editor has been able to discover nothing more than what Oettlé himself discloses. Though nothing seems to have come of the proposals herein put forward, the letters are of sufficient interest to merit publication. The exchange begins with a letter from Oettlé, which includes the postscript, "I believe I met you at Miss Carney's Forum: am not quite sure." The reference is to a symposium on the so-called Negro question conducted during the summer of 1934 at Columbia University by Mabel Carney, where invited experts, including Du Bois, lectured.

Chatham, New Jersey, October 13, 1934

Dear Sir,

The Carnegie Foundation has evinced much interest in South Africa, in the advancement of both white and black races.

Representations have been made by the Union Government of South Africa to the British authorities in the direction of taking over control of the Native territories, Bechuanaland, Basutoland, Swaziland, now administered by the Crown as native dependencies, provision having been made therefore at the time the Union obtained Dominion status.

The Union's native policy hardly warrants such action, unless these areas are to be reckoned as mainly native areas, and not to be exploited for certain white interests, at the expense of the blacks—witness the past history of the Union's native tribes and their loss of land for tillage and development.

You hold distinct views about segregation—judging from newspaper reports—and

1. Dorothy Detzer (b.1900), in her autobiography, *Appointment on the Hill* (New York: Henry Holt and Co., 1948), offers an account of her involvement in the Liberian episode of the 1930s (pp.124–37). She mentions Anna Graves and L. A. Grimes, consistently misspells the name of Edwin Barclay, Liberia's president at the time, and makes no mention of Du Bois at all and no reference to any activity on the part of the Black people in the United States.

the idea has occurred, that the Carnegie people have never sent a trained colored man to report upon the potentialities of the black races in Southern Africa, the only place on the whole of the African Continent where the black man is placed cheek by jowl with one of the best types of white civilization, where paternalism has been developed to a degree most amazing, and where the desire to be patriarchal to the native races around is mingled with fear lest the ruling classes be outnumbered by the blacks.

The writer was born and raised in South Africa, and from much observation and travel holds definite views about the native question in Southern Africa. Would it be possible, during one of your visits to New York, for us to meet to talk this matter over?

I would like to see an experienced colored educationalist of note sent out under their auspices, without the unconscious bias of white dominance, to report, especially bearing in mind the aspirations of the colored races in the United States: one who has been in touch with these movements should be able to throw valuable light upon what should be regarded as the black man's own responsibility in respect of progress, and suggest where the whites' duties lie in respect of both mulatto and blacks.

Such a proposal would be frowned upon by most politicians but I believe a real contribution to the problem of white and black would be served by such a visit. How do you regard this suggestion?

Segregation has been discussed many times in South Africa, and deemed impracticable; perhaps the addition of the above-mentioned territories to the Union might make segregation feasible. Quien sabe?

Naturally I write in confidence; am not naturally looking for the lime-light, but I would like to interest you in this idea, and if the Carnegie people can be persuaded, so much the better.

Sincerely,
George S. Oettlé

Atlanta, Ga., October 22, 1934

My dear Sir:

I have received your kind letter of October 13. I have long chafed over the unfair way in which the Carnegie Foundation and other funds have acted with regard to visitors to South Africa. I think it is a splendid thing that they should help South African students to study America, and that they should allow Americans to study the race problem in South Africa; but it is intolerable that they should confine American students to white men, and allow neither the South African natives nor American Negroes to come in contact with each other. Only now and then has this been affected, and at great expense.

I am quite well acquainted with Mr. Keppel of the Carnegie Foundation. I wonder if you would be willing for me to show your letter to him in confidence? Anything else that I can do in this matter, I should be glad to.

Very sincerely yours
W. E. B. Du Bois

Chatham, N. J., November 3, 1934

Dear Sir,

Yours of the 22nd is encouraging: I do not mind what you do with my letters, but I know that they will be misconstrued, for I am one of those peculiar men that call a spade a spade, and Dr. Keppel knows that I do not regard his work in South Africa with 100% approval: in fact, unconsciously his institution has given much impetus to the still greater domination of the Dutch race in that country. However, it would take too long to prove my point, and there is the equally important problem of giving the native black a square deal without forcing his civilization ahead of his needs, and without jeopardizing the white man's position—for no African race has maintained the standard of the European civilization apart from the white influence and presence. The real tragedy lies in the fact that under modern industrial conditions the greed for wealth plays off the one against the other to the detriment of both.

Frankly, in my opinion, the greatest disservice that has been done in recent years to the aboriginal races of Southern Africa was that conference arranged for General [Jan Christian] Smuts' benefit by Mr. JESSE (the capitals slipped in by mistake) Jones and Canon Phelps Stokes. I know both pride themselves upon their impression of the result, i.e. by what was said politely immediately afterwards by the chief participants. They do not know General Smuts: I do, being a South African. What do we find to-day? The Union Government making representations to the British Government with a view to taking over the native territories of Basutoland, Bechuanaland, and Swaziland—inferring that the British are not on the job in those parts. I recently had a private letter from the Prime Minister of Rhodesia in which he stated that there was a very strong insidious movement throughout Southern Rhodesia for union with the Union of South Africa. This has all taken place since the General's visit to this country and my firm conviction is that General Smuts—the world's shrewdest and astutest politician—had his eyes opened by the conference above referred to, and with the Dutch nature thoroughly imbued with the patriarchal attitude twixt white and black, he has made up his mind that it is not in the best interests of the whites to have a different native policy—especially as Rhodesia's is avowedly more liberal to the blacks than that of the Union—growing up in various parts of South Africa. And so a big drive is on to unite all Southern Africa under one control, and thus be in a position to dictate the policy of native race development!!!!

You will now understand the motive behind mine of the 13th ult. As you consider segregation workable, I thought I saw a way of having the position brought out into the lime-light by a visit as suggested therein by yourself. You will need all the wisdom that God has endowed you with, but I believe you can make a good job of it. I look forward to the day when a regular stream of keen South African blacks will come over to the Southern Universities, imbued with a sincere desire to advance the interests of their race, without antagonizing the whites, or allowing vested interests to exploit their folk to the detriment of the whites.

Hoping to see you when in New York, Sincerely,

George S. Oettlé

P. S. Dr. Keppel knows that I am not a persona grata with the Union Government. They do not want men who wish to be fair to the black races, and only want men who will 100% back them in their plans to establish a republic ultimately in Southern Africa. The whites need new blood from Europe, even as Australia, and to make that country a close preserve with one white race dominant will spell disaster. In fairness to the new combined party about to take over the control of the Union Government, the soft pedal has been put on 'Republic.'

Atlanta, Ga., November 17, 1934

Mr. dear Mr. Keppel:

My first letter this morning reminds me of another thing that I have been thinking of bringing to your attention, and I shall do so now.

In October, I received a letter from a white South African, evidently of Dutch descent. I am enclosing a copy of the letter with my answer and his rejoinder. I think you will be interested in the correspondence.

Very sincerely your,
W. E. B. Du Bois

Chatham, N.J. 10th December, 1934

Dear Sir,

I fear you found my letter of the 3rd ult. too much strong meat— hence your silence.

But I would be interested to know whether you ever received it, or whether it has been lost in the mails.

Experience has shown over many years that a super-imposed opinion never works out satisfactorily, and unless you are really honest in your determination to make an improvement—vide the second half of the 3rd sentence of yours of the 22nd October last—I suggest you forget mine of the 3rd ult.

Any move that is made, should emanate from the colored folk themselves, for the whites by tradition can only look at the problem from their own angle. Inter-racial committees were not established easily: even today they are still on trial. The difficulties besetting their introduction should provide a lead in understanding that your help will not come from the Carnegie folk at the outset: if some colored educational organization made the first move, and asked the Carnegie to supplement their own proposed expenditure, then something might be achieved: savvy?

I suggest you study the problem of South African blacks' development from the angle of restoring the authority of the Chiefs in purely native areas, with educated blacks as their right hand men. This would provide an outlet for educated men and women from Lovedale and Fort Hare.

Best Seasonal Greetings,

Sincerely,
George S. Oettlé

*For some forty years—from about 1905 to the end of the Second World War—the Black
intelligentsia, especially the younger among them, considered Du Bois not only as mentor but
more nearly as father. His correspondence is filled with reflections of such a role, as the first
volume of this work has shown, and Du Bois, with great seriousness, expended much time and
energy in encouraging and guiding others.*

*Illustrative is an exchange of letters between Du Bois and a young graduate student, whose
work in music and drama had already received public performance and attracted nationwide
attention; this was Shirley Graham, whose minister father had been a friend of Du Bois's, and
whose biographical studies of outstanding Afro-American personalities were later to be widely
acclaimed.*

Oberlin, Ohio, November 7, 1934

My dear Dr. Du Bois:

I have so often consulted your books for information along the lines which most
interested me that now I naturally write to you for advice.

In June, 1935, I hope to take my master's degree from Oberlin College in Music
History and Fine Arts. My graduate work, as did my undergraduate work, combines
both college and conservatory, but I am fulfilling all requirements for the college
degrees rather than for the conservatory. Before graduation I carried what constituted
a History minor in the college while majoring in Music.

It is my belief that Music History in its proper historical as well as artistic setting
should hold an important place in our (Negro) colleges. Such a department ought to
offer courses in the history, understanding and development not only of Music, but of
Painting, Sculpturing, Architecture and the Minor Arts. Upon the background of
History, the relation of these arts one to the other should be shown. This work should
be the center of classes which, on the one hand, teach Music Theory: Harmony,
Counterpoint, Composition, and on the other, Practical Music: Piano, Voice, Violin,
etc. Dr. Edward N. Dickinson, with whom I have been doing outside reading,
stresses the importance of Knowledge on the part of our potential musicians. It was
he and Dr. Herbert Miller who, greatly against the wishes of the conservatory,
insisted that I continue with my college work rather than allow myself to follow only
the artistic interpretation of music.

For so long have our schools been trying to send out students who could sing and
play that few of our administrators are going to see the importance of this approach to
music. I am faced with the problem of finding the place where I can put these theories
into practice. And so, I am writing to ask if you could suggest a college where such a
department might be seriously considered. I have had three years experience as head
of the department of music at Morgan College, Baltimore, Maryland. (1929–31)

It is true that I am deeply interested in dramatic music composition. I hope to yet
write the opera which will reveal the "Souls of Black Folks" in music. I have been
willing, however, to go back and prepare. The workmanship must be worthy of the
work.

In the meantime, I am writing a thesis on "The Survivals of Africanism in Modern Music." I should deeply appreciate it if you would suggest any material relating to this subject. I read French with ease and German (with a dictionary).

I trust that this letter does not sound presumptuous. It isn't meant to be. I believe that you will forgive an enthusiasm for a work which I believe is needed and will bear much fruit.

Sincerely,
Shirley Graham

Atlanta, Ga. November 17, 1934

My dear Miss Graham:

I am very much indeed interested in your plan of work and I am taking the liberty to show your letter to the President of Atlanta University where I think there ought sometime to be an opening of the kind which you suggest. Of course, the eternal matter of money will perhaps hinder anything definite immediately, and yet the department which you outlined is of major importance. I shall ask Mr. [John] Hope to write you and perhaps have an interview with you at sometime.

Of course, beside Atlanta University, Fisk ought to expand in that way but I do not know conditions there well enough to advise you. Howard University, I presume, is tied up with so many musicians of the older sort that it might be hard to start anything. On the other hand, the new Dillard University at New Orleans should be kept in mind and you might get in correspondence with Mr. Will Alexander who is the President. This institution opens in the fall of 1935.

With regard to your thesis, I suppose you are familiar with the work of Ballanta in West Africa. Also, there has been a considerable collection of music in South Africa. You know, of course, the intelligent work of Natalie Curtis and the books by Newman I. White, Odum and Johnson, and Miss Scarborough. The earliest collection of slave songs published in 1867 and edited by Allen, Ware and Garrison, has a splendid preface, but it's a rare book. Maud Cuney Hare, 160 Huckins Avenue, Squantum, Massachusetts, has done a good deal in Negro folk songs, and especially Creole music [1] Perhaps these references may help you.

1. Du Bois refers to Nicholas George Julius Ballanta (Taylor), *Saint Helena Island Spirituals Recorded and Transcribed at Penn Normal, Industrial and Agricultural School, St. Helena Island, Beaufort County, South Carolina* (New York: Institute of Musical Art, ca. 1925), with a foreword by George Foster Peabody; Natalie Curtis Burlin, a white woman to whose pioneering work in compiling and annotating the music of American Indians, Afro-American and African peoples Du Bois paid tribute in the *Crisis* 23 (February 1922): 170–71; Newman I. White, co-editor (with H. C. Jackson) of *An Anthology of Verse by American Negroes* (Durham: Trinity College Press, 1924); Howard Odum and Guy B. Johnson, *The Negro and His Songs* (Chapel Hill: University of North Carolina Press, 1925); Dorothy Scarborough, *On the Trail of Negro Folk Songs* (Cambridge, Massachusetts: Harvard University Press, 1925); William F. Allen, Charles P. Ware, and Lucy M. Garrison, *Slave Songs of the United States* (New York: Simpson and Co., 1867); Maud Cuney Hare, ed., *Six Creole Folk-Songs* (New York: C. Fisher, 1921); Maud Cuney Hare, a devoted friend of Du Bois's, was a pianist and music teacher living in Massachusetts. Du Bois described

I shall be glad to co-operate in any way I can to help your excellent plans.

Very sincerely yours,

W. E. B. Du Bois

November 17, 1934

MEMORANDUM TO PRESIDENT HOPE FROM DR. DU BOIS

I am enclosing a memorandum from Shirley Graham. You will perhaps remember that Miss Graham last year or the year before created quite a sensation in musical circles by the opera which she staged in Cleveland under the auspices of the Municipality.

She is a woman of talent and also broad education, which is rare among musicians. I have written her and told her that I was going to show you her letter and ask you to write her and perhaps talk to her. I have an idea that the kind of department which she outlines would be just the thing for graduate work in this university.

Oberlin, Ohio, November 27, 1934

My dear Dr. Du Bois:

Thanks so much for your kind letter of November 17th. I have written to both Mr. Alexander and Maud Cuney Hare. I have a copy of her book but a personal correspondence will be even more fruitful. I find that all of the other books which you mention are in our library.

My survey will not devote too much space to folk music and the Spirituals. That field has been pretty well covered. I am dealing specifically with African musical idioms as they appear in the larger forms of modern music. Such a study does not limit itself to Negroes or even to America. For instance, both Debussy and Ravel acknowledge their debt to Africa. Of course, William Dawson's symphony is a gold mine. I had the opportunity of going over the score with Mr. Dawson and I listened to the Philadelphia broadcast last week. I thought it was splendidly done. Now, some of the critics are accusing him of plagiarizing from Dvorak![1] Can anything be more ironical? Certainly somebody needs to go through the accumulation of "Nordic" music and draw broad, BLACK circles around many of his measures. That's a life-time job, but I can at least start it.

For many reasons, I should much rather work in Atlanta University than in any of the other schools you mentioned. Since you have been so kind as to take the matter up

<hr>

her exhibit on the history of Black music in the September 1924 *Crisis* (28:200–201). Upon her death in 1936, Du Bois devoted most of a column to her life and work in the *Pittsburgh Courier* (4 April 1936). That same year appeared her major book—*Negro Musicians and Their Music* (Washington: Associated Publishers).

1. William L. Dawson (b.1899) organized the School of Music at Tuskegee in 1930 and directed it for a generation. The Philadelphia Orchestra, under Stokowski, introduced his *Negro Folk Symphony* in a world premiere performance on 14 November 1934; the work was repeated at Carnegie Hall in New York City on 20 November. An account of this symphony and of its Philadelphia performance was printed in the *New York Times*, 18 November 1934, p. 6.

with Dr. Hope, I'll wait until I hear from him before writing. If he is seriously interested in such a plan of work I'd come under almost any condition.

With real appreciation, I am

>Sincerely,
>Shirley Graham

In reply to his memorandum to John Hope concerning Shirley Graham, Du Bois received the comment quoted in his letter below. Miss Graham was not hired by Atlanta, however, and shortly after this correspondence went—with her two young sons—to New Haven as a graduate student at the Yale School of Dramatics.

>Atlanta, Ga., December 3, 1934

My dear Miss Graham:

As I have stated, I have mentioned you to Dr. Hope and he has said: "I should like to talk with you about Miss Graham. I might sometime during the year, when I am near Oberlin, go to see her." Notwithstanding this, please write him directly. I am sure he would like to have you.

>Very sincerely yours,
>W. E. B. Du Bois

>December 8, 1934

My dear Dr. Du Bois:

Thanks for your letter of December 3rd. I am writing Dr. Hope today.

Thanks also for the recent reiteration of your stand on segregation. It must be terribly discouraging to have to say over and over again things which you have set forth once so clearly and so forcibly. I am glad that you pity my people's weakness. So many are still conversing with shadows thrown on the black walls which shut out all light. Mr. Johnson is indeed fortunate if he can remain "genial and calm." Many of us who are much younger are growing sharp and hard; witness Langston Hughes and his "Ways of White Folks."

Yet, I do believe that the walls are "a-tumblin' down." I'd like to know William B. Seabrook, the man who wrote "Magic Island" and "Jungle Ways." His books were recommended to me by a white friend as possible thesis material.

The article in the current issue of the "Crisis" on Oberlin has been noted here with a great deal of interest. The writer knew her facts. She, however, did not know the reasons for the facts. The students, black and white, are neither blind nor indifferent. As you have said, they are, for the most part, helpless. We do have strong and courageous friends, but for the last few years there has been here *one man* who is determined to change things. He has not been near as successful as he expected to be. The white students are with us.[1] After all, it is quite probable that Oberlin has been

1. The final "Postscript" column which Du Bois did for the *Crisis,* in June 1934 (41: 182–84), was devoted to a reiteration of his views on segregation. The "calm" Mr. Johnson is James

unduly sentimentalized. Negroes only entered Oberlin on a one vote majority and half the students threatened to leave when they heard the result of the ballot!

Sincerely,
Shirley Graham

With all his manifold activities, not least the final work on Black Reconstruction, *as well as his full teaching load at Atlanta, it was characteristic of Du Bois to seek additional tasks. In this connection, two letters written to the editors of leading periodicals contain matter of interest.*

Atlanta, Ga., November 19, 1934

The Editor of *The American Mercury*
My dear Sir:

I wonder if you would be interested in an article along these lines: the depression among American Negroes has made their economic and social situation critical. There has arisen inside the race a rather clear-cut difference in opinion as to just what ought to be done about it. For a long time, colored people have fought against segregation with the idea that eventually they are going to be so integrated into the nation that they would become full-fledged American citizens. On the other hand, the chances of this consummation are not bright and for economic and spiritual survival group organization has become necessary in work, in business organization, in education, in spiritual ideals. This group segregation, however, may and does encourage pressure from the surrounding race to increase in law and custom the separation of American Negroes from the rest of the citizenship. There arises a curious paradox which I should like to explain and criticize in your pages. Would you be interested?

Very sincerely yours
W. E. B. Du Bois

At this time Alfred A. Knopf was the publisher of the American Mercury *and Charles Angoff (b. 1902) the editor. Angoff replied favorably enough, but the article, if submitted, did not appear.*

Weldon Johnson; the reference is to a theme of his brief book *Negro Americans, What Now?* (New York: Viking Press, 1934). William B. Seabrook's books were sensationalistic and racist: *Magic Island* (New York: Harcourt, Brace and Co., 1929) dealt with Haiti, while *Jungle Ways* (New York: Harcourt, Brace and Co., 1931) had Africa as its locale; both sold very well. The article in the *Crisis* on Oberlin, written by Carolina W. Thomason, was entitled, "Will Prejudice Capture Oberlin?" (December 1934; 41: 360–61). Mrs. Thomason was a teacher whose daughter graduated from Oberlin in June 1934. Her article tells of discriminatory practices in various shops in Oberlin, student protest, but little college support. The *"one man"* Shirley Graham mentions probably was the Reverend William Herbert King of Detroit, then a graduate student at Oberlin and a Black man who led in the resistence to Oberlin's racism. Shirley Graham herself contributed an account of the situation at Oberlin, "Oberlin and the Negro," in the *Crisis* 42 (April 1935):118,124. Hughes's collection of short stories, *The Ways of White Folks*, was published in June 1934 by Knopf in New York City. "Sharp and hard" describes it well.

New York City, November 23 [1934]

Dear Dr. Du Bois:

All right. I shall be glad to see the article. Send it in at your convenience.

Sincerely yours,

Charles Angoff

Simultaneously, Du Bois suggested another kind of article to the editor of the Atlantic Monthly.

Atlanta, Ga., November 19, 1934

The Editor of *The Atlantic Monthly*

My dear Sir:

The recent election, just as the election in 1932, and in previous years, emphasizes the critical condition is which the United States stands with regard to a third party movement. I several times emphasized the fact that the emasculation of the 14th and 15th Amendments meant not simply the disfranchisement of the Negro but the disfranchisement of liberal opinion in the United States because of the rotten borough system of distortion of political powers [that] has resulted.

For a long time, any reference to these facts has been looked upon "as waving the bloody shirt," but it seems to me that it would be possible to make a dispassionate study of the returns of two or three elections to show that if the intelligence of this country is going to get a chance to vote on issues and express themselves on future policy, then there must be in the country a greater equality of political power among citizens.

I am writing to ask if you would be interested in an article along these lines?

Very sincerely yours,

W. E. B. Du Bois

Boston, Mass., 26 November, 1934

Dear Mr. Du Bois:—

It is very pleasant to hear from you after so many years. Your remarks are entirely justified, but I am sorry to say that we cannot at this time find a place in the *Atlantic* for political articles. We happen to be especially engaged on a number of social topics.

With many thanks for your kind offer, believe me,

Yours, sincerely,

Ellery Sedgwick[1]

1. Ellery Sedgwick (1872–1960) was editor of the *Atlantic* from 1908 to 1938. Du Bois contributed to the *Atlantic* beginning in 1897 and under Sedgwick's editorship in 1915.

On 19 November 1934, Du Bois wrote to *Harper's Magazine* a letter identical with that he wrote the same day to the *American Mercury*. In a letter dated 4 December, his suggestion was rejected. On 10 December, Du Bois wrote to *Harper's* suggesting an article on the third-party movement; there is no record of a response.

Indicative of Du Bois's humor and of his interest in drama, as in all aspects of education and of the functioning of his university, is a memorandum he sent to the person who founded the Atlanta University Summer Theatre in 1934 and served as professor of drama at Spelman College for Women.

Atlanta, Ga., November 19, 1934

MEMORANDUM TO ANNE COOKE FROM DR. DU BOIS

Lack of effective communication between us is due to my inability to be sure of the identity of "Ann Cooke" and "Anne Cook." Sometimes I think they are the same person, sometimes I am sure they are two sets of the same person, and at still other times, I am sure they are two quite different persons. Could you correct, guide, and help me in this rather abstruse matter?

The distance between the Atlanta University dormitory and Spelman campus makes it impossible for me to keep track of your work and the intricacy of your mental processes, as I should like. I am not sure of your all-embracing plans. I enjoyed "Mr. Pim" immensely, and I am waiting for the next thing on the bill of fare. But more particularly, I am waiting for the large and all-inclusive forecast of things to come.

I know how terribly busy you usually are, but if you find any extra time, won't you communicate with me?

[W. E. B. D.]

Spelman College, Atlanta, Ga.,
November 20, 1934

My dear Dr. Du Bois,

In spite of the fact that I found in my morning's mail a *Memorandum to Anne Cooke from Dr. Du Bois,* I am writing you a letter.

It would be difficult to write a full account of my all-embracing plans but as far as the public dramatic program is concerned—well we'll present some of the following plays this season:

1. *The Late Christopher Bean*—Dec. 14th
2. *Names in Bronze,* an original (New Haven) play—early part of second semester.
3. *The Life of Man*—Andreyev—later
4. Shakespeare???—Morehouse—March, 1935
5. Original Negro One-Acts—Spring 1935

I would like very much to have any suggestions you'd give. I appreciate your encouraging comments but it would be helpful to have some criticism at times. We know that we aren't as good as we think we are.

I have hoped that more people would feel themselves so much a part of our dramatic program that they would drop around to make suggestions and requests and tell us their honest opinions.

If you let me know your office hours or conference hours, I'll pull out walking shoes or have my bus overhauled in view of the long and hazardous trip to the Atlanta University buildings.

This invitation comes from the one and—only Anne Cooke.[1]

Elizabeth Prophet (1890–1960), born in Rhode Island, from an early age showed great talent as a painter and, especially, as a sculptor. Meeting blatant discrimination in the United States, she managed to get to Paris where she studied and soon gained recognition. Du Bois early became her friend and he and Mrs. Du Bois assisted her. He published a glowing tribute to her character and work in the December 1929 Crisis *(36: 407, 427–29); Countee Cullen devoted an essay to her career in* Opportunity *8 (July 1930): 204–5.*

At Du Bois's urging, Miss Prophet became an art instructor at Atlanta University beginning in 1933. The next year Du Bois wrote her in connection with his own classes.

November 20, 1934

My dear Miss Prophet:

I do not want to press you or take time that you ought to give to your own work, or establish a precedent for invasion of your time by other persons; but if you decide you can take my class, Sociology 471, in Room 116, Friday, November 30, the following facts will guide you: the class has been studying race problems, more especially the problem of the Jews throughout Europe, and now the problem of the Irish. I have in all cases taken opportunity to make comparisons with the Negro problem in the United States.

It seems to me that it would be very interesting for them to have a colored person who has spent so long a time in France as you, tell them frankly about the attitude of the French toward Jews, toward Negroes, toward Asiatics, toward Americans.

You can sit down and talk in just conversational tone, and be quite frank with them. If you give them opportunity, they may want to ask some questions.

Very sincerely yours,

W. E. B. Du Bois

George Streator (1902–55) was a leader of the student strike at Fisk University early in 1925; he received a bachelor's degree there in 1926, did graduate work at Chicago and Columbia universities, and taught briefly in Virginia and North Carolina. Du Bois brought him to the Crisis *staff at the end of 1933, but he remained only briefly after Du Bois left. When he wrote the letter that follows he was an organizer in New York City for the Amalgamated Clothing Workers. Later he worked for the International Ladies Garment Workers, held various government posts during the Second World War, served as a reporter for the* New York Times *after the war, and in his last years was editor of the* Pilot, *organ of the National Maritime Union.*

If Du Bois replied in writing to this letter, no copy has been found.

1. Now Anne Cooke Reid, professor of drama at the University of Maryland.

[New York City], Nov. 27 [1934]

Dear Doctor—

Abe Harris has a review of Lewis Corey's *Decline of American Capitalism*—December, *American Mercury*. Skipping the pyro-technics, he comes to excellent conclusions, to wit: that there must be leadership in order to win the masses from their present allegiances; that preachers, school-teachers, etc., must be broken away from their worship of the powers that be. O.K. When do we begin?

Why don't you persuade Hope to bring some of the consumers' cooperative people from such groups as the Finns have here, for talks to Atlanta students?

Also, why can't Atlanta promote quietly a series of conferences with labor leaders? It could be done.

I consider the main obstacles to your program to be the ignorance of your other university faculties. After all, an uninformed professor of English can wisecrack every other achievement away in ten days. So, for Spring; I suggest for A.U.—three conferences:

(1) Consumers' cooperatives, Finns; C.L.A., etc.

(2) Labor-radical conference

(3) Workers education

What about a "Southern" Brookwood?

As a good radical, I am afraid of college students who do not rub elbows with real workers' organizations, no matter how weak the latter.

I'd like to talk with you about these.[1]

G.S.

In the exchange of letters between Braithwaite and Du Bois (pp. 3–5 of this volume), reference was made to the Du Bois Literary Prize, established in 1931 with an endowment from Mrs. Edward Roscoe Mathews. Mrs. Mathews's daughter, to whom Du Bois refers in the letter published below, was married to Oliver LaFarge, the Pulitzer Prize novelist.*

DuBois's letter is addressed to Mrs. Mathews in Hawaii, where, apparently, she was vacationing. The letter from her that Du Bois mentions has not survived, but his letter contains important substantive material.

1. Abram L. Harris (1899–1963) was co-author (with Sterling D. Spero) of *The Black Worker* (New York: Columbia University Press, 1931). The CLA was the Cooperative League of America. Brookwood refers to Brookwood Labor College (1921–36) at Katonah, New York, the first resident school for workers in the United States; it was headed from 1921 to 1933 by the late A. J. Muste, and at its height it had the official support of thirteen national and international unions.

Harris's review of the Corey book is in the *American Mercury* 33 (December 1934): 504–7. Streator's summary is much too abrupt to do justice to Harris's analysis, which is still worth reading.

* Information on Mrs. Mathews, her prize, and Du Bois's reflections on it will be found in the *Crisis* 38 (April 1931): 117, 137; (May 1931): 157.

Atlanta, Ga., December 14, 1934

My dear Mrs. Mathews:

Mrs. Du Bois forwarded to me your letter from Los Angeles and I am writing on the bare chance that this will find you somewhere on the habitable globe.

I have missed not seeing you and the family the last year. I had to sever my connnection with the N.A.A.C.P. The organization has done a good work and still may but in order to do its best work now it must be thoroughly re-organized and have a new staff. I could not see how I could guide this re-organization without many months, if not years, of bitter and exhausting controversy. On the other hand, I had offered me here at Atlanta University a position which requires my presence only about eight months in the year and which gives me leisure for writing, and absence of friction. I, therefore, made the change comfortably, severing all connection from *The Crisis*, and the N.A.A.C.P., so as to have no long, drawn-out differences.

The first difficulty with the N.A.A.C.P. is that after twenty-five years' work it faces a changed world, and that the slogans and programs which carried it through its earlier career are glaringly insufficient today. We have got to lay down new goals and adopt new methods. I think, gradually, this can be done outside the N.A.A.C.P. and the organization will be influenced by this outside work.

The depression has had widespread effect upon the American Negro. First of all, it has greatly slowed up his literary and artistic output. There have not been in the last four years any distinctive contributions to Negro-American literature, except Mr. Johnson's anthology. I do not see this year anything really worth while in poetry, except possibly, Sterling Brown's little volume. Mr. Braithwaite has the matter of arranging for the committee and giving of the prize and I have written him saying that I did not see an outstanding work to which the prize could be given.[1] I am disposed to suggest that we wait again and hold the prize over until we see something outstanding.

Give my best regards to Mr. Mathews and to your daughter and family. I hope you will have a successful trip.

Very sincerely yours,
W. E. B. Du Bois

Du Bois had a geniality and humor that showed itself among friends; he also practiced a very courteous and gracious kind of living. These qualities appear in a letter he wrote to Mrs. Alice Ruth Dunbar-Nelson (1875–1935), a teacher and author and longtime friend. Mrs. Dunbar-Nelson began publishing short stories in the 1890s and later wrote important works in history. She taught in New Orleans, was married for a time to Paul Laurence Dunbar, headed the English Department at Howard High School in Wilmington, Delaware, for many years, and

1. Sterling Brown's book, *Southern Road*, is discussed in earlier correspondence between Braithwaite and Du Bois. The anthology edited by James Weldon Johnson was *The Book of American Negro Poetry* (New York: Harcourt, Brace and Co., 1931), a revised edition of a book originally issued in 1922.

was married to Robert J. Nelson. She was active in the NAACP, *in anti-war movements, and in efforts to break away from the two-party political system. In her last years she lived in Philadelphia.*

The illness which induced Du Bois's note was a fatal one and some nine months after this letter, Mrs. Dunbar-Nelson died.

Atlanta, Ga., December 15, 1934

My dear Alice Dunbar:

I see "be the paapers" that you are trying to be an interesting invalid and collect bales of sympathy from your friends and enemies. I hasten to comply. Nevertheless, it is impossible for me to be terribly sorry for anyone that has a chance to lie up in bed and do absolutely nothing, right along through here. I am sure I should thrive on it.

I arise here mornings with the sun, getting my mile walk by half-past seven, and I am sitting in my office bright and perky by eight; somewhere between nine and eleven, I go to bed. After this recital of my strenuous life, I am sure you will arise in sheer shame and write me that it is all very much exaggerated. That as a matter of fact, you had retired behind closed doors, and the camouflage of sickness, in order to do the week's wash or finish that novel.

Whatever the facts are, please have a good time and get strong and prosperous and let me hear from you. If you cannot write yourself, make that lazy niece of yours write me in your stead.

I have had virtuous intentions of calling upon you but somehow you don't belong in Philadelphia. I always get to Wilmington before I remember where you are. Sometime this spring, however, I am going to see you. Please notify that sister of yours so that the biscuit will be properly browned. (I came near saying burned, but don't tell her.)

With best regards to you and Mr. Nelson and all the household.

Very sincerely yours,
W. E. B. Du Bois

1935

Du Bois offers some interesting reminiscences in a letter of congratulations to Fred R. Moore
(1857–1943). Moore had been twice elected an alderman in New York City late in the 1920s;
before that he was owner of the Colored American Magazine *(1905), and in 1907 he*
purchased the New York Age, *of which he remained editor and publisher until his death.*

Atlanta, Ga., January 3, 1935

My dear Mr. Moore:

I have just heard that you are celebrating the 50th Anniversary of *The Age.* May I
congratulate you, and also myself, for I remember that my first printed words appeared in the New York *Age* sometime about 1882 or 1883 while T. Thomas Fortune
was editor of what was then the New York *Globe.*

I was the local correspondent in Great Barrington, Massachusetts. There were only
about a score of colored people in the town, so that I was rather put to it for news, but
I managed to sell about ten copies of the *Age* each week, and now and then got in
about two inches of current history from the Berkshires.

I can, therefore, claim that the New York *Age* started me upon my literary career.[1]

Very sincerely yours
W. E. B. Du Bois

Earlier correspondence between Du Bois and the young teacher Henrietta Shivery appears in this
volume (pp. 8–10). Another exchange between the young woman and her godfather conveys
a little of the realities of life for Black people, especially in the South.

Meridian, Miss., January 25, 1935

Dear "D. D.":

I know that you have called me a lazy individual. You are perfectly right. I am as
lazy as you have pictured me. I know that you had a merry Xmas therefore I wont ask
you about it. I was in Atlanta for a few days during the holidays and had a rather nice
time.

Since I've been back I've had a little run in with some members of the opposite race.
Therefore I have kept myself very low not daring to go into town. Hence I am quite
behind in my moving picture trips. It happened like this. I went into a shoe store

---

1. From 14 April 1883 to 16 May 1885, young Du Bois appeared in twenty-seven issues of the
New York Globe (or *Freeman*, as it was called in 1884).

namely The Cinderella Shop, sat down and waited for several moments; no one came to wait on me. The clerks were not busy because there was no one in the store. There was a white woman standing at the counter around whom the clerks were clustered talking. After waiting several minutes more I got up and started out of the store. One of the clerks looked across his shoulder and said, "Wait a minute girl I'll wait on you after while." I looked around at him and said, "how old do women grow in your country?" He grabbed a shoe and said—"God damn you I'll show you." As I was near the door I made my speedy exit, not exactly running but walking very rapidly. Before I could get half way the block they were behind me saying, "Wait a minute nigger. Where are you from?" I didn't answer him. He said, "You don't know it but I don't care a thing about a nigger. I'll throw you down and beat your brains out of you right here in the street." I still didn't answer. By this time several individuals had gathered around so he wound up by saying, "You don't know how niggers act down here in Meridian. You had better ask some of them or get back where you come from. Don't you think one minute that you are as good as white folk." The two of them then turned around and returned to the store. I proceeded to go on and do what few things I had come to town to accomplish, got a taxi and returned home.

Bearing all this in mind I haven't been in town for fear I should encounter those individuals again. To make things much worse I found last week when our semester ends that all of my classes had been taken from me, leaving me with three messy classes, Geography, Health, and sixth grade History. The other time is to be spent out on the yard rounding up children that he himself [the principal] can do nothing with. As for doing work in my own field, that's wholly out of the question. The more I ponder over this job the more I am convinced that I am fed up on this $45.00 a month job. True I am feeding myself and that's all.

I am still taking typing. I wont say how much progress I have made. I am going to New York and find me a job this summer if its doing nothing but washing dishes. Say hello to mamma for me.

Please come over here some time before my school closes. Do you know President Dogan at Wiley College?[1]

Love,
Henrietta

Atlanta, Ga., February 4, 1935

My dear Dimples:

Your experience was a trying one but we have all been through it in some form or other. I remember long before you were born going into a book store on Mitchell Street [in Atlanta] and waiting for a crowd of lazy clerks to get over their conversation and wait on me. I finally started out when one of them called out: "What do you want, professor?" I simply answered, "I'm not a professor," and went on out.

---

1. Matthew W. Dogan was the president of Wiley College in Marshall, Texas; Du Bois did not answer this question but there is no evidence of the two men knowing each other.

In some parts of the country, including Mississippi, this might have led to a row, and my technique since then has been this: I go into a store and wait a reasonable time. If I am not waited on I walk out and say nothing to any comment or question that may be made. There is much less of this thing today than there used to be, but there is still enough of it to make your blood boil.

On the other hand, do not avoid going to town. Simply avoid that store. In the long run, that kind of boycott made by intelligent people who have a little courage left— there are few of those, even in Mississippi—will bring very tangible results.

The treatment of Negroes in the stores of Atlanta has improved 100% in the last twenty years, as I can see as I come back.

You have a tough job in Meridian and I knew you were going to. But do it well. Jobs are scarce now and tough jobs have to be done, as I have intimated before. Your principal, undoubtedly, is up against it, and has to do his work with a miserable appropriation. Don't despise the poor shrinking children that you have to take care of too much. There is something to be said for them.

Moreover, if you do this job well, you can undoubtedly do better next year. I am reasonably sure that you could get a position with Charlotte Hawkins Brown,[1] but a private school as well conducted as hers is will be a tremendous improvement. Greensboro is also quite civilized as compared with Meridian. Last, but not least, I often stop in Greensboro going to and from New York. So buck up and expect me to visit the metropolis sometime this spring.

I have told your mother that I have heard from you.

With love

W. E. B. Du Bois

Du Bois's activities were astonishing for their range, but primary among all his interests was education. A revealing exchange on this subject occurred in questions put to Du Bois by a professor at the School of Education of the University of Southern California, who simultaneously held the position of assistant supervisor of attendance in the city school system of Los Angeles.

Los Angeles, Calif., January 18, 1935

Dr. W. E. B. Du Bois
Dear Sir:

The creation of a position in the city schools of Los Angeles to be known as "Special Assistant to the Superintendent" is being considered here. The place is to be filled by a Negro, who will discuss with the Superintendent all policies affecting Negro students.

It is desirous to secure the attitudes of a number of leading American Negro

1. Dr. Charlotte Hawkins Brown (1877–1961) was the founder, in 1902, of the Palmer Memorial Institute in Sedalia, North Carolina, near Greensboro, where she remained president until 1952. She was the first Black woman elected to the National Board of the YWCA.

educators regarding the value of such a position to the system, including special references to the social background of Negro students as it relates to their participation in secondary mixed schools.

The Department of Education of the University of Southern California is interested in collecting data of this nature in collaboration with the local Board of Education concerning this position. With your permission your letter will be handed to this Department.

Will you kindly let me have your unbiased opinion in detail on the matter at your earliest convenience?

Please accept my thanks for your cooperation.

Yours very truly,
J. McFarline Ervin

Atlanta, Ga., January 31, 1935

Mr. J. McFarline Ervin
My dear Sir:

Whether or not the appointment of a special assistant to the superintendent to give advice concerning Negro pupils will be a good thing or not depends on two matters:

1. The kind of superintendent which you have.

2. The kind of man that you appoint.

If your superintendent is persuaded that colored children are a liability to be suppressed or gotten rid of, and if in accordance with that idea, he appoints a man whose business is to give him excuses and reasons for doing what he has made up his mind to do, then of course the whole move is going to be disastrous.

On the other hand, if you have in Los Angeles a superintendent or a schoolboard who looks upon children with dark faces as having the same possibilities for the good of the future world that their paler fellows have, and if knowing that these darker children have had difficulties in environment and education it makes their adjustment to the city schools difficult, and if to help him with these problems he gets a colored man of education, manners, and courage, who is going to tell the truth about things, and take pains to find out the truth, then nothing but good can eventually come from such an effort.

I am afraid that so hypothetical an answer to your letter will not do much good, but it is the best that I can do.

Very sincerely yours
W. E. B. Du Bois

Frank S. Horne (1899–1974), educated in colleges in New York, Illinios, and California, was a dean and acting president (1926–36) of Fort Valley State College in Georgia. Thereafter he held positions in the Roosevelt administration and more recently served with federal housing agencies. A poem by him won the Crisis *award in 1925, and his work appears in many anthologies. Letters concerning his poetry and Du Bois's estimate thereof were exchanged early in 1935.*

Fort Valley, Georgia, February 4, 1935

Dear Dr. Du Bois:

You really brought this on yourself. Or maybe my senses are still reeling from the memory of that distillate formula of the wise old Benedictine monks. At any rate you were momentarily thoughtless enough to ask me whether or not I was writing anything these days. It so happens that I have completed a collection of what have been so liberally called my poems. They have been printed and now appear in various anthologies, collections, a text book or two and translations in German and Russian. Several times a year there come requests of one sort or another for permission to reprint some verse or other. The Interracial Commission includes a brief selection in its recently edited "Singers in the Dawn" pamphlet.[1] Several of my more enthusiastic friends have often asked why I have not had a collection of my own published. My answer has usually been that I have been simply unable to decide which of the myriad hungry publishers storming at my door I should so signally honor.

I would like you to steal a moment here and there from your busy routine to glance at these things and say a word or two about them. I can stand most anything. In fact, my audacity in asking this favor can only be explained by my understanding that of all the people in the world I know, I can depend upon you in a matter of this kind to speak your mind ruthlessly. I had thought that if such a slim collection were offered to a publisher, I should want it in such a modest format that the price would be so low that even Southern teachers and students might be induced to procure a copy or two. I have wondered, too, if you have thought of publishing something that would preserve your incisive viewpoints for the Southern student of today. It has seemed to me a great loss to a group of students just emerging into some consciousness of their problems in the midst of such tumultuous social and economic movements that they are deprived of the realistic thinking of one who could guide, clarify and crystallize their thinking through the written word.

Anyhow, read 'em and weep. The *Opportunity* magazine has asked me for an article on Industrial schools in the South. I am planning to tell them at least some of the unvarnished truth; if you need a good janitor, keep the job open a while for me.[2] Couldn't you come down during Negro History Week and tell us something of Africa? For the monks of the good Saint Benedict we will substitute an army of the collectors of dew-from-the-early-Spring-morning-blush-of-peaches. The masterpieces come under separate cover.

Frank Horne

1. Robert B. Eleazer, comp., *Singers in the Dawn: A Brief Supplement to the Study of American Literature* (Atlanta: Conference on Education and Race Relations, 1934). Horne's poem "To James" appears on page fifteen of this twenty-four-page pamphlet. The only collection of his poetry to be published is a forty-page booklet, *Haverstraw* (London: P. Breman, 1963).

2. Horne published two essays under the title, "The Industrial School of the South," in *Opportunity* 13 (May and June 1935): 136–39, 178–81. These are deeply critical and merit study today.

February 14, 1935
Memorandum on "Songs for a Lynching Bee."

I have just gone through these poems again. They merit publication. It will be a great loss if they are not published. They are good, and here and there is a line, a thought, that reaches greatness.

I am not sure about the title and the arrangement. I think I can see what you have in mind. All of these might be sung to lynchers but lynchers can't read and readers recoil from lynching bees. If you can catch them and hold them and make them read, all right. Possibly, however, you have to hit them with a smaller bludgeon at first.

A few titles are missing, 3 or 4. You probably know this, and have decided either to omit them or insert them later.

But it's a good collection. I like them. I hope you will get them into print.

[W. E. B. Du Bois]

Early in 1935, Du Bois proposed editing an anthology which unfortunately did not find a publisher. His description of the projected book is of interest. Its rejection came from John C. Farrar (b.1896) of the then fairly new house of Farrar and Rinehart. Farrar's mention of renewing "an old association" is unclear; he had been an editor of the Bookman *and was connected with Doubleday prior to founding in 1929, together with Stanley Rinehart, his own publishing firm, but there is nothing in Du Bois's biography to indicate any connection with those endeavors. Du Bois's letter was addressed to the editorial department of Farrar and Rinehart in New York City.*

Atlanta, Ga., February 9, 1935
Gentlemen:

In 1925, Albert and Charles Boni published a book called "The New Negro," edited by Alain Locke. It was designed to restate the position of the Negro with regard to his general problems and accomplishment.

Ten years have passed and ten years so filled with economic and social change that they could perhaps be fifty years in ordinary times. At any rate, the outlook of the Negro has perceptibly changed, and not only is there a younger generation struggling for expression, but also some of the older men are changing their points of view.

It has been suggested to me by a young Negro who is about to get his Doctor's degree in Sociology at Columbia University that it will be an excellent time just now for me to edit a volume on present currents of thought among Negroes. That my task would be to select the proper writers, and perhaps to sum up and interpret what they have said.

There are a number of persons, some of whom did not appear in the former volume, who might make excellent contributions to this. Among these are Abram Harris, a Doctor of Philosophy in Economics from Columbia, and professor at Howard University; Rayford Logan, former Captain in the A.E.F., and candidate for the Doctor's degree in History at Harvard, Ira Reid, who has done a good deal of social investigation, and is a Master of Arts from Columbia, Robert Weaver, a Harvard Ph.D., connected with the N.R.A., Sterling Brown, Howard University, author of several volumes of poetry, William H. Dean, a Harvard M.A. in Economics, who has made a notable record, and E. Franklin Frazier, a Doctor of Philosophy from the University of Chicago.

Beside these economists and historians of the younger group, there are artists and writers. Langston Hughes and Countee Cullen wrote before, but doubtless have a new message, and there is Welborn Jenkins, Claude McKay, George Schuyler, Arna Bontemps, George W. Streator, W. N. Rivers, the Cornell Doctor in Literature, V.B. Spratlin, a Ph.D. in Spanish Literature, and a number of others. I think I could get the co-operation of most of these.

I am writing to ask if you will be interested in such a volume, and would be glad to have your judgment.

Very sincerely yours

W. E. B. Du Bois

New York City, 21st February, 1935

Dear Mr. Du Bois:

I regret exceedingly that we cannot see our way to do your proposed book on the Negro. It would be fine to renew an old association, but we already have one or two omnibus books coming along and hesitate to extend ourselves further in this direction. You will most likely be able to place it elsewhere and I do hope so.

Yours sincerely,

John Farrar

Throughout his life Du Bois opposed anti-Semitism. Antagonism to appointing Joel E. Spingarn president of the NAACP in 1930 was based, in part, upon his being Jewish, and Du Bois—who loved Spingarn and dedicated his Dusk of Dawn *to him—resented and resisted this discrimination fiercely. Evidences of this facet of Du Bois's general detestation of vulgarity and cruelty appeared frequently; one such episode was his joining with other people of eminence soon after the First World War to denounce the so-called "Protocols of Zion" as the forgery they were and to castigate Henry Ford for his campaign to spread this poison.*

This background explains a letter from Herman Bernstein (1876–1935), written shortly before his death, to Du Bois. Bernstein, born in Czarist Russia, came to the United States in 1893. He was a European correspondent for both the New York Times *and* Herald, *and he published books of poetry, journalistic commentary, and studies (in 1921 and 1935) of the Protocols. It was Bernstein who sued Henry Ford for libel in 1921, a case that was settled out of court and that brought an apology from the automobile magnate. From 1930 to 1933, Bernstein was United States minister to Albania.*

New York City, February 11th, 1935

Dear Mr. Du Bois:

I have requested my publishers to send you, with my compliments, a copy of my

new book, "The Truth About the Protocols of Zion." The volume is dedicated to
"lovers of truth and justice and particularly to the one hundred and nineteen eminent
American Christians who, in January, 1921, signed the protest against the dissemination of the spurious 'Protocols of the Wise Men of Zion' and the 'vicious
propaganda' of prejudice and hatred, and who called upon 'moulders of public opinion—the clergy and ministers of all Christian churches, the publicists, teachers,
editors, and statesmen—to strike at this un-American and un-Christian agitation.' "
This book is thus dedicated to you as one of the signers of that splendid document,
which is reproduced in the book.

In this volume I am presenting the documentary evidence revealing both the motives and the methods of the fabricators of the so-called "Protocols of the Wise Men of
Zion," which have been and are still being used to invite religious and racial prejudice
and hatred. I believe that these documents show conclusively the various stages of the
literary forgery that has caused so much suffering to the Jewish people.

I would deeply appreciate any comment you may wish to make regarding the
subject discussed in this book.[1]

With high esteem and kind regards,

Yours sincerely,
Herman Bernstein

*One of the most persistent myths about Du Bois makes him the main foe of the Garvey movement.
At every opportunity Du Bois sought to set his position straight (see, for example, volume one of
this work, pp. 318–19, 464–65); a response early in 1935 to a correspondent not otherwise
identified is exemplary.*

New Haven, Conn., March 7, 1935

Dr. W. E. B. Du Bois
Dear Sir:

I have been interested by some members of the UNIA in their movement. Among
the discussion held at which I was to get the program and history of the movement
your name was mentioned several times in a derogatory manner. You were accused of
having sold out the organization and aided materially in causing its collapse. For
weeks I have been reading and writing to people whom I know to be against it in an
effort to reach something close to the truth. Why do you oppose it? The whole object
of the movement being:

"The objects of the Universal Negro Improvement Association and African
Communities' League shall be: to establish a Universal Confraternity among the

---

1. No comment from Du Bois seems to have survived. Earlier, however, Du Bois had
commented upon the anti-Semitism of Ford and the libel suit brought against him in the *Crisis*
34 (May and August 1927): 75,183. The book Bernstein sent Du Bois was *The Truth About "The
Protocols of Zion": A Complete Exposure* (New York: Covici, Friede, 1935).

race; to promote the spirit of pride and love; to reclaim the fallen; to administer to and assist the tribes of Africa; to assist in civilizing the backward tribes of Africa; to assist in the development of Independent Negro Nations and Communities; to establish Commissionaries or Agencies in the principal countries and cities of the world for the representation and protection of all Negroes, irrespective of nationality; to promote a conscientous Spiritual worship among the native tribes of Africa; to establish Universities, Colleges, Academies and Schools for the racial education and culture of the people; to conduct a world-wide Commerical Intercourse for the good of the people; to work for better conditions in all Negro communities."

To amend that and add more I would say that it will do just what you asked for in Chicago last week; establish race pride. It would tear down the dogmas upon which race prejudice and imputed inferiority are based; tear down the dogmas that make the American Negro look upon Africa as a dark continent and one to be shunned and despised as a homeland.

The movement does not say that all Negroes should return to Africa, the impossibility and futility of that being obvious, but don't you see the psychological effect, the stabilizing effect the idea has? If Negroes in America or the West Indies could feel that if they chose they could go to Africa, that some economic and social security was there or even that they could go there and help to work out their own salvation, to develop a new culture; would not that in a measure make them unite to break down barriers to their economic and cultural progress?

Upon rereading this, I find that I am far from clear but trying hard to see some light.

Please let me hear from you as soon as possible.

Yours truly,
Joseph Semper

Atlanta, Ga., March 11, 1935

My dear Sir:

I could not be accused of having sold out the U.N.I.A., since I was never a member of it, nor did I have anything to do with it. With its general objects, I agree, although they were much too vague and grandiose to be at all practicable. My attack upon the organization was an attack upon the dishonesty and deception of Marcus Garvey, and the reasons for that were set forth in detail in the *Crisis* for: December, 1920, January, 1921, August, 1924, January, 1923 and June, 1927.

Very sincerely yours,
W. E. B. Du Bois

Malcolm H. Bryan (1902–67), a professor of economics at the University of Georgia from 1925 to 1936, was a founder and editor of the Southern Economic Journal *(1933–37). In the latter years of his life he held government positions and served as an official of the Federal Reserve Bank of Georgia. Together with J. Thomas Askew he compiled* Readings to Accompany a Course on Contemporary Georgia *(Athens: University of Georgia Press, 1935); in connection with that effort he wrote Du Bois.*

Athens, Ga., March 7, 1935

Dear Dr. Du Bois:

Some months ago Chancellor Weltner of the University System of Georgia set me the task of getting up a textbook and a volume of readings to be entitled "Problems of Georgia," which I have changed to "Contemporary Georgia." Naturally many questions arise as to the relative status and condition of the Negro.

One of the first snags that I have struck in discussing the population of Georgia has to do with a satisfactory explanation of why there is a much greater tendency for the Negro population to drift out of the State than is true of whites, and in discussing this problem the question of whether or not the Negro is relatively exploited in the South must naturally come up for attention. I am exceedingly anxious, therefore, to get for my readings, and for my own information, material on this point. I wonder if you could assist me by suggesting articles of a scholarly and competent nature having to do either with the Negro's economic status in Georgia, particularly, or in the South, generally, that would, in your judgement, meet the intellectual capacities of sophomore students.

I might say that I am also exceedingly anxious to secure any data that you may know of tending to demonstrate for Georgia or the South the relative wage payments of Negroes and whites for identical services in identical employments—also anything tending to demonstrate factually the fact that the Negro in the South does not sell his labor on a free market.

I shall appreciate more genuinely than I can say any assistance that you can give me on these matters and will also appreciate your suggestion for other material that might be useful and suitable in this course.

Dr. Evans promised me that he would see you in regard to the possiblity of your doing an article for the *Southern Economic Journal.* I am wondering if he ever fulfilled the promise.[1]

Very sincerely yours,
Malcolm H. Bryan
Associate Professor of Economics

Atlanta, Ga., March 14, 1935

My dear Sir:

Answering your letter of March 7, I beg to say that you could get data on "The

1. Philip Weltner was chancellor of the University System of Georgia from 1933 to 1935 and later president of Oglethorpe University. Mercer G. Evans of Emory University was the secretary of the Southern Economic Association and in charge of programs from 1933 to 1936. The *Journal* was the organ of that association.

Economic Status of the Negro in Georgia and in the South" from the following works:

"The Negro Landholder in Georgia," Bulletin of the Department of Labor, Number 35, July, 1901; "The Negro in the Black Belt," Bulletin of the Department of Labor, Number 22, May, 1899; "Atlanta University Publications," Number 2, 1897, Number 6, 1901, Number 7, 1902, Number 9, 1904, Number 12, 1907, Number 14, 1909, Number 16, 1911, and Number 17, 1912. Also, Greene and Woodson, "The Negro Wage Earner," published by the Association for the Study of Negro Life and History, 1930; Spero and Harris, "The Black Worker," Columbia University Press, 1931; "The Negro in American Civilization," by Charles S. Johnson, Henry Holt and Company, 1930; "Georgia Nigger," by John L. Spivak, Brewer, Warren and Putnam, 1932, and "Black Reconstruction," Harcourt, Brace and Company, by myself, which is announced for April of this year; Carter G. Woodson, "The Rural Negro," published by the Association for the Study of Negro Life and History, 1930, and the recent book by Charles S. Johnson on "The Shadow of the Plantation." You also might consult Feldman, "Racial Factors in American Industry," Harper, 1931.

My own study of Georgia in the Second Volume of "These United States," edited by Ernest Gruening, and published by Boni and Liveright, could be consulted.

If you do not find what you wish in these references, I should be glad to give you others.

Dr. Evans has not spoken to me about the article in *The Southern Economic Journal*. I should be glad to prepare one sometime, if it was desired.[1]

Very sincerely yours,
W. E. B. Du Bois

Athens, Ga., March 18, 1935

Dear Professor Du Bois:

Thank you very much indeed for your letter giving me references along the lines of the questions I asked. I am really very grateful for this assistance and will try my best to examine all of these materials. I am sure that I shall be able to find something of service.

I very much want you one of these days to give me an article for the *Southern Economic Journal*. I am not going to suggest its immediate preparation, however, until such time as I can see the finances of the Journal more thoroughly for a longer time in advance. As you perhaps know, we threaten to suspend from one thin issue to

1. There is no record in Du Bois's correspondence of any letter from Evans. Du Bois wrote the Department of Labor *Bulletins* he mentioned, and edited the Atlanta University Publications. The man mentioned as a co-author with Woodson is Lorenzo J. Greene. Johnson's *Shadow of the Plantation* was published in 1934 by the University of Chicago Press. The Feldman referred to is Herman Feldman. The work edited by Ernest Gruening (later the United States senator from Alaska) was published in two volumes in 1924; Du Bois's essay on Georgia appears in volume two, pp. 322–45.

another, and I am especially dubious right now as to what is going to happen to us. You will hear from me again, however, on this point.[1]

In the meantime, again many thanks for your assistance.

Very sincerely yours,
Malcolm H. Bryan

In 1930, Gustav Oberlaender founded the Oberlaender Trust, with headquarters in Philadelphia, the stated purpose of which was "the development of cultural relations between the United States and German-speaking countries." The trustees, in addition to Oberlaender, were Carl W. Ackerman, Henry Allen Moe, and Wilbur K. Thomas, secretary-treasurer.

Sometime in late February or early March 1935, Du Bois applied for a grant from this fund so that he might visit Germany and study its educational system. Among the people approached by Thomas for an opinion as to the wisdom of making this grant was Frank Tannenbaum (1893–1969). Tannenbaum, after some work for the Brookings Institution in Washington and the publication of books on prison reform, the labor movement, aspects of life in the South and—especially—Latin America, became a member of Columbia University's faculty late in 1935, a position he held until his death.

On 11 March 1935, Tannenbaum replied from his Brookings post to Thomas's request for information, sending to Du Bois a copy of his letter that is now in the Du Bois papers.

Washington, D. C., March 11, 1935

Dear Mr. Thomas:

In reply to your letter of March 8 about Du Bois' application, permit me to say that I hope you will grant it.

Dr. Du Bois is, as you know, a person of very rarest gifts and a wide influence not only among Negroes but among other people interested in the Negro problem in the United States. He will learn a great deal more that will be of interest to us and to the American community than most other people to whom you could make available such an opportunity. An application from Du Bois to any foundation honors it.

Our whole educational program—not merely that of the Negro—is in a state of flux, and the best of our educators are going through a period of heart burning over the break-down of past efforts, especially in industrial education, and are blindly seeking for light wherever light can be found for the future.

Few people in this country are as sensitive or as intelligent as Du Bois, and your making a small fund available to him might in the end turn out to be the making of a great gift to the United States.

Sincerely,
Frank Tannenbaum

1. If Du Bois was ever asked to contribute to this journal no record of the request has been seen. It continues to be published, based at Chapel Hill, North Carolina.

Du Bois replied to Tannenbaum, and, in response to a request on 17 April 1935 for a detailed proposal, to Thomas.

Atlanta, Ga., March 14, 1935

My dear Mr. Tannenbaum:

I appreciate very much the kind letter which you sent to Wilbur K. Thomas.

Very sincerely yours,

W. E. B. Du Bois

Atlanta, Ga., May 3, 1935

My dear Mr. Thomas:

Answering your letter of April 17, I beg to submit the following plan:

1. I should like to investigate in Germany and Austria the relation of education to industry; that is, the extent to which the schools, elementary and higher, are used to furnish workers and leaders for the carrying on and development of industry in these countries. I shall want to do this with a special reference to our problems in the United States and more particularly to the Negro problem. My object would be to find out if possible through German experience the real cause of the partial failure of the Negro industrial schools in the South so ardently championed by the late Booker T. Washington and to be able to suggest methods by which these industrial schools instead of developing into ordinary colleges might again apply themselves to the problem of inducting American Negroes in industry.

2. For this purpose, I should like to spend 6 months as follows: a month in the Hanse cities and the Rhineland, a month in Bavaria, a month or 6 weeks in Prussia and East Germany, a month in Austria and the rest of the time for consolidating this study.

3. In this study, I would like to examine the laws and ordinances on industrial education, educational customs, the actual courses of study, the results of this instruction, the educational efforts within industries, including apprenticeship, and the social, class and race lines.

4. I hardly know how to estimate the cost of this from the data I have in hand. There would, of course, be—

A. Ocean passage to and from Germany and the travel in Germany.

B. Board and lodging for six months.

C. Some compensation for any salary which I would lose on account of my absence from my work at the University. This last matter I will take up with the President of Atlanta University as soon as possible.

5. My work for the next 5 or 6 months would have to be finished before I could go. It includes (a) a booklet on "The Negro and Social Reorganization"; (b) preliminary work on a proposed Encyclopedia of the Negro; (c) work on the history of the Negro in the World War which is partly finished.[1] I propose, therefore, to get these matters

---

1. Du Bois did write a brief book, "The Negro and Social Reorganization," for a series being edited by Alain Locke; he was paid for his labors but the manuscript was not published—

in such shape that they could be either finished or left by, say, April 1, 1936, and then spend the time from April 1 to October 1 in the proposed work in Germany.

I should be very glad to get your criticism of this plan.

Very sincerely yours,
W. E. B. Du Bois

Wilbur K. Thomas (1883–1953) had been executive director of the American Friends' Service Committee from 1918 to 1929 and in this capacity was especially active in Soviet Russia and Germany. In 1931 he became executive director of the Carl Schurz Memorial Foundation and the next year accepted his post with the Oberlaender Trust, a position he held until 1946. In his last years he served as a pastor of the Congregational Church in Otis, Massachusetts. His response to Du Bois was positive.

Philadelphia, Pa., May 9, 1935

Dear Dr. Du Bois:

The plan outlined in your letter of May 3 seems to me to be feasible. I believe such a study would yield interesting results, of real value in this country.

Since you could not plan to go until next year, there will be plenty of time in which to complete arrangements as to the amount of money you will need, etc., and to have these confirmed by our Board. I hope we shall have an opportunity to meet and discuss these questions. Will you let me know when you may be planning a trip north?

Sincerely yours,
Wilbur K. Thomas

Letters that Thomas and Du Bois exchanged between June and November 1935 tell the story of the completion of the arrangements for the Oberlaender grant. Du Bois actually left the United States in June 1936 and returned—after a trip that took him around the world—in April 1937. Later correspondence discusses Du Bois's objectives and some of the results of the journey. See pages 134–38 below.

Philadelphia, Pa., June 12, 1935

Dear Dr. Du Bois:

The Trustees of The Oberlaender Trust considered your application at their meeting on June 6. I am happy to report that they voted to appropriate the sum of $1600.00 to you, provided it will enable you to carry out your plans in a satisfactory way. We realize of course that this is not as large an amount as you had in mind, but it represents the sum which we felt was available for your particular object.

---

perhaps because it was highly critical of the New Deal—and remains unpublished to this day (see pp. 77–86 in this volume). The Encyclopedia of the Negro occupied Du Bois for years, indeed, decades, as he was working on it when he died in Ghana in 1963. The history of the Negro in the First World War he was never able to finish.

I shall be glad to hear from you as to whether or not this amount is sufficient to enable you to spend a year in Germany. If it is I shall be glad to be of assistance to you in working out plans, etc.

Yours sincerely,
Wilbur K. Thomas

New York, N. Y., June 22nd, 1935

My dear Mr. Thomas:

I have your letter of June 12th. Are you going to be in Philadelphia during the month of June? If so, I shall run down.

You say in your letter "a year in Germany"—you remember that we planned it for six months and I shall have to consult with you as to living costs, in order that I may see just what I could do in six months on the matter.

Kindly let me hear from you.

Very sincerely yours,
W. E. B. Du Bois

Philadelphia, Pa., November 23, 1935.

Dear Dr. Du Bois:

It is quite satisfactory to the Trustees of The Oberlaender Trust for you to go to Germany in May, 1936, for a six months' stay. A maximum of $1600.00 is available for the trip. We shall be glad to arrange to buy your steamship fare and then give you an order on our Mark account in Berlin for the remainder.

Will you kindly let me know at once what class you want to travel and on what ship. It is necessary for us to get reservations at once, as everything will be very crowded on account of the Olympic Games. I shall be glad to hear from you on this at your earliest convenience.

Yours sincerely
Wilbur K. Thomas

Atlanta, Ga., November 25, 1935

My dear Mr. Thomas:

Answering your letter of November 23, I beg to say that I would like to go to Berlin by way of London on any boat sailing after May 28. I should prefer to go on one of the slower, one-class boats, but if such a passage is not available, I would go second-class on one of the faster boats. I have no preference as to lines.

Very sincerely yours
W. E. B. Du Bois

William Leo Hansberry (1894–1965) devoted fifty years to a study of the history of Africa, inspired by Du Bois's Negro, published in 1915. Most of his academic life was spent as a teacher at Howard University, but in the 1950s he was a Fulbright scholar in Africa and then *taught African history briefly at the New School for Social Research in New York City. His last years he spent in Africa; in 1963, the Nigerian government established the Hansberry College of African Studies as part of the University of Nigeria, and Hansberry was appointed Distinguished Professor. In the year of his death, Hansberry published an appreciation of Du Bois, one of the few products of his pen to see print.* As this is written (1974), plans are well under way to publish the Hansberry papers in several volumes, so that at last Du Bois's continual urgings upon Hansberry will reach fruition.*

In response to a letter containing such urgings—a letter that seems not to have survived —Hansberry wrote to Du Bois from Howard University.

Washington, D. C., March 15, 1935

My dear Dr. Du Bois:

Your letter of some several days ago came just as I was leaving for lecture engagements in New England, hence my delay in the reply.

I regret to have to say that I have not yet published any of the work which I sent or mentioned to you in my last communications. Two years ago I completed the foundation-research on the History of Ancient Ethiopia. That done, I perhaps should have taken your advice and promptly published the material. Just about that time, however, Oxford University began the excavations of a most important site in Ethiopia. Knowing the value of what would be revealed through this effort, I decided to await at least the preliminary reports of the findings.

In the meantime, I turned my attention to a task I had long contemplated—a thorough examination into the sources on the history of Greater Ethiopia in the Medieval period. As I had anticipated, I found this a most engaging and fruitful field and in a short while was deeply absorbed with it, almost to the exclusion of anything else. By redoubling my efforts, I am now drawing close to the end of the basic research necessary to this study. I am now making a strenuous effort to be relieved from my teaching schedule next year in order that I may devote my full time to the final drafts of the manuscripts of each of these studies. In the event that the leave is granted, I shall have ready for publication next spring, the study *Imperial Ethiopia in Antiquity*—a study of the Ancient Negro in the Arts of War and Peace. By the end of the summer of 1936, I hope also to have in the publisher's hands the second study— *Imperial Ethiopia in the Middle Ages*—a study of the Medieval Negro in the affairs of Church and State.

Although Dr. [Charles H.] Wesley has strongly recommended my leave for next year, Dean [Edward P.] Davis, on the basis of a technicality, has taken a determined

---

* See William Leo Hansberry, "Du Bois' Influence on African Histoy," *Freedomways* 5 (Winter 1965): 73–87; and James G. Spady, "Dr. William Leo Hansberry: The Legacy of an African Hunter," *A Current Bibliography on African Affairs* 3 (November-December 1970): 25–40. In 1974 Howard University Press in Washington issued *Pillars of African History: The William Leo Hansberry African History Notebook*, edited by Joseph E. Harris.

stand against it. The matter is to be decided by the President and the Trustees at the Spring meeting of the Board.[1]

In connection with the appeal I am making to the President and the Board, I am now preparing certain materials which incidentally may be of some service to you in the projected revision of "The Negro."[2] I owe much to you for that work and consider it both a privilege and obligation to serve you in any way I can in the effort to bring out the new edition. Within the next two or three weeks I shall send you copies of the mentioned material, together with a list of some new publications—books and articles—which may have escaped your attention. Wishing for you much success in the new undertaking, I am

Very sincerely yours,
William Leo Hansberry

Soon after rejoining Atlanta University, Du Bois turned his attention to efforts at reinstituting the Atlanta University Conferences and Studies which he had directed during the last years of the nineteenth century and the first decade of the twentieth. One result of this was an approach, in March 1935, by President John Hope of the university to the Commonwealth Fund in New York City to assist in a study of the city of Atlanta and its Black population. The request was for a grant of fifteen thousand dollars.

The general director of the fund was Barry C. Smith, who had served in this capacity since 1921 and retired from it in 1947.* In response to President Hope, Smith wrote on 8 April 1935 that the Commonwealth Fund had given money since 1919 to various social studies, but that no practical results seemed to have been forthcoming; hence, "I should be interested to have from you a statement of a few of the practical concrete results which you would expect to follow from such a study and just how you would anticipate making use of the findings of the study to secure such results."

Du Bois replied on behalf of Atlanta University.

Atlanta, Ga., April 13, 1935

My dear Mr. Smith:

We too are not unmindful of the difficulties faced in securing concrete results from social studies. Yet, we know of no instrument that has been more effective in interpreting the problems of the Negro, and in securing recognition of the need for action than the well-conceived social study has been in recent years. Because of this belief

1. In 1936–37 Hansberry studied at the School of Oriental Studies, University of Chicago, and thereafter for two years, assisted by a Rockefeller grant, at Oxford and Cambridge universities in England.

2. This refers to what became Du Bois's *Black Folk Then and Now* (New York: Henry Holt and Co., 1939)—really a new book rather than a revision of the 1915 work.

* See *The Commonwealth Fund: Historical Sketch 1918–1962* (New York: Harkness House, 1963), pp. 3–17.

we have read very carefully the judgements expressed in your letter of April 8th.

In defending the utility of the proposed study of the American Negro in Atlanta, I am restating the contents of your letter in the form of three questions, as follows:

1. What concrete results are expected from the study?
2. How are these results to be secured?
3. What practical results have followed from other studies?

No social study can in itself effect changes and reforms. It can find the facts, present the findings and suggest ways for improving certain conditions. This study will propose remedial and constructive programs to be carried out in certain fields, depending upon its findings. We know that there are certain areas of maladjustment in the community. These relate to problems of work and income, home and neighborhood, life, leisure, citizenship and civil rights, health and education. We believe that some of these problems must be handled by the Negro community alone; others must be handled by the white community alone; and others, by far the largest group, must be approached through the combined effort of the white and the colored community. The study will ascertain the specific maladjustments, relate those to the groups believed best adapted to handle the problems, and propose certain programs and policies for action. The concrete results will be determined in part at least, by the type and character of community support the University can secure, as well as by the forcefulness of the study itself.

There is one concrete result of which we can be certain. That is the educating of the community with the problem studied. By making this information available to the public through the press, the movies, conferences, discussion, and practical demonstrations, the study should provide the basis for not only counteracting much of the subversive propaganda against Negroes now current in Atlanta, but for a constructive, intelligent approach to a persistent problem. If the study does no more than this it will serve an excellent purpose in the community, and will be well worth undertaking.

II

The techniques for bringing about concrete results are based upon the organization of an effective community committee. This committee will be composed of white and colored persons, and will represent all major groupings of activities, public and private, in which the matter of Negro adjustment is a vital one. The purpose of this committee will be fourfold:

1. To stimulate effective publicizing of the report's findings through the press, conferences, etc.

2. To prepare memorials to public and private agencies, and to confer with these agencies on the problems and programs suggested in the report.

3. To stimulate the interest of the Negro community and Negro neighborhoods in utilizing effectively their own resources.

4. To arrange for demonstrations of practical changes that may be effected when there is a concerted community effort. Such demonstrations may be in the fields of health, recreation, adult education by the University, in co-operation with the committee and the community.

These methods are not mere paper devices. They were used very effectively in a study of twenty-five Negro communities in New Jersey in 1931–32. This study was conducted by a member of our staff.[1] For such a program, Atlanta is virgin soil. Atlanta University realized the necessity for the program and is eager to take the initiative in stimulating the necessary community action.

III

The proof of the foregoing statements may be found in the experience of Atlanta University. From 1897 to 1911, Atlanta University conducted a series of conferences and studies. There was at the time no distinct plan of doing more than furnishing a sound basis of fact. Nevertheless, practical results did follow. We made, for instance, three studies on conditions of Negroes in cities, and efforts for social betterment, in 1896, 1897, and ten years later, in 1907. Out of these studies arose a great interest among Atlanta Negroes in social work, the first result of which was the kindergartens established by Negroes before there were any for whites in the city, and sustained by private contributions; and also, a general movement which gradually was crystallized by the organization of the Neighborhood Union, and eventually by the establishment of the School of Social Work, and efforts for inter-racial understanding and Adult Education.

The third study in 1898, continued in 1907, was on Negro business and economic co-operation among Negroes. This resulted in the founding of the Negro Business League, which still exists after more than thirty-five years of work, and has done a great deal for the guiding of Negro business. When the late Mr. Booker T. Washington heard of our conference and study, he asked for a statement of the results, objects, and especially lists of the business men with whom we had corresponded. On the basis of this list, he made his first call for the Negro Business League.

The study of education in colleges and common schools, done in 1900, 1901, 1910 and 1911, launched a lively discussion as to the place of the college and industrial school, and had its effect upon the subsequent course of Negro education. The study of the Negro artisan in 1902 and 1912, was participated in by Booker T. Washington and R. R. Moton, and led to attempts to bring Negro workers into trade unions. The results were largely abortive but this was mainly due to the attitude of the unions. No concrete movement followed our study of the Negro church, but the study of Negro crime in 1909 was later used as a part of the basis of an anti-lynching campaign under the N.A.A.C.P..

The efficiency of these studies was enhanced by the conferences which were held and the prominent persons who took part in them, and thus gave wide publicity to the results. Nearly all the leading social writers and workers of the day joined in this part of our studies. The appropriations, however, for the work were so small, less than $5,000 a year, including salaries, that at last the whole effort had to be given up.

In the proposed new set of studies, we are again compelled to make them because of

1. This was Ira De A. Reid; Du Bois called attention to the study he conducted in the March 1933 *Crisis* (40:70).

certain very definite problems which face us, and this is peculiarly true of the situation in Atlanta, where we want to make the first study.

In connection with this, we have the housing proposition about to be put into realization by the United States government. We have made a study of the people living in the area before it was cleared. This was to ascertain the exact type of community which the cleared area represented, their income and expenditures, and their demands in the matter of housing and other facilities. This study was put at the disposal of the United States government and used for comparisons in its other housing projects.

We have made a study of groups of Negroes in this and other parts of the city who represent the class of folk who would probably move in to this area. We have made some tentative estimates of the actual expenditures of the families who will occupy this area with the idea of seeing just what amounts of food, including meat and bread and vegetables, they are going to need in a year.[2] We plan to continue this sort of study with the idea of determining from this group, and from others, how far surrounding Negro farmers, or farmers who could be brought into touch with this group, could actually furnish the food that these people want. How far cooperative effort could help in the distribution of fuel, medical service, and possibly, some portions of the clothing.

This statement, Mr. Smith, I believe, accurately represents what we at Atlanta University conceive to be the possibilities of our proposed study.

Sincerely yours,
W. E. B. Du Bois

As shown in the first volume of Du Bois's correspondence (pp. 145–47), Du Bois projected the idea of an Encyclopedia of the Negro at least as early as 1909. In 1931 plans for such an undertaking were again announced and by 1934 the project had reached embryonic organizational form, with the backing of the Phelps-Stokes Fund and with Du Bois as the key responsible figure. For the remainder of the 1930s, the effort to bring into being such an encyclopedia was to consume hundreds of hours of Du Bois's time and large portions of his inexhaustible energy.

One of the organizations approached for help in funding the encyclopedia was the Rosenwald Fund, but Edwin R. Embree, president of the fund, responded in a letter to J. G. Phelps-Stokes with notable lack of enthusiasm for the venture. Embree's criticism was turned over to Du Bois for reply.

Atlanta, Ga., April 24, 1935
My dear Mr. Embree:

At a recent meeting of the directors of the proposed Encyclopedia of the Negro, Mr. [Phelps-] Stokes read your criticism of our project.

---

2. A description of this *Study of the Atlanta University Federal Housing Area,* prepared by Du Bois and issued in mimeographed form by the university in May 1934, will be found in Herbert Aptheker, *An Annotated Bibliography of the Published Writings of W. E. B. Du Bois* (Millwood, New York: Kraus-Thomson, 1973), p. 544.

I am venturing to disagree with you, not with the object of pressing the matter of any contribution from the Rosenwald Fund, but because I believe so thoroughly in the necessity of an Encyclopedia of the Negro now and not ten or fifteen years hence.

It seems to me that you forget that an encyclopedia is not a history. A history may have to be postponed in the writing until more source material is known, but even in that case, it should not be postponed until the collection of material is complete, because that would take a very long time. In any case and in the meantime, there should be some authoritative source from which children and the general public could learn at least as much as there is to be known about the particular period in mind.

With an encyclopedia, however, the case is even more imperative. An encyclopedia is not only a record of history, but a record of present conclusions and opinions and whatever an encyclopedia gains in factual accuracy by postponement of publication, it more than loses in lessening its grip on current opinion. For that reason encyclopedias are published and then at reasonable periods revised. But at any particular time there ought to be an authoritative collection of the opinion and historical judgements of that particular day. In no case is that more demanded than in the case of the Negro problem.

You recognized the demand when you published "Brown America."[1] What you did needs to be done on a larger scale by a wider group of scholars and public men, so that universities, colleges, schools and general readers will have a body of knowledge to which they can turn with the conviction that however incomplete it may be and it must be incomplete, it nevertheless expresses fairly well the current opinion of the best authorities of the day. In this time of crisis and inquiry to postpone such an undertaking for half a generation or more, would be not only unwise but calamitous. We need, of course, further source material, but nothing is likely to be gathered or discovered which is going to change the basic facts concerning the Negro in this country. And in the same way, the loss which the truth concerning the Negro has sustained in having no such authoritative statement, covering for instance the time of Reconstruction, or the day of Booker T. Washington, is irreparable.

May I call your attention, also, to the fact that Mr. Charles Johnson, who is on the Board of Directors, will undoubtedly be invited to be a member of the Editorial Board and has always expressed the greatest interest in this Encyclopedia and the need for it.[2]

1. Edwin Rogers Embree, *Brown America* (New York: Viking Press, 1931). Embree (1883–1950) was descended on both sides from well-known Southern abolitionists—Elihu Embree and John G. Fee. He was educated at the then-integrated Berea College in Kentucky, founded by Fee , and at Yale. He was connected with the Rockefeller Foundation for a time, but from 1927 to its termination in 1948, was a top administrator of the Rosenwald Fund.

2. Charles S. Johnson (1893–1956) was a prolific author and editor and probably the best-known Black sociologist in the United States during his lifetime. In 1946 he became the first Black president of Fisk University. He was a particularly close friend of Embree's, and from 1943 to 1948 served as a board member of the Rosenwald Fund.

As I have said, this has nothing to do with the question of money, but I should be very sorry not to have your good will and influence in what I regard as an epoch-making venture.

Very sincerely yours,
W. E. B. Du Bois

Chicago, Ill., April 30, 1935

Dear Dr. Du Bois:

Thank you for your letter of April 24. Next to Dr. [Charles H.] Judd, of the University of Chicago School of Education, you state complex matters more clearly and persuasively than anyone I know. From complete skepticism as to the value of a Negro encyclopaedia at this time, you bring me, by a page and a half statement, to believe in it. Hereafter, there will be no objections heard from me to this proposal on its merits.

There still remains in my practical—and fiscal—thinking, a question as to relative values. My present position might be stated as follows: I am unwilling to recommend an appropriation from the greatly restricted resources of our Board.[1] But I am ready to recommend use of anyone else's money that we can get our hands on.

Very truly yours,
Edwin R. Embree

Du Bois's associations with George Foster Peabody (1853–1938) went back to the early years of the twentieth century (see volume one of this work, pp.66–68). Because Peabody was a man of wealth and philanthropic inclinations and also of considerable political influence—a friend of Woodrow Wilson, Alfred E. Smith, and F. D. Roosevelt—Du Bois strove to get his aid also for the financing of the encyclopedia project. Peabody did make efforts to gain assistance for the project from agencies in the Roosevelt administration, although these were not successful.

Du Bois wrote to Peabody at his home in Saratoga Springs, New York.

Atlanta, Ga., October 4, 1935

My dear Mr. Peabody:

I want to ask for your aid and co-operation.

Perhaps you know that in 1931 on the initiative of the Phelps-Stokes Fund, a plan for the Encyclopaedia of the Negro was drawn up. It was received with favor and as you will note by the reference on this sheet, it has been endorsed by numbers of people of influence. The depression, however, has held up our effort to get funds, but we started again last year and I was selected as a Committee of One to correspond with various persons and have been doing so during the summer. My selection was made because the directors had nominated me as one of the editors-in-chief. This

1. The Rosenwald Fund made no grant for this project.

nomination, of course, must eventually be confirmed by the Advisory Board.

In the midst of my work, attention was called to the fact that the WPA of Washington might be induced to appropriate some money for a preliminary survey for gathering material for this project. Consultation with authorities at Washington seems to confirm this belief and we have made formal application to Mr. Alsberg, head of the Writers' Project.

However, in the glut of work in initiating new projects, I am afraid that despite its merit this matter may fall through, and I am asking if you will not be willing to say a word to President Roosevelt immediately so as to call attention to the merits of our plan and get the project approved.

I know this is asking a good deal, but will you not be willing to do it? I am enclosing a copy of the application which we made to Mr. Alsberg. The total cost of the Encyclopaedia has been estimated to be about $200,000 and we have fair prospects from the various funds and others of eventually raising this sum. In the meantime, if we could get something like $60,000 from the government for preliminary survey, it would decrease the total expense by that much, and give the enterprise such an impetus that the further raising of funds would be much easier.[1]

I shall await your reply with great interest.

Very sincerely yours,
W. E. B. Du Bois

During the 1930s, Du Bois wrote to scores of people in the United States and abroad discussing the encyclopedia and seeking financial assistance and scholarly commitments. Among those contacted was the distinguished American historian, Dixon Ryan Fox (1887–1945), at the time president of Union College.

Atlanta, Ga., October 10, 1935

President Dixon Ryan Fox
My dear Sir:

I have been told that you are connected in some administrative capacity with the WPA in Washington. My information may be wrong, but I am venturing to write you.

1. Guy B. Johnson of the University of North Carolina was to be co-editor-in-chief. The Alsberg mentioned is Henry G. Alsberg (1881–1970), who was national director from 1935 to 1939 of the Federal Writers' Project; Reed Harris was his assistant. See, on this, Jerry Mangione, *The Dream and the Deal: The Federal Writers Project, 1935–1943* (Boston: Little, Brown and Co., 1972). The encyclopedia project received no money from the United States government.

In the Du Bois papers there is a copy of a letter, dated 17 October 1935, which Peabody wrote to President Roosevelt; he enclosed the above letter from Du Bois—"of whom you know as one of the noted scholars of our country." On 4 November 1935, Frank C. Walker, executive director of the National Emergency Council, wrote Peabody that President Roosevelt had turned his letter over to M. H. McIntyre, one of his secretaries. Walker was certain that "full consideration was given to negro applicants."

You will see from the enclosed leaflet[1] and from this letterhead that a project for an Encyclopaedia of the Negro was started several years ago and is now being revived. It has been suggested to us by persons in Washington and elsewhere that it might be possible to get help for preliminary work on this project from the WPA. I accordingly sent an outline of such a project to Mr. Alsberg, who I understood was in charge of this. I am sending enclosed a copy of the letter.

Meantime, it has been suggested that I should write to you to see if such a matter would come under your jurisdiction. If it does and if there is any chance for favorable consideration of our plan, I should be very glad to hear from you at your convenience and to find out what steps it is necessary to take.

Very sincerely yours,
W. E. B. Du Bois

Schenectady, N.Y., October 16, 1935

My dear Mr. Du Bois:

I am sorry to say in reply to your letter of October 10th that the New York State Historical Association, of which I happen to be president, is involved in only one w.p.a. project, that of surveying and docketing the historical records of New York State and describing its historic monuments. I of course would warmly approve the project of an encyclopedia of the Negro and earnestly hope it may have attention in the proper quarters. But as I am unknown in Washington I suspect that my recommendation would have little weight. If you think it would and can designate the proper person to address, I will gladly write a letter.

Cordially yours,
Dixon Ryan Fox

Among those who replied to Du Bois's encyclopedia letter with more than merely formal responses were Henry L. Mencken (1880–1956); Roscoe Pound (1870–1964), the dean of the Harvard Law School; Margaret Mead (b. 1901), then assistant curator of ethnology at the American Museum of Natural History in New York City; Otto Klineberg (b. 1899), professor of psychology at Columbia University who was then studying and teaching in China; Harold J. Laski (1893–1950), the British Labour Party leader; Broadus Mitchell (b. 1892), then a professor of political economy at Johns Hopkins University; and E. Franklin Frazier (1894–1962), then head of the Sociology Department at Howard University.

The letters cover a span of over a year beginning in October 1935 and ending in November 1936.

---

1. This was a one-page printed leaflet of some seven hundred words giving a brief account of African and Afro-American scholarship and projecting a four-volume encyclopedia of some two million words, "devoted mainly to the American Negro, but [which] should include important related topics on the Negro in Africa and elsewhere."

Baltimore, Md., October 15, 1935

Dear Dr. Du Bois:

I think an encyclopaedia of the Negro is badly needed, and that the time for doing it is as soon as possible. Unluckily, I'd hesitate to offer to contribute to it. I am, of course, interested in the subject, but I know of no detail of it in which the information of other men is not greater than my own. I suggest that if possible it ought to be done principally by Negroes—indeed, it would be best if it could be done wholly by Negroes.

Sincerely,
H. L. Mencken

Cambridge, Mass., October 16, 1935

Dear Dr. Du Bois:

I quite agree as to the timeliness of an authoritative collection of articles concerning the Negro race in the form of an encyclopaedia. Also I should be glad to contribute an article or articles on some subject to be decided upon later, as you suggest. There are many important legal subjects which should find a place in such an encyclopaedia, and many of them would come within the purview of my studies. The law of slavery in this country differed in marked respects from the law on that subject elsewhere, and the encyclopaedia ought to have an authoritative article on that subject. The constitutional guarantees of individual rights after the Civil War, and their operation as securing to Negroes what the provisions were intended to bring about calls also for an authoritative article and could well be made the subject of a very useful and illuminating one. From the standpoint of a lawyer, the specific enforcement of labor contracts in the southern states running quite counter to the traditional doctrines of common law and equity would be another important subject. In fact, I think a legal editor, or a small group of competent lawyers, could very well work out a program of legal articles which would be of value not only in the encyclopaedia but generally.

Yours very truly,
Roscoe Pound

New York, N.Y., October 18, 1935

Dear Dr. Du Bois:

I was very much interested to hear of your plan for publishing an Encyclopedia of the Negro. I enthusiastically agree that the time is ripe for such a project.

I should be very glad to help in any way that I can. I am in no way an authority on any aspect of the Negro question, unless you intend to include such Oceanic peoples as have a probable very old Negroid strain in their racial constitution. In that case of course I would be glad to do something for you on Melanesia.

With very best wishes for the success of your undertaking.

Sincerely,
Margaret Mead

Peiping, China, February 9, 1936

Dear Professor Du Bois:

Please pardon my long delay in answering your letter concerning the plans for the Encyclopedia of the Negro.

The project appears to me an interesting and important one and would fill a real need for those who wish information about the Negro, and are frequently compelled to wander far afield in order to obtain it. I foresee a certain amount of difficulty in the fact that so many issues associated with the Negro are still controversial, so that the points of view presented may be expected to vary from one contributor to another. That problem also arose, however, in connection with the Encyclopedia of the Social Sciences, but the result is still a significant one. In any case, I shall be very happy to cooperate, and to contribute whatever articles you may wish to have from me.

As far as subjects are concerned, my work has been mostly in the field of race psychology. I would be willing to write on any of the following subjects:

The Problem of Negro Intelligence   Negro-Selective Migration?
Negro Psychoses   Crime and the Negro
Physiological Characteristics   Race Mixture
The Negro "Race" (anthropological
characteristics)

I shall be back at Columbia University in September, and can be reached there after that date.

With best wishes for the success of your project, I am

Sincerely yours
Otto Klineberg

London, England, August 7, 1936

Dear Dr. Du Bois

In general, thought the plan of your Encyclopedia excellent. The two points I would venture to emphasise are (1) the importance of really long articles on the principal topics touching contacts between Black and White (e.g. colonisation, slavery, indirect rule, etc.) and (2) an emphasis throughout on the intellectual and social achievements of the Negro. I want the Encyclopedia to be an armoury against current imperialistic anthropology.

With good wishes,

Yours sincerely,
H. J. Laski

Baltimore, Md., July 29, 1936

Dear Professor Du Bois:

I admire the plan of the section of the Encyclopaedia submitted to me. The attached notes[1] are hastily made and in some cases are unmindful of contents of the plan

1. These were not found.

which would be disclosed by more careful examination on my part. My chief recommendation would be that the controlling board have more men of your training and interest, and fewer University presidents, etc. The Encyclopaedia should be a scholarly work, not just an evidence of racial pride.

How is the work to be financed? On this depends the organization of it, I suppose.

If I can help in any way, please let me know. The project of an encyclopaedia is an important one, all will agree.

Yours sincerely,
Broadus Mitchell

Washington, D.C., November 7, 1936

Dear Du Bois:

I am replying to your letter in which you requested comments, criticisms, and suggestions concerning the syllabus of the proposed *Encyclopaedia of the Negro.* Before offering my comments and criticisms, I wish to make it clear that they have not been influenced in any way by the controversy relative to the *Encyclopaedia* which has been given considerable publicity in the Negro press.[1] My only reasons for offering these criticisms and suggestions are that I hope that the projected *Encyclopaedia* will not only be a source of authoritative information on the Negro, but also will be a monument to Negro scholarship.

My first criticism refers to the method which you are using to secure the opinions of competent persons on the organization and contents of the *Encyclopaedia;* for it seems to me that herein lies the fundamental weakness of the entire undertaking. If the counsel and opinions of competent scholars are to be of any value in an undertaking like the present, they should have been utilized before the syllabus was prepared. It is impossible to utilize in any effective manner the counsel and reflections of scholars when they are simply asked to comment and offer criticisms on a detailed syllabus after it has taken form. An *Encyclopaedia* worthy of the name would require the calling together of competent scholars to plan its organization and the principle which is to govern the selection of its contents. Only by such a procedure can one expect to secure the benefits of their knowledge and experience on an undertaking which in its very nature should be a cooperative enterprise.

While the second criticism which I have to offer refers specifically to the present syllabus, the defects which it points out are rooted in the shortcomings indicated in my first comment. As it is presented to us, the syllabus seems to be no more than a confused assortment of almost every conceivable topic and person related to Negro life. It is impossible to discover any rime or reason in either the selection of topics and persons or in the order in which they are thrown together. An *Encyclopaedia* to my way of thinking should give evidence of some definite principle of organization which

1. The Baltimore *Afro-American,* 30 May 1936, carried a feature story, beginning on page one, telling of a bitter attack by Carter G. Woodson upon the project and upon Du Bois and Benjamin Brawley in particular. Early in June, the Black press carried a reply by Brawley; Du Bois did not participate in this public debate.

determines the selection of topics and persons. Otherwise, it becomes a mere catalogue or at least a year book. Certainly, I assume, the aim is to produce something
more than a year book, since we already have a Negro Year Book. However, the
present form of the syllabus indicates that the proposed *Encyclopaedia* will not be
superior either in scholarly character or in usefulness to the present Negro Year Book,
the limitations of which may be excused on the grounds that it represents the pioneer
efforts of a single person [Monroe N. Work] who has been forced to work with
inadequate resources. Thus we are brought back to our first criticism that a work of
this magnitude can be carried on successfully only through real cooperation on the
part of competent scholars who will have the final say in its plan and execution.

My final comment is implicit in the last sentence. An *Encyclopaedia of the Negro*
should be the work of the most competent scholars available for the various topics to
be treated. If it is the plan to have it reflect as far as possible the achievements of
Negro scholarship, the Negro scholars should be invited to contribute articles on the
basis of their competency. In any case, the planning and the execution of the *Encylo-
paedia* should devolve upon scholars and not upon interracial "politicians" or "statesmen," white or black. It is no task for so-called "big Negroes" or whites because of
their good-will. An *Encyclopaedia*, I insist, is a scholarly undertaking. If the proposed
Encyclopaedia of the Negro is to represent the mature scholarship of Negroes working
with white scholars, then it should reflect this in its organization and in the character
of its articles.

The above criticisms lead to but one conclusion. The present syllabus should be
discarded and a group of competent scholars should be called together to plan the
general organization of the *Encyclopaedia*, including the principle according to which
topics and persons are to be selected for inclusion; and to work out such administrative matters as staff requirements and the assignment of subjects.

> Very truly yours,
> E. Franklin Frazier, Head
> Department of Sociology.

> Atlanta, Ga., November 9, 1936

My dear Mr. Frazier:

Permit me to acknowledge, in the absence of Dr. Du Bois, the receipt of your letter
of November 7. Dr. Du Bois, as you perhaps know, is on a trip around the world.
Your letter will be brought to his attention when he returns to his desk sometime the
early part of February.

> Sincerely yours,
> Ellen Irene Diggs
> Secretary to Dr. Du Bois

*In his campaign for the funding of the encyclopaedia, Du Bois sent Embree, president of the
Rosenwald Fund, copies of comments on the project from well-known scholars. Embree, in
responding, induced an exchange concerning Du Bois as novelist.*

Chicago, Ill., November 5, 1935

Dear Dr. Du Bois:

Thank you for letting me see the comments on the proposed Encyclopaedia of the Negro. They are certainly impressive. Thinking you may want to use these in other connections, I am returning the sheets herewith.

By the way, I have just read for the first time your "Quest of the Silver Fleece." I had supposed that I had read everything of yours of any consequence. This simply shows how unwise it is to assume that any writing of yours is not important. I was moved and impressed by this story. In the first place, it contains a searching interpretation of social conditions. But, quite aside from the social message, it is fascinating and gripping as a novel. The characters are real and the plot grips one with the intensity of real drama. Particularly significant among the mass of shoddy white characters stands the figure and personality of Miss Smith. You must have known some such person in your own early experience. If so, you have paid the lasting tribute to an early friend.

Very truly yours,
Edwin R. Embree

Atlanta, Ga., November 8, 1935

My dear Mr. Embree:

I am glad you liked "Silver Fleece." I always liked it myself, but the public apparently did not care very much for it. I have the same difference of opinion with the public with regard to my "Dark Princess."

I write to say that I am attempting a new novel. Nothing has been done, so far as I can see, to dramatize and put in form of a romance the development of a group. I once thought of doing this with regard to Haiti, but I was too far away. Now, I am planning to do it for the city of Atlanta.

Atlanta is a post-war city in all its essential development and was given its political opportunity by Negro votes and its economic development by a combination of poor white and carpetbaggers. It is a city which was deliberately planned and did not spontaneously grow and has become today one of the greatest centers for economic exploitation that the United States knows. Its history demands a three-volume novel; White, Poor White and Black; but of course no publishers would dare to attempt that. Therefore, I am going to make a single volume novel in three parts. At least, that is the plan I have. It presents, of course, enormous difficulties in technique and I may not be able to do it, but I am trying.[1]

---

1. *The Quest of the Silver Fleece* was published in Chicago in 1911 by A. C. McClurg Co.—the original publisher of *The Souls of Black Folk* (1903). *Dark Princess* was published in New York in 1928 by Harcourt, Brace and Co. For details on both novels see this editor's introductions to the Kraus-Thomson edition of Du Bois's works (1974). Du Bois's reference to a trilogy anticipates by a generation the appearance of his *Black Flame*, published by Mainstream Publishers in New York City, 1957–61.

Board of directors of the Encyclopedia of the Negro at Howard University, 1936.
Left to right, front row: Otelia Cromwell, Monroe N. Work, Charles H. Wesley,
Benjamin Brawley, Du Bois, Eugene Kinckle Jones; center: Willis D. Weatherford,
James Weldon Johnson, Charles T. Loram, Alain Locke, Waldo G. Leland; rear:
Arthur A. Schomburg, Joel E. Spingarn, Clarence S. Marsh, Anson Phelps Stokes,
William A. Aery, James H. Dillard, Florence Read, Mordecai W. Johnson.

Alain Locke. Photograph from the
New York Public Library.

E. Franklin Frazier. Photograph from
the New York Public Library.

Thank you for returning the sheets, I wish they had impressed you even more.
                                        Very sincerely yours,
                                        W. E. B. Du Bois

As Du Bois stated in his June 1934 letter of resignation from the NAACP *(see volume one of this work, pp. 479–81), that organization's program was excellent in an era "when a negative program of protest was imperative and effective," but—and especially with the fact of the Great Depression—the need in the 1930s was for "a positive program of construction and inspiration." Du Bois's efforts to achieve this change in the* NAACP *failed; he therefore left it but did not give up the idea of promulgating and seeking to fight for the kind of effort he thought necessary.*

Already in the summer of 1933 he had accepted a teaching position at Atlanta University— where he gave a course on Karl Marx and the Negro—and he had by then persuaded young George Streator to join the Crisis *staff. At Atlanta he worked especially hard, as letters have shown, on* Black Reconstruction, *on founding efforts for an Encyclopedia of the Negro, and on intense study of the economics of the country, especially as these affected the Black population, with particular emphasis on the impact of the New Deal upon his people.*

In the latter regard, with characteristic directness and practicality, Du Bois set about drafting a program of action and struggle for the Afro-American people which would, he thought, have a good chance of meeting at least minimum requirements.

In the Du Bois papers, an early reflection of this work appears in a Memorandum on the Economic Conditions of the American Negro in the Depression, which Du Bois sent from Atlanta on 20 November 1934 to a conference on that subject being held in Washington, D. C., by Edwin Embree, Charles S. Johnson, and Will W. Alexander. Alexander, a white man who had been head of the Commission on Inter-Racial Cooperation in Atlanta, was appointed in 1932 the first president of the new Dillard University in New Orleans.* The three men were among the professional advisers abounding in Washington at the time; at that moment they were completing a study of southern tenant farming, published in 1935 under the title, The Collapse of Cotton Tenancy *(Chapel Hill: University of North Carolina Press).*

The memorandum is presented here with emphasis as in the original. †

From long thought, I *am convinced that the solution of the present problem of the American Negro is a matter of organizing his power as a consumer* and entering, through this path, employment as a middle-man and producer.

I believe that the campaign of appeal for social justice has reached at present its limits. Every

---

* Alexander was one of the trustees of Howard University who supported the appointment, in 1926, of Mordecai W. Johnson as its first Black president. This action drew commendation from Du Bois at the time—see the *Crisis* 32 (August 1926): 164.

† The original of this memorandum is in the Alexander correspondence in the National Archives, Washington—Record Group 96; a carbon is in the Du Bois papers. I am obliged to Professor Raymond Wolters of the University of Delaware for assistance in this connection. The November 1934 conference was part of the work done in 1934–35 by the Rosenwald Foundation's Committee on Minority Groups in Economic Recovery. From 1935 through 1937 Alexander held important posts in the Department of Agriculture.

essential charge has been answered and every demonstration made. No one today can maintain successfully that Negroes cannot be educated; that they cannot work as free and skilled laborers; that they cannot contribute to science and art; and that they do not deserve civil and political rights under the same limitations that are applied to other American citizens.

Despite this, they still form in the main a servile caste on the edge of economic subsistence, largely deprived of civil and political rights, with limited chances for education and small opportunity to enter the higher walks of life.

Power is now needed to reinforce appeal, and this power must be economic power; that is, the nation must be shown that the Negro is a necessary part of the wealth-producing and wealth-consuming organization of the country, and that his withdrawal from these functions in any degree diminishes the wealth and efficiency of the country.

This fact might be demonstrated if a way were opened for the Negro to enter modern industry at a decent wage and with civilized treatment. This way might be opened by the employers, which was the plan of the late Booker Washington; or by trades-unions and labor organizations, which is the plan of many of the younger Negro economists and of the white radical groups.

Changes in industry and the profit which arises from using the Negro as a poorly paid and partly employed labor reservoir, checked the feasibility of Mr. Washington's plan. The attitude of labor leaders, the lack of education and vision among laboring classes, and the monopoly of certain lines of employment made possible by excluding Negro labor, is rendering the present chance of raising Negro labor through the trade unions improbable. The radical and revolutionary program lacks either the power or popularity to help the Negro. The Negroes' helpless condition is shown in current efforts of the Federal government. Wherever relief is to be administered by state and local agencies, wherever work is to be allocated, wherever [the NRA] codes are to be administered, the Negro must depend absolutely upon the good-will of his [white] neighbors and unless public opinion is unusually favorable, relief will come to him after everyone else has been relieved, jobs will be given him after all others are at work, and his wages will be held at the lowest point.

This throws the Negro back on his own efforts. These efforts should begin with the undoubted power of the Negro as a consumer.[1]

In February 1935, the Department of Philosophy and the Division of the Social Sciences of Howard University announced plans for a series of lectures and conferences, to be held on two successive weekends in April, on Problems, Programs and Philosophies of Minority Groups. A

---

1. Du Bois's memorandum continues from this point in very much the same way, and words, as his essay "A Negro Nation within the Nation," in *Current History* 42 (June 1935): 265–70. It is of interest to compare the above memorandum and the cited article with his paper "The Negro Citizen," delivered in December 1928 and published in *The Negro in American Civilization*, ed. Charles S. Johnson (New York: Henry Holt and Co., 1930), pp. 461–70, where Du Bois argues that the need is for political power: that is "the main problem . . . the question of political power for the Negro citizens of the United States."

chief organizer of this event was Alain Locke, professor of philosophy at Howard and one of the best known intellectuals in the Black world. *

Naturally, Locke wrote to Du Bois for his participation; letters between the two men in March arrived late or crossed each other, largely because at the time Du Bois was in Texas participating in another Economic Conference on the Negro held at Prairie View College. But Du Bois did agree to speak at the 6 April meeting at Howard on the subject, "Minority Tactics as Illustrated by Negro Experience."

The correspondence in connection with this matter was considerable; it is picked up here with a letter Locke wrote to Du Bois:

Washington, D. C. March 15, 1935

Dear Doctor Du Bois:

The larger audience of the Evening sessions will undoubtedly desire to hear you, and I trust you will not regard it an imposition if we ask you additionally to speak (if only briefly) at the Evening session of Saturday, April 6th on the topic: *Negro Group Alternatives Today,* as suggested in the enclosed revised program.[1] We will, of course, be under additional obligation to you, and unless there are vociferous protests by return wire, will take it for granted that you will oblige us.

Under same cover, goes an invitation to join us in another project,[2] which fortunately is a little more concretely remunerative. I look forward to discussing this with you on your visit—and hope most sincerely that you will react favorably.

With usual regard,

Sincerely yours,
Alain Locke.

Locke's letter did not reach Du Bois in Texas until 23 March.

Prairie View, Texas, March 23, 1935

My Dear Doctor Locke:

Your letter of March 15 has just reached me here where I am doing some special work for about two weeks. I immediately sent you a night letter saying that I did not want to speak but once on the sixth. I shall take a quick Pullman to Washington

---

* Locke was, with Du Bois, a central figure in the Harlem Renaissance of the 1920s; for evidences of the Du Bois-Locke relationship, see volume one of the present work, pp. 328, 352–53, 470.

1. Among those listed in the program as participants were: Raymond Leslie Buell of the Foreign Policy Association, Ralph J. Bunche and E. Franklin Frazier of Howard, as well as President Johnson of Howard, Broadus Mitchell of Johns Hopkins, Joshua Kunitz of *New Masses* magazine, Otto Klineberg of Columbia, William Ernest Hocking of Harvard, Abram Harris of Howard, and Sidney Hook of New York University.

2. This "project," of which more will be said later, was funded by the Carnegie Corporation and was aimed at producing brief textbooks on aspects of Afro-American life and history. Locke's reference to remuneration occurred because Du Bois received no money except travel expenses for his 6 April appearance.

stopping at Greensboro on the way back so that I will have to speak on the sixth and seventh and I am sure that I shall do a great deal better making one speech at Washington instead of two. Please excuse me from the second speech. I do not care when the first speech comes, in fact, rather prefer the night of the sixth. But that makes no difference.

As I said in my night letter, I shall be glad to supply one of the booklets which you are editing. The subject will be "Social Reconstruction and the Negro" and the length will be between thirty and thirty-five thousand words.

All of my writing is done through stenographers and subsequently corrected, so I should like as liberal allowance for stenographic help as possible.[1] I suggest that since this notice has come rather late and the booklet could hardly be finished before the last of June I bring my own secretary when I come to Washington. A fair allowance for her work would be fifty dollars on her salary and twenty-five dollars for her added expense of living in Washington, making a total of seventy-five dollars. I hope this will not be too much to ask.

I shall be glad to hear from you in Atlanta whither I return about the first of April.

Very sincerely yours,
W. E. B. Du Bois

Du Bois spoke at the conference the evening of 6 April. While in Washington, Du Bois and Locke discussed the projected brief book for the series Locke was to edit and made a tentative agreement to meet again in Washington on 20 April. This became impossible and Locke wrote Du Bois.

Washington, D.C., April 17, 1935

Dear Dr. Du Bois:

First, let me thank you, for myself personally and for the Division of the Social Sciences, for your appreciated participation in our Minorities Problems Conference. The Conference seems to have had reasonable success, and this is so encouraging that we may have another in the Fall.

Thank you also for your letter confirming our plans to meet for conference in Washington. I deeply regret now to find that I must be out of town in New York by or before April 20. I shall be glad to see you there if you are contemplating continuing on to New York. While there, I may be reached in care of the 135th Street Y.M.C.A.

Should we not be able to meet, I am sending you this memorandum re the subject of our conference.[2] We are delighted that you will undertake the booklet and hope to

---

1. Du Bois, who wrote with his left hand, was especially subject to writer's cramp; rare, indeed, are even letters from him written in pen or pencil.

2. The memorandum, two mimeographed sheets, was headed "Adult Education Series." It stated that a series of booklets, funded by the Carnegie Corporation through the American Association for Adult Education, was to be published. Each was to total not more than thirty-five thousand words; an honorarium of two hundred dollars per booklet was offered, plus some help toward secretarial assistance. Nine booklets were proposed: World Aspects of the Race

have it at your earliest convenience. However, since I find that the budget will not stand more than $35 or $40 as an additional allowance for secretarial help in its preparation, I suggest leaving it to your decision as to how this may be satisfactorily applied. With some regret we would be willing to wait until Fall for the submission of the manuscript, although that would entail publishing this booklet in the second rather than the first series. We had not contemplated simultaneous publication of the whole group anyway. That arrangement would possibly allow you to use resident secretarial help at Atlanta.

With regrets at missing you if that should be the outcome of this necessary arrangement postponing our meeting of April 20, I am

Sincerely yours,
Alain Locke

Du Bois, having accepted the assignment to produce the booklet, commenced work promptly. There ensued a fairly considerable correspondence between Locke and Du Bois on the subject, much of which is published below.

Atlanta, Ga., April 26, 1935

My dear Dr. Locke:

I want to suggest a change in the title of my booklet. I should prefer to have it read: "The Negro and Social Reconstruction" instead of "Social Reconstruction and the Negro." It makes a slight difference in the point of view.

I trust you have no objection.

Very sincerely yours
W. E. B. Du Bois

Washington, D.C., April 29, 1935

My dear Dr. Du Bois,

I very much enjoyed our breakfast together last Saturday, and write to confirm the agreements we reached at that time. Your letter about the change of title has since

---

Problem, by Ralph Bunche; The Economic Side of the Race Question, by Abram Harris; The Negro and His Music, by Locke; The Negro in American Drama, by Sterling Brown; The Art of the Negro: Past and Present, by Locke; The Negro in American Fiction and Poetry, by Brown; An Outline in Negro History and Achievement, by Carter G. Woodson; Experiments in Negro Adult Education, by Eugene K. Jones; and Du Bois's Social Reconstruction and the Negro. Professor Lyman Bryson, of Columbia, was to assist in "editorial revision of the manuscripts and the canvassing for agencies of publication."

This project eventuated in the Bronze Booklet Series, published in Washington by The Associates in Negro Folk Education, Inc. Ira Reid, rather than Eugene Jones, did the Adult Education Book; the projected work on Negro history did not appear; a booklet by Eric Williams, *The Negro in the Caribbean* (1942), became part of the series. No book by Abram Harris or by Du Bois was published; instead appeared *The Negro and Economic Reconstruction*, by T. Arnold Hill, of the National Urban League. The other books appeared as in Locke's original prospectus. The funding came from both the Rosenwald Fund and the Carnegie Corporation.

come, and of course it is entirely acceptable that you make the change proposed.

Just as soon as you look over your schedule, I will be happy to have your final answer as to the time you will choose for working on the manuscript.

With usual regard,

> Sincerely yours,
> Alain Locke

Atlanta, Ga., May 16, 1935

My dear Mr. Locke:

I have laid aside all other work for myself and office and worked on your booklet. The first edition of it is finished and I shall have the completed manuscript in your hands not later than June 1.

> Very sincerely yours,
> W. E. B. Du Bois

Atlanta, Ga., May 28, 1935

My dear Dr. Locke:

Enclosed is my booklet. There are some elisions in the center of the manuscript and the type of the last few pages is larger than that of the bulk of the work.

Nevertheless, I am afraid that as usual the work is too long. If so, it must of course be cut and I should be glad of any suggestions.

I enclose the bill in accordance with our understanding. My address during the summer will be: 226 West 150 Street, Apartment 5 Jay, New York.

I have put at the end reading notices for each chapter. I have not cited authorities. You mention the matter of topics for study, but I have done nothing about that until I know more nearly just what you want.

> Very sincerely yours
> W. E. B. Du Bois

Washington, D.C., June 4, 1935

My dear Dr. Du Bois,

I am acknowledging with appreciation receipt of your manuscript entitled: Social Reconstruction and the Negro.[1] At cursory glance it looks very interesting and adequate, and I am really glad of its length because that permits editorial pruning.

I also acknowledge receipt of your bill for $240.00, $200 as honorarium for the manuscript and $40 for secretarial service. The honorarium is really payable on final acceptance, and because [of] considerable possible delay in this, the Executive Committee have, I think, soundly decided to remit half the honorarium on receipt of the manuscript, with the other half payable on completion of editorial correction and proof reading by the author.

1. The manuscript was entitled "The Negro and Social Reconstruction," in accordance with Du Bois's letter of 26 April 1935 and Locke's agreement of 29 April. There were two additional versions of this manuscript; all bore the same title.

I am, therefore, certifying to the Treasurer through Eugene Kinckle Jones, Chairman, a voucher for immediate payment for $140.00.

With deep appreciation of your prompt and helpful cooperation.

Sincerely yours,
Alain Locke

On 27 June, Du Bois told Locke that he had not yet received the $140 promised in the letter of 4 June. On 2 October 1935 Du Bois again wrote Locke that he had "nothing from you during the summer concerning the booklet" and suggested that he would undertake revisions of two chapters to bring these up to date.

He wrote again, some months later.

Atlanta, Ga., February 27, 1936

My dear Mr. Locke:

What on earth has become of our booklets? I am not thinking mainly of the $100 still in escrow, but more especially of the real need of the booklets. One of my brightest students in sociology is about to write a master's thesis on the effect of the NRA program in the South. I could not refer her to my own work which I should have liked to have done.

I should like to hear from you.

Very sincerely yours,
W. E. B. Du Bois

Two letters followed rather quickly upon this complaint. The first was undated but was written sometime very early in March 1936, for the second was dated 6 March.

Washington, D.C.

Dear Dr. Du Bois:

You are certainly entitled to an explanation as to why you haven't heard from me sooner. There has been general delay on the part of the other authors in getting manuscripts in, which has held up the whole series, since we must for reasons of economy, print in one batch. I, too, have been negligent, based upon this knowledge of the practical situation, and have delayed editorial work unduly. During the holidays, I shall tackle it straightway, although I must send more than one manuscript forward for Professor [Lyman] Bryson's consideration when I do so. At present, the only Mss in hand is yours and one of my own.

With best wishes and the hope that you will appreciate the present state of things,

Sincerely yours,
Alain Locke

Washington, D.C., March 6, 1936

Dear Dr. Du Bois,

I quite sympathize with your inquiry and your legitimate impatience about the booklets. But we are dealing with "our ain folks," and you ought to know them. I have plead, cajoled, threatened, and finally welched to the committee. To date only three manuscripts are in hand and we cannot publish except in one printing because of the considerable saving on the printing bill for simultaneous publication. All I can say is that I hope to get them out before the end of the Spring, and will sit up Spring nights to get the responsibility over with—and never again! I was thinking of going to Russia this summer but I'd take a passenger booking on Webster's Rocket, if I could.

Thanks again for your patience and interest.

Sincerely yours,
Alain Locke

p. s. At Smith College last week, Professor Hans Kohn was discussing minority problems and tactics, and came to conclusions practically identical with your much criticized recent platform. I thought this was very interesting, especially since he did not know of your conclusions which I told him about afterwards. His basis was a generalization of the Jewish experience as well as of the Soviet program for minorities.[1]

A.L.

On 9 May 1936, Du Bois wrote to Locke again inquiring about the status of the booklet; he inquired "feelingly," he wrote, because he thought it was needed and also because he was leaving for a trip abroad on 5 June and "that other $100" also was needed. There is a gap in the correspondence, or perhaps the men spoke via the telephone. There is extant the text of a telegram sent to Locke by Du Bois from Atlanta on 15 May—"Will telephone you at [Howard] University Saturday morning at nine."

Apparently, the result of this call was Du Bois's receipt of an edited manuscript. On 22 May 1936 Du Bois returned the manuscript to Locke, with the memorandum given here.

I have gone over the book with considerable care and it is now in the shape in which I would like to have it published. If, however, you find it still too long, please cut the manuscript as follows:

1) Cut out the Introduction and Chapter I and substitute the page marked "1" attached to this sheet.

2) In case additional cutting down is still necessary, cut out Chapter II, prefacing Chapter III with page marked "2" attached to this sheet.[2]

1. In ink, Locke added, "Feel Mr. [John] Hope's death keenly"—referring to the president of Atlanta University and Du Bois's very dear friend, who had died 20 February 1936. Du Bois wrote of Hope very movingly in his column in the *Pittsburgh Courier,* 28 March 1936.

Hans Kohn (1891–1971), one of the scholars driven out of Hitler's Germany, published widely and especially on nationalism; see *Nationalism in the Soviet Union* (New York: Columbia University Press, 1933) and *The Idea of Nationalism* (New York, Macmillan Co., 1943).

2. Three versions of this manuscript exist. In the first, chapter one treats of revolt and chapter two of migration. Later versions shorten both and combine them into a chapter called "Violence and Migration." The originals of these manuscripts are in the library of Fisk University; copies are in the library of the University of Massachusetts.

Expand or change discussion and reading notes as you may wish.

I do not like paragraph headings such as you have suggested in some of the chapters. It smacks too much of newspaper headlines and does not seem necessary to me in a small book.

I do not like "The Way Out" added to my title, unless it must go on all the series.

I have followed some of your suggested corrections, but in other cases, it seems to me that my meaning has been toned down, and my style of writing unnecessarily changed. In some cases, I have restored certain suggested omissions.

Of course if you come across grammatical errors or serious mistakes of taste, I should be glad to have changes made, but on the whole, this is the manuscript that I want published.

I thank you very much for your work on this matter and shall be glad if you will remember that if remittance can be made, I shall be here [Atlanta] until May 28, and in New York until June 5.

My New York address is 210 West 150 Street, Apartment 3A.

A prompt and positive reply was forthcoming.

                                           Washington, D.C., May 30, 1936
Dear Dr. Du Bois:

Thanks for the prompt return of the manuscript. I have gone over it merely for proof-reading and press preparations and believe I can assure you of reasonably prompt printing now.

I am glad to enclose a check for $100, the balance now due. We all very much appreciate your cooperation, and wish we had had similar experience with other authors. Best wishes for your trip. If I do get to Germany, I will be glad to look you up, if you will let me know your forwarding address.

Just at present, I am of the opinion that it would be unwise to print the basic American Negro creed,[1] especially in view of the vigorous defense in the last chapter

---

1. This letter was written in Washington less than a week prior to Du Bois's departure for Europe and must have been received by him just a day or two before he left. There appears to have been no reply—none is in the Du Bois papers. Certainly, after the long delay and Du Bois's letter of 22 May stating that the manuscript as then submitted was what he wanted printed, in substance, Locke's assertion that Du Bois's "basic American Negro creed"—what Du Bois called BANC—was to be omitted must have been at least distressing and perhaps shocking. BANC constituted the final three pages of Du Bois's manuscript; he introduced it with this remark: "Finally, may I summarize my thoughts in the following words" and those words then meant a very great deal to him. They summarized the heart of his thinking at the time and he had put enormous effort into their formulation for many months and had sent versions to many people for their comment. These pages are published in Du Bois's *Dusk of Dawn: An Essay toward an Autobiography of a Race Concept* (New York: Harcourt, Brace and Co., 1940), pp. 319–22.

Du Bois remarks in *Dusk of Dawn* that he had worked out this "creed" after consulting "a number of younger scholars"—and something of this consultation will be seen in ensuing correspondence. After its text in *Dusk*, Du Bois wrote (p. 322): "This creed proved unacceptable both to the Adult Education Association [of the Carnegie Corporation] and to its colored

of the underlying point of view. I scarcely see how we could steer [clear] in that case of criticism on grounds of direct propaganda. But with all your other points, I find myself in complete agreement; so can assure you that the Mss will be printed substantially as is. In view of our haste after such prolonged delay, I suppose and hope you will trust me to proof-read.

    With usual regards,

Sincerely yours,
Alain Locke

P. S. Of course, if you have time to prepare it, we would welcome a page and a half of *general* summary.

While Du Bois was abroad—and of course his whereabouts were known to Locke and others connected with the series he was editing, not only because he had informed them of his plans but also because he wrote of his trip in weekly columns that appeared in the Pittsburgh Courier *for several months beginning in August 1936—the following letter was sent to Du Bois at Atlanta University.* *

Washington, D. C., November 30, 1936

My dear Doctor Du Bois:

    At last, after unavoidable delay, we are proceeding with the publication next month of the first batch of our Adult Education pamphlets, in which your early interest and prompt collaboration has been much appreciated both by myself and the Committee.

    However, after full Committee discussion at its last meeting, November 13th, it was decided that it would be inadvisable to publish your manuscript: 'Social Reconstruction and the Negro' in its present form,[1] largely because of its frequent references to specific situations of public program and policy which in the regrettable interim of delay since the manuscript was written have changed very materially. The Committee feels itself in no position, in view of the small honorarium given and the delay being not at all of your making, to impose or expect the additional trouble and work of extensive revision, that, in their judgment, would be necessary to make this manuscript appropriate for publication now.

    With the Committee's and my own best appreciation and regard,

Sincerely yours,
Alain Locke, Secretary.

---

affiliates. Consequently when I returned from abroad the manuscript, although ordered and already paid for, was returned to me as rejected for publication. Just who pronounced the veto I do not know." This entire affair is not mentioned in his posthumously published *Autobiography*, edited by H. Aptheker (New York: International Publishers, 1968).

    * Written on the letter in another hand is "12/5/36," probably the date of arrival in Atlanta, and: "Marked 'Please forward' and was not acknowledged"—presumably meaning that the envelope was so marked and that no acknowledgement of receipt was sent to Locke.

    1. The title is still given incorrectly!

The response, when Du Bois did get home, was brief.

Atlanta, Ga., February 4, 1937

My dear Mr. Locke:

   I found your letter of November 30, 1936, concerning my booklet on my return to my desk. May I ask you to return my manuscript at your earliest convenience?

Very sincerely yours,
W. E. B. Du Bois

One of the younger Black thinkers and activists upon whom Du Bois tested his ideas during the depression years was George Streator (see pp. 40–41 above). Streator was working out of the Virginia State Headquarters of the Amalgamated Clothing Workers in Norfolk, Virginia, early in 1936; he took the opportunity of attending in Washington the conference on Problems, Programs and Philosophies of Minority Groups organized, as earlier correspondence has shown, by Alain Locke and addressed by Du Bois on April 6. The section of the conference addressed by Du Bois was devoted to the question, Minority Tactics and Techniques of Minority Assertion. Du Bois entitled his fifteen page, so far unpublished, paper, "A Pragmatic Program for a Dark Minority." It was this paper which induced the rather savage letter from Streator to Du Bois, only part of which has survived.

Norfolk, Va., Apr 9 [1935]

Dear Dr. Du Bois:

   I have never felt like disagreeing with you so completely before, and I find it is hard to phrase my thoughts, for after all, I owe you a great deal for whatever stimulus to thought I have developed.

   Race prejudice outliving the present generation? So what? Is that a reason for creating illusions? But I challenge your argument on these points:

   1. There is no such thing as a separate consumers' economy. The best that can be expected is a cooperative system of distribution which will, of course, be unable to affect seriously the question of employment of Negroes. Subsistence homesteads are no solution. And for that matter, [neither is] separate TVA socialism; that is, separate from the rest of capitalist development. Nor can one expect social-democracy to be an efficient palliative in a period of decline. These objections can be sustained by an examination of the failure of the Weimar Republic in Germany, the collapse of the Vienna partial socialism, and of course, the doldrums of the English trade union cooperatives. (I wish that you could have heard Harold Laski on the latter, recently).

   2. You count on the Negro middle class to usher in this cooperation. What you need to do, Dr. Du Bois, is to cease dulling your vision to the fact that the Negro middle class is after all, a lousy minority bourgeoisie of which your late associates at the NAACP should have given you ample proof. Then too, after preaching for forty years to build up Negro business, I do not quite comprehend your incomplete shift to cooperation by these same business trained people. It is true that Harvard business school technique is stupid, but so is the variety of lesser breeds.

3. Mordecai Johnson was talking Ghandi [sic] passive resistance and picturing it unconsciously as a morbid blood lust.[1] One could feel that this waste of life which is characteristic of passive resistance could be directed in better channels. But he too, launched a vicious attack on Communism, although at one [the manuscript breaks off at this point].

Du Bois dropped Streator a note of acknowledgement, and then decided to write at greater length.

Atlanta, Ga., April 17, 1935

My dear Mr. Streator:

I wrote you today but I found I have an hour to spare, and, therefore, I am writing again.

1. *The persistence of race prejudice.* When I was at your age, I did not expect race prejudice suddenly to disappear, but I did think that under a barrage of facts and arguments, it would in a generation noticeably decline. This has been true in some respects, but the decline has not been nearly as decisive and rapid as I had expected, and I have come to the conclusion that we have got to regard race prejudice in this country as fairly permanent for practical purposes.

2. I am not thinking of a separate consumers' economy. I am thinking of consumers' co-operation in certain apposite things. For instance, there is no reason why colored farmers surrounding Atlanta should not furnish food for the 600 families in the new Atlanta housing project. Then, I am thinking beyond that to certain beginnings of producers' cooperation, like manufacturing, which should use the growing and cheap power, particularly in the southeast. All this is difficult, but with the careful planning of trained and honest persons, I believe that consumers' co-operation and producers' co-operation among American Negroes could be made just as successful as it has been in certain parts of Europe. The protective separatism of the Negro group here could be taken advantage of in economic lines.

3. I do count on a Negro middle-class to usher in co-operation. I count on the fact that not all of the young Negro leaders are selfish and stupid exploiters. At any rate, either we get leadership from the best part of this class, or we get nothing.

4. I have preached Negro business organization, but always with the philanthropic end of business in view, and as I have become more and more socialistic in my thought, with the idea of non-profit Negro business enterprise. It is true that the people who have led Negro business are not fitted by their training to lead co-operation, but they could be retrained, or others could be trained.

5. I think that radical reform in the United States is letting itself be hypnotized into extreme communism. I not only dabbled in Marx in the past, I still dabble in Marx. I think he is one of the greatest philosophers of our day. I believe in Marxism, but I do

1. President Mordecai Johnson of Howard University spoke at the same panel as Du Bois; his announced topic was "Non-Militant Tactics."

not believe that Marx said or implied that violent revolution must be the solution of our ills under all circumstances, and in all stages of development.

6. Even if it is true that there will be no radical change in America, except by revolution, it would be suicide for American Negroes to lead the movement. Their wisest and only attitude should be watchful waiting, and preparing themselves for such changes as may come.

7. I am not at all impressed by charges of changing my mind and methods. I shall always be willing to change my mind under any circumstances when I see reason to do so, but I shall always have what seemed to me adequate logic back of my changes, and in this logic there will be nothing selfish or self-seeking.

8. I am perfectly willing to listen to you or to anyone else who brings forward a coherent plan. So far, I have seen none. Your plan, as it seems to me, involves co-operation with organized labor. I have no faith in this. I should welcome just as much co-operation as was freely and honestly offered, as I believe it is in the case of the Amalgamated Clothing Workers. I have always advised Negroes to join unions when-ever they could. At the same time, the union movement in the United States, as a whole, is just as petty bourgeois and capitalistic as the capitalists themselves. I see no salvation in that direction.

9. I believe in the masses of Negroes, out of which continually leadership is rising, but after all, it is leadership, and on that leadership we must depend for guidance.

10. The enclosed "Atlanta Creed" represents the latest considered form of my economic philosophy. I am going to hold to it until I see something better. I am going to combine what I said in Washington; what I am going to say in Raleigh tomorrow night, and what I shall say at the Davis conference May 20, in a booklet which will be called "The Negro and Social Reorganization." I am going to firmly base our hope on co-operation, chiefly consumers', partly producers', carried on within the Negro race through segregated activities, partly forced and partly voluntary, and calculated to train the Negroes as socialistic citizens of whatever new state comes out of this depression. I should be glad to have you read the enclosed Creed and criticize it.[1]

There is only one thing in your letter at which I take umbrage, and that is the intimation that I have [been] or will be a tool for "Big boards and foundations." It is pretty easy to voice dirty accusations of that sort, but it is not true, and you know it.[2]

Very sincerely yours,
W. E. B. Du Bois

The very next day, Streator sent a long letter to Du Bois.

1. The "Davis conference" refers to another conference on problems of the depression whose main inspirer was the then young John P. Davis; it was held at Howard University 18–20 May 1935. This conference was part of the origins of the Joint Committee on National Recovery which, in a short time, became a main source of the National Negro Congress. The creed has been identified earlier, as has the "booklet" Du Bois mentions.

2. Du Bois here is clearly referring to a section of Streator's letter that seems not to have survived.

Norfolk, Va., April 18, 1935

Dear Dr. Du Bois:

Leaving here tomorrow, so address me at New York.

I do not think I am wholly wrong in criticizing your Washington address. As I recall, both you and Johnson said in whole or in part:

1. This is no time for philosophy, but for action. After Johnson's speech, your saying that dovetailed, and the crowd who are afraid interpreted it to mean, "Somehow, we can muddle through." Coming from one who had fought for thirty years a theoretical battle against inequality, it seemed to be a rejection of thought in favor of "action." I saw in it a recession to what Chas. [Charles S.] Johnson has gradually made putrid as "Objective scholarship." After all, what did your experience in Texas teach, if not that the contradictions of the operations of capitalism make for that poverty you described? Then what was your remedy? As far as I could understand, you had none except a derision of the very socialism you have preached all your life. It ought to be pointed out also, that your attitude towards violence is a purely liberal attitude. If the mild program you are preaching, that is, a mild social democratic program, were attempted in Atlanta, or in Texas, you would get as many Negroes killed aimlessly, as Ghandi [sic] has had killed in India to satisfy a childish passion for acting, and a not entirely non-Freudian love of flagellation.

2. Then, too, your attitude towards organized labor is a product of battling craft unionism and its multiple discriminations with words and letters. Your information on the present-day labor problem, its possible trends, your information on Southern white labor are on the whole poor. And there is no place for you to learn these things except from the "youngsters" you are tending to bawl out, these days.

3. Your economic thought is too much determined by the notion that the establishment of a Negro bourgeoisie is an essential first step to ultimate solution. What if the larger white bourgeoisie is crumbling? I went to Hampton the other day. A young Negro teacher of economics was talking about the great field for Negroes in building and operating filling stations. Does he know that there is already 1 to every 87 motor vehicles in the country? He does not. He simply has an injection of race pride. I am not saying here that the capitalist world is crumbling. I am saying that the monopolies are congealing. If white filling stations owners can't make a living, how will the Negro entrepreneurs make a go of it? They can't. Why quibble on that point.

Consumer organizations? The British associations flourished under a rising capitalism. Most of the social services and inner-economic organizations you are proposing were adopted by the English system through the Trade Unions, which are the only effective groups to put them in operation. And yet, your cooperation program would be based on the sympathetic interest of Negroes in themselves. And this is a flimsy interest. I always recall that the liberals at the NAACP were willing for me to work ninety hours a week for $100 a month. Or that few of the Negro colleges have a wage scale; that a top few of the "head men" get the only salary benefits; that the Norfolk *Journal and Guide*, which is typical of Negro business, pays the family a salary, but experienced and efficient men with wives and children of their own get $15 a week.

There is no such thing as a Negro *loving* his race in the matter of capital investment and profit.

And don't forget that the leaders of the English system—the MacDonalds, etc., were the first to sacrifice their interests to keep the systems going. I mean, were the first to sacrifice the English laboring masses.

I was particularly chagrined at your complete turning to the notion that a minority group can save itself. If so, why does not the majority group of Chinese save themselves from the minority Japs? Or the minority English? Am I contradicting myself? I am merely trying to learn to say what I know and feel deeply: that no one group can pull apart from world economy, no matter how spiritual and how resolved.

I heard that you were invited to the NC [North Carolina] Teachers. And I have a couple of letters from Bennett teachers who were equally hurt over your complete acceptance of the leadership of the stinking Negro middle class.

Of course, so far as local issues are concerned, you have a swell opportunity to urge political action on the matter of teachers' salaries. There is no need to call that communism. The wages have a mean of $56. But if in pointing out the failure of political democracy you destroy all germs of mass action, you have done them an injury.

Having successfully accomplished my task of breaking the ranks of the company union and of signing up Negro workers in the same union with the white workers, and of doing this in face of a stupid opposition from the Negro upper "clawses," I am going home for a little rest, returning here later in the summer.

Cheerio.

George Streator

Shortly after receiving Streator's letter, Du Bois sent him a response summarizing and illuminating his thinking as of that time.

Atlanta, Ga., April 24, 1935

My dear Mr. Streator:

I have received your two letters of April 9 and 18. As I wrote you, I did not have time to write you at length immediately, but I am writing now.

1. You must not be too impatient at the muddle in colored men's thinking just now. These are difficult times and we are all striving for clarity and for the firm road. Leadership is difficult to obtain, and unselfishness rare, but neither is entirely lacking.

2. Your main questions have to do with (A) The persistence of race prejudices; (B) The helplessness of minority groups.

A. It is natural for Youth to expect changes quickly. In the years from 1896 to the war, I expected that race prejudice in the United States was going gradually to crumble before scientific fact and agitation. I think now that we made some progress and inroads, but I am satisfied that we expected too rapid a solution, and as I said in Washington, it does not seem to me that any person now living is going to see essential change in the attitude of whites toward Negroes. Some change there will be, but race prejudice is going to persist for a long time in the United States.

If, now, we had reasonable economic independence, we could just wait, even though the waiting took a few generations. But our economic situation is such that while we are continuing to hammer at the false logic of race prejudice and continuing to bring forward scientific fact, we have got to live and earn a living, and therefore the immediate problem is how to do that?

B. I am not convinced of the helplessness of minorities. (1) They can agitate. (2) They can combine with other forces for good. (3) They can take some lines of independent action.

The only possibility of combination that seems fruitful to me today is that which can stress, mainly, combination with the newer forms of trade unionism as contrasted with the older craft unionism. This is the point in your program which is to me most reasonable. But the point that I make is that even there progress is going to be slow, and that in the interim, minorities, like the Negro, must do something for themselves. I am convinced from wide contact with the working people of the United States, North, East, South and West, that the great majority of them are thoroughly capitalistic in their ideals and their proposals, and that the last thing that they would want to do would be to unite in any movement whose object was the uplift of the mass of Negroes to essential equality with them.

I know that the vertical trade union is against this, and that it is growing in power. I think that Negroes should keep in closest touch and co-operation with it; but I think you exaggerate the rapidity of its growth, and the prospect of its triumph. It represents to my mind, a minority and a small minority of the labor movement in the United States. I hope I am wrong.

C. I am still convinced that the organization of consumers is an immediate program for minorities. I do not mean by this simply consumers' co-operation on the old lines, although I want to use this method. I mean a complete change in that ideology among Americans, both white and black, but especially among colored people, which puts production first and consumption as its tool. I want to get Negroes thinking from the consumers' point of view, which is the only way to gage their real power. A people who spend (even according to [Eugene K.] Jones' faulty estimate) $185,000,000 a month, have got economic power, and of that there can be no doubt. Now, I propose that they use a new method for protecting themselves by the very segregation of which they are victims; that they concentrate this consuming power for mass buying, elimination of the middle man's profit, and an increasing number of productive operations. I know this is difficult. I know it has vast chances of failure, but I believe it has clear possibilities of success, if it is led by trained men of unselfish character, and if it eliminates the private profit motive.

3. I believe in Karl Marx. I am an out and out opponent of modern capitalistic labor exploitation. I believe in the ultimate triumph of socialism in a reasonable time, and I mean by socialism, the ownership of capital and machines by the state, and equality of income. But I do not believe in the verbal inspiration of the Marxism scriptures.

First of all, I do not believe that Marx ever meant to say that under all circumstances and at all times, a violent revolution is necessary to overthrowing the power of capitalists. Even if he did say this, I do not believe that it is true, and I am not interested in working out a perfect dogmatic system on the basis of the Marxism brand of Hegelianism. What I want is a realistic and practical approach to a democratic state in which the exploitation of labor is stopped, and the political power is in the hands of the workers.

4. I am a pacifist. I regard with astonishment militarists who agitate against violence; and lovers of peace who want the class revolution immediately. It is quite possible that there have been times in the world when nothing but revolution made way for progress. I rather suspect that that was true in Russia in 1917. I do not think that it is true in the United States in 1935. But whether it is true or not, Negroes have no part in any program that proposes violent revolution. If they take part, they will make the triumph for such a program more difficult, and they will bring down upon the mass of innocent Negroes, the united vengeance of the white race. The result would be too terrible to contemplate.

I am, therefore, absolutely and bitterly opposed to the American brand of communism which simply aims to stir up trouble and to make Negroes shock troops in a fight whose triumph may easily involve the utter annihilation of the American Negro. I, therefore, attack and shall continue to attack American communism in its present form, while at the same time, I regard Russia as the most promising modern country.

5. Under any circumstances, and whether I am right in my line of thought, or only partially right, or altogether wrong, I see but one path of salvation for American Negroes, and that is the one which I have been striving desperately for ever since I left the N.A.A.C.P.; and that is to get a growing group of young, trained, fearless and unselfish Negroes to guide the American Negro in this crisis, and guide him toward the coming of socialism throughout the world. I think the path for such guidance leads along the path of consumers' organization, but if I am wrong here, I am perfectly willing to be shown.

I think your worst difficulty is your assumption that no such body of young leaders can be found. You think that they are all bourgeois and reactionary and of the type of those in the N.A.A.C.P. office. I am convinced that you are quite wrong. Streator and Du Bois are not the only unselfish people among Negroes, nor does the fact that a Negro has a first-class college education disqualify him from being among the real leaders of the Negro race. The difficulty is today that so few of this class of young men and women have had any opportunity to hear the truth. They did not get it at all, or only partially, in their college course, particularly if they were trained in reactionary Northern institutions. They are not hearing it today in Southern colleges, for the most part, and they do not get it in social intercourse.

What you are attacking, therefore, is not their character, but their teaching, and what has got to be done is to teach the Negro intelligentsia that either we get such a group leadership of the Negro race or we are lost. In this procedure, we are no different from other groups. Karl Marx was not a worker. He was a university teacher [sic]. Socialism in the modern world has been led by intellectuals, and while they can be blamed for much of its failure, they must also be credited for most of its success.

This is my present philosophy. I shall change it when I think it ought to be changed, and no jibes from critics will keep me from following in the future as in the past, the truth as I see it.

I have been working on a basic creed, as you know, for some time. I am enclosing the seventh edition. I shall be very glad to have your criticism of it.

Very sincerely yours,
W. E. B. Du Bois

Streator replied quickly.

New York, N. Y. April 29, 1935

Dear Dr. Du Bois.

I have your letter, and regret that you are interpreting my impatience as purely youthful impetuousness. Not that at all; not even a question of sincerity, etc. Once and for all, while I know that half of the new programs and the followers even, of your new program are rank opportunists, I am still hoping that you have not turned back on all thought in an effort to take advantage of certain handouts under the New Deal. Frankly, while I am quite able to see that most of this talk about new programs of action for the Negro is proceeding quite logically from (1) The Rosenwald confer-ence, and (2) the Amenia conference,[1] it is nevertheless my fond hope that you will not turn completely back on the energetic years when Du Bois stood for clear thought and not for obscurantism.

Your present activity is a recognizable short range program growing out of a desire to see certain jobs under NRA and its many offspring fall into the hands of Negroes. To that end you have made a bargain with yourself which leads you to begin one of the most intense efforts at self deception I have ever witnessed. While willing to grant that there is always a place for immediate objects, that Negroes must eat, and be clothed and housed, etc., I am certain that you are finding some trouble in convincing yourself that the following are ways out:

1. Subsistence homesteads, which mean "concentration camps," as witness the latest New Deal talk about 5,000,000 permanent unemployed. Can you visualize 5,000,000 permanent unemployed making rag mats, door knobs, and boon doggles, in an effort to build a civilization?

2. A separate Negro TVA at Atlanta, where the colored folk under the aegis of the University will have a small piece of socialism, while at your back door (however remote because of "slum clearance") you have sharecroppers living and dying like

1. Both conferences were held in 1933 and were devoted to working out programs to combat racism and its results. Du Bois described the Rosenwald Conference in the *Crisis* 40 (July 1933): 156–57 and the (Second) Amenia Conference in the *Crisis* 40 (October 1933): 226–27.

dogs. Of course, to the Negro intellectual, these people have hardly counted, although occasionally you used to take up the pen for them.

3. All Negro intellectuals hoping to work either for relief or in some government job. This is the traditional way out for the Negro intellectual. Postoffice, schools, and now relief. What of the future? Will not these black bureaucrats behave precisely as Britain's Nigerian chiefs & priests? Will not a little 5 per cent serve as a more efficient buffer than say, the Americo-Liberians for Liberia?

4. Consumer organization to a peaceful end. What about the very efficient organizations like CR [Consumers' Research]? What have they been able to do? Why with the pressure of intelligence and 50,000 members they could not pass a decent pure foods law, and yet, under the leadership of a group of young Negroes who for the most part are too great cowards to stay out of back alleys to see a cheap movie, you would marshall 12,000,000 poverty stricken Negroes and that thing called buying power. I am unable to grasp your scheme of organization, to begin with. But I can report the reactions your scheme is getting, and I shall later on.

5. The "diplomatic," that is Booker Washington "hand-out" approach through the great foundations, which, somehow, you are trying to make me believe, are interested in fundamental changes such as catapulting Negroes [a section of the original letter is lost at this point; it continues:]

Your program is singularly like [Father Charles] Coughlin's. He will divorce the world and live in a state of economic onanism, and you will divorce the white race, and live in a state of racial-economic onanism.

You will denounce bitterly American Communism which simply aims to stir up trouble. This is your key sentence. Suppress it from your other letters. Here is where the fascist trend is unmistakably clear.

You can't have your cake and eat it too. Don't kid yourself by thinking that capitalism is going to hand over industry and sacrifice even 12,000,000 customers for your mild program. How the hell do you suppose the TVA got choked off? What happened in every single power scrap? What happened to the "low-cost" housing? And by the way, Sunnyside development was not a "workers' co-op." Sunnyside was a limited dividend affair like the Dunbar. It was a "fooler" just like the Dunbar, and typical. Not a single voice has ever been raised by you or others in New York against the mental corruption that was encouraged by calling the Dunbar a co-op. Why these tenants are afraid of co-operative milk buying!!!! And not a single tenant with the power to see spoke out in the beginning.

You attack American Communism, but you do not send any of your students out of Atlanta fired with the determination to work in the labor movement which you have talked about but never studied.

I can also attack the American Communist Party—get the distinction—but I can do my part in building the labor movement and in fighting Jim-Crow in the labor movement. And I find in all local instances, the educated Negroes who are led by the type of thought I have been criticizing in these pages, are lined up in every single instance (when they are opposed, as they usually are) because they do not know the difference between a trade union of craft workers and a shop union, and because too, for $$$$ they can "be had." It is singularly noticeable, that the "leadership" knows how to support a company union. In fact, it is rather remarkable how well your pet Negro intellectual can discover his class interests!

You have not satisfied me that you are working for the ultimate coming of socialism. You had me believing that once, but lately you have almost convinced me that your objectives are hardly removed from the end of your nose. If you are working for socialism, why are you hitting off on an entirely new trail. It can't be because you do not know what is going on in the world. At present, you are in the same camp with McDonald, Thomas, Mussolini (of the days when he was out of power), the Social Democrats, and the Mensheviki of Kerensky's brief regime. You want security, prestige, and the good life, and socialism without a sacrifice. And you are easily fooled by flatterers.

Yes, you are a pacifist in peace-time, and when war comes you will enter it with vigor when you discover that the race pride of Negroes is being hurt because there are no Negro puppets to lead them to the trenches. This is hard for me to say, but don't forget your last confusion. I am pretty close to this war business you know. I was at West Point yesterday, and learned plenty. But you would sacrifice millions of Negroes by feeding them taffy. 'Twould be better to feed them nothing. Let them learn empirically.

As I get your program: Socialism is coming. We will work for it separately. We will work for a socialist Negro to be handed over to the movement when fully developed. But who are your teachers? Young men brought up on the Foundations and suckled on teaching jobs. Young men and women who have three hours credit in labor history taught by persons who decry the class struggle. In short, you want only conservative young intellectuals who live as they can beg, who abhor violence without knowing that the class in power determines that.

Violence? The CP of USA is led by stupid men, but it is nevertheless a working man's organization. The SP is confused and inept for the reason that its leaders feel just as you are writing and talking. I am sending you the criticism that our group has got out on the SP leadership. Read it. In writing about violence, you write like an apostle of Abdul Bahia.[2] We are criticized for being the communists that we are, but certainly we are not above criticizing the CP. But in criticizing the CP we are not doing so in the belief that the big interests with their private police, gas guns, etc., are going to say:

Come here, Streator; you and Dr. Du Bois! We are handing over the mass buying power of the exploited Negro. Take it and use it to challenge our power. In order to

2. Abdul Baha (Sir Abdul Baha Bahai, 1844–1921) was a Persian leader of the international mystic religion Bahai, founded by his father, Baha Ullah. Bahai aims to unite people of all races and faiths in such causes as universal education, the equality of the sexes, and world peace.

help you work it out, here is $50,000 from GEB.[3] Make a study of it and train your leaders in Atlanta and Fisk.

Very sincerely yours,
George Streator

From his colleague in the sociology department at Atlanta University, Ira De A. Reid, Du Bois received a memorandum responding (in a quite different manner) to his request for commentary on his program. Reid (1901–68) was educated at Morehouse College, the University of Pittsburgh, and Columbia University. From 1924 to 1934 he held offices with the National Urban League and from 1934 to 1946 was a professor at Atlanta University. Thereafter he was on the faculty of New York University and Haverford College; he headed the latter's sociology department by the time of his retirement in 1966. His comments on Du Bois's creed are of significance themselves, and several of them were taken into account by Du Bois in finally publishing its text in Dusk Of Dawn.

April 30, 1935

To: Dr. Du Bois
From: Ira De A. Reid

Your letter to Streator rings with conviction. He must have said some very rash things in his two letters.

This memorandum, however, is to discuss the seventh edition of the Atlanta Creed. Several things have occurred to me in connection with both its form and content. I have tried to think of it in the light of what I should subscribe to, and how it would strike me most effectively.

1. I believe that BANC [Basic American Negro Creed] is a much more appropriate naming for the creed than anything else you have called it.

2. I would eliminate the lengthy foreword and encouch whatever is necessary as a plaint in a few gripping and emphatic sentences. This preamble, I think, should avoid anything that would need interpretation. Items 1, 2, and 3 of the current foreword, to which might be added another concluding paragraph, reflect fully what I conceive the purpose of the statement to be. The remaining items should be made a part of BANC. In so doing I would combine 4, 5, and 6 into a trenchant statement. Paragraph 7 I would clarify. What is the exact relationship between "our own masses," "the whole group" and "our working class"?

3. The GEB was the General Education Board. Exactly what Streator meant by "our group" is not clear. It was probably made up of the individuals who, later in 1935, called themselves the Conference on Social and Economic Aspects of the Race Problem and published a quarterly, *Race*, in New York City, with the first number dated Winter 1935–36. Black and white men and women constituted the board of directors of this conference, including Abram L. Harris, Martha Gruening, George Streator, Henry Lee Moon, Bertram D. Wolfe, Loren Miller, Howard A. Kester, and others. This first number published articles severely critical of Du Bois by E. Franklin Frazier and George Streator.

3. I fear the inference of paragraph 8, particularly that part which refers to "the darker races of men." Do you not introduce one of the sore points in any program when you introduce this idea of international racial solidarity? Would it not be better to have that evolve from a creed, after the group has achieved the first step?

4. BANC is the most convincing part of the plan. Yet it has no direct reference to the broad cooperative economic action proposed in the foreword. I think it should be inserted.

5. In section "B" I think the wording should be changed from "we would avoid" to something like "We repudiate" etc.

6. Should not the Talented Tenth, "trained to think and do," do more than "determine"? Should not this paragraph end with something of action?

7. I simply suffer an aesthetic revulsion to the combination of Employment, Education and Art. Employment, Education and Culture, strikes me as much better, but is not yet satisfactory. Furthermore one doesn't plan one's Art, does one?

8. Paragraph "F," particularly the last sentence, is not consistent with the economic philosophy you have advocated previously. Why restrict the avenues of poverty-abolition to reason, sacrifice and the ballot? Is not the economic program in which you believe and which you advocate something more than reason and sacrifice? Is it not a dynamic that can be put into the hands of youth? One that should be included in this powerful statement? And in the last line, instead of saying that we will not join or abet such movements, why not state what we will join—the movements that will do so and so are the movements that will receive our support?

9. Item 7 of the summary I would make a part of the creed.

10. Item 1–6 of the summary I would state in fewer words, ending the summary with paragraph 9.

And finally, am I too sensitive about the expression "and for the Life Complete and Beautiful, in a world of Peace for all men"? I would let that rest until we had achieved the more basic things presented. And why couldn't that sentence end with "accomplishments"?

Thank you for permitting this outlandish type of criticism.

Ira De A. Reid

Robert C. Weaver (1907–73), whose correspondence with Du Bois in 1931, when he was a student at Harvard, appears in the first volume of this work (pp. 434–35), obtained his doctorate in economics from Harvard in 1934. He was then appointed advisor on the economic status of Negroes and in this capacity served with Clark Foreman, who had been named by Secretary of the Interior Harold Ickes as his assistant concerning Negro affairs. Foreman, a white Georgian, had served on Atlanta's Inter-Racial Committee and then years later was to be among the founders of the Southern Conference on Human Welfare.*

* Du Bois had commented upon Foreman's appointment in the *Crisis* 40 (October 1933): 236–37. He observed that the appointment of Ickes, a member of the NAACP, was perhaps the best Roosevelt had made; he called Foreman "an estimable young man" but felt it was an

Du Bois, in his work on the booklet requested by Locke and through his intense concern about the economics of Black life and the impact thereon of the New Deal, had written to Foreman and to Weaver for information especially on the influence of the National Recovery Administration (NRA) upon the Black people.

Washington, D. C., May 1, 1935

My dear Dr. Du Bois:

Dr. Foreman has asked me to answer your letter of April 26, addressed to him, at the same time that I am answering the one addressed to me.

I am not sure that I understand exactly what you want in connection with the NRA. I am assuming that you use "NRA" in its technical sense, rather than in its popular implication; that is to say, I assume you are interested in the National Recovery Administration *per se*, rather than in the Recovery program as a whole. There is much discussion concerning the effects of the codes of fair competition under the NRA upon Negroes. I know of no comprehensive study. There are, however, certain fragmentary data available.

At the inception of the controversy over the NRA and the Negro, the Atlanta Urban League and the Inter-Racial Commission of Atlanta made a study of the displacement of Negroes by the NRA. This study is available, I believe, at the Inter-Racial Commission in Atlanta. About two months ago, John P. Davis had an article in the *New Republic* concerning the Negro and the New Deal, and in Norman Thomas' most recent book there is a chapter which conerns itself with the effect of the Recovery program upon Negroes, and reference is made to the NRA in this chapter. I need not, of course, call to your attention the recent files of the *Crisis* and *Opportunity* magazines. While I was connected with the Joint Committee on National Recovery, I prepared a study on "The Negro and National Recovery." That study was prepared for the organization I name above and, if you desire to obtain a copy of it, it will be necessary to secure it through the Joint Committee on National Recovery. The NRA held a series of hearings concerning the effect of the codes upon labor and the country in general last year. At those hearings John P. Davis presented a resume of the effects of the codes upon Negroes. No doubt he has copies of his testimony available for distribution. More recently Mr. Davis appeared before a Congressional committee and discussed the same subject.

I fear that the references indicated above will give a one-sided picture of the situation in that most of them are written from a most critical point of view. Unfortunately I do not know where the other side of the picture has been presented except in a recent article in the *Crisis* by Howard A. Myers of the National Advisory Board of the National Recovery Administration. I am sending you this material in a rather informal form in order to avoid delay; consequently, in many instances I have

---

"outrage" that even "our best friends" think it necessary still to have white people designated as our spokesmen. Weaver became the first Black member of the cabinet in 1966, serving until 1968. From 1969 to 1970 he was president of Baruch College in New York City.

not been able to give you exact dates or accurate references; however, I believe that you will find it fairly simple to secure the material I suggest.[1]

I trust that this is the type of thing you want and will be glad to send you additional information if this is not the type of material you desire.

Sincerely yours,
Robert C. Weaver,

A. *Philip Randolph, the national president of the Brotherhood of Sleeping Car Porters* (AFL), *wrote Du Bois about a historic development in the ten-year history of the organization he had helped found.*

New York, N.Y., May 24, 1935

Dear Dr. Du Bois:

On the 27th of May or a few days after, the Pullman porters, by order of the National Mediation Board, will be given an opportunity to vote in a national election for the organization they want.

This is the first time that Negro workers have had the opportunity to vote as a national group in an election under federal supervision, for their economic rights. It is an extraordinary occasion. It is the result of 10 years of militant, determined and courageous fighting by a small band of black workers against one of the most powerful corporations in the world. It may be interesting for you to know that on the Pullman Board of Directors sit J. P. Morgan, R. K. Mellon, Alfred P. Sloan, George F. Baker, Harold S. Vanderbilt, George Whitney and others. These men rule Wall Street, America and practically the world of capitalist finance and industry. And yet the Brotherhood of Sleeping Car Porters has, in the face of nameless opposition and terror, stood its ground through one of the worst depressions ever witnessed in America, and has come to the point where it has caused a national election to be called to determine the organization the porters really want.

Now the election will be secret and off Pullman property. On the ballot will be the names of the Brotherhood of Sleeping Car Porters and the Pullman Porters and Maids Protective Association or the Company Union. The Pullman Company caused the Pullman Porters and Maids Protective Association to be formed when the amendment to the Railway Labor Act by the 73rd Congress killed the old company union known as the Plan of Employee Representation. The law does not allow railroad companies

1. The article by John P. Davis was "Blue Eagles and Black Workers," *New Republic* 81 (14 November 1934): 7–9. The chapter Weaver had in mind in Norman Thomas's book, *Human Exploitation in the United States* (New York: Frederick Stokes, 1934), was the twelfth, "The Negro," pp. 258–83. The reference to Howard A. Myers as the author of the article favorable to the NRA is in error; the writer was Gustav Peck, also part of the National Recovery Administration, and the article, "The Negro Worker and the NRA," appeared in the September 1934 *Crisis* (41:262–63,279). It was rebutted by John P. Davis in "NRA Codifies Wage Slavery," *Crisis* 41 (October 1934): 298–99,304.

to finance employees' organizations and so this new company union was planned to come within the law from the point of view of appearance. The Company, however, is financing the Pullman Porters and Maids Protective Association secretly.

Because of the great significance of this election to Pullman porters in particular and the race in general, I am herewith requesting that should you make any addresses at any time during this election, which will extend from May 27th to June 22nd, will you say a word on behalf of the Pullman porters' union in its fight to break down the company union? The porters who have suffered, sacrificed and struggled to conquer the Pullman monopoly will be grateful for your cooperation. When the Brotherhood wins this fight, it will probably be the most significant economic victory and stride of substantial and constructive progress the Negro has made in history.

The story is yet to be written of the great sacrifices that were made to bring this fighting organization to this point where we are quite certain of winning the fight.

If the porters, who are the vanguard of the black workers of America, feel that their press, church and education are backing them, it will mean much to their morale when they face the organized millions of the Pullman Company.

The election will be held in 66 districts and agencies, from coast to coast, through-out the country.[1]

Sincerely yours,
A. Philip Randolph

It was not only Streator who wrote sharply critical letters to Du Bois in the 1930s. The author of the following letter was born in Mississippi but lived most of his life in Los Angeles. He wrote and published his own pamphlets and books, including It Was Not My World *(1942) and* Letters to My Son *(1947). Du Bois's response has substance as well as restraint.*

Los Angeles, Calif., June 15, 1935

My dear Dr. Du Bois:

It was with pleasure I read your article, "A Nation Within A Nation," in the June issue of *Current History.* I was glad to read you as I was just wondering what you were doing with your pen since leaving the *Crisis.* I thought perhaps you were working to astound the world with another book.

With your article in mind I must confess, as others have, you are indeed a learned and scholarly man. It was just a few days ago my professor of Sociology spoke of your scholarly ability in high esteem. Yet I must agree also, as others have, that you are not a thinker. Judging you from your recent article I would say you are a man without

---

1. No reply to this communication seems to have survived. Du Bois from the first ardently supported the struggles of the Pullman porters and wrote of his support and of Randolph's leadership quite frequently. Consult the indexes in H. Aptheker, *Annotated Bibliography of the Published Writings of W. E. B. Du Bois* (Millwood, New York: Kraus-Thomson, 1973). The Pullman elections resulted in an overwhelming vote for the union—5,931 against 1,422 for the company union. There was a full story on the election in the *New York Times,* 2 July 1935.

ideas. Your article tells me that you are sincere in aiding the Negro masses by pulling him out, making him a separate entity. Perhaps in order that he can look upon himself as does the Japanese, or any race which has been taught to worship their race and ancestors, keeping forever an eye on some Great Sun, as it were. Perhaps become a power, or perhaps a Black Menace. Or perhaps insane with Nationalism.

You state that the Negro has been left out in the cold from the early dawn of America's rise to power. But I am afraid, Dr. Du Bois, you but mean that there is nothing for the Negro under Capitalism, which succeeds only by exploiting the minorities. Would it not be better if the Negro would turn his attention to a New Order which seems to give him his chance by overthrowing Capitalism which, as you have stated even if you did not know it, has kept him out in the cold.

The world seems to be headed not towards Nationalism which has inherent in it prejudice but towards Internationalism, Socialism, Communism and Assimilation. A Nation Within A Nation does not go far towards building up the brotherhood of man. With these thoughts in mind I can but say your best place seems to remain forever shut up in a classroom. As for me, I can not agree with such unfair but somewhat prevalent philosophy. I am seeking the brotherhood of man and not self-assumed segregation. If you must write let it be your memoirs.

Very cordially yours,
Deaderick F. Jenkins

New York, N.Y., August 30, 1935

Mr. Deaderick F. Jenkins
My dear Sir:

Answering your letter of June 18, I beg to say that I am a Socialist although not a member of the party and have voted the Socialist ticket for a dozen years or more. I am seeking the brotherhood of men just as you are, but I am not attaining it and I see no way of reaching it as other people are not willing to recognize me as a brother. Certainly the laboring class of the United States is not willing to recognize black men as fellow workers. Until they do there is nothing for black workers to do but to unite with each other in order eventually to realize the new social state.

Very sincerely yours,
W. E. B. Du Bois

Writing again from Norfolk, the very intense Mr. Streator returned to the attack. His final sentence in this letter—written at the precise time of Hitler's atrocities—is somewhat shocking; Du Bois's reply again suggests his great self-control.

Norfolk, Va., July 7, 1935

Dear Dr. Du Bois:

I want to add a postscript for emphasis to a recent letter to you.

In Norfolk, an AF of L union—the Amalgamated—has been making a strenuous effort to organize colored workers along with the white in one union in a particular plant here.

Some headway has been made, but on the whole, in spite of some lip service to the cause, not a single instance has been noted of any unified interest, to say nothing of cooperation on the part of the colored community. On the contrary, there are a dozen evidences of sabotage. Open advocates of the open shop; the usual drivel about "being careful about the AF of L" in spite of the fact that a genuine effort to organize is being made.

I ask again, where are your racial loyalties? The leading business man of the town is opposed to a union because first and last some one will try to unionize him. The leading colored business man gave me the same statement. He thought I should go to Detroit and organize rich Henry Ford instead of stirring up things in Norfolk.

Again I want to know how you arrive at your conclusions that the lower middle class Negro who has absorbed the capitalist ideology will somehow be enlisted for socialism without disturbing his class allegiances? My leading colored business man pays skilled mechanics fifteen dollars a week and fires them if they look like asking for a raise. In public utterances the man deplores the "discrimination against Negro wage earners." Once or twice you listed him among your list of liberals. However, he believes that Dr. Moton will influence world affairs, that Booker Washington ranks with Marx and Malthus (!), that Jesus was probably colored. As if that mattered.

You didn't see fit to answer my last letter to you, and I am sure that it's too hot to answer this one. But for me, I am through with any doctrine of "racial solidarity" as a way out. I have watched the capitalist Jews too long, now.

Sincerely,
George Streator

New York, N.Y., July 9th, 1935
My dear Mr. Streator:

It will be just as difficult to enlist colored business men and students who have received capitalistic education in the cause of Socialism as it is to enlist American labor members of the A.F. of L. in most of the unions. Nevertheless, by education and propaganda, this can be done. It will be slow work, but no one need be astonished or discouraged if the miracle of their conversion does not happen in a month or in a year.

I did not answer your last letter and I do not usually carry on an argument unless there is reason for it. That is: individual understanding of facts or lack of clearness in the opinions expressed. In our case, I do not think there is anything of the sort. I understand your position, I think, perfectly. You believe in Socialism as I do. You think however, that Socialism is coming through the leadership of the workers led by a few men of intelligence like yourself. I believe in the same thing, but I believe that the intelligent leaders need not be confined to a few like you, but can be spread through the young Negroes when they are properly taught. Our difference therefore is a matter of degree and also I think, a matter of willingness on my part to believe in the essential honesty of human beings a good deal further than you do. Your tendency is to think that everybody is a scoundrel who does not agree with you. That may be but it is wisest to wait for proof.

Very sincerely yours,
W. E. B. Du Bois

Du Bois and Lester A. Walton (1882–1965) maintained a warm friendship for decades. Walton, born in Saint Louis, worked as a youth on various newspapers in that city and from 1908 to 1919 served in an editorial capacity on the New York Age. *He was among the journalists covering the Versailles conference concluding the First World War and later was a reporter for the* New York World *and the* New York Herald-Tribune. *He returned to the* New York Age *early in the 1930s and from 1935 to 1946 served as United States minister to Liberia. Upon the announcement of his diplomatic appointment, Du Bois wrote to him.*

New York, N.Y., July 9, 1935

My dear Mr. Walton:

May I give you sincere congratulations on your appointment to Liberia. It is a great chance and a touchy job! Advice is cheap, but I have some for you:

(1) The villain in this play is the Firestone Company and on the other hand they are going to be so nice to you and your family in a country where entertainment and society is scarce that you will have a hard time escaping them. Nevertheless, if you play your game right, you can save the independence of Liberia.

(2) The Liberians are just ordinary humans that need new blood and modern ideas, but they have done a rightfully good job in keeping their independence in the face of the world for over 100 years. They deserve more sympathy than criticism.

(3) Your great difficulty is going to be your health. The English have this all worked out for their civil servants. They have a tropical school which is the best on earth in London, and they see that their appointees get proper medical care and dress properly. You can get a good deal of medical advice, etc. here in this country, but I think you ought to stop by the London school, if possible.

Also, use light summer clothes—linens and white ducks, in spite of the fool regulations and customs of the United States officials. Talk to the people in Washington about this.

Before you go we must have luncheon together at my expense. I am going to be here until July 18th and again August 20th to September 20th. Let me hear from you.

Very sincerely yours,
W. E. B. Du Bois

New York City, July 18, 1935

My dear Dr. Du Bois:

I wish to thank you for your letter of July 9th in which you congratulate me upon my designation by President Roosevelt as American Minister to the Republic of

George Streator. Photograph from the *New York Times*.

Lester A. Walton. Photograph from the New York Public Library.

Liberia. I appreciate the suggestions you were good enough to make and hope to discuss the subject more fully when I see you.

Relative to lunching together *at your expense,* I shall get in touch with you by telephone before you leave town.

Sincerely,

Lester A. Walton

With satisfying frequency, Du Bois's writings brought him letters of commendation. One such that perhaps surprised him came from a member of the Supreme Court of Pennsylvania, George W. Maxey. Maxey (1878–1950) received a law degree from the University of Pennsylvania in 1906 and practiced in Scranton until 1920. He was a district judge from 1920 until his appointment, in 1930, to the Supreme Court of the state, and from 1943 until his death, he was chief justice of Pennsylvania's Supreme Court.

Scranton, Pa., July 15, 1935

Mr. W. E. Burghardt Du Bois
Dear Sir:

I wish to tell you how much I enjoyed reading your article: "Does the Negro Need Separate Schools?" which appears in the current number of "The Journal of Negro Education." Your article is a masterpiece of sound reasoning, good sense, and superb diction. You say many things which the members of the Negro race should comprehend, well consider, and act upon. You wisely counsel them to believe in their own power and ability and to cultivate their innate qualities. You rise to the level of statesmanship when you write: "What he [the Negro] needs more than separate schools is a firm and unshakable belief that twelve million American Negroes have the inborn capacity to accomplish just as much as any nation of twelve million anywhere in the world ever accomplished, and that this is not because they are Negroes but because they are human." Your summing up, or closing, paragraph is the quintessence of wisdom.

You possess that practical sense of realism which every person must have if he is going to make any worth-while contribution to the solution of present-day problems, whether these problems be racial, social, economic, or political. As Spengler says in substance in his comments on Bismarck: "The highest art of statesmanship is the art of the possible."[1]

With best wishes,

Very truly yours,

George W. Maxey

1. Du Bois's article appeared in the *Journal of Negro Education* 4 (July 1935): 328–35. The quotation from Spengler reads: "What, then, *is* politics? It is the art of the possible . . . ," in *The Decline of the West* (New York: Alfred A. Knopf, 1932), 2:445.

New York, N.Y., August 29, 1935

My dear Sir:

Your kind letter of July 15 has been received. I appreciate very much your approval.

Very sincerely yours,
W. E. B. Du Bois

Sadie Tanner Mossell Alexander (b. 1898) was the first Black woman to earn a Ph.D. degree in the United States (in economics from the University of Pennsylvania in 1920) and the first woman to be granted a degree in law by that university. In 1927 she was admitted to the Pennsylvania bar (once more the first Black woman to achieve this goal) and in the late 1920s and early 1930s was assistant city solicitor of Philadelphia. In later years she was secretary of the National Urban League, active in the work of the American Civil Liberties Union, and a member of the United States Commission on Civil Rights during Truman's presidency.

She and her attorney husband, Raymond Pace Alexander, were longtime friends of Du Bois's. In the summer of 1935 she wrote to Du Bois, then, as usual during August, vacationing in Litchfield, Maine.

Philadelphia, Pa., August 10, 1935

My dear Dr. Du Bois:

May I intrude upon the peacefulness of your vacation in the interest of a mutual friend of ours, who I can assure you is enjoying anything but quiet and peace. You have probably learned through Virginia that Raymond and I recently returned from Haiti. We spent much of our time in the company of and as the guests of Dantés Bellegarde, whom I am certain you know and admire. You probably do not know that he is apparently persona non grata with his government at the present time, because he opposed the agreement under which the American troops were withdrawn from Haiti. The financial control of the country, as you know, remained in the hands of foreigners. Even today the Bank is only nominally under the control of the Haitian Government—in fact the control of the Bank and the Port is in the hands of Americans.

The government has left no stone unturned to insult and embarrass M. Bellegarde. Can you imagine that, after the Haitian Government sent his eldest son, Auguste, to Ohio State University to study Veterinary Science and after the boy returned with his degree, the only person on the island with this training, the government refused to employ him in any capacity. He is today teaching at Tuskegee. One or two of his daughters were teachers in the public schools. They too were relieved of their positions. The husband of his only married daughter, a recent bride, was committed to jail along with Jacques Romaine, where he is still confined. M. Bellegarde, himself, is being constantly attacked by supporters of the government. I enclose herewith some paragraphs from a letter which he sent me under date of July 31, 1935. Have you received the letter to which he refers? If not, it probably awaits you at your office.

I am certain that it would be a source of great mental comfort to M. Bellegarde, if you would address a letter to him and send a copy to the Haitian press, protesting the maligning of the character of such an honest man. I am equally certain that you will be happy to do what you can to relieve the suffering of one who has been so unjustly attacked.

As further evidence of the treatment M. Bellegarde is daily receiving, I should tell you that when we were departing from Port au Prince, the government sent not less than ten Haitian guards to examine our luggage. There, in the noon day sun, on the floor of the dirty dock, we were compelled to go through the most exhaustive search of every article, even the lining of our shoes, pockets and the pages of books, including "Black Reconstruction." This was done in the presence of Mr. Bellegarde and for the obvious purpose of embarrassing and insulting him, because we were his guests and friends.

Because of the close surveillance the government keeps over M. Bellegarde's mail, I suggest that you do not mention to him in your letter any of the facts which I have stated in this letter. The government would gladly attribute to him, rather than to me, many of the conclusions that I have drawn. Furthermore, it would not help him for the government to know that I, his friend, have divulged them to you. If, however, there are any further facts you need in order to comply with my request and his desire that you send him a letter, I shall be glad to send them to you.

Raymond wishes to join me in kindest regards to you and your family. Mary Elizabeth also sends regards to DuBois. We hope that you have had an enjoyable rest. I also wish to express my appreciation of the attention which I am certain you will give at your earliest convenience to the matter herein presented.[1]

Very sincerely yours,
Sadie T. M. Alexander

1. The Du Bois papers do not disclose what action Du Bois took; the enclosure mentioned above and the letter from Bellegarde also were not found. Louis Dantes Bellegarde (1877–1966) was perhaps the single most distinguished public figure produced by Haiti in the twentieth century. Author of several significant books in history and contemporary affairs, teacher, Haitian ambassador to France and to the League of Nations and to the United States, he was a staunch opponent of imperialism in general and United States imperialism in particular. Du Bois's contacts with him went back to 1921 when Bellegarde participated in Pan-African efforts in France. An unsigned essay by Du Bois, "Dantes Bellegarde: International Spokesman of Black Folk," appears in the *Crisis* 31 (April 1926): 295–96. While Du Bois was at Atlanta University, Bellegarde served as guest professor in the department of French; under Du Bois's editorship, *Phylon*, in its issue dated Second Quarter 1940 (1:125–35), published an account of his life by Mercer Cook.

The Jacques Roumain mentioned in this letter was the poet and novelist; a grandson of a former president of Haiti, Roumain was a founder of the Communist party in Haiti and frequently suffered imprisonment. He was born in 1907 and died in 1944. One of his books, *Masters of the Dew*, translated by Langston Hughes and Mercer Cook, was published in New York in 1947 by Reynal and Hitchcock and reissued as a Liberty Book Club selection in 1956.

Mary Elizabeth was the Alexanders' daughter; DuBois was Dr. Du Bois's grand-daughter.

Du Bois's friend and colleague at Atlanta University, Ira De A. Reid, presented plans concerning the Encyclopedia of the Negro idea to officials of the Federal Writers' Project (FWP) in Washington, hoping that this action might lead to government support. The Reed Harris mentioned by Reid was the same person expelled from Columbia University in 1932 for having written articles for the Columbia Spectator—*of which Harris was the editor—distasteful to President Nicholas Murray Butler and assorted trustees. Henry G. Alsberg (1881–1970) was in 1922 director of the American Joint Distribution Committee providing relief against famine in Soviet Russia; thereafter he directed the Provincetown Theatre. On the Federal Writers' Project—and the work of Harris and Alsberg therein—see Jerre Mangione,* The Dream and the Deal *(Boston:Little, Brown, 1972).*

Du Bois's letter to Alsberg in accordance with Reid's suggestion is a good description of the encyclopedia project. Nothing came of these efforts to interest the FWP *in helping fund the effort.*

[New York, N. Y.], September 12, 1935

Dear Dr. Du Bois:

I presented this data [outlining the encyclopedia concept] for a hasty review to Mr. Reed Harris, Assistant Director of the Federal Writers' Project of the WPA. He was tremendously interested and took it up with Mr. Alsberg, the Director. Mr. Alsberg did not have time to go into it thoroughly but expressed the opinion that it is the "most likely" project that has come to his attention.

It seems that this division has received money to do only four things, of which the Encyclopaedia is not one. But both Mr. A. and Mr. H. are willing to go forward with it and request money if further study confirms their initial views.

I brought the materials back because I know them to be originals. However, Mr. A. wishes to go into it more carefully. I suggested in your behalf that you would send him copies. My suggestion now is that—

Copies of the important documents regarding the Encyclopaedia be prepared and sent to:

Mr. Henry G. Alsberg
Director, Federal Writers' Project
Works Program Administration Auditorium
Washington, D. C.

Your accompanying letter might state that this is the material I discussed with Mr. Reed Harris, his assistant, on September 11. You might request his opinion on requesting Federal monies to get some of the preliminary work out of the way—to employ from twenty-five to one hundred persons (do not emphasize the clerical aspect, these people should be classed as research aides, or something of that sort) for a period of one year, at the centers we mentioned.

Your letter might state, also, that if a formal project application should be made, that my assistance and experience is available for its construction.

Frankly, the reception accorded the project was very cordial. I think it is one of the most plausible things that the FWP has seen, and the men are ready to do something about it, if they can. Of course, they do not have the final say-so, but the character of the first step is important.

I may be reached at home—Edgecombe 4-4049—for the remainder of the week.

Ira De A. Reid

Du Bois wrote at once.

New York, N. Y., September 12, 1935

Mr. Henry G. Alsberg
My dear Sir:

This letter is in further explanation and amplification of the project presented to you and your assistant, Mr. Reed Harris, by Mr. Ira Reid September 11.

November 7, 1931, there was a conference of white and Negro scholars and of educational leaders, especially interested in the advancement of the Negro, and held at the invitation of the Phelps Stokes Fund at Howard University. Later, January 9, 1932, the conference reconvened and adopted a memorandum on the project of an Encyclopaedia of the Negro. The conference made a statement concerning its general objects, part of which has been printed and is herewith enclosed. Later, contact was made with representatives of various institutions and learned societies and a Board of Directors elected with officers. The names of these persons are printed on the letter-head of this sheet.

The first problem before this board was the expense of such a project and the method of raising the money. It was estimated on the basis of conferences made with the Encyclopaedia of the Social Sciences, the Catholic and Jewish Encyclopaedias, that an encyclopaedia of four volumes, containing about 500,000 words each, would take about four years for writing and publication of it would entail the total expense of $225,000 for four years.

It was proposed that the Board of Directors try to secure from foundations, groups and individuals interested, a fund of $200,000 with the assumption that all expenses of preparing and publishing the material in excess of this figure would be paid for by receipts from the sale of the Encyclopedia.

The increased severity of the depression brought to a halt for three years all active effort to raise the money required, but last spring the directors held another meeting and determined to make active effort to raise the sums required. It was stated that there seemed to be a fair chance to raise this money in time. Meantime, however, it was regarded as essential that some preliminary work be started. I was, therefore, appointed as the Committee of One to take charge of preliminary correspondence.

I had letterheads printed, opened a small, temporary office at 200 West 135th Street in New York for the month of September and hired a stenographer and library assistant. We began a tentative list of experts who might aid in the preparation of such an encyclopaedia and whose interest we would like to have. A series of letters to such persons is being sent out.

Meantime, it was suggested to us by Mr. Ira Reid that possibly the Works Progress

Administration might be interested in this project, at least to the extent of securing for us government aid for preliminary work. For such work, we could employ from 25-100 persons as research aides for a period of a year, grouping them in Washington, New York, Chicago, Atlanta and New Orleans, and in this way we could lay plans, prepare preliminary bibliographies, collect books and manuscripts, and begin the actual gathering and writing of special data.

I am writing, therefore, to ask your opinion on the advisability of requesting Federal monies for this project and with the assistance of Mr. Ira Reid, we would be glad to work out a formal project application.

I am enclosing copies of some of the official data. I beg to refer, also, to Dr. Anson Phelps Stokes of Washington, the President of the Board of Directors, and Professor Benjamin Brawley of Howard University, the Secretary, for any additional information that you might wish.

I shall be glad to hear from you at your convenience.

Very respectfully yours,
W. E. B. Du Bois

*Horace R. Cayton (1903–70), born in Seattle, was the grandson of Hiram R. Revels, the first Black United States senator. He received his bachelor's degree from the University of Washington and was a graduate student at the University of Chicago from 1931 to 1935. The next year he taught at Fisk and from 1936 to 1937 at the University of Chicago. From 1940 to 1949 he was director of the Parkway House in Chicago; he was co-author of two significant books—*Black Workers and the New Unions *(1935, with George S. Mitchell) and* Black Metropolis *(1945, with St. Clair Drake), and author of* Long Old Road: An Autobiography *(1965).*

Despite the extraordinary tone of his letter, Du Bois's reply is marked by his normal courtesy.

Seattle, Washington, September 14, 1935

Mr. W. E. B. Du Bois
My dear Sir:

Perhaps your latest book creation [*Black Reconstruction*] will be of great economic, civic and social benefit to the Negro and his environments throughout the United States of North America, even elsewhere, in the way of solving or overcoming the hundred and one incongruities, which daily confront him, here, there and everywhere; yea verily, prove to be the long sought for desideratum for all inter-racial ills and complaints; but, if so, I am at a loss to decipher, how.

Though its pages are full and overflowing with historical reminiscences, not only of the Negro, but likewise of the dominant citizenry of this country which transpired in bygone days, yet in spite of their voluminous facts and figures, the signs of the times lead one to conclude, it is absolutely preposterous to think of the Negro in the United States in the light of a distinct individuality, to say nothing of a separate nationality, both mildly suggested in your book preface. Living as he is under the ban of the law of Might Makes Right, and it never losing an opportunity to subject him to its unrelenting cruelties, all superinduced by the bullet and the ballot, he has but a slim chance, if chance at all, to assert individuality, personality or provinciality; therefore, of him it may be truly said, a man he is, but without either a cause or a country.

To build up a black race within a white race, or vice versa, with the one or the other largely predominating, is as hopelessly impossible as to try to drink the ocean dry, and using the language of a plantation philosopher, "hit jest can't be did." History fails to recount of two distinct races occupying the same land and territory, at least for any great length of time, without violent clashes and clangors of words and arms sporadically as well as spasmodically occurring, which sooner or later resulted in the extermination of one or the other and often the both.

However your book is a splendid reference compendium for such human fossils as lived through the periods of the golden and tragic eras of United States quasi Negro citizenship days, but it holds no brief for the men and women of the morrow, who will live in the determination realm of, fusion if possible, but fight if forced. Under such circumstances, it is safe to say, the Negro of this country is either headed for wholesale amalgamation or for the "Beautiful Isle of Somewhere," paraphrasing another, but of which he knows nothing. In other words he is facing extinction, which may come either by absorption or by violence, the latter, however, being only problematical.

Therefore to parade his past incompatibilities with Uncle Sam's dominant group before the eyes of an unsympathetic youth, whose minds are set on the burning issues of the age, will in no wise foster fraternal fusionism between whites and blacks, who are struggling to combat the spread of fascist wars and economic concentration, and to persist in doing so may hasten the focalization of extinction by violence.

But the lines and language of your book will further convince the general public that you are one of the foremost writers of the United States, if not the world, and I therefore hasten to congratulate you on the book's successful "broad-cast." May your literary star grow bigger, better and brighter in the galaxy of those of 'steen' magnitude. May the sales of the book bring to you much of that, which, under the influence of the capitalistic system, makes the world, go 'round and 'round.

Very truly,
Horace R. Cayton

Atlanta, Ga., October 6, 1935

My dear Mr. Cayton:

I thank you for your letter of September 14 concerning my book. I think you make the usual mistake of many people in minimizing the importance of careful knowledge and study of the past. The people of the 15th Century used to call themselves Moderns and show vast disdain for the world that had gone before. But out of the past is spawned the present and only by a study of the past can we be wise for the future.

Very sincerely yours
W. E. B. Du Bois

A remarkable exchange of letters between editors of the American Mercury *and Du Bois
occurred late in 1935. Gordon Carroll, the managing editor, was born in Baltimore in 1903; he
served on the* American Mercury *from 1934 to 1938, was a senior editor of the* Reader's
Digest *from 1938 to 1941, and was editor-in-chief of* Coronet *through 1952. Most recently he
has been a director of the Famous Writers' School in Westport, Connecticut. The letter to Du
Bois from the other* Mercury *editor, Paul Palmer, was not directly answered by Du Bois,
though he referred to it occasionally in later years with as much wonder as disgust. (See his
column in the* Pittsburgh Courier, *8 August 1936, and in the* Amsterdam News, *6 March
1943.)*

New York, N. Y., September 27, 1935

Dear Professor Du Bois:

After reading an article of yours in a recent issue of *Foreign Affairs*,[1] it occurred to me
that you might have on hand other manuscripts which would be suitable for publication
in the Mercury.

If this is the case, I will be glad to read any articles you care to submit.

Sincerely,
Gordon Carroll

Atlanta, Ga., October 2, 1935

My dear Sir:

Answering your letter of September 27, I beg to suggest certain subjects for
treatment in the American Mercury which might interest you. I should be glad to
know which one you think might be suitable.

A. The American Negro During the Depression.

(This would deal with the way in which the depression, the New Deal and
the Recovery had affected black folk.)

B. Recent Currents of Thought Among American Negroes.

(This would deal with the new outlooks concerning economic conditions, the
Ethiopian crisis, and imminent World War.)

C. The Present Plight of Negro-American Literature.

(This would review the renaissance of Negro literature about ten years ago and
its results as shown today.)

D. The Possible Future of the Negro in America.

(This would examine anew the possibilities of amalgamation, more complete
segregation, migration and extinction as ways of settling the Negro problem.)

Very sincerely yours
W. E. B. Du Bois

1. The reference is to "Inter-Racial Implications of the Ethiopian Crisis: A Negro View,"
Foreign Affairs 14 (October 1935): 82–92.

New York, N. Y., November 4, 1935

Dear Mr. Du Bois:

Mr. Carroll turned your MS over to me. The only possibility I see in it is an article stating what effect the New Deal has had upon the Negro. If you care to write such an article, and it is distinctly unfavorable to the administration, I will be glad to read it. Please submit a piece of this type on approval if you feel that it will make interesting reading.

Sincerely,
Paul Palmer[1]

In an earlier letter (to Streator, 17 April 1935) Du Bois made reference to his intended participation in a "Davis conference" in May. This was a national conference, sponsored by the Joint Committee on National Recovery—whose leading spirit was John P. Davis—and the Social Science Division of Howard University. Its theme was The Position of the Negro in our National Economic Crisis; it was held at the university, 18–20 May. Du Bois spoke the evening of 19 May on "Social Planning for the Negro, Past and Present."

It is with this paper that the following correspondence deals; Ralph J. Bunche (1904–71), then a young professor at Howard, was to be the Nobel Peace Prize winner in 1950 and the United Nations Under-Secretary from 1955 until 1971.

Washington, D. C., November 8, 1935

Dear Dr. Du Bois:

I have been requested by the Committee on Publication of the Proceedings of the Economic Conference held at Howard University last May to request your permission for the publication of your address. It was noted in going over the manuscripts delivered at the Conference that a notation appeared on yours to the effect that the material was not to be published.

In sending out the invitations to the speakers who addressed the conference and other literature in connection with it, Mr. Davis of the Joint Committee and I indicated that the proceedings of the conference would be published. All of the other speakers have consented to the use of their manuscripts and we are very anxious to receive your consent for publication, in order that the proceedings may be complete. We are using the January issue of the *Journal of Negro Education* as the vehicle for publication. We will be happy to send you the proofs for correction, or revision, if you desire us to do so.

Sincerely yours,
Ralph J. Bunche.

1. Paul Palmer (1889–1942) was born in Philadelphia, moved to Yonkers, New York, and served there for several years as a reporter and editor of local papers. After his employment at the *American Mercury*, he served in the public relations department of the Westchester Lighting Company of New York.

Atlanta, Ga., November 11, 1935

My dear Mr. Bunche:

The speech which I delivered at Howard will be published in my booklet in the Adult Education Series which will appear, I imagine, sometime this winter. If the January number of the *Journal of Negro Education* is going to be published before the first of January, I should be glad to have my paper appear there. However, I would like to correct the proof.

Very sincerely yours,
W. E. B. Du Bois

Washington, D. C. November 15, 1935

Dear Dr. Du Bois

I wish to thank you for your note of November 11 concerning your manuscript. I have consulted with Dr. Locke concerning the matter and he has informed me that, since the *Journal* is to appear with your article the first week in January, there will be no conflict with the publication of the adult education series.

We thank you for the privilege of publishing the manuscript and will be glad to submit you a proof as soon as we get it.[1]

Sincerely yours,
Ralph J. Bunche

Among Black people in New York City the most widely read newspaper was (and is) the Amsterdam News. *Its stance was pro-labor until its own workers demanded a union shop through the Newspaper Guild, whose president at that time was Heywood Broun. A strike began on 10 October 1935, held solid for twelve weeks, and the workers won a union shop at the end of December.*

The paper had been established late in 1909 by Edward A. Warren; upon his death in 1921, its direction was assumed by his widow, Sadie Warren-Davis; she was in charge when the strike occurred. She wrote a lengthy letter about it to Du Bois in response to one from him (his letter has not been found).

New York, N.Y., November 26, 1935

Dear Dr. Du Bois:

We are pleased to give you the following description of the history of the dispute between the publisher of The Amsterdam News and a number of its employees who are on strike.

The Amsterdam News has been in debt for some years. In May of this year (1935), the suggestion was made and carried out that new features be added to the newspaper

1. Published as "Social Planning for the Negro, Past and Present," *Journal of Negro Education* 5 (January 1936): 110–25.

and the price be increased to ten cents. It was thought that if this might be done without a great loss in circulation the income of the paper could be increased.

The experiment was costly. From May until October, the obligation to our printer increased $8,000. Circulation dropped 14,000 from an original figure of 32,000. Each week the deficit grew until it reached $800 and the firm's reserves and credit were exhausted. It was imperative that some economies be effected if the business were to continue.

Our plant divides itself into three departments; business, editorial and printing. During the past year, nearly a dozen persons had been dropped from the business department without being replaced. We retain a skeleton force in that department. We first applied ourselves to the printing department. We had been printing seven different editions. We reduced these to one at a saving of more than $200. We then decided to prune in the editorial department. A total of 51 persons was on the payroll in that department, ranging from the home office staff to correspondents, special writers and artists. The first discharges struck three of the nine persons in the home office and five part-time workers outside the office.

Five of the six persons left in the home editorial office rebelled when three were discharged. The first open breach between employer and employees was then created.

Before that time, however, there had been some disaffection, a description of which is necessary to a complete understanding of the controversy.

Early in 1934, a unit of the New York Newspaper Writers' Guild had been formed among the employees of the editorial department of The Amsterdam News. The employer took no position in relation to this except that in her own mind she saw little necessity for it and was somewhat apprehensive that the new unit might be the cause of future trouble. Every member of the home office staff belonged to this guild unit. None was discharged in more than a year of membership.

It had been the custom of the employer to give her employees two weeks' vacation with pay in the summer. Lack of money forced her to withdraw this concession this summer. She permitted vacations but was unable to give wages during the vacation period. As noted above, she was steadily going further in debt and losing circulation as a result of the increase in the price of the paper to ten cents. These payless vacations resulted in considerable grumbling and became the basis of agitation to require the publisher to sign employee contracts with the New York Guild. The publisher declined to negotiate contracts with the Guild. There were two reasons:

First, she felt that recognition of the Guild would give control of the personnel of her editorial office to the Guild, a primarily white organization. She had no prejudices against the white leaders as such, nor against whites. She had four white reporters on her pay roll. But she was fearful that whites would not be able to understand the special problems of a Negro business and would lack the sympathy and spirit of sacrifice necessary to maintain it.

Second, her income was constantly decreasing and she was aware that she could not sign any contracts covering pay which she was sure she would not be able to fulfill.

It should be recognized that the Guild issue was divided into two parts: Did the publisher of The Amsterdam News oppose the membership of her employees in the Guild and did she oppose signing labor contracts with the Guild? The answer to the first question is no and to the second, yes.

The payless vacations had caused dissatisfaction. The discharge of three employees intensified this discontent.

These employees were given notices of dismissal Monday, October 7, effective October 12. They were members of the Guild. The six retained in the home office were also members of the Guild.

On the night of Tuesday, October 8, a meeting was held of all the Guild members of the staff, inside and outside the home office, except one. At that time, it is reliably reported to the publisher by one of her loyal employees who was there, that a proposal to strike in behalf of the three discharged employees was discussed by the other employees, Guild members, who had not been discharged.

Some were in favor of a strike and some were not. The editor of the paper expressed the hope that a settlement involving the three discharged employees might be effected with the publisher. Others suggested that an approach be made to the publisher on the matter of finances. These suggestions were coldly turned down by the unit leader. He advocated a walkout and insisted that there must be no recognition of the financial condition of the publisher. He suggested that the Guild be permitted to take the matter in hand and that a fight should be made on the grounds that the publisher had ignored the rights of labor.

It was not true that the publisher had been indifferent to the welfare of her employees. Her lowest-paid reporter received $30 a week. The editor was paid $45. The salary of the sports and theatrical editor, a veteran employee, was $50. The society editor was paid $35 a week. These were "depression"wages, much lower than those formerly paid, but still as good or better than those paid by any other Negro newspaper. The employees had the five-day week; in fact, they worked only four and one-half days. They had no fear of losing their jobs. Only one person had been discharged in the editorial department in 15 years.

Nevertheless, it was decided at this meeting to make the "cause of labor" the strike issue. No unit vote was taken on the walkout. Instead, over the objections of some, a committee of three was appointed and invested with the power to command a walkout.

The next day, Wednesday October 9, the publisher was placed in a dilemma. The paper goes to press Thursday night. She learned that no copy had gone to the printer, nor any pictures to the engraver. No work had been done and material which had come into the office through the mail was missing. There was more than $2,000 worth of advertising scheduled for that week's issue which would have been lost or jeopardized if the paper had failed to come out.

She therefore approached her employees and asked them what they intended to do. They refused to state, insisting instead that she see the white secretary of the Guild. This was their reply, with the exception of one, to her question as to whether or not they were going to put the paper out.

When they refused to give her an answer and referred her to the Guild, she asked them for their keys and paid them for the week.

That afternoon pickets appeared before the plant bearing placards reading: The Amsterdam is opposed to organized labor.

A vicious campaign has been waged against the paper. Aided and abetted by the Guild and other union organizations, eight members of the home office staff and all but two of the outside staff who were members of the Guild, took their case to the public and described the publisher as a malevolent persecutor of labor. The sympathy of many intelligent and influential citizens was won through this deceitful plea. These citizens never took the trouble to find out the publisher's side. A vigorous campaign was waged against circulation and advertising. The circulation was not injured, but valuable local advertising was forced out of the paper, not because the advertiser supported the strikers in principle, but because he did not want his establishment picketed.

Some persons sought to effect a compromise which would involve recognition of the Guild and the re-employment of the publisher's old employees at reduced salaries. She was unable to entertain any so-called "compromise" because she knew that there was no compromise which would enable the paper to operate.

The institution is more than $43,000 in debt and is completely without funds except those which come from circulation and some national accounts. The present editorial staff is only half as large as the former in the home office, and the number of outside workers has been reduced so that the total is now 18 instead of the former 51. Furthermore, the publisher is unable to pay her present employees. They are working without salaries for such sums as she can spare them when Saturday comes. This means that the paper can only survive by investment of new capital. Even the re-insertion of the local advertising would not enable her to operate at a profit. She had a weekly deficit of $800 when this advertising was in the paper.

This brings us to a consideration of the second paragraph of your letter. You quote the charge that some Negro business men are making considerable profits, but are paying much lower wages to their workers than similar white businesses. We believe that some Negro business men do make profits and pay low wages. We do not know whether these Negro businesses pay lower wages than white businesses of similar standing. It has been our impression that a trained Negro young man or young woman expects more for similar service than the white person gets in so-called white-collar jobs. It has not been true that the publisher of The Amsterdam News has made profits at the expense of low wages. She is as insolvent as her business, except for a few minor and unconvertible properties.

Is a Negro weekly newspaper prosperous enough to pay current union wages to its employees? Most of them are not. We know of only one Negro publisher who has grown wealthy and has had part union help. That publisher was Robert S. Abbott. He was finally forced to rid himself of union help and although once wealthy, is reported to be in straitened circumstances today. The Amsterdam News has never been able to pay union wages. More than $30,000 of the $43,000 owed by The Amsterdam News today is for union printers and engravers. These bills have been allowed to accumulate while she was trying to pay her employees in the business and editorial departments. Her employees in these latter departments were colored; in the other, white. She paid fair wages to her colored employees and forced the whites to wait. Most Negro businesses, harassed by union prices, try to solve the problem by paying low wages to the colored employees.

The reason that Negro newspapers cannot pay union salaries throughout and exist is simple. Negro newspapers are shut off from the best local and national advertising accounts. We believe that most persons, considering this question, think of Negro newspapers in comparison with white dailies. The Negro newspaper should be compared to weekly rural white publications of the second grade.

Yours very truly,
Sadie Warren-Davis

Du Bois, deciding prematurely that this strike would be lost, wrote to the editor of the Forum,† then an important national magazine published in New York City, suggesting an article; his letter illuminates his thinking in this period.*

Atlanta, Ga., December 10, 1935

The Editor of The Forum Magazine
Dear Sir:

May I bring to your attention the following situation which seems to me to call for an article in your magazine:

In the fall of 1935, a strike took place among the editorial writers and reporters on the Amsterdam News, a colored weekly published in Harlem. These writers had joined the new union in which Heywood Broun and others are interested.

The strike was unsuccessful and the young writers lost their jobs and since they are colored, there is practically no opportunity for them to get other jobs of the same sort, except on other colored papers in New York or elsewhere.

This shows a peculiar dilemma. From most of the labor unions, Negroes are excluded, either in the constitution or by the ritual or by local action. In unions where they are admitted, they are in most cases discriminated against. It is fair to say that in the union movement, Negroes are barred from nine-tenths of the best paying jobs. In cases where they have underbid the union workers are scabs, they have often met the

---

* There is an analysis of the strike by Henry Lee Moon in *Race* 1 (Winter 1935–36): 41–42. Reportage on the strike was fairly full in the *New York Times*, beginning on 10 October and ending with an account of the workers' victory in its issue of 25 December 1935.

† At the time, this was Henry Goddard Leach.

treatment of the molders in Chattanooga some years ago. The molders struck; non-union Negro laborers took their places; the molders obtained their union and asked Negroes to join; the Negroes joined; the employers made peace with the union and re-hired the white molders, leaving the Negro molders out.

The result is that in the best paying and new technique, Negres cannot get an industrial foothold and in the older branches, they are being forced out, as for instance, as locomotive firemen.

In partial compensation for this industrial exclusion, the Negroes have long tried to establish their own businesses and hire Negro workers. Here they have had some success. There are manufacturing establishments, like Pero and Walker's Hair Preparation; there are insurance organizations with a number of employees and there are newspapers and retail stores.

In most of these cases, the Negro managers worked along with their employees and their income was from wages far more than from profits. In some cases, however, the Negro manager has become a capitalist.

There are, for instance, four or five Negro weekly newspapers which have proved to be profitable investments and yielded their owners considerable incomes, from $5,000 to $25,000 a year, and most of this income has been profits and not wages.

Suppose now, the employees of these Negro business institutions should join the labor movement and strike for higher wages. First of all, the Negro employers would complain that it is only by paying lower wages that they can make their businesses grow and that for the most part, their profits are rewards for hard labor in the past; that if they try to pay union wages and value, that the black laborers could not get jobs with white institutions; that the low wage paid by colored institutions is, therefore, better than no wage at all.

On the other hand, the white labor leaders say that unless Negroes are going to join in the labor movement and cease scabbing labor cannot successfully raise the rate of wages. The Negroes in rebuttal point out that by the action of white laborers themselves they are getting smaller and smaller chance for remunerative work in any line and that, therefore, they must take what is offered in order to live.

Here is an extraordinary dilemma and a real one, and the only way out, as I see it, is producers' and consumers' co-operation among Negroes, the possibility of which both the Negro intelligentsia and white labor leaders and white economists deny.

Do you not think the above situation calls for an article? I shall be glad to have your judgment.[1]

Very sincerely yours
W. E. B. Du Bois

1. The article was not desired.

1936

After Du Bois left the Crisis *in 1934, he had no medium by which he could regularly reach a significant component of the Afro-American people. For a brief period in 1927 he contributed a regular book-review column to the* Amsterdam News, *and for several months in 1931 he did a weekly column for the Black-owned Eastern Feature Syndicate, which appeared in several newspapers. Early in 1932 he contributed a column to a venture undertaken by George S. Schuyler, called the* National News, *which was issued from New York City; but this paper expired quickly.*

By 1935, Du Bois missed this regular readership among his own people; late that year Robert L. Vann wrote inquiring whether Du Bois would be interested in writing a column for the Pittsburgh Courier, *a nationally circulated paper owned by Vann. From this offer dates an important feature of Du Bois's post-*Crisis *life, for beginning with the* Pittsburgh Courier *of 8 February 1936 and ending with a piece in the* National Guardian *in May 1961, hardly a week went by in those twenty-five years that Du Bois's ideas were not published in the papers named or in the* Amsterdam News, *the* Chicago Defender, *the* People's Voice *(issued in New York City by Adam Clayton Powell, Jr.), the* Chicago Globe, *or* Freedom, *a paper published in New York City through the efforts of Paul Robeson and Louis E. Burnham.* *

This aspect of Du Bois's life is illuminated in his correspondence with Vann (1887–1940), an attorney in Pittsburgh, a power in politics, and, above all, publisher of the influential Courier.†

Atlanta, Ga., January 4, 1936

My dear Mr. Vann:

Your letter of December 27 has been received.

Ever since leaving the *Crisis,* I have contemplated a weekly or monthly letter to the American Negro, but the two or three offers which have come did not seem to me to indicate any real demand for my services. On the other hand, letters and personal talks in various parts of the country have led me to believe that eventually there would be such a demand.

What I want to write about divides itself into three parts:

1. The pithy and caustic comment on general matters such as I used to write under the caption "As the Crow Flies" in *The Crisis.*

---

* Du Bois's connection with the *Courier* lasted through January 1938. In October 1939 he began a regular column in the *Amsterdam News* that ran until October 1944.

† There is a recent biography, *Robert L. Vann,* by Andrew Buni (Pittsburgh: University of Pittsburgh Press, 1974).

2. An attempt to try and clarify the thought of the American Negroes in the basic matter of making a living, especially during this time when the whole economic structure of modern society is going to be revolutionized.

3. To prevent the American Negro from considering his problem as local and provincial, but rather as a part of the whole international development of the modern world, especially with regard to the darker races.

I think these three subjects might fit into a weekly column: the first to popularize it; the second, to give real information; and the third to make Negroes think of Europe, Asia and Africa.

In addition to these three features, I should like to have a weekly picture and instead of following the custom of having a picture of the columnist, I should like to have it a one or two-column picture of something closely connected with the subject of the week's column.

To do such a column and do it well would mean time and work. It should not be simply a weekly stunt done at the last minute and calculated to fill space. Rather it should stimulate thought and give real information.

I contracted once with the *Amsterdam News* and a syndicate of colored papers for a weekly letter which would pay $12.50. This I soon found was not enough for my services and too much for their resources, and I gave it up after six months' trial. Personally, I think that $25 a letter would be a fair compensation, but I am afraid that this is more than a Negro weekly can bear. On the other hand, $15 would not pay me.

I have three books in contemplation: one almost finished; one which I am writing, and one on which a publisher is considering a contract.

I have also a growing amount of magazine work. Both the *American Mercury* and the *Forum* have approached me recently and I shall probably do an article for the *Forum*. It seems to me, therefore, that $20 a week would be reasonable for my point of view.

May I also add in confidence that I am going to have an unusual opportunity for study and observation during the coming year. On June 6, I am leaving for a six months' residence in Europe, chiefly Germany, for the purpose of studying the relation between education and industry. This trip will be financed by the Oberlaender Trust which has in the past sent out a number of American scholars for similar studies. The Grant given me is small, but if I can piece it out by lectures, I shall return by way of Japan and China. You will realize that the opportunity to be in Europe during this most critical time perhaps in the world's history will be of tremendous advantage.

I am writing you frankly and at length and would be glad to hear from you at your convenience.

Very sincerely yours,
W. E. B. Du Bois

Pittsburgh, Pa., January 13, 1936

My dear Dr. Du Bois:

Let me acknowledge with thanks your letter of January 4.

I like the idea of dividing your writings into three parts. I shall be glad to see you give us a diversified column.

Now as to price. I suppose you know that I am well aware of the sacrifices you have made to improve the status of the Negro. I also know that no one has attempted to compensate you. I have long since learned that anyone who expects Negroes to invest any money in their own advancement is certainly mistaken. I am going to pay you one hundred ($100.00) dollars a month, payable on the 1st and 15th. I wish I could do more, and as time goes on, I believe I will be able to do more. I could put all the profits in my pocket, but I really have no use for money except as a tool with which to work. I know that we are to make our millions, if we make any, off ourselves. The Negro will never get any wealth from the white man. I am dedicated to the idea that the Negro must derive his wealth from himself. We make plenty of money, in a way, but it all gets away from us. Some day we will find this out and invest our earnings a little more wisely. We are segregated and we can't do very much about it, but one thing is certain, we can make segregation pay. I have done it. Therefore, I speak with authority so far as my own activities are concerned.

Let us start the column February 1. In order to do this, please place in our hands before February 1, material for at least two weeks. This will always give us a column in the office in the event some emergency arises to interfere with your schedule.

Of course, you understand that this matter is exclusively our property, since we are paying for it, and we will copyright your column. I am selfish enough to do this because I cannot get other Negro editors to invest any money in building up their product; and since I have to carry the burden myself, I am going to appropriate the column and copyright it. You are the judge of what you say in your column. We are going to treat you as an independent columnist and you are going to have full and free hand to say what you please—observing, of course, the rules of journalistic ethics.

Your first check for fifty ($50.00) dollars will be mailed this week so that our payments will stay in advance. I hope your studies in Europe will not interfere with the column; in fact, your visit to Europe should make your column more interesting. We now have more than a half million readers, and at the rate we are increasing, we should have three-quarters of a million by June 1.

I do not know how you would like to have this column headed, but since it is your opinion and it represents the subject matter as you see it, suppose we put at the top of the column something after the following: "The Way I See It" by Dr. W. E. B. Du Bois. If you think of something more suitable, let me have your suggestion.

Yours very truly,
Robert L. Vann

Atlanta, Ga., January 16, 1936

My dear Mr. Vann:

I have your letter of January 13 and shall be glad to furnish a weekly column for the Pittsburgh Courier for the remuneration of $100 a month, payable in installments of

$50 on the 1st and 15th. I shall have material for two columns in your office before February 1.

I should rather prefer the caption, "As the Crow Flies." This caption is pretty well known and I think would be recognized. I should be glad, however, to have your reaction.

In the same mail with your letter came a request from the re-organized *Amsterdam News* asking for a column. I told them that I had already contracted with you.

Very sincerely yours
W. E. B. Du Bois

Pittsburgh, Pa., January 16, 1936

Dear Dr. Du Bois:

Pursuant to promise, I am inclosing you herewith our check, made payable to your order, in the sum of fifty ($50.00) dollars, payment in advance on account of services for column to be supplied to *The Pittsburgh Courier*. Our next check will go forward February 15.

We are planning to announce your column the first week in February, and begin your column the second week in February. This is a slight change from the plan indicated in my last letter to you, but in order to make the announcement in the way we prefer to make it, we find a little more time is necessary.

Sincerely yours,
Robert L. Vann

Pittsburgh, Pa., January 21, 1936

Dear Dr. Du Bois:

I have yours of January 16th, which confirms our arrangement about payments; namely one hundred ($100.00) dollars per month, payable in installments of fifty ($50.00) dollars on the first and the fifteenth. I note that you will have your material, two columns, in our office before February 1.

I think I should explain why I do not take kindly to the caption "As the Crow Flies."

In the first place, it smacks too much of the *Crisis* and I prefer not to borrow any ideas from the *Crisis* for journalistic reasons. Second, there is a peculiar association connected with the crow. Many of our people who are not able to rise above petty things think of Jim Crow, the Two Black Crows and even nicknames that are applied to Negroes in certain sections of the country. For this reason, I did not like the caption when you were using it in the *Crisis*. Of course, in its higher and more elegant sense, it means, in a straight line, bearing close resemblance to the mathematical truth that a straight line is the shortest distance between two points, but I cannot resist the attitude of the masses who, after all, constitute our larger reading public. The psychology of the Negro is just something we have to deal with. I hope we can agree on something else as a caption.

Personally I prefer "As I See It" because, after all, what you write represents the subject as you see it and regardless of what you write, it will represent your point of view. Then too, a newspaper is unlike a magazine. It has to subscribe to modern suggestions and even commercial suggestions. The newspaper is more akin to the fellow in the street than a magazine, and it has to be clothed in garments comparable with the fellow we find in the poolrooms, barber shops, garages, factories, etc. Think it over. I shall, of course, seek to please you since you are to write the column.

I have some personal knowledge of the so-called reorganized *Amsterdam News*. In fact, I declined to buy the business myself, due to too many obligations outstanding and pressing for payment. While I hope to the contrary, I very much fear the boys are in for a sad experience.

Very sincerely yours,
Robert L. Vann

Atlanta, Ga., January 23, 1936

My dear Mr. Vann:

Answering your letter of January 21, I see the objection in the caption "As the Crow Flies." On the other hand, I do not like "As I See It." It is too much like Heywood Broun's "It Seems to Me." I suggest three other possible titles. How do you like them?

"The Far Horizon."

"The Opinion of W. E. B. D."

"Shadows of Dawn."

I may think of some others. I am sending herewith two pictures of African nurses in or near Ethiopia. I think possibly one of them might be used in connection with my column.

As I have said, I object to my picture in the column every month. It might be done once, but I think the repetition is cloying. I shall try to send a suggested picture each month, or you may have something better. Otherwise, perhaps all pictures might be omitted.

Very sincerely yours,
W. E. B. Du Bois

Pittsburgh, Pa., January 27, 1936

Dear Dr. Du Bois:

I have gone over the manuscripts you sent me, and while I agree with you that they are a little heavy, nevertheless, it is time our so-called thinkers adjusted their glasses and minds to something grave and weighty. Therefore, I am going to use the manuscripts just as you sent them.

I note you still have the crow flying and I don't believe the bird has sufficient historic backround to say nothing of family history to warrant using him in connection with such grave and weighty matters as are treated in your manuscripts. Therefore, let us use the following: "A Forum of Fact and Opinion" by Dr. W. E. B. Du Bois. Under this title, you can talk about anything under the sun and the title will still be appropriate.

We looked around here for a good cut of you, and not being able to find a very good one, we wired your office in Atlanta, only to receive a reply that your desk is locked and you are out of town. Therefore, you will have to bear with us and forgive us when you see the cut we are using. It is the best we have. After all, you know you were never very handsome except in that white flannel suit, and this is no season for white flannels.

Sincerely yours,
Robert L. Vann

P. S. Please address all manuscripts to *The Pittsburgh Courier*—and not to me—since I do leave town once every month or so—Vann.[1]

An exchange between Du Bois and James T. Shotwell (1874–1965) contains much substantive thinking. Du Bois's effort to publish a history of the role of Black people in the First World War was unsuccessful; the papers and various drafts of chapters connected with this effort are in the library of Fisk University—with micro-film reproduction in the library of the University of Massachusetts.

Shotwell was on the faculty of Columbia University from 1900 to 1942, when he became emeritus; he was perhaps the most distinguished scholar in international relations in the United States. He was a trustee of the Carnegie Endowment for International Peace from 1924 on and in 1949 was its president. In 1945 he was chairman of the United States consultative group advising the delegation founding the United Nations.

It is of some interest that Du Bois's first letter to Shotwell was addressed in care of the Carnegie Endowment for Inter-Racial Peace.

Atlanta, Ga., January 16, 1936

Mr. James T. Shotwell
My dear Sir:

For some time I have been engaged on a history of the Negro in the World War, chiefly American Negro troops, but with a good deal about black troops in the English, French and Belgian armies. At first, I conceived this simply as an historical record and since 1918 when I was in France with the press ship directly after the Armistice until today, have collected a mass of material, some of it unique and very valuable. I got it partly in shape for publication five or six years ago, but realized that it was too bulky and had to be cut down to readable and publishable size. Last year the Social Science Council made a small grant to help me work it over.

I am planning to get it ready for the press next year, but in the meantime, the more I study the material and the general literature that has come out about the war, the

---

1. The column began in the issue dated 8 February 1936. It had a picture of Du Bois then and thereafter—despite his request and objection. Its title was "Forum of Fact and Opinion," and it was headed: "This column represents the personal opinion of Dr. Du Bois and in no way reflects the editorial opinion of the *Pittsburgh Courier*—the Editor."

more I conceive of this history as a potent tract for peace. The unnecessary suffering and intrigue, the effect of the war upon the Negro peoples today, the Italian-Ethiopian aftermath, all makes me certain that I could write a volume which would be an effective attack upon the war from the point of view of the so-called lesser peoples.

I write to ask you if your foundation or any other of the peace foundations would be disposed to help me further in getting this volume ready for the press and getting it published. It may be, of course, that when it is once ready for the press I can find a publisher. On the other hand, it is equally possible that no publisher would undertake it unless some [word illegible] were made.

The work of getting it ready for the press involves the entire rewriting, verification of authorities and copying of documents. I estimate that this, with the clerical and skilled help, would cost about $3,000.

I would be very glad if you could give me any advice as to how I might secure aid and co-operation.

Very sincerely yours
W. E. B. Du Bois

New York City, January 27, 1936
Dear Professor Du Bois:

I am very much interested indeed in the plan of your history of the Negro in the World War, of which you wrote me in your letter of January 16. I only wish I had known of it earlier, for I am by no means clear as to how the Endowment could support it at the present time. The War History, which I edited,[1] was financed by a special fund of the Carnegie Corporation so that it did not come out of the budget of the Endowment. That fund was definite and limited; it is now exhausted.

Could you send me a table of contents of the volume you have in mind? I should like to see what possibilities there are and am sincerely interested.

With all best wishes,

Faithfully yours,
James T. Shotwell

On 4 February 1936, Du Bois responded to Shotwell's letter by promising to send further information soon thereafter. In about two weeks, he did so.

Atlanta, Ga., February 26, 1936

Mr. James T. Shotwell
My dear Sir:

In accordance with my letter of February 4, I am sending you enclosed an outline

---

1. He refers to a colossal project of scores of volumes in English, German, Italian, and French, published in the 1920s and 1930s; it was under the general editorship of Professor Shotwell with the overall title, *Economic and Social History of the World War.*

of the manuscript concerning which I spoke [the enclosure was not found]. I wish very much that you could examine the manuscript itself and that I could emphasize a little better my feeling that this could be a most effective, practical peace document. Usually we talk about peace in the abstract, but here is a chance to see what war means in the concrete as applied to people who are already under social difficulties, and what interest American Negroes and the Negroes in the world have in world peace.

Repeatedly in the history of the United States, this argument has been made and it will come again. No matter what the cause of war is, Negroes ought to support the war policy loyally and fully, because by fighting shoulder to shoulder with America, they will gain recognition as American citizens. This was the argument in the Revolutionary War and the War of 1812, in the Civil War, in the Spanish-American War, and in the World War. Results prove that it was justified only in the Civil War, where Negroes were after all fighting for their own freedom. In the other cases, they got little or no credit for their effort. They fought in many cases against their own conscience and simply helped further to muddle a muddled world.

Very sincerely yours
W. E. B. Du Bois

New York City, March 12, 1936

Dear Dr. Du Bois:

I am sorry for the delay in answering your letter of February 26, but I have been lecturing in the Middle West and in John[s] Hopkins, and have got behind with my correspondence.

I think you know my sympathy for the kind of work you are doing, but I am sorry that the Endowment is not in a position to help. As I told you in my letter of January 27, the Economic and Social History of the World War has not been supported by the Endowment from its own funds but on a definite and limited fund from the Carnegie Corporation, and with no possibility of additions being made to it. I am, therefore, not in a position to sponsor the publication of this volume under the Endowment. I know that the volume also has another appeal and a very strong one, but that would not come directly within the purview of this Endowment. It would be more like something that the Sage Foundation or the Milbank Fund, or some such organization devoted to American problems, could undertake. My Division is distinctly International and the trustees are obliged to interpret it that way owing to the terms of the trust.

With best wishes and sincere regret,

Sincerely yours,
James T. Shotwell

Aspects of the right-wing attack upon liberal and radical groups and forces in the 1930s are reflected in a letter to Du Bois signed by the distinguished Columbia University professor George S. Counts, the eminent theologian Reinhold Niebuhr, and the dramatist Elmer Rice.

New York City, February 7, 1936

My dear Mr. Du Bois:

We are anxious to have you become one of the sponsors for the Progressive Inter-collegiate Alumni Association of America.

This organization, recently formed, consists of alumni from universities through-out the country. We are appealing to those university men and women, representing a diversity of professional activities, who are disturbed by a growth of illiberal forces in America, particularly on the college campus. Our anxiety has been sharpened by the savage attacks directed against university administrations, faculty members, and stu-dents, by the Hearst press, the American Liberty League, vigilante societies and other reactionary elements in American Society.

We should help protect civil liberties and democratic rights wherever they may be endangered on the university front. Alumni associations have not, up to the present time, been very active in the campaign to safeguard these values. They have usually been cut off from all but a small group of university graduates. This is the first time an attempt has been made to form a national alumni group with a definite liberal pro-gram. In addition to the maintenance of civil liberties and democratic rights, we favor freedom of learning and teaching and the advancement of learning through govern-ment appropriations of funds for scholarships and research. Our program is elabo-rated in our Constitution, a copy of which we are enclosing.

The success of this organization will depend on the endorsement of persons like yourself who occupy positions of leadership in American cultural and political life. We shall appreciate your interest in the Association, and hope to receive a favorable reply.

Sincerely yours,
George S. Counts
Reinhold Niebuhr
Elmer Rice

P. S. Kindly address all communications to Sydney Prerau at the above address.

It is worth noting that this letter was addressed to Du Bois at the address of the Crisis, *though of course he had left it and the* NAACP *two years before. Perhaps this explains the delay in Du Bois's response.*

Atlanta, Ga., March 16, 1936

Dear Mr. Prerau:

Answering the letter of Messrs. Count, Niebuhr and Rice, I beg to say that I should be glad to become one of the sponsors of the Progressive Intercollegiate Alumni Association of America.[1]

Very sincerely yours
W. E. B. Du Bois

1. The constitution of the Association—a four-page printed document—mentions in its intro-ductory section that Heywood Broun had endorsed its formation. It was pro-union, anti-

*Richard Robert Wright (1855–1947), born in Georgia, and educated at Atlanta University, was
a high school principal for a decade toward the end of the nineteenth century and president of
Georgia State Industrial College from 1891–1921. He served with distinction in the Spanish-
American War (gaining the rank of major). In 1921 he moved to Philadelphia and became
president of the Citizens and Southern Bank and Trust Company of that city. From 1880 to
1898 he was a trustee of Atlanta University. In his eighty-first year, he wrote Du Bois.*

Philadelphia, Pa., February 20, 1936

Dear Dr. Du Bois:

I happened to notice today in the paper that you will be near your three-score years
and ten on next Sunday, February 23rd. I had no idea that you were so near being a
septuagenarian.

Please accept my sincere congratulation. My, how time flies. I remember when I
was in Hartford, Conn. after having visited the corpse of Harriet Beecher Stowe and
sat as Vice-President and acting Chairman of the Trustee Board of Atlanta University
when they were all discussing the engagement of a young Professor, W. E. B. Du
Bois. You will perhaps be surprised to know, if you do not already know, that every
one of these splendid Trustees has passed away. I do not recall that a single one of
them is still in existence. I am satisfied that all of the colored have passed away
beginning with Dr. Joseph E. Smith, L. B. Maxwell, Edgar J. Penney, Dr. [Horace]
Bumstead, Dr. [Joseph H.] Twichell, Professor [F. A.] Chase and perhaps members
whose names I did not just this moment recall. I am sure that this gruesome reminis-
cence will not disturb you, for if you are as robust and healthy as your picture
indicates, you will be here long after all the rest of us have answered the final roll call.

I am happy to congratulate you upon the great record which you have made and the
great service which you have rendered to mankind. May your days be increased and
your splendid service enhanced by the additional service which you will be able to
render.

With the highest regard, I am

Very truly yours,
R. R. Wright, Sr.

Atlanta, Ga., February 26, 1936

My dear Mr. Wright:

I appreciate deeply your kind letter of February 20 with congratulations on my
birthday. I am glad to know that you are still well and able to carry on.

Very sincerely yours,
W. E. B. Du Bois

---

militarist, anti-fascist, and affirmed as an "ultimate objective" the achievement of "free public
education for all students in the colleges and universities as well as in secondary and elementary
schools." This "increased and equalized" educational program, it stated, was to apply to all
persons of all ages and "races, colors, beliefs, or affiliations."

The secretary of the District of Columbia branch of the NAACP *raised an interesting question—one that still persists—and received a clear answer from Du Bois.*

Washington, D. C., March 9, 1936

My dear Dr. Du Bois:

I am anticipating a question which is likely to come before me, hence, the inquiry that I am about to make of you.

What was the policy of the *Crisis* under your direction with respect to the printing of the word "nigger"? Did you permit short stories and the like to be published where that word was used?

Sincerely yours,
A. S. Pinkett

Atlanta, Ga., March 11, 1936

My dear Mr. Pinkett:

My policy when I was editor of the *Crisis* was to let a writer use the word "nigger" or "darky" if it served an artistic purpose in his story. Of course I tried not to have this occur too often. The point is if an author is quoting a Southern white man, and the white man is addressing a Negro, he will say "nigger." To make him say anything else would be rather a strain upon credulity.

Very sincerely yours,
W. E. B. Du Bois

After Du Bois left the NAACP, *there were occasional rumors concerning his possible appointment to the presidency of one or another Black university. Following the death of John Hope of Atlanta, the idea of Du Bois as his successor came to the fore. Illustrative is a letter written on behalf of a section of Sigma Pi Phi, a Black fraternity of which Du Bois was a member, by its secretary—or "grammateus"—Henry K. Craft (1883–1974). Craft at this time was executive secretary of the Harlem Branch of the* YMCA. *Born in South Carolina, he attended both Brown and Harvard Universities and was a teacher at Tuskegee (1908–11). After a career as an electrical engineer in Chicago for several years, he went into social work and served the* YMCA *in many cities, and finally in Harlem, from 1932 to 1946.*

New York City, March 26, 1936

My dear Dr. Du Bois:

At a recent meeting of Zeta Boule the general discussion turned around to the question of who was to be the next president of Atlanta University. Immediately and almost simultaneously several of the men presented your name which led to the offering of the Boule's services to this end, providing you were willing to have it so act. I was, therefore, instructed to write and inquire whether or not you would be interested in having the Boule work toward the end of your selection for this very important and serviceable post.

I shall be glad to receive your early reply and will, of course, treat it with whatever confidence you desire.

Sincerely and fraternally yours,
Henry K. Craft

Atlanta, Ga., March 31, 1936

My dear Mr. Craft:

I thank the archons very much for their kind intentions, but I do not wish to be President of Atlanta University or any other university. I have plenty of work mapped out and time, peace and content to do it. I do not want to be distracted by difficult, if not impossible, executive duties.

With best regards

Very sincerely yours
W. E. B. Du Bois

An exchange with Edwin Embree of the Rosenwald Fund is substantive, and Du Bois's response provides an early reference to what became Phylon, *the quarterly begun by Atlanta University in 1940 and edited by Du Bois until 1944, when he left the university.* Phylon, *of course, continues its illuminating existence.*

Chicago, Ill., April 8, 1936

Dear Dr. Du Bois:

I have just read your interesting comment on *Island India* in the *Pittsburgh Courier*.[1] I was impressed, as I always am in your writing, with the amount of matter that you can pack into a short space and in beautiful and readable English. The other thing that impressed my was that this is much too good writing for the ephemeral column of any weekly newspaper. In fact, it is so much above the newspaper level that I doubt if, from the standpoint of the publisher of the newspaper, it is even good for his business.

Reading this column of yours started me thinking again about the state of Negro journalism. In the old days, under your editorship, the *Crisis* was a power in the land. The same was true of *Opportunity* during the brilliant early years when Charles Johnson edited it. Both have now fallen into the doldrums and there is not left a single journal of Negro expression that is even respectable, to say nothing of excellent. I don't know whether anything can be done about it, but there is some responsibility on your head simply because you have proved what can be done.

Very truly yours,
Edwin R. Embree

1. The column appeared on 4 April 1936. The book by Edwin Embree, Margaret Simon, and B. Mumford was *Island India Goes to School* (Chicago: University of Chicago Press, 1934).

Atlanta, Ga., April 10, 1936

My dear Mr. Embree:

I appreciate your letter of April 8. I have just written the Editor of the *Courier* and suggested myself that perhaps my articles were a bit heavy.

I deplore with you our present lack of a journal of Negro opinion and I do not know what ought to be done about it. Last year, I suggested and urged on President Hope a quarterly journal to be published at this university; either (a) a journal of Negro sociology; or (b) the Atlanta University Quarterly. My idea was that under either name, we could secure a considerable amount of valuable literary and scientific articles of permanent value. Mr. Hope was always slow in his decisions and unfortunately died without coming to any conclusion concerning this quarterly. I think, myself, that a quarterly of this sort, rather than a monthly magazine, is what we need now. News and current controversy can be carried very well by the weekly newspaper, but we need something between the weekly and the book. Just now, of course, our plans are in abeyance until the University is re-organized.

Very sincerely yours,
W. E. B. Du Bois

Not long after taking up his ministerial post in Liberia, Lester Walton (see pp. 103–4 above) wrote Du Bois.

Monrovia, Liberia, April 14, 1936

Dear Dr. Du Bois:

I am delighted to know that you are a weekly contributor to the *Pittsburgh Courier*. Since your divorce from the *Crisis* I have often thought it a great pity that there was no medium for the regular publication of your views. Both you and the *Courier* are to be congratulated upon the new alliance.

The death of Dr. Hope came as a shock to me. I note by the Negro Press that there is much speculation as to his successor. After your answer to my statement sometime ago that I thought you the logical choice of the Presidency of Howard University, I guess there is little hope of your becoming an aspirant for selection as Atlanta University's President.

We are well. President [Edwin] Barclay and I continue to work harmoniously together. Much of our business is transacted informally. Conditions are on the up-grade in Liberia and prospects of the three-year plan succeeding appear bright. President Barclay is dominating the situation on every hand.

Sometime ago I wrote you affirmatively relative to cooperating with you on a Negro encyclopedia. Are there any new developments to proposed project?

From what I can read and also hear on my short wave radio set which picks up United States of America programs, the Presidential campaign bids fair to be very hectic.

Please write me now and then. I promise to give you a "banquet" at Lüchow's[1] when I get back.

Faithfully,
Lester A. Walton

Atlanta, Georgia, May 9, 1936

My dear Mr. Walton:

I was glad to get your letter of April 14. I, too, was pleased to have the offer come from the *Courier*. I wanted to do some writing, but only in case there was a real demand for it, and so I turned down two or three small offers and waited until something which seemed worth while should come along. I hope the series will go well.

The death of Dr. Hope came as a shock to us all. I still believe it was quite unnecessary for four or five years. But at any rate, as I am planning to live those four or five years myself, I haven't the slightest desire to commit suicide by accepting any such job.

I am glad that you think Liberia is on the upgrade. I have heard very little about it recently, and have wondered just what was happening.

The plans for the Negro Encyclopaedia are coming on very well. I am just sending today a proposed list of subjects which it should treat. The Phelps Stokes Fund is making a small, annual appropriation. I hope that in a year or two, we may get some real money. I shall be sure to call upon you when we once do get started.

I am glad to know of that banquet at Lüchow's and I am pleased to know that you say banquet and not luncheon. By the bye, I am taking a vacation. I leave here June 5 for Germany to spend five or six months there, after, of course, going to London and Paris. I shall then go to Russia and come home by way of China, Japan and Hawaii, arriving to take up my work here February 1; the second term.

I wish I could see you on the way, but I am afraid I shall not get that far South. My best regards to your family and to the President of the Republic and others whom I know.

Very sincerely yours
W. E. B. Du Bois

The most distinguished anthropologist in the history of the United States was Franz Boas (1858–1942). He was born in Germany and received a doctorate in 1881 from Kiel University. Shortly thereafter he emigrated to the United States, became an editor of Science *and joined the faculty at Clark University. From 1899 to 1937 he was a professor at Columbia, and thereafter*

---

1. Lüchow's was (and is) a well-known restaurant in the Union Square section of New York City. It features German food—and beer—and from his student days in Germany Du Bois developed a taste for both that never left him. From time to time Walton and Du Bois took turns buying each other meals at this restaurant.

emeritus. In 1931, Boas was elected president of the American Association for the Advancement of Science.

Boas was a passionate opponent of racism and reaction and his early lectures and writings had a profound impact upon the young Du Bois.

In 1936 letters were exchanged between the two men.

New York, N.Y., April 22, 1936

Dear Dr. Du Bois:

The decline of culture in Nazi Germany, accomplished by the suppression of free speech, assemblage and discussion, by the regimentation of education and intellectual and political life, is threatening to destroy in one decade what has taken centuries of effort to build. For us who hold precious the progress of civilization, this reversion of mankind to the jungle-pit appears as an incalculable calamity. It seems therefore that the very least we can do in defense of our common humanity is to reaffirm our faith in free intelligence against brute force.

To this end the *American Committee for Anti-Nazi Literature* is being founded: to wage a campaign of education and enlightenment against the Nazis. It plans to hold an educational exhibit in New York and in other large cities of anti-Nazi literature, in memory of the burning of books by the Nazis. Steps are being taken to establish an anti-Nazi archive, to serve scholars, writers, students and educators. Organized educational activities will be carried on, in American colleges and universities; lectures and symposia on the various aspects of the anti-Nazi movement will be given. Moreover, as the center of its educational activities, it will supply through subscription, copies of underground literature now being courageously disseminated in Germany by all progressive elements, regardless of party, class or religious faith.

We feel that we need your assistance in this important educational venture. We would like you to lend your name and valuable influence as a sponsor of this Committee.

We need not assure you that we anticipate with pleasure a prompt indication of your support.

Yours sincerely,
Franz Boas
Chairman

Atlanta, Georgia, May 5, 1936

My dear Mr. Boas:

I have your kind letter of April 22. I am sure you know where my sympathies are in the terrible outburst of race prejudice in Germany, but it happens that I am not in a position to join your committee for the following reason: I have been given by the Oberlaender Trust a commission to make investigations in Germany for six months. At first, I wanted to study race prejudice or the question of colonies directly, but that did not fit in with their objects, but they are allowing me to make a study of education and industry. Of course there is no limit set upon what I may say after I come back. It would not, however, be wise for me to publicly join any committee before I went, otherwise I probably would not be allowed to study.

I am sure you will appreciate my reasons for not joining your effort. When I come back, I hope to be able to join it with much useful accumulated knowledge.

Very sincerely yours
W. E. B. Du Bois

New York, N.Y., May 11, 1936

Dear Prof. Du Bois:

I was much interested in receiving your letter of May 5. I am wondering how much you will be able to see in Germany. With the officially stimulated race prejudice you might have difficulties, although, on the other hand, it is also possible that they might try to be particularly courteous to you and show you Potemkin villages. The real difficulty would be to see behind the scenes. I know that the people in Germany are so terrorized that nobody dares to say anything except to his oldest and most reliable friends. Visitors are always impressed with the quiet and order which I understand prevails at the present time. It is true enough where there is a good government there is orderly conduct of the people but that does not mean that where there is orderly conduct there is good government. I wish I could direct you to some people who might allow you to look behind the scenes but I do not know of any. I am going to make some inquiries and if I find any names of people who would be willing to talk freely I will send them to you.

Yours very sincerely,
Franz Boas

Atlanta, Georgia, May 11, 1936

My dear Mr. Boas:

I thank you very much for your letter of May 11. I realize that it's going to be a little difficult for me to see and know anything in Germany, but the offer was made and it is too good an offer not to take advantage of. I have had a good deal of experience in seeing beyond surface indications, which may stand me in good stead this time.

Meantime, if you should by chance know of any persons from whom I could get information, I should be greatly obliged. My address in Germany will be:

% Dr. Georg Kartzke
Oberlaender Trust
Hegel Haus
Am Kupfergraben 4a
Berlin N 24 Germany

I am sailing June 5.

Very sincerely yours
W. E. B. Du Bois

1937

Du Bois returned from his trip around the world late in January 1937 and went almost at once to Atlanta and his teaching duties. His seven-month journey crystallized an idea for a book on the great theme that really preoccupied his entire life—the meaning and the practice of democracy. He wrote at some length of his idea to his friend and publisher Alfred Harcourt, but no reply seems to have survived. Certainly the book proposed was never done.

Atlanta, Ga., February 11, 1937

My dear Mr. Harcourt:

As perhaps you know I have just returned from a trip around the world. I was in England when [Anthony] Eden announced the failure of sanctions; I was in France at the time of the devaluation of the franc; I made short trips to Belgium and Austria; and I spent nearly six months in Germany visiting all the chief regions; I was ten days in Russia traversing the Trans-Siberian from Moscow to Otpur; I spent a week in Manchukuo, ten days in China, ten weeks in Japan, and stopped in Honolulu on the way home.

On the basis of this trip I have in mind, and partially written, a book of about two hundred pages to be called "A Search for Democracy." I want in this book to try to compare, in the different countries that I have seen, the effort to carry on government in accordance with the popular will and especially to discuss the means and methods by which governments today are trying to face new problems of work and wage, income and wealth. I want to see how far I can induce Democracy, Fascism, and Communism to speak the same language and to draw into the picture the colored peoples of the world; the people of China, Japan, and India, and the peoples of Africa.

My main thesis is that government today, whether it will or not, must regulate and in part conduct industry; that the world is too near unity to leave colored labor and the wishes of colored peoples out of the equation; I want to emphasize the fact that the fundamental differences between governments today are not differences between Democracy, Fascism, and Communism, but differences as to how far and in what way governments are going to attack the problem of work and wages and the distribution of wealth, and that that problem being settled the next problem is one of method and ability.

I want to put this book into popular form by beginning with the difficulty of discussing problems and politics and economics in a small, southern, Negro college. Then I am sending my colored professor on leave of absence without pay and having him correspond with the woman friend whom he has left behind. She writes from time to time about democracy in America and particularly the practical application of democracy in committees, boards of trustees, group organization, and local government. He, on the other hand, writes of democracy in England and France, of Hitler and the Nazis, and of Russia. Then he plunges into the contradictions and implications of the new political and economic revolution in China and Japan and its inevitable extension in other parts of the East. He then comes back to the newer aspects of the African question, disfranchisement and land monopoly in South and East Africa, the conquest of Ethiopia, and industry and raw materials in West Africa, and the influence of all this on incipient war in Europe.

What would you think of a book like this and would your firm see a chance to handle it? I could have it ready by April 15.

Very sincerely yours,
W. E. B. Du Bois

Sometime in February 1937, a student at Oberlin College put a series of questions to Du Bois that evoked answers of consequence.

Oberlin, Ohio [undated]
My dear Mr. Du Bois,

I am writing a thesis for the Political Science Dept. here on the Significance of the change in the Negro vote in 1936. My professor here thinks the change is indicative of reform for both the major political parties. Do you think the Negro is sincerely interested in the Democratic cause—or do you think the Negro has learned race solidarity and will change his political affiliation to better the group as a whole? Do you think the Southern Negro can afford to vote for the party that has been traditionally anti-Negro? Do you think there is possibility of disfranchisement?

I shall be obliged for any and all you will say on the matter. I want this paper to be notable. You might remember my parents, Dr. and Mrs. J. E. Brown of Keystone, W. Va.[1] You met them when you were guest of Pres. [R. M.] Simms of Bluefield [Institute].

Anna Vivian Brown

Atlanta, Ga., February 23, 1937
My dear Miss Brown:

Answering your letter without date, I beg to say that the Negro is interested in the Democratic Party only so far as the Democratic Party is interested in him. During the New Deal he has received much consideration at the hands of the Democrats, and in turn voted for them largely in the elections. The attitude of the democratic South still inhibits him from wholesale espousal of the Democratic Party. More than that there is

1. Dr. Joseph Edward Brown, a physician who practiced for many years in Keystone, West Virginia, was active in the NAACP in that state.

no real division between Democrats and Republicans so far as national objects are concerned. The rotten borough system in the South prevents any real third party movement. The result is that in local affairs, particularly, the Negro goes with the party which distributes the largest amount of employment, appointments, and other consideration. In New York the Democrats[1] are overwhelmingly democratic for this reason and in Chicago overwhelmingly Republican. You know, I presume, such studies as Negroes in Politics,[2] a recent book by Harold F. Gosnell published by the University of Chicago Press in 1935.

Very sincerely yours,
W. E. B. Du Bois

One of the best-known of the Southern white liberal scholars who came to the fore in the New Deal period was Arthur F. Raper (b. 1899). Two of Raper's books that made a considerable impact in this era were The Tragedy of Lynching *(1933) and* Preface to Peasantry: A Tale of Two Black Belt Counties *(1935)—this latter an examination of the farm economy in Greene and Macon counties, Georgia—both published by the University of North Carolina Press.*

When Raper was a professor at Agnes Scott College in Decatur, Georgia, Du Bois wrote to him. The Du Bois papers do not have a reply from Raper, but Du Bois's brief note and particularly the enclosure sent with it are noteworthy.

Atlanta, Ga., March 1, 1937

My dear Dr. Raper:

The colored organizations of Georgia are trying to get the proposed bill for Federal Aid to Education amended as you will see by the enclosed draft of a letter. Can you furnish me data of any sort that would support our contention?

Very sincerely yours,
W. E. B. Du Bois

[Enclosure]

To the Members of the Senate Committee on Education

Gentlemen:

The undersigned organizations representing the colored people of Georgia, deeply regret that they did not know of the hearings which were held on the Harrison-Black-Fletcher Bill for Federal Aid to Popular Education.

They wish to say that they are deeply interested in this matter and have long believed that there is nothing that the Federal Government could do of so great importance as to attack the dangerous illiteracy in this country, and particularly in the South. They sincerely hope that some action to this end will be taken by the present Congress.

1. The word "Democrats" appears in the original; obviously Du Bois meant Negroes.
2. The precise title is *Negro Politicians: The Rise of Negro Politics in Chicago.*

They believe that Federal monies in aid of popular education should be distributed among the states in accordance with illiteracy; but since in many states there are separate systems of schools for black and white they ask that such states be required to divide Federal money between these systems according to the school population in each system. This would not interfere with the reasonable power of the states to administer the monies as they see fit, but it would insure that Federal funds be expended for attacking illiteracy where it is worst. More and more in the future the Federal Government must come to the rescue of local governments in certain matters of national concern; and while as much latitude as possible should be given to the judgment and initiative of local administration, yet one thing the nation must certainly insist upon and that is, that the main object of Federal help be attained and not hindered or obstructed. Less than this the government could not ask.

We are deeply appreciative of the fact that money spent on Negro schools in Georgia has considerably increased in the last quarter century; but at the same time we are apprehensive when we realize that the disparity between the amounts spent on Negro and white schools is steadily growing rather than decreasing. It should be impossible in the future to have recur that which happened in 1933 and 1934 when the Government granted to the state of Georgia $4,961,881 for aid in education; of this sum $4,338,148 or 87.3% went to the white schools in spite of the fact that colored children formed 39.1% of the school population.

For these reasons we ask your honorable committee to amend the bill under consideration, before it is reported to the Senate, so as to provide that in the case of states having separate and compulsory school systems for different classes of their citizens, the monies appropriated must be allocated to the separate systems according to the school population in each. We are unable to see how any person who honestly wishes to be rid of illiteracy could object to this proviso.

If it is possible, we would be very glad to send representatives to appear before your committee in order to state our case more in detail.[1]

                                        Very respectfully yours,

March 1, 1937

Robert Ezra Park (1864–1944) was one of the most eminent sociologists of his time; from 1914 through 1933 he was on the faculty of the University of Chicago, and thereafter he served as a visiting professor at Fisk University. He was a president of the American Sociological Society (1925–26) and in 1933 studied problems of race relations while visiting India, Brazil, and West Africa. He was prominently associated with the efforts to launch an Encyclopedia of the Negro; it

---

1. Du Bois testified on 2 April 1937 before the Committee on Education of the House of Representatives in Washington; he appeared as Chairman of Education, Georgia Association of Negro Colleges and High Schools. His testimony led to a sharp exchange with Representative Graham A. Barden of North Carolina, which made headlines in the Black press. For details see Aptheker, *Annotated Bibliography*, p. 503.

was in this connection that Park visited Du Bois at Atlanta early in 1937. When Park returned to Fisk in Nashville, Du Bois wrote to him there.

Atlanta, Ga., March 3, 1937

My dear Dr. Park:

It was very pleasant indeed to have you and Mrs. Park here. We enjoyed your visit. I hope you had a pleasant return trip.

I am sending herewith a hundred sheets and envelopes of the Encyclopaedia letter-heads; also I am sending some data about the Encyclopaedia Africana. You will find Mr. Woodson's version of his Encyclopaedia Africana on page 15 of the January, 1937, issue of the "Journal of Negro History." You will note that he refers to action on the Encyclopaedia Africana in 1921. If you will consult, however, the reports in 1921 (*Journal of Negro History*, 1921, Volume VI, pp. 126–130), you will find there is no notice or mention of any such Encyclopaedia in the proceedings of the annual meeting of 1920, nor is there any notice in the meeting of 1921 reported in Volume VII, 1922, pp. 121–126. I believe both of these meetings took place during the time you were president of the Association.

My project never went far enough to give me any claim to exclusive occupation of the field. It was merely one of my large ideas which never got down to earth or finance. It is barely possible that I should have pushed it further had it not been for the World War; but as a matter of fact I didn't. I never heard of Mr. Woodson's project until after the Phelps-Stokes Encyclopaedia movement was started. When he mentioned it I immediately tried to find out when the idea was first made public, but [he] got angry and refused to give any specific answer. In the case of my Encyclopaedia Africana, I conceived the idea in 1909, and in 1911 while attending the Races Congress in London I talked about it with Sir Harry Johnston, Dr. W. M. Flinders-Petrie, and others. Previous to that I had correspondence with Professor William James, President [Charles W.] Eliot, and all of the Negroes whose names appear on the letter-head.

I trust you will find time to carry out the correspondence with the men of science according to your kind proposal while here. Meantime I think that Mr. [Rayford W.] Logan and I will concentrate on getting a pretty clear idea of the possible size of the projected Encyclopaedia. Perhaps we can actually make some sort of dummy. I will let you know just what we plan to do in this line as soon as we get our plans in hand. Also I shall send out a questionnaire to a selected number of perhaps fifty or one hundred persons asking them "if you consulted an Encyclopaedia of the Negro, what information would you specifically seek?"

I hope from time to time you will write me freely of any thoughts or criticisms that occur to you.

Please give my best regards to Mrs. Park, and express my pleasure at the opportunity of becoming better acquainted with her.

Very sincerely yours,

W. E. B. Du Bois

An inquiry from a student in Texas, written on a postcard and postmarked 2 March 1937, asked Du Bois's opinion about a then burning issue, one with lasting significance; characteristically, Du Bois answered promptly and plainly.

Prairie View State College, Prairie View,
Texas [undated]

Dear Sir:

I am making a study of the Supreme Court [and] the present plan of [the] President for the reorganization of the court. I want to get the opinion of prominent Negroes on this subject. I would like very much to get your opinion. I will appreciate it very much if you will let me know at once just what you think of the President and the Supreme Court.

Yours respectfully,
Jesse H. Sterling

Atlanta, Ga., March 10, 1937

Mr. Jesse H. Sterling
My dear Sir:

I believe very strongly that the power of the Supreme Court should be curtailed. I should prefer a constitutional amendment but that would take too long for present pressing necessities. Meantime and while such an amendment is being considered, I think President Roosevelt's plan[1] the best practical effort.

Very sincerely yours,
W. E. B. Du Bois

Barry Hyams, born in Brooklyn in 1911, graduated from Brooklyn College in 1934 and moved at once into the life of the theater, serving as editor of the National Play Bureau from 1935 to 1937, and as press representative and production associate for Sol Hurok. Thereafter he served as associate producer and/or press representative for such plays as "The Emperor's Clothes," "Bus Stop," and "Touch of the Poet." More recently, he has written plays for television and drama criticism for leading publications.

Early in 1937 there was a significant exchange between the very young Hyams and Du Bois.

---

1. This was Roosevelt's so-called "court-packing plan." The president sent his proposal to Congress on 5 February 1937; it provided that whenever a federal judge who had served at least ten years did not resign or retire when he was six months past his seventieth birthday, the president might appoint a new judge—though in the case of the Supreme Court, no more than six new justices might be so appointed. The impulse for this suggestion was the Supreme Court's decisions declaring the National Recovery Act and the Agricultural Adjustment Administration unconstitutional and a New York State minimum wage law invalid. It was feared the Court would rule against the Wagner Labor Act. Roosevelt's plan was defeated, but beginning in 1938 the Court began reversing former conservative decisions and rendering pro-New Deal findings. In May 1938 Justice Van Devanter resigned and Hugo Black replaced him.

Brooklyn, N. Y., March 12, 1937

W. E. Burghardt Du Bois
Dear Sir:

I am engaged in research preparatory to writing a play about Nat Turner. Through bibliographies and through questions put to friends acquainted with the history of the Negro your name was impressed upon my mind. Your work in this field and your knowledge of the Negro, his life and struggle against injustice, as well as your records and information concerning Nat Turner, about whom so little has been written, all these engender in me a respectful solicitation of your aid and advice.

Nat Turner to me always represented the heroic surge toward liberty of a people whose will to live centuries of enslavement could not destroy. He was and is the symbol of revolt which springs from the heart and soul of man, which cries out against inhumanness and seeks to destroy it. His failure was Promethean. History was against him. Lack of class-consciousness both on his part and the part of the White prevented him from ascertaining the only method to fruition: the union of Black and White toward a common end.

To write this play I shall need material and information concerning the day of Nat Turner and the background and development of the Negro in America. I hope for your kindness and trust that you will suffer no inconvenience. I am looking forward to as early a reply from you as your time will permit.

Very truly yours,
Barry Hyams

Atlanta, Ga., March 17, 1937

Mr. Barry Hyaml[1]
My dear Sir:

The life of Nat Turner should make an interesting basis for a play, but authentic material concerning him is unfortunately rare. The best available account is in [Benjamin] Brawley's *Social History of the American Negro*, New York, Macmillan, 1921, pages 140 and following. There is a so-called history by W. S. Drewry, 1900, a very poor and prejudiced account. The only reliable source of information is the "Confessions of Nat Turner." This pamphlet is very rare and the only copy that I know of is in the Harvard University Library. Of course contemporary newspapers would throw much light on the situation at the time.

Very sincerely yours,
W. E. B. Du Bois

During the years of Lester A. Walton's service as United States minister to Liberia, he maintained a regular correspondence with Du Bois. Illustrative is this exchange.

1. Hyams's signature lends itself to this mistaken reading.

Monrovia, Liberia, April 12, 1937

Dear Dr. Du Bois:

I have been following your around-the-world tour with much interest and I am sure you enjoyed yourself as is customary on your visits to the various countries.

During the month of August, I was in Paris with my family en route to the United States. I was also in the French Metropolis for nine days on my return to Monrovia. Naturally, I thought of you. I was sorry that we did not meet abroad.

I am happy to state that conditions continue to improve in Liberia and indications point to a successful termination of President Barclay's three year plan. The American Government is giving President Barclay 100 percent moral support; in fact, I think I can state without fear of contradiction that at no time in history have relations between the two countries been so friendly and our Government so cooperative.

In 1936, there was an increase of 30 percent in revenues over 1935 and the budget for 1937 is the largest in history except 1928.

Since late in December, President Barclay has made two trips into the interior. He is now on his second tour. He is giving much time and consideration to improving hinterland administration. He regards as fundamental the construction of roads into areas which should be tapped, thereby improving the economic status of the natives and increasing the internal revenue of the Government.

The Department of State is giving me whole-souled cooperation. Before long the erection of the new $100,000 Legation will be started. When completed, I shall invite you to "come up and see me sometime."

I hope you are enjoying good health and that you are finding your work in Atlanta pleasant. I look forward to seeing you on my next visit to the United States, and if I am not mistaken I owe you lunch at Lüchow's. I presume your appetite is as hearty as ever.

With kindest regards and best wishes,

Cordially yours,
Lester A. Walton

Atlanta, Ga., May 26, 1937

Personal

My dear Walton:

I have your kind letters of April 12 and 20, and was glad to hear from you. I had a very delightful trip around the world and was sorry indeed that I could not include Liberia. I am glad to know things seem to be going better, but I am still deeply suspicious of the Firestone monopoly. They did all they could to hurt Liberia in Europe, and of course their chief object is to make money. Years ago after I had been with the Firestone representative viewing the rubber forests I wrote Firestone urging him to employ American Negroes in Liberia. I received no answer.[1] Recently, how-

1. That letter was dated 26 October 1925; it is published in volume one of this work (pp. 320–23). As he states, Firestone did not reply, but a W. D. Hines did, in Firestone's name (p. 323).

ever, I have heard that one such clerk or official has been employed. Is that true? I would like to know the facts.

I am glad you are going to have a fine modern dwelling. You will need it in that climate. I was glad to have the clipping which you sent.

My best regards to you and to President Barclay and other officials whom I know.

Very sincerely yours,

W. E. B. Du Bois

From the 1930s until his death in 1963 one of Du Bois's central interests was the effort to bring into existence an Encyclopedia of the Negro—or an Encyclopedia Africana, as the projected work was called in the late 1950s and early 1960s. Some of the very considerable correspondence that developed concerning the project, particularly with Anson Phelps Stokes, has been presented earlier.

Efforts were made, as has been seen, to interest the federal government in supplying some funds through its Writers' Project, and similar efforts were directed toward such foundations as the Carnegie, the Rockefeller, and the Rosenwald; but little success was achieved. Work nevertheless went forward and a report of its progress by mid-1937 appears in a letter from Du Bois to Stokes.

Atlanta, Ga., May 19, 1937

My dear Dr. Stokes:

We have finished the following work on the Encyclopaedia: the preparation of a manuscript of about one hundred and twenty-five pages giving a list of possible subjects for an Encyclopaedia of the Negro with a short bibliographical note under each subject. These subjects have been carefully revised from my original list of last year in light of criticism sent in from various scholars, and have been arranged alphabetically.

In addition to that we have made a careful estimate of the space these articles would occupy by the following method: three of the longest articles on Africa, the Negro Race, and the African Slave Trade; five long articles on the Negro in the United States, Negro in the West Indies, Negro in South America, Race and Miscegenation. These articles will occupy 350 pages and 280,000 words. Then we have allowed space for 250 chief articles occupying a thousand pages with 800,000 words. We have next allowed for 700 biographies covering the world and including Negroes, persons of Negro descent, and white persons connected with their history. This will occupy 560,000 words. In addition to this we have allowed for 550 pages and 440,000 words for minor articles and an index of 200 pages or 160,000 words. This makes a total of 2,800 pages and 2,240,000 words. This calculation has been based on the *Encyclopaedia of the Social Sciences* and we have allowed 400 words to a column.

The next step according to my original plan would be actually to space these articles on dummy volumes, but the sheer physical labor involved in this is too much for us to finish this spring although we might do it this summer. It promises, however, this difficulty: the spacing would involve a judgment as to the length of each single article. None of us would be competent to make a final judgment now in the case, even if it were desirable, and it is not as it would have to be gone over entirely again by the editorial board.

I shall, therefore, bring with me to New York to the meeting June tenth the material that I have described.

This study has led both me and Dr. [Rayford W.] Logan to a consideration of the matter of biographies. The biographies in an encyclopaedia are usually done according to a single pattern and worked out by the editorial staff. I am wondering, if in addition to the conference which I proposed for next year, I might not undertake next year the matter of such definitive collection of biographies so that the editorial board would have all the facts beforehand and could more easily make choices. This matter of biographies is going to be a point very difficult to decide and the longer it is worked upon beforehand the more satisfactory the final decision will be.

I hope this will find you in good health as it leaves me.

Very sincerely yours,
W. E. B. Du Bois

With some regularity, Du Bois received from schoolteachers—especially Black teachers—the kind of letter that follows here.

Louisville, Ky., October 4, 1937
Dear Dr. Du Bois:

The Fifth B Grade of the Virginia Ave. School Lousiville Kentucky is making a special study of your life during the first two weeks in October. The study will end with a program in Chapel Thursday morning, Oct. 14, 1937.

I am asking you to please send a message of encouragement to the girls and boys of the Virginia Ave. School, if time will permit you to do so.

I would like to have the message read in Chapel on that morning.

Prof. C. A. Liggin is the principal of the school.

Thank you.

(Miss) M. L. Buckner
Teacher—5B.

Atlanta, Ga., October 7, 1937
To the Students of the
Fifth Grade of
The Virginia Avenue School
Lousiville, Kentucky

I am glad to send greetings to the Fifth B Grade of the Virginia Avenue School. I thank the pupils for their interest in what I have tried to do and hope that my life has had some lessons for them.

Very sincerely yours,
W. E. B. Du Bois

A significant exchange occurred by wire between Dr. Harry F. Ward and Du Bois late in 1937, reflecting the fact that Du Bois made a great distinction between opposition to Hitler and Mussolini and opposition to Japan in its expansionistic course in Asia. Of course, he detested fascism and loathed war and aggression, but in connection with British and United States opposition to Japan's course in Asia in the 1930s he discerned hypocrisy so vast as to deter him from joining in any denunciation of the Asian country.

Harry F. Ward (1873–1966) was in the tradition of such Social Christians as Walter Rauschenbusch. Born in England, he came as a youngster to the United States, was educated at Northwestern and Harvard Universities, became a Methodist minister and was a chief founder, in 1907, of the Methodist Federation Social Service. He was a professor at the theological school of Boston University from 1913 to 1918 and then began his illustrious career as a teacher at Union Theological Seminary (1918–44, thereafter emeritus). He headed the American Civil Liberties Union (1920–40), and chaired the American League against War and Fascism (1934–1940). His books, spanning the years from before World War I to the close of World War II, had a very wide influence. In his position as chairman of the American League Against War and Fascism he wired Du Bois.

New York NY Oct 7 1937

W E B Du Bois

Eager for your reply to our invitation to endorse peoples congress for democracy and peace at Pittsburgh November twenty six twenty eight Stop Would like to add your name to second printing of call Stop Please reply collect via postaltelegraph

Harry F Ward   American League Against
War And Fascism

Atlanta Ga. October 7 1937

Mr Harry F Ward

Am bitterly opposed to present effort of American and English capital to drive this nation into war against Japan Stop Such miserable war would be based on color prejudice and would put forward as false friends of China a nation which fought the opium war and is today the most ruthless exploiter of Chinese labor and a nation that passed and maintains the Chinese Exclusion Act.

W E B Du Bois

Harrison J. Pinkett (1881–1960), born in Virginia, was educated at Howard University and received a law degree from Columbia University. He practiced law in Omaha, Nebraska, for

fifty-three years and served the NAACP *in several civil rights cases. Something of his life and work is conveyed in a long letter he sent Du Bois.*

Omaha, Nebraska, October 8, 1937

My dear Dr. Du Bois:

Many thanks for your articles in the *Pittsburgh Courier* on Co-Operatives.[1] For many years I have been interested in the subject and at one time made an intensive and extensive study of it. At the time I made the study I was associated in the law practice here with a prominent white attorney who devoted all his time to the formation of corporations which dealt in foods. Much of the research work for the basis of the companies he formed I did. It was during that study that I examined the structures of such companies as Standard Oil, International Harvester Company, The Great Atlantic and Pacific Tea Company and the Shell Oil Company. I made a brief of these studies at the time. These studies led me into an examination of the Co-Operatives. I soon found that I was living in the section of the United States where there had already been much progress made along that line.

As the years have passed I have continued my interest in them and my study of them. About eighteen years ago I formed a corporation for a group of Negro citizens which embodies the principles of the Co-Operatives. And when I issued the prospectus, great excitement prevailed among the old line merchants. The company remained in business for about two years and failed, largely because of inefficient management. One interesting thing about it was that Bradstreet and Dun examined the plan and recommended a monthly credit up to $5,000.00. And this before any business had begun.

I am writing you of this experience, because I know that the Co-Operative plan for production and consumption must be adopted by all the people, if we are to survive. The Y.W.C.A. is making a study of this subject here. I know of this, because I have given a number of young women material on the subject.

You must bear in mind that the greatest difficulty is to be found in the lack of experienced persons among Negroes in this field. Indeed, I know of no attorney in the country of our group who has had anything like as much as my experience in the theoretical and practical phases of the subject. May I suggest that you ascertain the whereabouts of persons who are informed in this field. They will all be needed.

Upton Sinclair made the only sane proposal thus far made respecting the spending of the Government WPA funds. He suggested several years ago that the U. S. Government finance the set-up of Producers Co-Operatives on a scale large enough to absorb all the unemployed, and, of course, maintain the undertaking through a period. At the end of a certain period, Sinclair claimed, the people would be self-sustaining. To to sure, the money advanced by the government would not be repaid, but we would be rid of the particular unemployment problem. Otherwise, Sinclair claimed, we will

---

1. Du Bois's columns in the *Pittsburgh Courier* from 12 June through 25 September 1937 were devoted, in large part, to explaining the nature and history of co-operatives.

spend the money and still have the unemployed.[2] Sinclair was right and the *exploiters* were wrong.

I am social minded, without being a Socialist in the sense that Carl Marx was one.

I think it a very fine thing that you are writing a column for the *Pittsburgh Courier*. Your contribution has been very great in this respect, greater than that of any American writer. Emerson, of course, gave us some standing among men of letters in the older states, but your writing has taught a whole nation the lesson of intellectual equality among men. And it is a very fine thing to see you writing now with the same clarity and incisiveness that characterized your earlier style, with this addition—a maturer thought.

During the passing years I have been able to read books outside my *art*. I have always been active in community life, as well as at the bar. And I make the boast among the attorneys of the state that I have aided more individuals with their intellectual development than any member of the Nebraska Bar. In other words, I have used my acquirements for service and not for the arrogation of wealth to myself. I am much amused now-a-days when I hear public men talking about becoming "*social minded*." All educated men and women are "Social Minded." I held these views when I was yet a youth, thirty-four years ago, when I first met you. I was then in my twentieth year. You had but recently published your Immortal Book, *Souls of Black Folk*. And I was trying to write for weekly papers. I have remained young and open-minded and forward looking, and at fifty-four years of age I am just beginning to learn many things. I can appreciate your attitude and outlook.

I am fearful that Roosevelt like Wilson will seek release from his fiscal blunders through *war*. His Chicago speech after his return from the Pacific Coast where he had imbibed anti-Japanese sentiments, was highly inflammable.[3] He will find it so when the German and Italian blocs go into political action against him later on.

I have written a short sketch of the Omaha Negro which I am having printed.[4] I have done it as a sort of racial service to encourage them a little in the midst of myriad discouragements. I will send you a copy of it when it is off the press. I do not dignify it by calling it a book, but it will serve the purpose for which I wrote it.

2. Upton Sinclair ran for governor of California in 1934 on a program based upon his End Poverty In California (EPIC) plan—and very nearly won. Basic to it was the idea of co-operatives. See his *The Way Out: What Lies Ahead for America* (New York: Farrar and Rinehart, 1933) and *We, The People of America and How We Ended Poverty: A True Story of the Future* (Pasadena, Calif.: National EPIC League, 1935).

3. President Roosevelt's Chicago speech was delivered 5 October 1937. It is sometimes referred to as his "quarantine" speech, for he advocated such a course for those nations—unnamed in his address but clearly Japan, Germany, and Italy—who were "creating a state of international anarchy and instability from which there is no escape through mere isolation or neutrality."

4. Pinkett did not succeed in getting his manuscript printed. In typescript, under the title "An Historical Sketch of the Omaha Negro," it is now in the library of the Nebraska State Historical Society in Lincoln. I am indebted to Mrs. Alice E. Station of the Omaha Public Library for assistance in tracking down this information. Pinkett's essay was used extensively in the book *Negroes of Nebraska*, Writers' Project, WPA, Omaha Urban League Community Center, 1940.

The Negro in this section of the country is growing toward freedom through education and otherwise. Economically, the Negro here is much better off than in other communities of similar size. I give the reasons in the little booklet I have written and will not give them here.

I was saddened by your leaving the N.A.A.C.P. I fear it is doomed to failure, because it confines its fight within too narrow limits as you pointed out at the time. It, like the Negro church, will perish, unless it adopts a program which is comprehensive enough to include not only the life that is and is to be, but the means of life.

When I was writing for Negro papers thirty-five years ago, at the peak, I sent a syndicated letter to eight papers each week. I was the foremost columnist of that era. What writing! The things I lacked in literary style I made up for in my flaming vigor. My writing here has been largely newspaper writing for daily papers and political propaganda.

Keep up your good work of writing. I do not always agree with your conclusions, but I appreciate the value of the service you have rendered and are rendering, even now.

With kindest personal regards, I am

Sincerely,
H. J. Pinkett

Atlanta, Ga., October 15, 1937

My dear Mr. Pinkett:

I appreciate very much your kind letter of October 8, and I am using a part of it without quoting your name in my *Courier* letter. You, of course, put your finger upon our real difficulty and that is the right kind of leadership for co-operative enterprise. So far as that is concerned our lack of leadership is felt in many other directions. It isn't a lack of ability but the deterioration in ideals which has gone on in America and the assumption that every man can work for himself and achieve the good of all which simply and unfortunately is not true.

Very sincerely yours,
W. E. B. Du Bois

Another meaty exchange between Anson Phelps Stokes and Du Bois concerning the Encyclopedia of the Negro occurred late in October 1937. Stokes was then in Washington participating in federal efforts to combat unemployment.

Washington, D.C., October 27, 1937

Dear Dr. Du Bois:

This is a note to report various things to you: (1) A letter was received from Dr. Alvin Johnson yesterday. It read as follows:

October 25, 1937

Dear Mr. Stokes:

I have your letter of October 20th and the copy of the estimated expenses of the Encyclopaedia of the Negro. This appears to me entirely adequate and satisfactory.

Sincerely,

Alvin Johnson

This ought to carry great weight with Dr. Keppel as he specially asked us to get Dr. Alvin Johnson's advice. It means that we will have to increase our total budget from $225,000 to $260,000.

(2) At the luncheon at the Town Hall Club yesterday to the group of visiting African educators Mr. Jackson Davis came up to me and spoke of his interview with you in Atlanta. He told me frankly that he was very favorably impressed with your objective attitude towards the whole proposal and with the significance of the material you had collected and of the letters of endorsement from the scholars of the world. Indeed, the interview created such a favorable impression that he informed me he had arranged with Mr. [David H.] Stevens, who is Director of Humanities with the General Education Board and the Rockefeller Foundation, to have me see him about the possibility of our renewing our application. Of course he did not commit the Boards in any way, but his attitude is distinctly favorable to our project, although he says that most of the money that they have set apart for Negro work in the next few years is going into higher education. I think we can show, however, that nothing will advance the cause of Negro higher education more than our project, both for the authoritative information it will provide, and for the opportunity it will give young Negro scholars.

(3) I had a meeting with Mr. Raymond Fosdick later in the day about an entirely different matter. He is, as you know, both the new President of the Rockefeller Foundation and of the General Education Board, so I took the opportunity of telling him a word about developments. He seemed interested.

(4) Would you be good enough to let me know what times between now and Christmas you can be in the east, for I want to arrange for an interview with Mr. Stevens when you can accompany me, and it may be advisable for us to get the Executive Committee together. Among other things we must discuss the matter of an Associate Editor. It is clear that we must have a younger man than Dr. Park. You will remember Dr. Johnson's reaction on this subject. The two possibilities that have appealed most to me are that we find one of the younger men from the University of North Carolina, or that we get the Assistant Editor of the Encyclopaedia of the Social Sciences, about whom Dr. Johnson spoke to us—I think that his name was Bernhard J. Stern. Perhaps you will give this matter special consideration. I am asking Dr. [Charles T.] Loram, who has just been spending a few weeks at the University of North Carolina, where a good many of the liberal white leaders of the country were present to meet the African educators, to give me his reactions.

(5) I will have to go away again for meetings in Southern Virginia, but on returning

I will draft a letter to Mr. Keppel of which I will send you a copy. This will be for the purpose of transmitting to him our revised budget.

(6) I am not without hope that we can get the General Education Board and Rockefeller Foundation each to give a hundred thousand dollars to our project. Of course if they would each give $130,000, it would be better yet, but I doubt whether this will be possible, and I think that by hard work we could get a few Foundations or individuals who would make up the remainder.

(7) As to the possibility of the Atlanta University connection, I think that this should only be considered as a last resort for in the long run we will gain by being at the national Capital with its libraries and other collections, in accordance with our Act of Incorporation and previous decision. If we should leave here I think that New York would probably be the best place and anyway I think that there is more chance of our getting the money and carrying the thing through successfully if we retain our independence of any institution.

(8) The Phelps-Stokes Fund meets for its Fall meeting on November 17th. I will see that the $2500 appropriation is renewed. I think we have enough in the amount set aside for the Encyclopaedia of the Negro project to carry us up to the first of January, 1939, by which time we shall hope to have the project fully financed.

I can't over emphasize my appreciation of what you and Dr. Logan have done in collecting all this invaluable material. It will be of vital importance both in interesting the Foundations and in enabling the Encyclopaedia staff, when it gets together, to make a running start.[1]

Sincerely yours,
Anson Phelps Stokes

Atlanta Ga., November 1, 1937

My dear Mr. Stokes:

I have your letter of October 27. I am very glad we have Dr. Johnson's approval. I can come up at any time between November 6 and Christmas. There is no particular preference as to date except that it would be better if it could cover a week end. Kindly let me know as far in advance as possible.

With regard to the Associate Editor. I should be very glad to talk this over at length with you and the committee and to interview some people, but I hope that the

---

1. Alvin Johnson (1874–1971) was the chief editor of *The Encyclopedia of Social Sciences*. His assistant was Dr. Bernhard J. Stern (1894–1956), an instructor in sociology at Columbia University and the author of many books in the sociology of medicine and the family. In 1937 he edited, with Alain Locke, *When Peoples Meet*. Dr. Guy B. Johnson, born in Texas in 1901, received his doctorate at the University of North Carolina and from 1924 on was on the faculty of that university; in 1936–37 he was a Fellow of the Social Science Research Council. Dr. Charles T. Loram, a professor at Yale, chose not to live in his native South Africa. He was on the encyclopedia's board since its inception. Du Bois wrote admiringly of Loram in his column in the *Pittsburgh Courier*, 25 April 1936, and again, 19 October 1940, commenting upon his recent death.

decision will not be arrived at too quickly. In fact I think that perhaps it would be better to have a decision after we get enough money in sight to make a pretty definite offer. A large part of the responsibility of the Encyclopaedia would fall upon the Associate Editor and I should want to know the candidate personally pretty well. In the case of Guy Johnson of North Carolina, for instance, I should have some objection: I cannot see how a man who seriously argues that Negro folk songs originated and were developed by white people has exactly the mental balance for this work. But as I do not know Mr. Johnson personally I am not in a position to make final judgment.[1] There is another southern man for whom I have the highest respect, Arthur Raper, who is more or less in hot water at Agnes Scott because of his outspoken stand on lynching. On the other hand, I am very much impressed by Mr. Johnson's recommendation of Stern. He seems to me theoretically exactly the kind of man: well trained, impartial and a hard worker, but I have never met him.

I do not think we can afford to choose a man because he is a liberal southerner. There are several kinds of that sort of person and I have had some experience with them. Some are liberal because it pays; some are liberal in certain matters with regard to the Negro and reactionary with regard to all other matters, other questions and other people; and so many are apt to regard their liberality as calling for praise and reward when as a matter a fact it ought to be simply human. On the whole then I should like to canvas the possibilities or have the committee canvas the possibilities without seeking a decision immediately.

With regard to Atlanta University. It would of course be absolutely necessary that the work of the Encyclopaedia be carried on largely if not entirely in the North, whether the University came into the project or not. I do not think there would be any question or objection on the part of the University to such a plan.

I just have your letter from Malone this morning.[2] I think it is splendid backing for our calculations.

Very sincerely,
W. E. B. Du Bois

Lillian E. Smith (1897–1966), the novelist, was born in Florida and educated at the Peabody Conservatory in Baltimore; she taught music for three years in China and then returned to the United States and lived out her life in Georgia. Her novel Strange Fruit *(New York: Reynal and Hitchcock, 1944) was a phenomenal best-seller—reaching a sale of three million copies; its plot was the love of a Black man and a white woman in the South and the eventual lynching of*

1. Du Bois's comment on Johnson's attitude toward Negro folk songs is somewhat severe, as one may see from the book Johnson did with Howard Odum, *The Negro and His Songs* (Chapel Hill: University of North Carolina, 1925), especially pp. 150–52. In fact, Johnson was appointed joint editor with Du Bois on the encyclopedia project.

2. The reference is to Dumas Malone, chief editor of *The Dictionary of American Biography*, who had written Stokes commending the idea of the Negro encyclopedia and confirming estimates Du Bois and Stokes had made of probable costs.

the man. Other books came later—Killers of the Dream *(1947)*, Now Is the Time *(1955)*, One Hour *(1959)*, Memory of a Large Christmas *(1962)*, *and finally*, Our Faces, Our Words *(1964)*. *In 1950 she received a special citation from the National Book Award Committee. In addition to her literary work, Lillian Smith was active in the battles against racism and repression: she was, for example, a member of the national board of the American Civil Liberties Union.*

In 1936, Lillian Smith and her friend Paula Snelling started a literary quarterly, Pseudopia, *whose name was happily changed to* North Georgia Review *in 1937, reflecting its place of publication and the editors' home in Clayton, Georgia. In 1942, the name was changed again to* South Today, *and by 1943 the quarterly had five-thousand subscribers; but with the increased demands upon Lillian Smith's time after the appearance of her best-seller, the* South Today *ceased publication in 1945.*

In 1937 Du Bois subscribed to the North Georgia Review *and appended a note wishing the venture well. A result was a series of letters.*

Clayton, Ga., December 13, 1937

Dear Mr. Du Bois:

Please let me thank you for your subscription to the *North Georgia Review* and for the little notation in your letter which we enjoyed.

We should like very much for you to review John Dollard's *Caste and Class in a Southern Town* for us if you have the time and interest to give it. We know you are a very busy person and shall be grateful to you if you can be so generous with your time. *The Review* can pay only with the book itself. We personally think the book of unusual merit and hope you will care to do it. Kind wishes,

Sincerely,
Lillian Smith

Atlanta, Ga., December 17, 1937

My dear Miss Smith:

I shall be glad to review Dollard for you if you will let me do it after the holidays.

Very sincerely yours,
W. E. B. Du Bois

Clayton, Ga., December 22, 1937

Dear Mr. Du Bois:

I am writing Yale University Press today to send direct to you a copy of Dollard's *Caste and Class*. The winter issue of our *Review* goes to press about January 15th if our reviewers can get their material in by then. If not we shall have to hold it up a few days. The book is not so long and I hope you will find it interesting and fruitful reading.

Please criticize our efforts frankly whenever you feel a desire to do so. I have lately had the feeling—a kind of frustrated feeling too—that we say too much (or I do) scold and nag, are too fault finding. Not that these strictures are not deserved and obviously so, but from a more pragmatic angle are we going to succeed in doing what we set out to do? If our little paper ever grows into a journal of any influence in the South it must be read by southerners. At the present time we have more northern subscribers than southern—a significant commentary, isn't it? We have at present almost 200 paid subscribers. We send the little paper out to 1000 people. Each issue steadily brings us in new subscribers and our old ones are renewing nicely but it costs $500.00 a year just to print and distribute the four issues. We should be paying our contributors too. It seems to me a monthly magazine of the same size would stimulate more interest and sustain it better and would quite possibly increase our subscription list in greater ratio-speed than at present. Because we can publish only four times a year we are restricted by lack of physical space in our scope of interests. I think we should for instance have two or three pages for a forum of letters; a page or two for the arts, articles on folk culture movements, on crafts etc., etc., more reviews of significant European books, more fiction, and a one-page biographical sketch of a southerner who is making a real contribution to the South and more photographs, cuts, draw-ings, etc. Our policy, as I think perhaps you have already perceived, is to make no distinction in white and colored contributors (that is, no racial discrimination of any kind but some stress on racial prejudices and their evils) or artists or themes but we do believe it advisable to limit usually (there should be some exceptions) the bulk of subjects treated to those which have a direct relevancy to the South—yet always extending our line of vision to include even if obliquely, international affairs and thought. More explicitly when we review a book we should not only appraise it in relation to other southern books but extend our critical values to include comparison with the 'best' in its line wherever found: American, European, or Oriental. That is, I realize with more humility than I perhaps suggest, an ambitious plan but perhaps not too apt to fail entirely if the editors discipline their minds and emotions rigidly enough.

I have several little projects in mind for awakening more interest among the colleges and for securing more cooperation and help from our subscribers (although they have shown already a generosity beyond our dreams). If from your wide experience and your wisdom you can offer us advice we shall be deeply grateful to you.

Please come by to see us if you are ever up here or passing through. In January we plan to be in New York for a month. Just now we are spending the winter in my mother's little summer cabin near Woodland Lodge. June, July, August, September we spend up at my camp, Laurel Falls Camp. But at any time we can be easily located by telephone and shall be so glad to have you come out to our home.

Good wishes for a happy Christmas.

Sincerely yours,
Lillian E. Smith

Atlanta, Ga., January 4, 1938

My dear Miss Smith:

I have your letter of December 22, and I shall try to get a review of Dollard to you by the fifteenth.[1]

I can follow with deep understanding your desires for the *North Georgia Review*. I had the same ambitions for a periodical over the space of a quarter of a century. I saw the thing planted, struggle, grow to astonishing dimensions and then decline. The fundamental difficulty with any periodical in the United States is the surprisingly small number of intelligent people who are willing to take time to read and think. Even those who have sufficient intelligence are not willing to pay for thought. In England people pay five, ten and fifteen dollars a year for a review simply printed without adornment but with a high standard of literary skill and real penetrating thought. In the United States people simply will not do this. They demand that the magazine live principally by advertisements and therein, of course, lies death. I think perhaps that the policy of the *Survey* is the one which intellectuals will have to follow: securing a body of associates whose voluntary contributions support the magazine and then go on and do the work. I should have done this with the *Crisis* and would have succeeded but the Association with which the *Crisis* was tied up was itself making continual appeal to the charitable and it was impossible to make a separate appeal for the *Crisis* that would not confuse the issues. There are in the United States sufficient people of intelligence to support an *Atlantic Monthly* and a *North Georgia Review* but it is a hard thing to find them and to support your enterprise while you are searching them out. I should avoid expanding the physical size of the magazine as long as possible for two reasons: the increased cost and the fact that people are appalled by a large magazine with its various appeals. We were most successful with the *Crisis* when a person could sit down and read it through at a sitting. I think it better to omit a good many things, select the cream and put that before the Lord's anointed rather than to cast any large variety of pearls before swine.

I hope that if you are in Atlanta you will come out to the University.

Very sincerely yours,

W. E. B. Du Bois

1. Du Bois's review of John Dollard, *Caste and Class in a Southern Town* (New Haven: Yale University Press, 1937) appeared in *North Georgia Review* 2 (Winter 1937–38): 9–10. It may be added that Du Bois commented very favorably upon *Strange Fruit* in his column in the New York *Amsterdam News*, 10 June 1944.

1938

Karl R. Wallace (1905–73) was educated at Cornell University and taught English and public speaking at several universities, including Iowa State, Cornell, Washington, Virginia, Illinois, and the University of Massachusetts; from 1945 to 1947 he edited the Quarterly Journal of Speech. *At the time he wrote to Du Bois he was an associate professor of public speaking and chairman of the School of Speech at the University of Virginia.*

Charlottesville, Va., January 8, 1938

My dear Mr. Du Bois:

For the past three years I have been making a study of Booker T. Washington as a speaker. The study, now nearing its final form, was undertaken at the invitation of the Committee on Research in American Oratory, sponsored by the National Association of the Teachers of Speech. The committee hopes to publish next fall a volume called *A History of American Oratory*, and Booker T. Washington is to be one of the twenty-six major American speakers included in the volume. You can appreciate that I am particularly anxious to make an accurate appraisal of the great colored leader; hence, I wonder whether you would be willing to read the manuscript in its present form, and write me your criticisms of it.

Very sincerely yours,
Karl R. Wallace

Atlanta, Ga., January 10, 1938

My dear Mr. Wallace:

I should be very glad indeed to read the chapter on Booker Washington in your forthcoming book and make any comments that occur to me.

Very sincerely yours,
W. E. B. Du Bois

Charlottesville, Va., 12 January 1938

My dear Mr. Du Bois:

I greatly appreciate your willingness to look over the paper on Booker T. Washington. I am particularly anxious that you look for any errors in judgment, whether of interpretation or of emphasis. If, however, you have suggestions as to clearer or more interesting method of treatment, I hope you will not withhold them.

Sincerely yours,
Karl R. Wallace

Atlanta, Ga., January 21, 1938

My dear Mr. Wallace:

I read your paper on Booker T. Washington and am returning it herewith. I think it on the whole excellent and I have very little criticism to offer.[1]

Possibly if I had been drafting this paper I would have put a little emphasis on Mr. Washington's uncanny insight into personalities and his indefatigable study of men, particularly in the case of white people, both North and South. He made it his business to sense what they were thinking, what they liked and disliked. I remember his saying to me once when we were on a committee to interview Andrew Carnegie "Have you read his book?" I said, No. "You ought to. He likes it." It was doubtless painstaking observation like this that secured Tuskegee's endowment.

On the other hand, there were two classes of people that Mr. Washington deliberately wasted little time in knowing: one was the group of educated Negroes particularly in the North. He was undoubtedly prejudiced against them on account of his experience at Wayland Seminary which afterwards became Howard University.[2] He did not often address them; was very sensitive to their criticism and perhaps discounted their influence. The first time, at his request, I had an interview with him he simply listened, tactfully encouraging me to do all the talking. Two slight references in your paper reflect something of a similar attitude: on page three you speak of the Negro urban group "perhaps better educated and somewhat less moral and upright." Again on page fifty-six you intimate that Negroes expect to see flashily dressed leaders with a diamond. Neither characterization is quite true. Mr. Washington was not the first Negro orator that used the colloquial style. Frederick Douglass' approach was very homely and everyday. He soared to heights of loud eloquence and sometimes too Mr. Washington took the oratorical tone but, of course, not so often.

The second group that Mr. Washington usually ignored was the white laborer, the poor whites of the South and the trade unionists of the North. He probably was educated into the traditional Negro attitude toward the poor white and apparently he knew absolutely nothing of the labor movement. The subject was not taught at Tuskegee. He did not take the side of the employer against the employee because he did not sense any real opposition. The employer was of course right and normal. The only recognizable ambition of an employee was to become an employer or to serve humbly as a worker. It is possible that in Mr. Washington's book *The Man Farthest Down* there is some reference to the white labor class but if so it was probably primarily the thought of Dr. [Robert E.] Park. Certainly it never came out in Mr. Washington's speeches.

1. Wallace's essay, "Booker T. Washington," will be found in *A History and Criticism of American Public Address*, ed. William N. Brigance (New York: McGraw-Hill, 1943), 3:407–33.

2. Precisely what Washington's "experience at Wayland Seminary" was remains in doubt—see Louis R. Harlan, *Booker T. Washington* (New York: Oxford University Press, 1972), 1:96–99. Du Bois was mistaken in writing that Wayland became Howard University; it merged with Richmond Institute in 1899 to form Virginia Union University.

Perhaps, these thoughts will be of some interest.

Very sincerely yours,

W. E. B. Du Bois

Charlottesville, Va., March 1, 1938

My dear Dr. Du Bois:

I want to thank you for your kindness in reading my paper on Booker T. Washington as a speaker. I was pleased to have you emphasize that Washington, for the most part, addressed his remarks to influential and substantial Southerners and concerned himself but little with the poor white. I had had the same impression, but in view of some of the early speeches in the North, in which Washington pled the case of the poor white as well as of the Negro, I hesitated to make much of the point.

I appreciate knowing of the incident in which Washington advised you to read a book that Carnegie liked. It is a splendid bit of evidence that Washington ever had his attention on the interest and attitudes of his audience.

Very sincerely yours,

Karl R. Wallace

As already noted, Du Bois's correspondence with Lady Kathleen Harvey Simon went back to early 1930 and was induced by her response to his review of her book on Slavery *(1929). Her reference to her husband is to Sir John A. Simon, at the time Britain's chancellor of the exchequer.*

London, England, February 28, 1938

Dear Mr. Du Bois:

I was very glad indeed to get your letter. I knew you had severed your connection with *The Crisis* a long time ago and were working at a University in the South but I did not know your exact address so I wrote to Walter White. I am now wondering who gave you my address as Old Queen St. for, though it is the official head quarters of the Liberal Nationals, I do not live there. However I got your letter of course. We are expecting to move into Downing Street soon—the two residences of the Prime Minister and Chancellor of the Exchequer.

I wish so much I could take a trip to the States for I would welcome another talk with you and, at the moment, I with others, am trying to see justice done to the natives of the Protectorates in South Africa and your views and help would be most valuable. I am one of the trustees of Aggrey House—a club in London for African students and I sometimes go and address them and advise them. It is a really good home for the poor lads away from home. I do not know if you saw any account of my husband's and my action in Scotland because of the treatment meted out to Bishop Heard and his great-niece Miss Caldwell.[1] My anger was roused to white heat at the

1. In August 1937 the second World Conference on Faith and Order met in Edinburgh, Scotland; present were some four hundred delegates from almost every Christian denomination

refusal of a hotel to accommodate them because of their color. We invited them out and showed them publicly with us and I learned that the poor old man was comforted by our action. Curiously enough several people in Edinburgh whom I did not know, came and thanked me for my action which "took the slur from our city." The poor old Bishop died when he got home. If you did not see anything about it I have cuttings I could send you.

Did I ever tell you of a conversation I had with the wife of an American Judge who was visiting here? I was driving to a hospital to speak for them and we were talking of my Anti-Slavery Crusade. "But Lady Simon, you don't know what a problem we have in our coloured population." I replied quickly and indignantly: "Yes, and you deserve every bit of your problem. They never asked to come to your country from their home. You brought them there by force and now you blame them for being there—it is *most* unjust." She turned to me and said with wonder in her eyes "My Lands! I never thought of it like that." "Well," I replied bitterly, "you had better, and all your people had better start thinking it out in fairness to the poor people you speak of as a 'problem.' "

Are the Scottsboro boys out yet? I sent my contribution towards their defence. My husband's legal mind is appalled at the case. Have you read "The Story of the American Negro" by Ina Corinne Brown? I have just got it. I have read "I am Black" recently and think it very good. But of all the books which impressed me in my life on this burning subject was your "Dark Water."[2] It is the most beautiful and pathetic piece of literature. Let me know when your book comes out. You have a wonderful talent for beautiful writing.

I have been to Atlanta when in my early years I was in Athens, Georgia and later in Tennessee—Knoxville, the latter place being where I saw what burned into my childhood's mind—injustice to Amanda—when I was told not to speak to her as she was descended from slaves. I went right out and took her hand in mine for, child as I was, the thing struck me as cruel and wrong. The white man could do as he liked but the coloured man must be lynched for the same sin. I belong to some Anti-Lynching Society in America but I don't think it means much to have an English-woman, or rather an Irishwoman, on it. You had some ideal which you would not give up so left the *Crisis* I know. I then stopped taking it.

---

except the Roman Catholic. Among the delegates was Bishop William Heard of the African Methodist Episcopal Church; he was the eldest delegate present, being in his eighty-seventh year, and was accompanied by his niece. Both were unable to obtain accommodations at any of the larger hotels in the city, though they finally managed to rent a room at a small establishment. The archbishop of York invited them to stay with him but Bishop Heard said he was comfortable. Sir John and Lady Simon were vacationing in Edinburgh at the time, protested the insult, and invited the bishop and his niece to dine with them. Brief accounts appeared in the *New York Times*, 8 August 1937 (p. 29) and 9 August 1937 (p. 34).

2. The books referred to are: Ina C. Brown, *The Story of the American Negro* (New York: Friendship Press; London: Student Christian Movement Press, 1936); J. Grenfell Williams and H. J. May, *I Am Black* (London: Cassell and Co. 1936); and Du Bois's *Darkwater: Voices from within the Veil* (New York: Harcourt, Brace and Co., 1921 [© 1920]).

I have been very near death in the last year but I am beginning my work again. My husband has a very stiff time as you can imagine but he works for his country very earnestly.

Yours very sincerely,
Kathleen Simon

Written from bed!!

Atlanta, Ga., May 2, 1938

My dear Lady Simon,

I have your letter of February 28. Five days before I received it I celebrated my 70th birthday. I am sending you herewith a copy of my address on that occasion.[1]

I am revising my little book *The Negro* in the Home University Library and making it really a new book which I think I shall call *Black Folk Past and Present*.[2] I have been reading most of the recent literature on Africa and especially noted Perham and Curtis on the Protectorates of South Africa and books by Miss Hunter, Miss Mair, Orde-Browne, Merle Davis and others.[3] I have been trying to promote an Encyclopaedia of the Negro and we have some assurance of getting funds. I have been in correspondence with [Bronislaw] Malinowski, [Harold J.] Laski and others in England. I was in England a few weeks during the summer of 1936 on my way to Germany and thence around the world by way of China, Japan and Hawaii. I believe you were not in town at the time.

I trust this will find you in renewed health. I note the burden which your husband is bearing.

Very sincerely yours,
W. E. B. Du Bois

1. Du Bois's birthday was 23 February; hence he meant to write of her letter, "five days before you wrote it" rather than "five days before I received it." The copy of the address was entitled, *A Pageant in Seven Decades: 1868–1938;* privately printed at Atlanta in 1938, it came to forty-four pages. The occasion was a university convocation held 23 February 1938 to mark Du Bois's birthday; the address was autobiographical in form but basically historical in content.

2. Du Bois's *Negro* was published in 1915; the "new book" he refers to was *Black Folk Then and Now: An Essay in the History and Sociology of the Negro Race* (New York: Henry Holt and Co., 1939).

3. Du Bois refers, in all likelihood, to the following works: Margery Perham and Lionel Curtis, *The Protectorates of South Africa: The Question of Their Transfer to the Union* (London: Oxford University Press, 1935); Monica Hunter, *Reaction to Conquest: Effects of Contact with Europeans on the Pondo of South Africa*, with an introduction by General J. C. Smuts (London: International Institute of African Languages and Culture, by Oxford University Press, 1936); Lucy P. Mair, *An African People in the Twentieth Century* (London: G. Routledge and Sons, 1934), and the same author, through the same publisher, *Native Policies in Africa* (1936); several books by Granville St. John Orde-Browne, perhaps especially *The African Labourer* (London: International Institute of African Languages and Culture, by Oxford University Press, 1933,) and *Report Upon Labour in the Tanganyika Territory* (London: H. M. Stationery Office, 1926); and John M. Davis, ed., *Modern Industry and the African* (London:Macmillan and Co. 1933).

London, England May 28, 1938

My dear Dr. Du Bois

I do not know how to thank you for giving me such a delightful treat as the reading of "A Pageant in Seven Decades" has been. I have always had great pleasure in reading your books for your style is elegant, pure and simple. Your philosophy in your ending of your address is very telling and shows us who come along after you how to greet the end. It is almost like the remarks of one of the French politicians who was retiring and someone who was consoling him asked him sympathetically "Whatever will you do now?"; the reply sums us all up: "Do? I shall now live until I die."

I wish I could meet you again. I have been so near leaving the earth that now I want to meet my friends in case I start to die again, and, though you don't know it, I count you as one of my friends. I have worked so hard during my life for *justice* for all those races who are often scorned by their inferiors that I feel drawn to all who suffer. Remember I lived in Georgia and Tennessee and know what I am talking about when I speak of cruelty, injustice and oppression.

My husband is a very hard worked man but he likes it and he has a really wonderful brain and a most lovely character. We are moving into the official residence of the Chancellor of the Exchequer in Downing St. in the auturm. *Be sure* to let me know if you are coming over as you must let me see you. Again thank you very, very much for giving me so much pleasure by reading your address.

Yours very sincerely
Kathleen Simon

I suppose you know Garland Anderson.[1] He has married again and this time a white wife and most intelligent lady. I see them sometimes.

We are having a club for African students and Mrs. Anderson and I are doing all we can about it. We want playing fields for them too.

K. S.

The relationship between Mary White Ovington and Du Bois was remarkable not only in its length—some forty years—but in its depth, each profoundly respecting the other yet often disagreeing. Their exchanges always were of substance.

1. Garland Anderson (1886–1939) was a Black man, born in Kansas, who served as a bellhop in San Francisco and then in 1924 wrote a play, *Appearances*, that attracted the attention of Al Jolson and David Belasco and was staged on Broadway for three weeks in 1925. He went to Europe in 1929 and this play was produced in Brussels, Paris, and London. He settled in the latter city, married a white woman named Doris Sequira, conducted an "advice-to-listeners" program on London radio, and in 1933 published *Uncommon Sense: The Law of Life in Action* (Fowler and Co). He and Mrs. Anderson toured the United States in 1935, creating something of a sensation. She wrote of their lives together in a book much better than its title—*Nigger Lover* (London: Fowler and Co, 1938). He died in Harlem while trying to produce another play in the United States.

New York, N. Y., March 11, 1938

Dear Dr. Du Bois,

I have been reading your "Seven Decades" and am writing to ask if you will send it to the Gt. Barrington library if you have not already done so. They bought, of their own initiative, your "Black Reconstruction," though they apparently spend less than a hundred dollars every year for books; and I think they ought to have this account of your life, particularly as it is interesting reading to any one.

I wish I had any hope that a minority group can achieve its economic place in a nation against the wish of the majority but since the Nazis attitude to the German Jews, exiling Einstein, my only hope is in Communism.

I am glad if you are a Rabbi Ben Ezra in your old age, old, counting the years only. Not so with me. I am just beginning to understand a little how to live. I want more time.

"The lyf so short, the craft so long to lerne."[1]

Yours,
Mary White Ovington

Atlanta, Ga., March 21, 1938

My dear Miss Ovington:

I thank you for your letter of March 7, and I have sent a copy of the "Seven Decades" to the Great Barrington Library.

A minority group can and must achieve an economic place as the price of its survival and this achievement may not necessarily be against the wish of the majority. Indeed the majority in numbers of cases will help it on with the cynical confidence that it will fail.

Communism is the hope of us all but not the dogmatic Marxian program with war and murder in the forefront. Economic communism by the path of peace is possible.

Very sincerely yours,
W. E. B. Du Bois

Du Bois's attachment to Fisk University was profound. It was his alma mater; from it his daughter graduated; at it he waged fierce struggles in 1908 and in 1924–25, and in both cases helped force the removal of the university's presidents. Hence, his pleasure must have been keen indeed in learning that, in his seventieth year, Fisk wished to bestow upon him an honorary doctorate.

The president of Fisk at the time, Thomas Elsa Jones (1888–1961), was born in Indiana and educated at Earlham College, the Hartford Theological Seminary, and Columbia University. He taught in Indiana public schools, was national secretary of the Young Friends' Movement during the First World War and directed YMCA work in Vladivostock, Siberia, 1918–19. For some years thereafter he taught and worked in Japan, and in 1926 he was appointed president of

1. From Chaucer's *The Parlement of Foules* (1380–86). Mary White Ovington died in 1951.

Fisk. He was a member of the International Commission studying conditions in South Africa in 1938—which explains several references in the letters that follow.

Nashville, Tenn., April 13, 1938

Dear Dr. Du Bois:

At the meeting of the Board of Trustees of Fisk University, on Monday, April 11th, 1938, it was decided by unanimous vote to depart once more from our time-honored custom of not granting honorary degrees to bestow upon you the honorary degree of Doctor of Letters, and to request you to be present in person on our Commencement Day, June 8th, 1938, to receive this the third honorary award given in the history of Fisk University.

Your distinction as a scholar, author, and great American causes your Alma Mater to wish to honor herself by bestowing this mark of recognition upon you. It is a matter of sincere regret that I cannot be present in person to award this degree. Either Mr. Paul D. Cravath, Chairman of the Board of Trustees, or Mr. L. Hollingsworth Wood, Vice-Chairman of the Board, will render this service in my absence.

It is with genuine pleasure that I inform you of this decision by the board and I sincerely hope that you will make us happy by being present to receive the degree.

Sincerely yours,
Thomas E. Jones
President

Atlanta, Ga., April 15, 1938

My dear President Jones:

I have your letter of April thirteenth and I am deeply sensible of the honor which Fisk University proposes to bestow upon me. I shall be glad to be present June 8, 1938.

Very sincerely yours,
W. E. B. Du Bois

Nashville, Tenn., April 19th 1938

My dear Dr. Du Bois:

We are delighted that you can be with us at Commencement to receive the honorary Doctor of Letters Degree.

At the request of the Senior Class of 1938 and our alumni, we should like you to deliver the Commencement Address on June 8th. You may choose any subject you wish. Mr. L. Hollingsworth Wood, Vice-Chairman of the Board of Trustees, will preside in my absence and confer the degree upon you.

I wish I could join the festivities but since I cannot, I shall be thinking about you between conferences at Capetown.

Sincerely yours,
Thomas E. Jones
President

Atlanta, Ga., April 22, 1938

My dear President Jones:

I have your kind invitation of April 19. I shall be glad to deliver the commencement address June 8. My subject will be "The Revelation of Saint Orgne the Damned."

For your information I will say that this cryptic subject covers the following thesis which I have been developing for some years, namely: the path which young American Negroes today must follow if they are going to attain a secure place in modern culture. It calls

1st for the rehabilitation of the family as a cultural more than a biological center, to begin the real education of the child.

2nd the reorientation of the church for teaching ethics in a day when questions of right and wrong are inextricably mixed and ignoring "revelation" and dogma.

3rd the school as a center of imparting knowledge and not for the discipline or character both of which, if not already attended to, are impossible subjects for school activity.

4th work for service and service alone, and service as the only basis of income.

5th freedom for Art, untrammelled by convention.

6th the development of Race as cultural activity, rather than blood relationship and

7th the development of the State and patriotism solely as a method of realizing a world wide humanity.

I want to put this in a literary form which I began many years ago on a European trip. Of course, how much time I am going to have to develop all of this is a question but I will try it.[1]

I hope you and Mrs. Jones are going to have a pleasant trip.

Very sincerely yours,

W. E. B. Du Bois

Cyril Clemens (b. 1902), kinsman of Mark Twain, was educated at Washington University in Missouri. He has been president of the International Mark Twain Society and was the founder, in 1936, of the Mark Twain Journal. *In addition to books devoted to Twain, Clemens is author of early biographies of Harry S. Truman (1945) and of Clement Attlee (1946). His request to Du Bois in 1938 brought a significant response.*

Webster Groves, Mo., May 22, 1938

Dear Mr. Du Bois:

It gives us great pleasure to inform you that you have been unanimously elected to

1. Originally published, with title as given above, in *Fisk News* 11 (November-December 1938): 3–9, and reprinted by Du Bois in 1939 as a sixteen-page pamphlet. The cryptic title becomes clearer when it is realized that Orgne means Negro. This essay appears—with a brief introductory comment by Du Bois—in his *Education of Black People: Ten Critiques, 1906–1960,* ed. H. Aptheker (Amherst: University of Massachusetts Press, 1973), pp. 103–26.

W. E. B. Du Bois. Photograph courtesy of the *Crisis*.

Du Bois at the Cambridge Rod and Gun Club, Litchfield, Maine, during his annual vacation. Photograph courtesy of the University of Massachusetts Library.

the Society's Historical Committee whose Chairman is George Macaulay Trevelyan.
  With all good wishes

Most sincerely

Cyril Clemens

P. S. I am editing a book to be called "The Humor of Different Peoples," in which well known authors will discuss the humor of their various races. Would you honor the book by writing on Negro humor? Complete liberty of treatment would be allowed you. If Mark Twain were alive you would be his choice.

  Will you do me the great favor of filling out the enclosed questionnaire?

Atlanta, Ga., June 2, 1938

My dear Mr. Clemens:

  I have your letter of May 22 and thank you for its information. I am returning the blank which you asked me to fill. Concerning the contribution to the book of humor of different peoples, I might undertake a short statement on Negro humor sometime next year.[1] I could not do anything before September first. Perhaps you will write me again concerning the time limit.

Very sincerely yours,

W. E. B. Du Bois

[Enclosure]
My best virtue—grit
My worst fault—sensitiveness
My favorite actress—Bernhardt
My favorite actor—Richard Harrison
My chief hobby—a motor car
My favorite song—Go Down Moses
My favorite book (by myself) *Souls of Black Folk*, (by another) *Three Musketeers*
My pet vanity—a beard
Usual time of rising and retiring—6 a.m. and 10 p.m.
My favorite food—Bread and milk
My favorite drink—ginger ale
My favorite sport (outdoor)—walking
My favorite sport (indoor)—reading
My favorite character in history—Toussaint L'Ouverture
My favorite animal—the dog
My earliest memory—Tongs and the fire place
My favorite study in School—History
My favorite study (outside my native land)—Sociology

---

1. The requested time limit was forthcoming and Du Bois wrote briefly on "The Humor of Negroes." This piece was published in *Mark Twain Quarterly* 5 (Fall–Winter 1942–43):12.

A letter from a worker and a Communist is itself revealing and brought from Du Bois a significant reply. Efforts to identify George Cook in more detail than he gives in his letter have not succeeded. The names he mentions are all familiar, with the possible exception of "Jim Allen," meaning James S. Allen, then a Communist organizer in the South, editor of The Black Worker, *published in Alabama, and author of* Reconstruction: The Battle for Democracy *(New York: International Publishers, 1937); Tim Holmes was, at that time, a leading Black Communist in New York City.*

Yonkers, N.Y., July 22, 1938

Mr. W. E. B. Du Bois

Dear Sir:

I do not often write to authors of books telling them what I think, but you are an exception, for your book on *Black Reconstruction* is an exception. I am a southern white man with ancestors who fought in the Civil War to keep your people in slavery; I grew up in the tradition of white superiority and southern justice; I attended college in the North without having my beliefs shaken. I had advantages, of course; my grandfather, although illiterate (legally so), believed that your people should have had their forty acres and a mule; my father fought with all his strength, and successfully, to prevent our county from separating Negro and white tax funds for school purposes; I got more out of college than the average student; I work in a factory and am a member of the Communist Party. Yet your book is a revelation, showing me for the first time what a powerful force your people have been, can be, and are for progress and Democracy. I am sorry that I did not come to it earlier. It is a sort of call to arms to blot out the wrong that my people have done to yours, and I take the call. I have no illusions about becoming a Thad Stevens, an Earl Browder, or a Jim Allen, but the little I can do is at the service of your people and mine, split into two artificial halves by their common enemy and oppressor.

I used to spend all my time trying to be a writer, but the strain of day after day in a steaming dyehouse, night after night pounding the streets to rouse union members, meetings and shop papers have rusted my typewriter and made fingers lose their cunning and my brain its search for pithy phrase and well-turned sentence. There I want to suggest to you the thing I want to do myself. Why don't you prepare a series of booklets and pamphlets to be sold for two, five, ten cents on Negro history, the truth about such things as Nat Turner's rebellion, the glories of Haytian revolution, the story of Reconstruction in simple, easily read language for our people? The Communist Party, The Workers' Library, International Publishers would help; Modern Age books would take a small volume with illustrations; James Ford and Tim Holmes would add their knowledge to yours. There is a need for such things, and not many workers, black and white, can or will go to the pains to read through volume after volume to get the truth. I have tried to do that, and I have found the glory of the Negro people shining through even the pages of [Claude G.] Bowers and [Walter L.] Fleming, but, as I have said, I am more fortunate than most workers.

I know you are no Communist, you are not even a follower of Marxian analysis in your study of the second American revolution, but you must recognize our sincerity in working for all labor and in fighting for the obliteration of the color line between humans. And you must know that we have the ear of labor more than any other group within the country and must respect our propaganda distribution facilities. It is a bit presumptuous for me, a very lesser member of the Party, so freely to offer you its machinery, but I am hereby starting an awful yowl for it to do that very thing, and there is still enough of the rebel left in me to yell. Your people want this knowledge; my people must have it, else we face the degradation of Hitler Germany. My part is a small one; you can do a big job. You write the pamphlets, or get them written, and I'll sell ten dollars of them here in Yonkers. Damn little for me to do, but I'll do more when I can.

> Sincerely yours
> George W. Cook

> Atlanta, Ga., November 7, 1938

Mr. George W. Cook
My dear Sir:

Your letter of July 22 has been in my hands for some time and I have meant to answer it before this but I have been transporting my family to Atlanta and opening my school year and finishing a book so that I have put the answer off.

I thank you for the letter. Such frank appreciation and criticism are always welcome and I am especially glad that my attempts to show the fundamental problem of Reconstruction have in some degree been successful. I appreciate your advice concerning pamphlets and have for a long time had something of the sort in mind but the publication game in the United States at this time is pretty difficult and my twenty-five years of experience in publishing a monthly magazine, the *Crisis,* has made me perhaps over-timid in starting anything else and yet I may be able to do it myself or inspire it in others. I am not a communist but I appreciate what the communists are trying to do and endeavor always in my classes and elsewhere to give a fair and balanced judgment concerning them.

> Very sincerely yours,
> W. E. B. Du Bois

Charles Edward Russell (1860–1941) began his remarkable career as a newspaper editor in New York and Chicago and was among the leading muckrakers in the era of Lincoln Steffens and Ida Tarbell. Unlike them, however, he went on to become an active socialist and frequent candidate for public office on that ticket. He was among the founders in 1909–10 of the NAACP and thereafter for over thirty years was Du Bois's friend. He wrote very many books, including a biography of Wendell Phillips (1914) and The American Orchestra and Theodore Thomas *(1927), which brought him a Pulitzer Prize.*

An exchange between Russell and Du Bois in the 1920s appears in the first volume of this work (pp. 262–63). Another of great interest was begun by Russell in 1936 but, because of Du

Bois's extended absence abroad, did not bring a response until over two years had passed. That Du Bois was engaged in a study of the Reconstruction era had been announced in the press in 1933, so Russell knew about this work. Meanwhile, as earlier pages have made clear, works by James Truslow Adams and Claude G. Bowers were appearing, taking a deeply racist view of the period, and were being widely advertised and sold. Du Bois's book appeared in the spring of 1935 and received good and extensive reviews, as noted previously, but somehow Russell did not know of its appearance. This background explains his letter written in the summer of 1936.

Danville, Vermont, July 17, 1936

My dear Doctor Du Bois:

I have grown so weary of the continual appearance of books stuffed with lies about the Reconstruction Period and of the efforts of our book reviewers to boom such books, that I am driven to ask you when we may expect your book, upon which we rely to controvert this flood of falsehoods. It seems to me that such a book as yours was never so much needed. The Southern propagandists are succeeding in fastening upon the American mind the notion that the Reconstruction narrative, as now presented to this public, is final proof of the inferiority of the Negro race. We need some such authoritative and convincing statement of the facts as yours will be. I note with the utmost disquietude the spread of racial antipathy in the North, which, it seems clear to me, [is] the direct result of text book and other widely spread prevarication.

I hope you are well and that all goes well with you and that we may soon have your book,

With best wishes

Yours very truly
Charles Edward Russell

In a letter dated 21 July 1936, Russell was informed by W. A. Shields, serving as Du Bois's secretary at that time, that Du Bois was abroad, was expected back early in 1937, and that Black Reconstruction *had been published by Harcourt, Brace in 1935.*

Du Bois did not find it possible to reply to Russell until the winter of 1938, and in doing so then he made the error of referring to Russell's letter as having been written in July 1937, rather than 1936. Du Bois sent his reply to Washington, D.C., where Russell was serving on an interracial committee.

Atlanta, Ga., November 8, 1938

My dear Mr. Russell:

I have long had your letter of last July concerning Black Reconstruction. I was very much pleased and heartened with it. It has had varied reception: it received a large number of very favorable reviews at first and then was treated with rather prolonged silence. Every once in a while I get a letter from somebody who seems to think the job was not badly done. I put a lot of time and trouble into it. It indicated a number of paths which I should like to pursue further. My largest effort just now is toward editing and publishing an Encyclopaedia of the Negro race. The Phelps-Stokes Fund is financing the promotion and we have a rather imposing list of editors, advisers, etc. The financing will cost about $250,000 and that means that we have got to get support from the "Funds." That, of course, is a problem especially in the case of a person as suspect as I am. There is however a chance and if you can push it along any place, do so. I am enclosing one of our letter-heads.

I am also about to finish what started out to be a revision of my little book *The Negro* in the Home University Series for Holt. It has turned out to be an entirely new book of three or four hundred pages. I hope to have it published this winter and I know you will be interested in it.

My best regards to you and Mrs. Russell.

Very sincerely yours,
W. E. B. Du Bois

Washington, D.C., November 10, 1938

My dear Doctor Du Bois:

I am glad indeed to hear from you again. Anything I can do to help along your beneficent project I will do with great satisfaction.

I am still resentful because I did not know of *Black Reconstruction* until a year and a half after its appearance. There is one book I should like to review. Look at it from any point of view within the scope of truth and reason, and it is a most remarkable and admirable performance. As research, as history, as narrative, as the revelation of the trials of a race misunderstood and horribly maltreated, as an irresistible appeal to justice, as a demonstration of the real nature of slavery and its real reason to be, as illuminating economics, as a complete handbook of actual happenings in the South in the Reconstruction period, it is beyond ordinary praise. There are so many good features about it that one could not tell them all in an ordinary article. Among them I want to thak you most sincerely for these, that you put the cause of the Civil War exactly where it belongs, without equivocation and with absolute proof. That you show relentlessly the real origin of the campaign against the colored Americans growing out of the post-war period. And, incidentally, you refer continually to that infallible source of true information about the Civil War causes, the old *Congressional Globe*. It rejoiced my heart to find another writer that had been peering over those neglected volumes. How foolish they cause to appear the fantasies chased by Ford[1] and the rest! A great work you did. I have been trying ever since I came upon it to boom it. My talk at the Columbus Convention about poisoned text books referred to *Black Reconstruction* as the sure source of accurate knowledge wherewith to antidote the

---

1. Russell's reference to Ford is somewhat obscure; probably he meant to refer to James Ford Rhodes, the well-known author of *History of the United States from the Compromise of 1850* [to 1877], published in seven volumes from 1893 to 1906.

venom of the text-books and since then I have had several inquiries for further light all of which I have referred to the same source.[2]

I hope you keep well. It is reassuring to know that your energies go on unabated in this great cause. We shall not see it win out in our time but our grandchildren will see it and we are working for them.

Yours very truly
Charles Edward Russell

Atlanta, Ga., November 25, 1938

My dear Mr. Russell:

Thank you for your letter of November 10. Let me say right off that I am in excellent health and hope to put in a few more years of work. I am just today sending off a manuscript of five hundred pages which is a history of the Negro race with enough of Marx lugged in to make some of my friends unhappy but it is a good, well documented history. I will see that you get a copy when it comes out next spring. Holt is publishing it. I received from time to time very encouraging letters about *Black Reconstruction*. Two came recently from working men which pleased me very much.

My best regard to you and Mrs. Russell.

Very sincerely yours,
W. E. B. Du Bois

Washington, D. C., December 1, 1938

Dear Dr. Du Bois:

I rejoice to know that you have done another book and thank you earnestly for remembering me about it. I look forward to it with keen interest. You have set such a pace in research, clarity, accuracy, interest, everything that make historical writing worth while, that I am eager to see this new achievement. We need a book on the subject you have chosen.

About the Marxism, Good Lord! how can any reasoning man look over the world today and fail to see that there is no way out of this mess except the way indicated by Marx? It's either Marxism or the return to serfdom.

I am glad to know that your health is good. May you have many years of it.

Yours very truly
Charles Edward Russell

Du Bois in his letter to Russell of 25 November 1938 referred to two letters he had recently received, treating of Black Reconstruction, *that had given him pleasure. That from George Cook appears earlier. Augustus M. Kelley wrote from New York City (he is now a publisher*

2. He refers to the NAACP Convention held in June 1938 in Columbus, Ohio. The *Crisis* in reporting this convention (August 1938; 45:270), noted Russell's "analysis of the manner in which text books used in the public schools have omitted or distorted or absolutely falsified the accomplishments of the Negro in this country. . . . "

there) affirming that the book had been an eye-opener for him and telling Du Bois that he, young Kelley, was the grandson of Florence Kelley, one of the earliest translators of Engels, a pioneer in reform efforts aimed at child labor, one of the earliest organizers of consumers, and an active supporter of both the NAACP and the Pan-African movement. Du Bois's reply to Kelley touches on his approach to history writing.

Atlanta, Ga., September 28, 1938

My dear Mr. Kelley:

I knew your grandmother and counted her as one of my most valued friends. She was a fine collaborator in my work for many years.[1] I appreciate your kind words concerning *Black Reconstruction*. It has been criticized for its bias and enthusiasm and I have sympathy for the ideal of cold, impartial history; but that must not be allowed to degenerate as it has so often into insensibility to human suffering and injustice. The scientific treatment of human ills has got to give evil full weight and vividly realize what it means to be among the world's oppressed. Thank you for your letter.

Very sincerely yours,

W. E. B. Du Bois

The various interracial and intercultural committees and commissions which proliferated, beginning in the 1920s and growing in consequence during the New Deal years, reflected a kind of liberal approach to "race problems" which, it was hoped, might be resolved by an educational program that demonstrated how all peoples of all backgrounds had contributed to the United States. This effort reached even the federal government by the end of the 1930s; illustrative is the correspondence between the United States commissioner of education and Du Bois.

The commissioner—appointed to his post in 1934—was John Ward Studebaker, born in Iowa (1887), a teacher and principal in various schools in that state, and then superintendent of schools in Des Moines, from where he had accepted the federal appointment.

Washington, D.C., November 1, 1938

Dear Dr. Du Bois:

Thinking people agree that the foundation of our democracy is the spirit of tolerance of the other man's viewpoint, regardless of his race or place of origin. People of many races and places have come to this country and contributed to its upbuilding.

In order to promote a keener appreciation of the interdependence existing among the various stocks with which our land has been peopled, this office is planning a series of 26 one-half hour broadcasts, over a nationwide hook-up of the Columbia Broadcasting System, under the title "Immigrants All."

1. At a memorial service for Florence Kelley, 16 March 1932, Du Bois offered a loving—and critical—estimate of her life; it was published, with notes by the editor of this volume, in *Social Work* 11 (October 1966): 99–100.

To assist us in attaining the objectives of the series I am inviting a number of leaders like yourself to act as consultants. Those accepting this invitation will be called upon from time to time to offer suggestions for the guidance of those whose primary responsibility it will be to organize the content of the program.

Mr. Gilbert Seldes, outstanding author and playwright, has been chosen to write the scripts for "Immigrants All." Mrs. Rachel Davis DuBois, Director of the Service Bureau for Inter-Cultural Education, has been selected as Consultant on Inter-Cultural Education, to coordinate the research cooperation which we expect from the various racial and national groups in this country. These two people, in collaboration with this Office, are now at work on the formulation of definite plans for the series.

I can assure you that the acceptance of this invitation will not impose upon you an arduous burden. I sincerely hope you will find it possible to cooperate with us. Upon being advised of your acceptance we will send you a brief synopsis of the proposed series to which we would be very glad to have your reactions involving criticisms and constructive suggestions.

> Cordially yours,
> J. W. Studebaker
> Commissioner

Atlanta, Ga., November 4, 1938

Honorable J. W. Studebaker
My dear Sir:

In accordance with your letter of November first I shall be glad to act as consultant in the planning of your series of broadcasts "Immigrants All." I am glad that you have the cooperation of Mrs. Rachel Davis DuBois. I think she is one of the best authorities in the United States.[1]

> Very sincerely yours,
> W. E. B. Du Bois

Washington, D.C., November 7, 1938

Dear Mr. Du Bois:

It is with great deal of pleasure that I learn that you will act as Consultant in connection with our "Americans All—Immigrants All," radio series whenever necessary, with regard to the subjects upon which you may be able to cooperate with us.

I am advising our Research Director that you have consented to do this, so that he may get in touch with you whenever the occasion presents itself.

Your helpfulness is most assuredly appreciated.

---

1. Rachel Davis DuBois—no relation to Dr. Du Bois—was a Quaker, originally from New Jersey, whose work and writings in the field described by Studebaker were several times commended by Du Bois; see, for example, *Phylon* 1, no. 2(1940):191–92, and the *Amsterdam News*, 12 February 1944.

I feel certain that those of us who contribute to this very significant educational effort will have ample reason to feel proud of our participation in it.

Cordially yours,
J. W. Studebaker
Commissioner

A teacher of English at Temple University in Philadelphia (not otherwise identified) in November 1938 posed an important question to Du Bois.

Philadelphia, Pa., November 21, 1938

My dear Dr. Du Bois:

My class in *The Novel* would value a statement from you relative to the following question about novels concerning the Negro. Does the Negro fictionist's portrayal of the Negro correspond with that of his Caucasian brother? Kindly give us the reason for your answer and specify novels we might read to corroborate your statement.

This will be of great value to us. We hope you have the time to make this contribution.

Thank you very kindly.

Very truly yours,
(Miss) Grace V. Postles

Atlanta, Ga., November 25, 1938

Miss Grace V. Postles:
Dear Madam:

Some Negro novelists agree in their portraiture of Negro life with white novelists; others do not and I think the latter persons are right because, of course, the authentic portrait must in the long run come from the persons within. The ones who represent what I regard as a correct portraiture are among others: Jessie Fauset—*Plum Bun, There Is Confusion, Chinaberry Tree;* Charles W. Chesnutt—*Conjure Woman, Wife of His Youth, House Behind the Cedar;* and Walter White's *Fire in the Flint.*

Very sincerely yours,
W. E. B. Du Bois

Gunnar Myrdal (1898), one of the most renowned social scientists of the twentieth century—a recent (1974) recipient of the Nobel Prize in economics—was born in Sweden and educated there in the law but soon turned his major attention to economics and sociology. In 1927 he joined the faculty of Stockholm University; in 1938 he was Godkin Lecturer at Harvard University and that year became director of the Study of the American Negro Problem for the Carnegie Corporation, a position he held until 1942, which resulted in the publication in 1944 of An American Dilemma: The Negro Problem and Modern Democracy *(2 vols., Harper and Bros.). Myrdal's staff was numerous, and quite early in his undertaking he consulted many people, among them Du Bois.*

New York, N. Y., November 26, 1938

Dear Dr. Du Bois:

Now that we have returned to New York from our trip to the South I should like to take this opportunity of thanking you for your kindness to me when I was in Atlanta.

The most interesting discussion I had with you on the social and racial question was extremely valuable to me in understanding the magnitude of our problems, and I have the deepest appreciation for the time you devoted to me.

I am looking forward to coming back to Atlanta although probably not before the beginning of next year, and shall avail myself then of your offer of a further conference.

Yours very sincerely

Gunnar Myrdal

Letters from Lillian E. Smith to Du Bois in 1937 have already been presented. Late in 1938 she wrote him again.

Belem, Brazil, November 30, 1938

My dear Dr. Du Bois:

I am writing to ask a favor of you. I hope the request does not presume too much upon your scant knowledge of us, or upon the kindness you have already shown in writing to us encouragingly about our little magazine.

Miss Snelling and I are planning to apply for a Rosenwald Fellowship. We have in mind making a joint application, as the project for which the application is being made is one on which we are both working: a book of criticism of Southern Literature. It is our belief, founded upon years of desultory reading and supported by more recent specific study, that the creative output of any section or group is to a large degree limited by those prejudices which the artist and his people share. We will tend, in the book we are working on, to form our judgements in part on the basis of our intimate knowledge of the South, in part on the aesthetic criteria of literature which are available to any student of art, and in perhaps larger part upon the theory that life and art are so interrelated that health or poison in one realm will evince itself in the other. An essay in the summer issue of the *North Georgia Review* (Southern Fiction and Chronic Suicide) indicates the trend of the proposed book more clearly than anything I can say here.[1] The general effect of the book should be towards a clearer understanding of racial relationships in the South, and so perhaps would warrant our applying for the fellowship on that basis.

You probably know much better than I do what projects and qualities the Fellowship Committee values. We shall be most appreciative if you will write the Committee mentioning our qualifications, as you see them through reading the little magazine, for the proposed undertaking.

1. The essay, with cited title, was by Paula Snelling and appeared in *North Georgia Review* 3 (Summer 1938): 3–6, 25–28.

Miss Snelling and I are spending a few months in South America, and left home before securing details from the Committee. Until I hear from them, I am uncertain who Mr. Potey's successor as Director of Fellowships is.[2] Otherwise the address is Director of Fellowship, Rosenwald Fund, 4901 Ellis Ave., Chicago, Ill. If you prefer to write directly to them, please do so; otherwise if you will be so kind as to enclose your letter in an envelope addressed to me at Clayton it will, in our absence, get to the hands of our secretary who will be instructed to mail the assembled data to the committee near the end of December.

We have been completely out of touch with happenings in the States for the past month. But we hope that things are going at least normally well with you and your undertakings. And when we return home and are again in Atlanta we hope to have the pleasure of calling by the University and of seeing you.

We shall appreciate anything you may do for us in the matter of the fellowship, but do not bother with it if you feel your knowledge of us is insuficient.

Very sincerely
Lillian E. Smith

Atlanta, Ga., December 10, 1938

My dear Miss Smith:

I shall be very glad to say a word to the Rosenwald people concerning your project and to recommend it. You can refer to me in your application. The application must be in, as I presume you know, by January tenth. I shall hope to see you and Miss Snelling when you come back.

Very sincerely yours,
W. E. B. Du Bois

Atlanta, Ga., December 10, 1938

My dear Mr. Embree:

I understand that Miss Lillian E. Smith and Miss Snelling are going to make application for a Rosenwald fellowship. They are two young southern women who have been publishing at Clayton *The North Georgia Reviw*. I think they have done a stunning and courageous piece of work and if you can possibly encourage them I am sure it will be worth while.

Very sincerely yours,
W. E. B. Du Bois

Hugh H. Smythe, born in Pittsburgh in 1913, did graduate work at Atlanta University in 1936–37 under Du Bois. He went on to a doctorate from Northwestern University in 1945 and a

2. She refers to Raymond R. Paty (1896–1957), who was director for fellowships from 1936 through 1937; he was succeeded by George M. Reynolds, who held the post from 1938 to 1941. Both Lillian Smith and Paula Snelling received Rosenwald Fellowships for creative writing in 1939 and 1940.

career as a professor of sociology at various institutions—most recently Brooklyn College. He also served as United States ambassador to Syria (1965–67) and to Malta (1967–69). The letter published below relates to an effort to obtain the Rosenwald Fellowship that he was granted for 1939 to 1941. From 1938 to 1939 he pursued graduate studies at Fisk and it was from there that he wrote Du Bois.

Nashville, Tenn., December 1, 1938

Dear Dr. Du Bois:

Since coming to Fisk I have been engaged with a study of Haiti, its race and culture, carried on in conjuction with the Race and Culture Seminar here, conducted by Dr. Robert E. Park. Learning of my interest in the specific locality Dr. Park took me under his personal guidance and has assisted me in developing a project for thorough investigation which I have decided to use as the basis for doctorate study in the field of Sociology.

In view of the conditions existing in various parts of the world today, especially in regard to the matter of race, it seems pertinent that such a study as I propose to carry on should have significance and contribute toward an understanding of the racial situations wherever they may be found. Haiti with a background rich in racial lore affords a fertile field of study for a project of this nature and its importance towards the comprehension of problems created in any center that has become a locus for race contact does not seem out of place here.

Dr. Park has given me his sanction and is urging me to continue with the work. Since I too see the great possibilities involved in such an undertaking and have increased and developed my personal interest in the field through research of my own, I am desirous of carrying through the work which I already have begun. To further the work, or rather to enable me to continue with it, I have applied to the Rosenwald Fund for aid, and gave your name as one of my references. I am asking if you will please give me your support on the project and attest my ability to pursue the work, when they contact you for my qualifications and ask your opinion relative to the work and value of the proposed project.

Thank you in advance for your consideration and courtesy and I hope that I shall continue to advance in my chosen field as only a student of yours should do.

Respectfully yours,
Hugh H. Smythe

Atlanta, Ga., December 15, 1938

My dear Mr. Smythe:

I shall be very glad to recommend you for aid from the Rosenwald Fund at any time they refer to me. I am glad you are doing interesting research work.

Very sincerely yours,
W. E. B. Du Bois

1939

Perhaps the most condemnatory letter in all those within the Du Bois papers is that which Du Bois wrote to Willette Rutherford Banks early in 1939 protesting the suggestion that Walter White be elected to the board of trustees of Atlanta University. (White was not in fact chosen.) The recipient of this letter, born in Georgia in 1881, was a student at Atlanta University from 1901 to 1909, during Du Bois's first stay there. He went on to administrative posts in schools in Alabama and Texas and from 1926 to 1947 was president of Prairie View State College in Texas. He was, at the time of Du Bois's letter, a member of the board of trustees of Atlanta University.

Atlanta, Ga., January 11, 1939

My dear Mr. Banks:

I think it would be a calamity to elect Walter White to the Board of Trustees of Atlanta University. I was closely associated with Mr. White from 1917 to 1933 and was instrumental in bringing him to the Association. He is an intelligent and hard-working man but I do not think that in all my career I have met a man more utterly selfish. He is absolutely self-centered in everything that he does or thinks. In the earlier years his concentration on himself became the joke of colored New York. Later he curbed a little of the outer expression of it but it became all the more dangerous and difficult to deal with. One of the reasons that I left the National Association was because staying there would have involved a bitter fight with White's methods and objects, and especially with his utter lack of principle and broad ideals. If he [be] came associated with Atlanta University, you need not think that his contacts would help the University. Rather he would use the University for his own objects. It was due to his selfishness and refusal to cooperate that James Weldon Johnson was compelled to resign as secretary of the NAACP. If White had been loyal and devoted, Johnson could have kept the position and would have been glad to.

All of his executive colleagues united in December, 1931 in a complaint to the Board of Directors of the NAACP concerning Mr. White. I am enclosing a copy of the concluding words of this indictment with the signatures and the figures indicating the length of service of each person. The statement was prepared by me at the request of my colleagues; written out and given to them for consideration; then signed on the next day and presented at a meeting of the Board of Directors. I am sending you this statement at the request of Elizabeth.[1]

1. The Editor does not know to whom "Elizabeth" refers; Elizabeth Prophet, the distinguished sculptor, was then in the art department at Atlanta and close to Du Bois, but whether she is the one meant or not is pure conjecture.

It is noteworthy that in Du Bois's autobiography, *Dusk of Dawn*, published in September

I hope you are still in good health after your travels. My best regards to Mrs. Banks.

Very sincerely yours,
W. E. B. Du Bois

[Enclosure]

TO THE BOARD OF DIRECTORS:

" . . . It is our solemn and carefully considered opinion that unless the power of the Chairman of the Board over the appointment of committees is curtailed and unless Mr. White is going to be more honest and straight-forward with his colleagues, more truthful in his statement of facts, more conscientious in his expenditure of money, that the chief question before this organization is how long he can remain in his present position and keep the N.A.A.C.P. from utter disaster?

"We make this statement with our own free will and at the solicitation and suggestion of no single one of us; and with a full realization of the gravity of what we say and the utmost willingness to abide by the consequences. We have all had considerable and varied experience, but in our several careers, we have never met a man like Walter White who under an outward and charming manner has succeeded within a short time in alienating and antagonizing everyone of his co-workers, including all the clerks in the office."

		Years of Service
Signed	W. E. B. Du Bois	21
	Herbert J. Seligmann	12
	William Pickens	12
	Robert M. Bagnall	11
	Roy Wilkins	1/2

Du Bois's exchanges with Lester Walton were always of interest; early in 1939, the United States minister to Liberia wrote to Du Bois.

Monrovia, Liberia, January 14, 1939

Dear Dr. Du Bois:

In transmitting a copy of my commencement address delivered [November 30, 1938] to the members of the graduating class of Liberia College, I hope you will forgive me for having the temerity to invade the field of education of which you are an authority. My wish, however, is that the sentiments expressed by me are very much in accord with your own.

I regret that during my visits to the United States on leave I have not had the

---

1940, Walter White is not in the index; but in his *Autobiography*, written in 1959–60 and published posthumously (in 1968), White appears several times. This incident is related there on page 294; the letter above is fuller, however, than the book's account.

For further discussion of the 1931 complaint, see pp. 300, 318–19 below.

opportunity of enjoying your company and indulging in an eat-fest at Lüchow's. I sincerely trust this privilege will not be denied me upon my next trip.

Liberia has again balanced its budget in the face of a decrease in revenues in 1938 due to world conditions. President Barclay is doing all in his power to justify the existence of this black republic and it affords me considerable satisfaction to know that I am playing some part in Liberia's heroic efforts to preserve its sovereignty and autonomy. Despite rumors of probable aggression by European powers, I think I can authoritatively say to you as long as Liberia continues to make progress along economic and social lines and it receives the strong moral support of the United States Government, I have little fear of it losing its political and territorial independence in the near future.

I think I can point with pardonable pride to my record as diplomatic officer at this post during 1938. Three important treaties were negotiated and concluded at Monrovia by the United States and Liberia. A United States cruiser made a memorable courtesy visit to this capital last October when the new Legation site was dedicated. I feel that you will be interested to know that my efforts during the year have won praise from time to time from the Department of State.

Please let me hear from you at your convenience.

With every good wish for a prosperous and healthful 1939, I am

Sincerely yours,
Lester A. Walton

Atlanta, Ga., February 27, 1939

My dear Walton:

I was very glad to have your letter of January fourteenth. I wish you would send me some exact figures concerning the income and expenditures and the imports and exports of Liberia covering say the period from 1930 to 1940. I am greatly interested in its development. I have just been lecturing for a committee of colored students in the University of Nebraska. Its president is Charles C. Blooah who is a native Liberian. I should think the government would eventually want his services. I am very glad to hear of your success and hope to meet you when you come again.

My best regards to you and Mrs. Walton and my regard to His Excellency, the President, and such other persons I may know.

Very sincerely yours,
W. E. B. Du Bois

Alpha Kappa Alpha, a national sorority of Black women, financed and conducted a free health service for tenant farmers and sharecroppers in Mississippi, beginning in 1934. One of the founders of the sorority, Norma E. Byrd, a schoolteacher in Washington, D. C., then persuaded two chapters of the sorority to establish a lobbying organization in the capital with the objective of eliminating discriminatory practices and laws. As a result, in 1938 there appeared the Non-Partisan Lobby for Economic and Democratic Rights; its first employee was a young Black *attorney, Willam P. Robinson.* It is in response to a letter from Robinson—which seems not to have survived—that Du Bois succinctly expresses elements of his political thinking at the time.*

Atlanta, Ga., January 26, 1939

Mr. W. P. Robinson
My dear Sir:

The right to vote is the only effective weapon of democracy and disfranchisement deprives any individual or group of its opportunity to realize and guide democracy. At the same time since the War, I have become increasingly impressed with the fact that any people deprived of their right to earn a living or discriminated against in income are unable to use their vote effectively or intelligently. Therefore, I favor all practical efforts toward inducing the colored people to maintain our right to vote and vindicate it in the courts; nevertheless unless such effort is supplemented and accompanied by successful efforts to earn a living, the vote will be nullified. These efforts to earn a living must not be merely efforts to gain employment under any circumstances and at any wage. They must be efforts to establish and carry out democracy in industry through which the government will control income and maintain decent standards of living as well as encourage production.

Very sincerely yours,
W. E. B. Du Bois

Note has been taken earlier of Du Bois's tendency to sympathize deeply with Japan and, especially, to be suspicious of those who condemned her aggressions in China and "forgot" the record of Western aggressions against colored peoples. His 1937 visit to Japan and to Manchuria (then called Manchukuo) certainly did nothing to diminish this feeling. The result was the kind of rumor reflected in a letter written to Du Bois early in 1939. Du Bois's response exudes the anger of which he was quite capable.

New York, N. Y., February 13, 1939

Dear Dr. Du Bois:

As an individual, I have fought for many years for the rights of the Negro people. I am supporting the efforts of the NAACP in attempting to secure the passage of anti-lynching legislation.

While in Washington over the past week-end, a number of liberals in Congress interested in this legislation asked me if it was true, as has been rumored, that you are receiving funds for Japanese propaganda work in this country. They indicated that some speeches coincided with those of official Japanese propaganda agencies' propa-

---

* The Non-Partisan Lobby in turn evolved into the National Non-Partisan Council on Public Affairs, a significant anti-racist pressure group of the 1940s. See the article on that council by Ida Louise Jackson in *Opportunity* 20 (November 1942): 327–29.

ganda in this country. The December 10th issue of the *China Weekly Review* in an editorial names you as a suspect in the dissemination of Japanese propaganda.[1]

If these allegations are true, you can readily understand how it is going to reflect not only on you as an individual, but upon the whole Negro people in this country.

I would like to have a statement from you indicating your official position on the Sino-Japanese conflict, so as to lay at rest, once and for all, these ugly rumors; for I am sure that you are still on the side of peace and democracy and not an agent of Japanese fascism.

Sincerely yours,
Waldo McNutt[2]

Atlanta, Ga., February 25, 1939

Mr. Waldo McNutt
My dear Sir:

Perhaps it is a miracle for an American to have an opinion which is not paid for. If so, the miracle has happened; it is true in my case. I have never received a cent from Japan or from any Japanese and yet I believe in Japan. It is not that I sympathize with China less but that I hate white European and American propaganda, theft and insult more. I believe in Asia for the Asiatics and despite the hell of war and the fascism of capital, I see in Japan the best agent for this end.

Very sincerely yours,
W. E. B. Du Bois

A young woman studying at Mount Holyoke College propounded some significant questions to Du Bois, and, as was Du Bois's habit when he felt he had a serious questioner before him, answers came quickly and with no equivocation.

South Hadley, Mass., March 8, 1939

Dear Dr. Du Bois:

I am spending a year on an honor paper at Mount Holyoke College which deals with the attitudes of Negro leaders on economic and social questions and I am now

1. There is an editorial essay, "Serious Racial Element in the Sino-Japanese Struggle," on page 32 of the cited *China Weekly Review*. It notes that Japan is using the color issue as one of its propaganda lines, especially among Afro-Americans. It continues: "There were rumors that Prof. W. E. B. Du Bois, of Atlanta University, outstanding educator and [former] editor of *The Crisis*, who recently toured the Orient, had expressed pro-Japanese sympathies, but this was not confirmed."

2. Waldo R. McNutt was an officer in the Consumer-Farmer Milk Cooperative, Inc. and is mentioned in its publication, the *Link* (New York City) for November 1940, and in the *Organized Consumer*, also issued by the Cooperative, in May 1941 and October 1941. He is mentioned and quoted, in line with his work with the milk cooperative, in the *New York Times*, 2 August 1941. Further data have not been obtained.

working on labor problems.[1] I would appreciate it very much if you could possibly answer the following questions, as I am anxious to obtain a representative cross-section of opinion.

    I.   Is the Negro worker benefited by trade union organization?

    a) How widespread has been the use of Negroes as strikebreakers?

    b) Are you in favor of separate trade unions for Negro workers?

    c) What do you consider the advantages and disadvantages of separate organization? Would you advocate a different policy for the South as compared to the North?

    d) Do you know of instances where segregation in work has been practiced in the North?

    II.   Is there any difference in regard to Negro labor in the policies pursued by the A.F.of L. and the C.I.O.?

    III. What political objectives should Negro unionization have?

I do hope that you will find it possible to answer these questions soon. Thank you for your courtesy.

                                Respectfully yours,
                                Dorothy Goldstein

                         Atlanta, Ga., March 13, 1939

Miss Dorothy Goldstein

My dear Madam:

    Enclosed are answers to your questions of March 8:

    I.   Yes

    (a) They have been widely used

    (b) Separate social institutions for racial minorities should only be resorted to when the use of the general group institutions is denied; or when, if permitted, there are such limitations and conditions laid upon their use that the persons involved suffer and do not get the full benefit of membership.

    (c) The one and only advantage of a separate social institution is that it will do for the members of the race what the group insitution cannot or will not do. Any difference in policy between the North and the South as to such a matter would depend entirely upon the specific circumstances.

    (d) Yes

    II.   Yes, the CIO welcomes Negro membership much more generally than the AF of L.

    III. The political object of any union movement should be to bring economic

---

1. In the library of Mount Holyoke College there is a typewritten honors paper for 1939 by Dorothy Goldstein entitled, "Negro Leaders and Their Attitudes toward Social and Economic Problems of Today"; a copy is in the Schomburg Center of the New York Public Library.

matters, that is, questions of the production and distribution of wealth, within the democratic control of the nation.

Very sincerely yours,

W. E. B. Du Bois

Professor Reid, Du Bois's colleague in the sociology department at Atlanta University, was on sabbatical in 1939. Aboard the Queen Mary *he wrote a brief note to Du Bois that evoked a long and news-filled response; in it Du Bois referred to, among other activities, his teaching— something he took very seriously and for which he carefully prepared. Reid's reference at the close of his letter to a sense of danger was prompted by the imminence, widely sensed at the time, of the war which erupted a few months later.*

March 28, 1939

Dear Dr. Du Bois:

Somehow I do not remember writing you from New York, though I planned to do so.

While there I mailed you a copy of *The Negro Immigrant,* one of the publications of the Department of Sociology for 1939. It is amazing what shortcomings an abbreviated publication can contain. But I do hope you'll like it.[1] If not, I hope you will tell me so.

One of the things I planned mentioning to you concerned the theses of Misses Graham and Calloway. When I was in New York I went over the copies they sent and made written suggestions which were to be shown to you for final approval and comment. You may do what you wish with them, though I tried to ease the burden for any one who would have to carry on.

So we—Mrs. Reid and I—begin the second phase of the wanderings. If Europe is as rough as the sea we are going to have one awful time. Yet the nearer we get to Southampton the less dangerous it all seems—perhaps I mean less imminent. Anyway, we shall see.

Please remember me to your family, and to Miss [Irene] Diggs.

Cordially,

Ira De A. Reid

April 14, 1939

My dear Reid:

I was so glad to get your letter of March 28. I have received *The Negro Immigrant.* I think it makes a fine and impressive book. I have only had a chance to glance at it but I am going to read it from cover to cover very soon.

---

1. Ira De A. Reid, *The Negro Immigrant: His Background, Characteristics and Social Adjustment, 1899–1937* (New York: Columbia University Press, 1939). This 261-page book was a pioneering study of the West Indian immigrant to the United States.

We are getting on very well. The President [Rufus Clement] has shown no marked activity or plans. I, at the instigation and prodding of [Mercer] Cook, asked him for an interview and talked with him the other day. Cook thought that his attitude when the faculty discussed a periodical was not favorable and in general the discussion was rather poor. I was away on my lecture trip. I heard nothing of it until I went to him the other day. Then I wrote him a memorandum and said I should like to see him with regard to the periodical and the housing proposition in which you and I were interested. He asked some preliminary questions as for instance whether all members of the faculty would be compelled to contribute to the periodical and I felt like saying that they should be compelled not to in most cases. He asked if two thousand dollars would start us and I told him that I thought it would. He promised that he would recommend to the Board an appropriation of $2,000 for next year and mentioned of course budget difficulties but said that they had an accumulated surplus and he saw no reason why the appropriation should not be made. The Board will meet in a week or two and we shall see what they will do. It looks as though we might get an appropriation of $2,000. In that case I am thinking of approaching [Charles S.] Johnson again. I saw him in New York just for a minute at the YMCA. He has not mentioned the periodical by word or letter for over a year and I haven't mentioned it to him. But I will consult the President on the matter and if he is willing and we do get the appropriation, I shall write Johnson somewhat like this: I have not heard from him and do not know what his mind is at present but we have $2,000 and if he is still minded to come in with us that he might get Fisk or his department to give $2,000 and then we should endeavor to get a third party to give from one to six thousand. If we could start next year with ten thousand dollars we could issue a periodical which would restore to the American Negro his rightful hegemony of scientific investigation and guidance of the Negro problem.[1] I shall also intimate gently that if I do not hear from him or he is not prepared to go into the proposition that we are going to publish something anyway.

The President seemed interested in the housing proposition and the next day called in Daley for a consultation.[2] I have heard nothing more.

1. Du Bois's reference is to what became, in 1940, the quarterly *Phylon*, issued by and at Atlanta University. He had labored on the idea of a quarterly for some years and had invited Charles S. Johnson, head of the sociology department at Fisk, to participate and make the journal a joint product, but this plan did not eventuate. Du Bois here also expresses his distress that centers at Southern universities—especially Duke and the University of North Carolina (both at this time, of course, barred Black people)—had been producing book after book on the so-called Negro problem and had become national "experts" on that subject. Du Bois commented in print upon this phenomenon and noted particularly that white scholars—he cited Thomas J. Woofter, Jr., as an example—received generous grants for their studies but Black scholars did not. See Du Bois in the *Crisis* 37, (November 1930): 378,393 and 38 (March 1931): 81–83.

2. Tatham A. Daley was a member of the Romance Language department at Atlanta. Other faculty members mentioned in the letter are: Matthew S. Davage, president of Clark University; Hersey H. Strong, from the sociology department at Atlanta; Walter R. Chivers, who taught

My classes are getting on very well. I have one very excellent class in Social Institutions. We are using Hertzler which is a pretty bum book but I really have gotten a good deal out of it by way of knowledge and inspiration[3] and I think that my next class in Social Insitutions is going to be worth something. We are going to do some original studies of methods of changing social insitutions among Negroes particularly in economic lines. The other class of six is in racial problems which I am changing to cultural problems and putting on a geographical rather than a racial basis. This is getting on fairly well although I have a couple of lazy Morehouse students. This is balanced by one very bright Clark student.

By the way Davage was in yesterday asking advice about his speech before the general conference of the Methodists this summer. He said that they were having a hard time in raising the money for moving the institution but that they must get it this year or fail and he didn't know what they would do in that case.

The seminar is very successful. We are having it upstairs in the lounge opposite the faculty conference room on the third floor of the Administration Building. There are about seven or eight attending in addition to Strong, Chivers, myself and Miss Diggs. We devoted the first part of the year to discussing the Papacy, the Jews in Germany and the college curriculum. Last Wednesday Miss Graham started off with an excellent exposition of her thesis. Next Wednesday Miss Calloway will have the floor. Always good eats!

Chivers has been busy with a number of lectures and trips out of town which he seems to have enjoyed. Strong is in the depths. He came to talk to me saying that he had been warned that his services would not be wanted next year. He said, and I agree with him, that it had taken seventeen years for them to find this out and that they ought to have found out earlier. I told him that the only thing he could do was to make a calm statement of that fact to the Trustees. He is in a tough spot.

I am looking for the final paged proof of my book every day. It was held up a week or so for a curious reason. The attorneys of the Henry Holt and Company reported to them that they might be liable for some libel suits because I had "accused" several people of Negro blood. In addition to that I had spoken disrespectfully of several English colonial governors. I laid aside my work for a week and at the risk of putting Miss Diggs out of commission entirely presented them with a memorandum that was simply unanswerable. They wrote back expressing their thanks for my thoroughness, etc., and so on. I am expecting the paged proof now any day and the book will appear before May first if nothing else goes wrong.

I have two other books very nearly ready to submit to publishers: one a sort of biography with essays which is an amplification of the *Seven Decades* and addition of some other stuff. I am hoping to send that out this month. I shall probably have to

---

psychology and sociology at Morehouse College; Otis W. Caldwell, a visiting professor of biology at Atlanta; and Nathaniel P. Tillman, from the English department at Atlanta.

3. He probably refers to Joyce O. Hertzler, *Social Institutions* (New York: McGraw-Hill Book Co., 1929).

hunt for a publisher. The other book is a series of speeches which I have made at critical times on Negro education: first my criticism of Hampton in 1906 on account of which I did not get an invitation to return for thirty years and the other my Fisk speech, Saint Orgne. I have had the latter reprinted and I am sending you a copy herewith.[4]

We had a meeting of the AAUP last week in my office. They wanted to know something about research projects which I had on hand. I piled up the stuff until they gasped and were properly impressed. I hope it will make some of them go to work. I have had the Tiffany windows wired for electricity and turned them on to impress the visitors.

This past week I went to speak in North Carolina and returned, as usual, by way of New York. There I saw Oscar Wilde, Hells a Poppin and Judith Anderson in the Family Portrait which is another excellent Christmas play. I had dinner with the Alexanders and saw Arthur Spingarn. He says that Joel cannot recover; that it is simply a matter of his lingering on until death. It is very sad and a great strain.

Caldwell returned for a week, looked pleasant, said little and did nothing.

The faculty has had one meeting beside that on the periodical. They discussed the grading system and the inspiration of teachers. Tillman led the thing unaided by his committee and it was a pretty poor exhibition. I kept still.

I had an unusually successful lecture tour: three engagements in Chicago, one with the University of Chicago, one at a Sunday evening meeting at Orchestra Hall and one at the colored Church of the Good Shepherd. In addition to that I spoke in Nebraska, Detroit, Wheeling, Springfield, Ohio, etc. Also I made five talks before the junior colleges of Chicago. It was the most successful trip I have made in years.

Marian Anderson, of course, is the talk of the town and the union. She sang here Wednesday night, April fifth, in the city auditorium. It was divided into two bands: Negroes to the left of the throne and whites to the right. But everybody seemed happy. She sang gloriously and did she wear clothes. And of course you have heard of her tremendous triumph in Washington where she sang before seventy-five thousand people, before cabinet members, justices of the Supreme Court and senators.[5]

Mr. Myrdal and his wife called on me on Saturday afternoon. We had quite a talk. He left a copy of the memorandum concerning the work which he is proposing to do

4. The three books to which Du Bois refers are: *Black Folk Then and Now: An Essay in the History and Sociology* (New York: Henry Holt and Co., 1939); *Dusk of Dawn: An Essay toward an Autobiography of a Race Concept* (New York: Harcourt, Brace and Co., 1940); and a book on education, the manuscript of which he submitted to the University of North Carolina Press in 1940. Letters in connection with this effort and the fate of the projected book at the time are in this editor's preface to Du Bois's *Education of Black People: Ten Critiques, 1906–1960* (Amherst: University of Massachusetts Press, 1973).

5. He refers to the sensational concert given by Marian Anderson at the Lincoln Memorial on Easter Sunday 1939, after the DAR had refused to allow a Black artist to perform in Constitution Hall in Washington. Contemporary accounts are in *A Documentary History of the Negro People in the United States, 1933–1945*, ed. Herbert Aptheker (Secaucus, New Jersey: Citadel Press, 1974), 3: 352–53.

with me and asked for my criticisms. I sent him a few criticisms yesterday. My chief feeling is that he has bitten off a pretty big bite and is going to have a hell of a job in finishing it up in two years; but it is on the whole well conceived. He did not discuss any details as to whom he was going to ask to help but he did say that on his immediate staff he was going to have Ralph Bunche.[6]

I think this is all the dirt I can dish at this writing. The weather is lovely here with flowers and green things in spring glory. My best wishes to you and Mrs. Reid and I hope you will have a fine rest and ignore all wars and rumors of wars.

With best regards,
W. E. B. Du Bois

In a letter not yet located, Du Bois wrote to Will W. Alexander concerning the efforts of the Farm Security Administration. The reply was meaty. Alexander (1884–1956) was born in Missouri, received a B.D. from Vanderbilt (1912), and from 1901 to 1917 served in the Methodist Church, South. In the latter year he withdrew from the ministry and devoted himself thereafter to interracial efforts. He was president of Dillard University in New Orleans from 1931 to 1935 and an officer of the Rosenwald Fund. In the 1930s he held several offices in the New Deal and from 1937 to 1940 was administrator of the Farm Security Administration. In the latter capacity he responded to Du Bois.

Washington, D. C., April 14, 1939

Dear Dr. Du Bois:

Your letter of April 4 brought me as much satisfaction as anything that has come to my desk in a long time.

I am attaching a list of Farm Security Administration projects in which Negroes are involved.[1] All except the one in Virgina are purely agricultural. The ones marked with asterisks are new communities, such as that at Montezuma, made up exclusively of Negro families. The others are projects involving both white and Negro families. I wanted a few communities where we could demonstrate that Negro farmers could prove without question their capacity to succeed if given an opportunity. On the others, I wanted to demonstrate, if possible, that whites and Negroes could work together in the solution of their problems. That accounts somewhat for the wide variety of these projects. The project at Roanoke, North Carolina, and the one in Missouri are particularly interesting examples of white and colored families working together in the same community.

As usual, Mississippi has presented one of our most difficult problems. We have set

6. On the mechanics of the Myrdal study and Bunche's part therein, see Ralph J. Bunche, *The Political Status of the Negro in the Age of FDR*, edited and with an introduction by Dewey W. Grantham (Chicago: University of Chicago Press, 1973)—especially Grantham's introduction.

1. The enclosure—a one-page mimeographed sheet—stated that as of 1 April 1939 there were 31 homestead projects in 13 Southern and border states, with 1,185 Black families in residence. Eight of these projects were all-Black.

aside, out of funds that were available, a sufficient amount of money to purchase and develop as a Negro project 12,000 acres of splendid delta land near Yazoo City, Mississippi. We are now negotiating for this land and I think we will be able to complete the purchase soon. In most of these projects we have selected the families with great care. On this proposed Mississippi project, I hope we can take the families who are already there and start them from scratch without any selection to demonstrate what can be done with the ordinary run of sharecroppers if they are given a chance. I hope we can make this proposed Mississippi project 100 percent cooperative. In most of the others, we have introduced at the beginning only a minimum of cooperative enterprises, hoping to develop the cooperative idea just as far as the people themselves can be made to understand it.

As you no doubt know, the homesteads projects constitute a relatively small part of our program. The principal function of the Farm Security Administration is to make small loans, coupled with guidance in sound farming practices, to needy and low-income farm families, who cannot obtain adequate credit from any other source. This is an effort to reach the mass of sharecroppers, to give them some capital goods with which to work and credit under reasonable conditions, and to get them out from under the landlord system. Such loans run from about $300 to $500 for the purchase of work stock, seed, tools and other equipment necessary to carry on farming operations. Rehabilitation loans of this type have been made to approximately 50,000 Negro families since the program was initiated three years ago. I have been pleased with the fact that almost without exception these families have, as a group, made better progress than other farm families in the same area. These families are for the most part set up on individual family-sized farms, and the supervision and farm management assistance which is provided by our county supervisors plays a very important part in the success of this program.

We have found it difficult to do anything for sharecroppers on large plantations where the landlord finances them. However, in some 40 instances, we have enabled the tenants to organize themselves into cooperatives and lease the plantations themselves for a period of five years with an option to purchase. These groups thereby become their own landlords, and with our financial assistance at a reasonable rate of interest, are able to get free from their efforts whatever the plantations will produce. On a great many of the plantations we have bought, as well as on the ones we have leased, there is a cotton gin and a plantation store. These are being operated cooperatively, and we have been interested to discover that on the average these gins will earn, clear of all costs of management, insurance, depreciation, etc., about $3,000 a piece a year. This goes back into the pockets of the tenants and has been found to be one of the best means of teaching them the value of cooperative effort.

Health, of course, is a great factor in the success of these families. They have had almost no medical care. Their incomes do not enable them to pay for it at the going rates. We have, therefore, organized, both on our projects and among the rehabilitation clients, health cooperatives on a county wide basis, in which the families set aside about $2.00 per month which is put in a common health fund. A contract is made with the County Medical Society to give necessary medical care to the group for the combined amount that the families contribute. Physicians seem satisfied with the arrangement, and the families are getting good medical care. We are inclined to believe that we have a pattern here that may have wide application.

One of the principal factors involved in these rehabilitation programs is one of management. Our project managers and county supervisors must be efficient as farm managers, but they also need qualities of leadership and inspiration which are more difficult to find than mere technical ability.

The development of this sort of thing is very slow, and the success depends in large part on the soundness of the educational program carried on by the project managers and county supervisors.

I hope you will have an opportunity to see more of our work as you are travelling through the country. I am particularly interested in the Gee's Band project in Alabama. Here, there is a very primitive and undeveloped group of people, who have been on this land since before the Civil War with very little contact with the outside world. They have developed a form of cooperative life that has impressed us very much. We are trying to preserve this, as we give them an opportunity to have permanent tenure on the land which they have worked for generations.

You may be interested in the fact that the Lakeview project is in Phillips County, Arkansas, near Elaine where there was once serious trouble.[2]

Under separate cover I am sending you some printed material which may be of interest.

With appreciation, I am

Sincerely,
Will W. Alexander

A letter that surely pleased Du Bois very much was sent him by a young professor of sociology at Howard University. It is to be read in light of the fact that its author was then among the younger Black people who considered themselves a good deal to the left of Du Bois and who had made public their disagreements with him in rather sharp terms.

Washington, D. C., August 2, 1939

Dear Doctor Du Bois:

I had the University of Chicago Press send to you a copy of my recent book, *The Negro Family in the United States*. In this book I have noted your pioneer contribution to the study of the Negro family. In fact, my feeling in regard to the work which some

2. In the fall of 1919, Black sharecroppers in Phillips County, Arkansas, who had formed a union to secure better conditions, were attacked by planters and police; at least twenty-five of them were killed and, through Black resistance, five whites also. Twelve Black men were sentenced to death and almost eighty others to long prison terms. The case was widely reported; it was fought through the courts for years, with final success, by the NAACP. See the editor's *Documentary History*, 2: 279–82, 320–21, 420–25.

of us are doing has been that we are building upon a tradition inaugurated by you in the Atlanta studies.

My chief purpose in writing to you is to apologize for a mistake in the spelling* of your name which appears in a footnote in the Author's Preface. I can't understand how this error slipped by. However, I am writing to the Press, and will see that they make the correction in subsequent printings.

Sincerely yours,
E. Franklin Frazier

* i. e. a small d instead of capital D in Du Bois [Frazier's note].

New York, N. Y., August 7, 1939

My dear Mr. Frazier:

Thank you very much for the copy of your recent book. I shall not see it until I return to Atlanta but I shall be glad to have it and to read it.[1]

Very sincerely yours,
W. E. B. Du Bois

As is evident throughout Du Bois's correspondence, any inquiry for information or for opinion that he thought was made seriously and in good faith drew a careful response from him. An example is a letter to him from a white man in West Virginia who was the minister of the First Presbyterian Church in Bluefield.

Bluefield, West Virginia, August 5, 1939

My dear Dr. Du Bois:

I am seeking some help on the preparation of a study of the relationship between The Southern Presbyterian Church and The Southern Negro. I am writing to ask if you will give me a brief statement of your opinion regarding the effect on the Negro Race of the Failure of White Southern Christians to measure up to a Christian standard of dealing with the Negro; and what we can do now to meet our responsibilities.

I do not expect you to deal with the relationship of our own Church to the Southern Negro. Since that relationship has been practically the same as that of all the other Southern White Churches, you do not have to know our specific history. I am attaching hereto a copy of a letter I am sending to a number of our Church leaders with the thought that it may be a guide to you.[2]

1. In his *Amsterdam News* column, 28 October 1939, Du Bois called attention to Frazier's "excellent" book. In his review of the work published in the *Journal of Negro Education*, April 1940 (9: 212–13), Du Bois hailed it as "an astonishing and revealing study."

2. The enclosure was not found.

Would you tell me of any sources of information that might be particularly useful to me in this study?

I shall appreciate your help very much.

Yours very truly,
William Crowe, Jr.

New York City, August 9, 1939

Reverend William Crowe, Jr.

My dear Sir:

Answering your letter of August 5, I beg to say that I think the chief effect of the attitude of white Christians toward Negroes in the United States is to establish in their minds a double standard of truth. They have come to think that one must expect in this world professions and expressions of ideals which have nothing to do with actual conduct and consequently all truth has two sides: one, an ideal expression; the other, a practical series of acts. Although the first may be of the highest and finest promise, the latter may be the most selfish and self-seeking.

Back of all this as far as your church is concerned rises the fundamental fact that your church is an expression of economic organization, a group for social purposes with members composed of persons for the most part who receive an income above the average and whose primary solicitude is to protect that interest. Whatever ethical action does not interfere with that income is permissible and encouraged and often exceedingly well done. On the other hand, any action or program that threatens income has little chance for recognition and none for adoption.

The best work that I know of with regard to the relation of the Presbyterian Church to the Negro is the book by a Reverend Matthew Anderson entitled *The Negro and the Presbyterian Church*, published in Philadelphia between 1890 and 1900. The other works are other writings, pamphlets and published sermons of the Reverend Francis J. Grimké, a colored man who for many years was the minister of a large and intelligent group of colored folk in Washington. He is dead but the church is still there and a letter to the present minister would bring you information.[1]

Very sincerely yours,
W. E. B. Du Bois

1. Matthew Anderson, *Presbyterianism: Its Relation to the Negro*, with introductions by Francis J. Grimké and John B. Reeve (Philadelphia: J. McG. White and Co., 1897). For half a century the Reverend Francis J. Grimké served as pastor of the Fifteenth Street Presbyterian Church in Washington, D. C. Both Anderson and Grimké were graduates of the Princeton Theological Seminary. The works of Grimké have been edited in four volumes by Carter G. Woodson (Washington: Associated Publishers, 1942), and a good recent work is Andrew E. Murray, *Presbyterians and the Negro* (Philadelphia: Presbyterian Historical Scoeity, 1966). There is an account of the life of Matthew Anderson, with a photograph of him, in the April 1928 *Crisis* (35:117).

Left to right, W. E. B. Du Bois, Richard Harrison, John Hope, and Will W. Alexander. Photograph from the Marr Family Papers, by permission of the Amistad Research Center.

Incessantly, in published criticisms and in private communications, Du Bois was confronted by lamentations from white people about the alleged "bitterness" of his writing. A typical example—with a characteristic reply—appears in this exchange.

Indianapolis, Ind. [undated]

My dear Dr. Du Bois:

I am preparing in story form a little book of the accomplishments of the outstanding people of your race.

I have read much about you and have also read your books.

The Souls of Blackfolk was very interesting but I regret extremely that in it you show so much bitterness toward the white race.

There are many educated white people reading your book today and sincerely striving for a better understanding of your people. They have the same regret that I have for bitterness engenders bitterness.

I wish you would write to me a few lines with a more hopeful outlook for the Future.

I would like to have something that might be helpful to both races, and cause a better understanding.

Sincerely yours,
Julia Belle Tutweiler
(Mrs. H. D. Tutweiler)

Atlanta, Ga., October 17, 1939

Mrs. H. D. Tutweiler
My dear Madam:

I have your letter without date. If white people are reading my books for the purpose of learning what black folk are thinking, it would be dishonest for me to hide or gloss over the bitterness which we quite naturally feel over our treatment in the United States past and present; and if knowledge of that reaction engenders further bitterness on their part I am sorry but I can do nothing about it.

I am enclosing a list of my publications of which the *Souls of Black Folk* is only one. You may be interested.

Very sincerely yours,
W. E. B. Du Bois

[Enclosure]
Books by W. E. B. Du Bois
The Suppression of the Slave Trade
The Philadelphia Negro
The Souls of Black Folk
John Brown
Quest of the Silver Fleece
The Negro
Darkwater

The Gift of Black Folk
Dark Princess
Black Reconstruction
Black Folk Then and Now

A Black woman in Los Angeles named Dorothy V. Johnson sent Du Bois a sketch of his life as a youngster—this to be part of a projected collection of such accounts of outstanding Black people. Du Bois's comments on it offer significant glimpses of the young Du Bois as he remembered himself.

Atlanta, Ga., November 30, 1939

My dear Miss Johnson:

I have the little story which you sent me November fifth and have been interested in reading it. There are some little matters that might be changed but not of great importance. In New England it was always bad form to talk about princes. We were exceedingly democratic. I was widely known as Willie Du Bois which was the way in which all children were designated, one given name and one surname. Secondly, our town was too small to have a park. I would have been found sitting somewhere on the mountains overlooking the valley or on the bank of a river. I think your idea of these little biographies is interesting.

Very sincerely yours,
W. E. B. Du Bois

Late in November 1939, Du Bois asked the editors of Harper's Magazine *if they would be interested in publishing an account of developments in Mound Bayou, Mississippi. As it turned out, they were not, but Du Bois's letter outlining the proposal is significant. At this time Lee F. Hartman was* Harper's *chief editor.*

Atlanta, Ga., November 15, 1939

My dear Sir:

There have taken place recently some culminating facts in a long story which has to do with Mississippi. Before the War, Isaiah T. Montgomery, a Negro, was a slave on the plantation of the brother of Jefferson Davis. Eventually as a freedman he bought that plantation. The plantation was near the Mississippi River in the celebrated Delta region half way between Memphis and Vicksburg. It was near the place where recently social studies have been made by Powdermaker and Dollard and near where Theodore Roosevelt appointed a colored post mistress who was a center of fierce anti-Negro controversy.[1] In the capital of the state, Jackson, a hundred miles away,

1. The books Du Bois had in mind are: Hortense Powdermaker, *After Freedom: A Cultural History of the Deep South* (New York: Viking Press, 1939); and John Dollard, *Caste and Class in a*

during Reconstruction times, John R. Lynch who died this month at the age of ninety-two* was Negro Speaker of the House of Representatives and was commended by that House, whose majority were Southern white men, as being unusually fair and efficient. He was given a gold watch for his services. Later Mississippi disfranchised Negroes and Isaiah Montgomery was a protesting member of the convention which did it. He later established on his plantation a Negro city of refuge, Mound Bayou, which attained considerable notoriety during the heyday of Booker T. Washington's Negro Business League. Montgomery's daughter married a man named [Edmund] Booze and a second daughter fought for part of her father's fortune but was kept out of it by Booze. Between Booze, representing the disfranchised Negroes, and the surrounding whites an agreement was entered into so that Booze as a leading Republican helped the whites to office and preferment. The wife of Booze became a member of the Republican National Committee from Mississippi.

Recently the disinherited sister, almost poverty stricken, forced herself into the Montgomery home where Booze lived and from which she had been restrained by court injunction. Booze called in white officials and they shot and killed her. Thereupon the black citizens of Mound Bayou or of the neighborhood shot and killed Booze.[2]

Here are an extraordinarily interesting series of dramatic events which I should like to combine into an article for *Harper's*. In order to do this I should have to make some local investigation. Would you be interested in giving me such commission?

Very sincerely yours,
W. E. B. Du Bois

* Buried in Arlington! [Du Bois's note]

New York, N.Y., November 22, 1939

Dear Mr. Du Bois,

We wish to thak you for your letter of November 15th, but the story which you kindly offer us of Mound Bayou and the Montgomery-Booze feud would not fit into our heavily crowded schedule. Discussions of the war and related subjects have

---

Southern Town (New Haven: Yale University Press, 1937). The town with the Black woman postmistress was Indianola, Miss.; the incident occurred during Theodore Roosevelt's first administration and he refused to dismiss his appointee despite protests of white citizens. Indeed, the post office of the town was closed for several months, until finally the president yielded and reopened the office with a white male appointee.

2. The struggle around Mound Bayou and especially the effort to keep it an all-Black community was of very long duration. In the May 1927 *Crisis* (34: 93) was published a letter from M. Estello Montgomery, I. T. Montgomery's daughter, concerning this matter, and in the first volume of Du Bois's *Correspondence* (pp. 349–50) is another letter on this situation. See also Joseph Taylor, "Mound Bayou: Past and Present," *Negro History Bulletin* 3 (April 1940): 105–6, 109–11 and Saunders Redding, *The Lonesome Road* (Garden City, New York: Doubleday and Co., 1958), pp. 93–100, 105–21.

preempted so much of our limited space that we are obliged to say "no" to articles which in more normal times would have claim upon our consideration.

We appreciate none the less your kindness in making the suggestion to *Harper's*.

Sincerely yours,
The Editors

As part of Du Bois's efforts to establish a scholarly quarterly edited by and speaking for the Black intellectual world, he had written to the General Education Board, which had its origins in the post-Reconstruction efforts to help finance Black education. An exchange following Du Bois's original request for some financial support illuminates some of the particular projects Du Bois had in mind at this time.

Jackson Davis (1882–1947) spent his early years as an educator in his native Virginia; his association with the General Education Board began in 1915, when he was appointed a general field agent. He later served the board as assistant director and from 1933 to his death was associate director; from 1939 until his death he also held important posts with the Phelps-Stokes Fund.

New York, N.Y., December 2, 1939

Dear Dr. Du Bois:

I have delayed replying to your letter of November 22nd until I could discuss it with my colleagues. Dean Mann, Mr. Stevens, and I are interested in your proposal to publish a quarterly journal as a means of encouraging research and creative work in literature and art.[1] Your effort to undertake this project on a cooperative basis with Fisk seems a wise approach. However, it does not seem advisable that the Board should be in any way responsible for its publication.

Could your purpose be advanced if there were available a modest fund for productive studies? This might take the form of assistance to a member of the staff to cover the additional expense to which he would be put in making a study, or it might take the form of assistance to a graduate student who needs the maturing experience of a field study under the guidance of and in cooperation with members of the University staff.

I should like to discuss this matter with you and President Clement. I am not sure what we could do but I know how much concerned you are with giving encour-

1. The references are to Albert R. Mann, director of Southern Education and vice-president of the General Education Board, 1937–46, and David H. Stevens, a vice-president of the GEB from 1930 to 1938. The GEB had a long history of providing funds for Southern schools, particularly those serving Black people: from 1931 to 1935 it granted $400,000 to 27 Black colleges. See Raymond B. Fosdick, H. F. Pringle, and K. D. Pringle, *Adventure in Giving: The Story of the General Education Board* (New York: Harper and Row, 1962). In 1964, the GEB published its *Review and Final Report, 1902–1964*. See also L. R. Harlan, "The Southern Education Board and the Race Issue in Public Education," *Journal of Southern History* 23 (May 1957): 189–202.

agement to young students of ability and promise who are just getting a start in social studies. Activity in this field would assist the University in making contributions to some of the basic social and economic problems of the South.

The next time I am in Atlanta I hope to discuss this matter with you and Dr. Clement. In the meantime, if you care to write me your further thoughts on the subjects, I should be glad to hear from you.

With kindest regards,

Sincerely yours,
Jackson Davis

Atlanta, Ga., December 7, 1939

My dear Mr. Davis:

I enclose outlines of four special research problems which the Department of Sociology in Atlanta University would like to take up with the object of eventual publication of the results in *Phylon*, our new quarterly.

1. Much attention is being given to the problem of the rural life of the American Negro. Little attention has been given to the problem of the Negroes in Cities, save as the problem related to social welfare. The Department of Sociology is undertaking a comprehensive approach to this problem from the point of view of social fact, by beginning the construction of an Atlas of Urban Negro Communities. This Atlas will be a statistical and social reference on all aspects of urban living, with special reference to the problems in Southern cities. Our initial inventory is covering the eighty-six cities in the United States having ten thousand Negroes or more. This inventory will be supplemented by special studies, such as a carrying on of the studies in Negro immigration initiated by Ira De A. Reid. These will be continued in Florida cities.

2. The use of graduate students in social sciences in planned research projects in Southern cities. This is to be done on a work-study basis wherein students will spend from eight to sixteen weeks on a field project in some Southern city, working under the supervision of the Department. This work will be a necessary requisite for a degree in the field of sociology for those undertaking a social research major.[1]

3. There is a Negro rural community in Mississippi which since Emancipation has been carrying out a communal economic life evidently traceable to African influence. Mr. Will Alexander's resettlement work is entering this community and Mr. Alexander has suggested to Dr. Reid how interesting it would be if a careful study of the past economic activities could be made before they entirely disappear. We would like to send a member of the staff, a graduate student or both, to live in that community for three months or more.

4. Dr. [Rushton] Coulborn, head of the History Department, tells us that he has a graduate student who is engaged upon a study of isolation or segregation of certain

1. Something like this proposal was effected: "With this in view [assisting graduate studies] the Board appropriated to Atlanta University $10,000 toward support of graduate assistantships during a period of five years beginning in 1941 . . . in English, sociology, and education." *Annual Report, 1941* (New York: General Education Board, 1942), p. 73.

racial groups in the British Empire and possibly in other parts of Europe. He thinks the man is doing unusually good work but needs funds for supporting the work a year or more until completion.

Very sincerely yours,
W. E. B. Du Bois

In connection with the impending seventy-fifth anniversary of the Nation, *Freda Kirchwey, editor of the magazine from 1932 to 1955, wrote Du Bois of plans for marking the event and requested a contribution from him. Despite the concluding sentence of her request, Du Bois's characteristically candid response was not published in the special issue. Perhaps, as Du Bois suggests in his reply, it did arrive too late.*

New York, N. Y., December 5, 1939

My dear Dr. Du Bois:

Early in February *The Nation* will celebrate its 75th Anniversary. For us this will be a great event, and in honor of it we are planning a special issue. We hope to make it both important and exciting. It will be several times the usual size of *The Nation* and will offer us an opportunity to take stock of our period and of our own record, as well as to look ahead into the stormy future.

Although I realize how busy you are, I wonder whether you would be willing to tell us in a few words what you think of the *The Nation*, now and in the past. Such a comment would be much appreciated and the sooner we have it the more help it will be. And I should prefer an honest expression of opinion to a conventional "testimonial."

Sincerely yours,
Freda Kirchwey
Editor

Atlanta, Ga., December 13, 1939

My dear Sir:[1]

Your invitation of December fifth was directed to 150th Street, New York and has just reached me in Atlanta. This reply will probably be too late but I am sending it.

The *Nation* was for many years my standard and reference for advanced thought in social lines. As a student in Harvard from 1888 to 1892, I repeatedly went back over its field to complete my knowledge of the meaning of that great fight for democracy which crossed the color line and sought to include all Americans between 1865 and as far forward as 1915.

Since the war, however, and especially in recent years I am not so sure of the *Nation*. It seems to me that this weekly is trying more to be consistently radical than

---

1. The face of the letter shows it to have been addressed to "Miss Freda Kirchwey" at the *Nation*, so that this salutation was apparently just a typist's slip, unnoticed by Du Bois. Perhaps it did not add to Freda Kirchwey's eagerness to publish the communication.

inconsistently true. I do not follow its unreasoning attitude toward Japan and its friendliness for British China. I am not sure of its wobblings in the case of Russia and I sometimes think that the *Nation* has quite forgotten that there are still twelve million Americans of Negro descent whose plight is of more pressing importance than the *Nation* usually seems to think. In all these matters I may be wrong and therefore I still read the *Nation* weekly but I am not always happy when I have finished its perusal.

Very sincerely yours,

W. E. B. Du Bois

A Ben F. Rogers, Jr., of Saint Paul, Minnesota—not otherwise identified but apparently, from Du Bois's closing line in his letter, a white person—had written Du Bois asking specific biographical questions. This letter produced a reply of great value, though unfortunately quite brief.

Atlanta, Ga., December 20, 1939

My dear Sir:

A manuscript of mine partly biographical is in the hands of publishers for their decision. This manuscript would answer most of your questions. I have time in this letter only for some brief statements:[1]

First of all the change of environment from Atlanta to New York was not as sudden as you assume. I was born and trained in Massachusetts, educated in Tennessee as well as at Harvard and taught in the west[2] and in Pennsylvania before going to Atlanta.

The Niagara Movement was a revolt against the doctrine of Booker Washington and took place in 1906 at Fort Erie on the Canadian side of the river opposite Buffalo. It was in a sense the beginning of the National Association for the Advancement of Colored People which was incorporated in 1910.

The Pan African Congresses are reported in the *Crisis* at length. If you can get at a file for the years 1919, 1921, 1923, they may be helpful.

The founding of the NAACP has been written up several times. You could get information by writing to 69 Fifth Avenue, New York City.

I left Atlanta because my work of scientific investigation of the Negro problem did not find sufficient financial support. I went to New York to continue investigation if possible but found my vocation in editing the *Crisis* magazine. I certainly have been back to Atlanta since. For the last six years I have been head of the Department of Sociology in this institution. During my first sojourn in Atlanta, 1897–1910, half my time was given to research and writing, the other half to teaching. At present something like three-fourths of my time is given to writing and research. I formerly taught high school and college students in history, economics and sociology. I am at present teaching graduate students in sociology.

1. Du Bois refers to *Dusk of Dawn*, published by Harcourt, Brace in 1940.
2. Wilberforce, Ohio.

I began my study of Reconstruction in 1910 but did not give continuous and concentrated time on it until about 1930. From 1930–1935, I gave most of my spare time to it which varied in amount. My novels and essays were done at various times and places and in intervals and then collected in book form.

I was extremely emotional on the race problem while I was a student at Harvard and my emotion was curbed by the philosophy of William James and the historical research under [Albert Bushnell] Hart. They did not quench; they directed it. I was never "primarily a historian." If anything, I had the urge to be a creative artist but the literature which I wanted to write was not the kind which the public was willing to read. My attitude toward history and historical writing you will find in the seventeenth chapter of *Black Reconstruction*. I did not want to be a historian. I wanted to be an unhampered intelligence but history pointed a path.

There were three main crises in my life: first, openly to oppose a part of the doctrine of Booker T. Washington whom I admired in many ways. This was in 1906. Second, to give up my social investigations at Atlanta University and go into propaganda in New York City in 1910. Third, to give up the *Crisis* and go back to teaching in 1933.[3]

I hope these brief notes may help you. There is no color line in the NAACP. You can become a member. Write them. I should be very glad to have a call from you if I were in New York but as I say I live in Atlanta and am only in New York for short visits now and then.

Very sincerely yours,
W. E. B. Du Bois

3. Du Bois tended throughout his life to be careless with dates. The first meeting of the Niagara Movement occurred in 1905, not 1906. Du Bois certainly did not begin his studies of Reconstruction in 1910, for his pioneering paper on "Reconstruction and Its Benefits," while published in 1910, was delivered in December 1909 at the meeting of the American Historical Association. His open opposition to Booker T. Washington dated not from 1906 but at least from 1903 with his *Souls of Black Folk;* even earlier, in 1901, he had written a critical review of Washington's *Up From Slavery* in the 1 July *Dial,* published in Chicago. And he actually "gave up" the *Crisis* in 1934, not 1933.

1940

Du Bois, in his column in the Amsterdam News, *24 February 1940, mentioned receiving a letter from Henry L. Stimson requesting Du Bois's aid in opposing Japan and—Du Bois thought—suggesting in fact the likelihood of war between the United States and Japan. Du Bois announced that he would not help Stimson's efforts because he believed that the United States was not motivated by concern for China but wanted to exploit Asia itself. Though this state of affairs did not make Japan right, he continued, it certainly did not make the United States right, either. Du Bois added that he did not recall any letters from Stimson suggesting concern about Italy's ravishment of Ethiopia. So far as Du Bois's papers show, this was his only answer to Stimson.*

Stimson (1867–1950) had been trained in the law at Yale and Harvard and was a member of prestigious law firms in New York City, was secretary of war under Taft, governor general of the Philippines from 1927 to 1929, Hoover's secretary of state, and secretary of war from 1940 to 1945 under FDR *and Truman. Here is his letter to Du Bois.*

New York, N. Y., January 24, 1940

My dear Dr. Du Bois:

The struggle taking place in Asia today is essentially a conflict between two types of civilization—the one, pacific and evolutionary; the other militaristic and aggressive in its foreign policy. The outcome will be of enormous significance for the world.

American policy in the Far East has been based upon the conviction that a friendly, progressing, independent China would be the best guarantee of future stability and peace in the Pacific, and a great safeguard for the welfare and security of this hemisphere.

On January 28, the commercial treaty between the United States and Japan will come to an end. It is my conviction that prompt measures should then be taken by our Government to restrict, by such measures as may be appropriate and effective, the very substantial aid that Japan is receiving through the procurement of essential war materials from the United States. What action can and will be taken must depend in large measure upon the extent to which the people as a whole are informed upon this question and alive to the far-reaching consequence involved in our present position.

I consented, a year ago, to become Honorary Chairman of The American Committee for Non-Participation in Japanese Aggression because I felt that the members of this Committee were endeavoring, intelligently and honestly, to place before the American people one of the most significant issues that we must face in our foreign policy during this critical period in our own history and that of all nations. Subsequent experience has confirmed that confidence. I am glad to bespeak for the

Committee such cooperation and support as you may be able to give for its important work.

Sincerely yours,
Henry L. Stimson

The breakthrough in what are today called Black Studies does not date from the 1960s, as is commonly asserted and believed, but rather from the 1930s. Indeed, by 1940 even the American Historical Association was aware of this development, with the result that, for the first time in its history, it planned to devote one session in an annual meeting to Negro history. Naturally, Du Bois was in the center of the activity, and the ensuing letters relate to this development.

Mary Wilhelmine Williams (1878–1944) received her degrees from Stanford University, taught there and at Wellesley briefly, and then began her long association with Goucher College in 1915, becoming emeritus in 1940. She specialized in Latin American history and published several books in that field; she also was an editor of the Hispanic-American Historical Review *(1927–33), was active in the women's rights movement, and was a member of the Women's International League for Peace and Freedom.*

Her first letter to Du Bois addressed him as W. E. Burkhardt Du Bois.

Baltimore, Md., January 24, 1940

Dear Dr. Du Bois:

The 1940 convention of the American Historical Association meets in New York, and the program committee of which Dr. Merle Curti is chairman and I am a member has decided to have a session on Negro history, with the program supplied by Negro historians for the most part. I have been asked to arrange the program for this particular session, and I am now writing to ask if you would be so good as to preside over the session.

The program is, as yet, only partly planned; but it is settled that the first part of the two-hour session will be composed of papers by Dean [Charles H.] Wesley and Dr. [Rayford W.] Logan of Howard, both of them probably relating to abolition—that of Dean Wesley being on abolition work of Negroes and that of Dr. Logan probably being on Negro colonization projects in [the] Americas. We intend these two papers to be limited to twenty minutes each, which would leave about fifteen minutes for informal discussion from the floor. After the first hour we may have a short inter-mission—of perhaps ten minutes—and then another hour session in which we are thinking of having Carter Woodson and a sympathetic white Southerner engage in discussion. But Dr. Woodson *has not yet been asked*, so there may be a change in this part. If the plan for the latter half of the session on Negro history is carried through, each of the two scheduled speakers will be limited to twenty minutes, and the remaining part of the hour could be devoted to discussion from the floor.

The duty of the chairman would not involve any formal speaking at all. In fact, there was criticism of the recent AHA program because some of the chairmen used their positions to deliver addresses, in some cases stealing the thunder of those having papers. The chairman of the session on Negro history would be expected to introduce the speakers briefly, recognize those desiring to take part in the discussion from the floor, and perhaps—if necessary—to start the informal disucssion by means of a question or remark. We may decide to have discussion leaders. That is not yet settled.

I forgot to say that because many speakers at the recent AHA meeting far exceeded their time the present program committee made a rule that each participant on the program must promise to keep within the time set, and that the chairman of the session be asked to agree to hold them to the time agreed upon.

Would you be willing to preside over the session? And, if so, would you hold the speakers strictly to the time limit?

Very sincerely,
Mary Wilhelmine Williams

Atlanta, Ga., February 1, 1940

Miss Mary W. Williams
My dear Madam:

I shall be glad to preside at the session of the 1940 convention of the American Historical Association if I can get away from my duties here at the time. Unfortunately you did not say just what date the convention meets. If you will let me know that and the date of the proposed Negro session, I will let you know if I can be present.

Very sincerely yours,
W. E. B. Du Bois

Baltimore, Md., February 11, 1940

Dear Dr. Du Bois:

The dates for the meeting of the American Historical Association in New York this year will be

Saturday, Dec. 28,

Monday, Dec. 30,

Tuesday, Dec. 31.

I hope that these may be convenient for you and that you can, therefore, definitely accept the chairmanship of the session on Negro History, which, I think, will come on the 30th.

Sincerely,
Mary Wilhelmine Williams

Atlanta, Ga., February 20, 1940

My dear Madam:

I shall be glad to accept the chairmanship of the session on Negro history at the meeting of the Historical Association in New York, December 30.

Very sincerely yours,
W. E. B. Du Bois

Baltimore, Md., April 9, 1940

Dear Professor Du Bois:

At last I have the personnel of the A.H.A. session on Negro history settled, and I am sending inclosed a copy of the program so far as it is arranged.

You will note that two hours are allotted to it. As I said before, chairmen are expected to hold participants strictly to the time set.

I suppose that it might be well for you to limit in advance the time for each who wishes to speak from the floor.

So far, I have not received the specific titles of the papers. Dr. Wharton wanted to confer with President Bond, who is to discuss his paper, before he decided.

The program seems to me interesting, and I hope that you like it. You will note that three white men appear on it, and that the papers by Negroes are to be discussed by whites and the paper by a white will be discussed by a Negro.[1]

Many thanks for consenting to preside.

With best wishes,

Sincerely,
Mary Wilhelmine Williams

A letter reflecting conditions characteristic of much of the northern United States at the time of writing and still of more than historical interest came to Du Bois from a young college student in California. Its author moved to Oregon and has published several books which serve as introductions and guides to that state; he also is the Oregon correspondent of the Nation.

Chico, Calif., January 29, 1940

Dear Professor Du Bois:

I am a student at the Chico State College in California and recently completed a paper on "Cotton in the South—Its Economy and People." I had spent months in research—all, of course, in secondary sources—and when I completed the paper I turned it over to some members of the faculty for study. All, without exception, commented thusly: "Very interesting, good background and analysis, but where did you get that slant on the Reconstruction Period? That's the first time I've seen that viewpoint."

1. Page 15 of *The Annual Report of the American Historical Association, 1940* (Washington: U. S. Government Printing Office, 1941), states that a morning session on 27 December 1940 was devoted to "The Negro in the History of the United States" and that its chairman was "W. E. Burghardt Dubois." Charles H. Wesley of Howard delivered a paper, "The Negro in the Organization of Abolition, 1831–1837," with comment by Alex M. Arnett of the Woman's College of the University of North Carolina; Rayford W. Logan of Howard offered "Some New Interpretations of the Negro Colonization Movement," with comment from A. Ray Newsome of the University of North Carolina; and Vernon L. Wharton of Millsaps College in Mississippi spoke on "The Race Issue in the Overthrow of Reconstruction in Mississippi," with comment by Horace Mann Bond of Fort Valley State College in Georgia.

The "viewpoint" I had taken was that the Reconstruction Era was not a period of meddling and ravishing carpet-baggers but an attempt by the rank-and-file of the South to advance democracy to include all the people. Some of the laws passed during those years, I wrote, are far more progressive and intelligent than laws now in effect throughout the cotton belt.

It was surprising to me to find that even the professors in history and economics had not known of this. Frankly, my detailed knowledge was lacking, but I had studied Marx enough to know a little of social dynamics. Furthermore, I had been through the South and lastly, I have faith in the efforts of the People to work out their own destiny, provided they are given a chance.

Asked by the Professor to corroborate my view with a whole string of bibliography I started another search and this time discovered your most excellent and thorough book, "Black Reconstruction in America." A faculty member to whom I showed your book said, "If this is true more people ought to know about it."

It seems somewhat odd that books like "Gone With The Wind" (more aptly re-titled by my friends, "Gone With The Truth") should be so popular in the North and that the North should be so quick to support the ante-bellum nostalgia of the South.

Furthermore, there is tremendous race-prejudice against the Negroes even in the pioneer towns—traditionally democratic in behavior—of the Sacramento valley of California. In our town one of largest restaurants has on its window "Only White Help Hired." The theatres discourage with subtlety the attendance of Negroes. At the college, however, the one or two Negro students in recent years have been very welcome.

I wish someone would write a history of Negro migration to the north and the setting-in of race-prejudices. Have you read "History of The American Negro People—1619–1918" by Elizabeth Lawson of the History Department of the Workers' School of New York? You can get it for 40 cents at the Workers' Book Shop at 50 E. 13th St., New York, N.Y.

Again thanking you for writing such a splendid book.

Ralph Friedman

Atlanta, Ga., February 4, 1940

Mr. Ralph Friedman
My dear Sir:

I thank you for your letter of January 29. Although my book *Black Reconstruction* received some good reviews in the *New York Times* and elsewhere, it isn't, I am sure, widely known. I thank you for your kind words.[1]

Very sincerely yours,
W. E. B. Du Bois

1. In his *Amsterdam News* column of 2 March 1940, Du Bois commented on this letter from "a student in California" and noted the astonishment of his professors on the viewpoint he called to their attention.

The letter from Ralph Friedman—like the 1940 session of the AHA—*reflected the developing interest in Afro-American history. Another indication of this growth was a letter from a graduate student in Indiana, which reflected also the rising concern about women's position and the common tendency to combine the two interests. Further information on the writer of this letter has not been found.*

Hammond, Ind., February 5, 1940

My dear Dr. Du Bois:

As a graduate student and a candidate for the Master's of Arts degree at Ball State Teachers College, Muncie, Indiana, I am preparing a thesis in American history. Especially am I interested in the contributions which women have made in the history of our country.

I have selected forty-nine women who have been significant leaders in the suffrage and abolition movements, and in the fields of social welfare, public nursing, medicine, law, and education.

In order to have a more representative selection of personalities, it is my desire to include in this group of contributors a negro woman, either one who is living or one who is deceased but who has been of special help to her race in this country.

As I am rather poorly informed about the leaders of the negro race, I am writing to you for suggestions. Your assistance will be greatly appreciated.

Thanking you for your attention and courtesy, I am

Sincerely yours,
Florence Van Duyn
(Mrs. Robert Van Duyn)

Atlanta, Ga., February 7, 1940

Mrs. Robert Van Duyn
My dear Madam:

I would suggest as colored women of importance, one or more of whom might be included in your thesis: Catherine Ferguson, founder of Sunday Schools in the United States; Phillis Wheatley, one of the first of American poets; Sojourner Truth, early advocate of abolition and women's rights; Harriet Tubman, leader in the underground railroad; Maria L. Baldwin, principal of a public grammar school in Cambridge, Massachusetts. All these are dead. Among living colored women the most outstanding are Mary McLeod Bethune, head of the Negro division of the National Youth Administration, and Marian Anderson, contralto singer.

A good book on the subject is *Homespun Heroines* by Hallie Q. Brown published by the Aldine Publishing Company, Xenia, Ohio. There are published biographies of Sojourner Truth and Harriet Tubman.[1]

Very sincerely yours,
W. E. B. Du Bois

1. The book by Hallie Q. Brown was published in 1926. Available at the date of this letter were two biographies each of Soujourner Truth and of Harriet Tubman: Olive Gilbert, *Nar-*

In his adult years Du Bois was consistently hostile to established (white) churches, but he retained a religious sense and belief—in the years just before World War I he prepared a book called Sermons for Dark People, *not yet published, reflecting this feeling. His frankness on the established churches and their failures to practice the teachings of Christ marked many of his addresses and essays; as may be expected these evoked responses. One such came from an Episcopal clergyman in Ohio.*

Euclid, Ohio, February 10, 1940

Dear Dr. Du Bois:

I listened today with great interest over the radio to your address before the City Club of Cleveland. And especially to your answers during the question period— with most of which I was in complete agreement. But I confess one of them was puzzling, and so I write to ask you to please explain just what you meant when you said that the Episcopal Church had never shown any particular interest in the education of the Negro in the south. I am an Episcopal Clergyman who happens to have been born in Savannah, and so I am interested both in the south and in the Episcopal Church.

I know that you must be familiar with our American Church Institute for Negroes.

When I was rector of a church in Richmond, Va., I went once or twice to St. Paul's School, Lawrenceville. It is the only school under the jurisdiction of the Institute of which I have any first-hand knowledge. My impression has always been that our church has shown great interest in the Negroes in that section, and of course you know that Archdeacon Russell, its founder, was a clergyman of the Episcopal Church.[1]

I know of some of the other schools under the Institute such as Fort Valley, St. Augustine in Raleigh, etc., only by reading about them.

But we are appealed to for funds to help support all those schools and are given the impression that our church is very much interested in educational work among the Negroes of the south.

Is it possible that we are being misled? Or did I misunderstand your reply to the question?

I assure you I will be grateful for any explanation you may be willing to give me.

With highest regards for you and your work and your courage, I am,

Sincerely yours,

A. C. Tebeau

---

rative of *Sojourner Truth* (Battle Creek, Michigan: Review and Herald Office, 1884); Arthur H. Fauset, *Sojourner Truth* (Chapel Hill: University of North Carolina Press, 1938); Sarah E. Bradford, *Harriet: The Moses of Her People* (New York: J. J. Little, 1901); and Robert W. Taylor, *Harriet Tubman: The Heroine in Ebony* (Boston: G. H. Ellis, 1901).

1. He refers to the Black clergyman and educator James Alvin Russell (1885–1952), educated at Oberlin, the Philadelphia Divinity School, and the University of Pennsylvania, ordained a minister in the Episcopal Church in 1915, and from 1916 to his retirement in 1950 active in St. Paul's School in Lawrenceville, Virginia, and rector of St. Paul's Memorial Chapel in that town.

Atlanta, Ga., 20 February 1940

Mr. A. C. Tebeau
My dear Sir:

I did not mean in my Cleveland speech to give the impression that the Episcopal Church had done nothing for the Negro but I did mean to say that it had done less than almost any other of the large churches in the United States and considerably less in proportion to the wealth which it represents.

The Episcopal Church, as of course you know, did not sever its relations with the South on account of slavery. The result was that during Reconstruction when Congregationalists, Methodists, Baptists and Presbyterians were pouring money into the South for the education and social uplift of the freedmen, the Episcopalians as a Church did very little though I doubt not that many contributed through extra-Church channels. The result is that today the leading Negro schools owe their establishment in few cases to the help of the Episcopal Church. Howard, Atlanta, Fisk, Talladega, Wiley and others, the leading Negro colleges according to the estimate of the General Education Board, were in no cases founded by Episcopalians or supported by them. It was not until comparatively late that the Church Institute for Negroes was organized and helped schools like St. Paul's and St. Augustine. They also came to the rescue of Fort Valley which had been established without their aid. St. Paul has done some excellent work; St. Augustine, considering the small support which it has received, has struggled bravely on; Fort Valley being no longer able to carry on with what the Episcopal Church and others gave them has been taken over by the state.

What I meant then to say was that considering the great wealth and prestige of the Episcopal Church their work for Negro education has been pitifully small. Even their work in proselytizing among Negroes has not been notable. My own grandfather was once a member of an Episcopal Church in New Haven, Connecticut but was asked with other colored people to withdraw and he became the first senior warden of St. Luke's, a little church which still exists. Negro Episcopalians have a long tradition and are jealous of what they have been able to accomplish but they have had a hard fight within your Church.[1]

Very sincerely yours,
W. E. B. Du Bois

In his Dusk of Dawn *(1940), Du Bois tells on page 115 of his application in 1908 to become a member of the Sons of the American Revolution, of acceptance by the Massachusetts branch, and rejection by the national headquarters in Washington as a result of racism. Actions of this character by organizations with such names provoked increasing dissent; the climax came with*

1. Earlier comments by Du Bois on churches and Black people, and the Episcopal Church in particular, will be found in volume one of this work (pp. 130–31).

the banning of Marian Anderson by the Daughters of the American Revolution. From this
discrimination came the organization in New York City of the Descendants of the American
Revolution, whose founders and members included Mrs. Sherwood Anderson, Professor Ruth
Benedict, Stuart Chase, and Malcolm Cowley.

Early in 1940 Du Bois wrote to the Descendants; the correspondence presented here ensued, and
Du Bois became a member.

New York City, February 13, 1940

My dear Dr. Du Bois:

Our National Executive Committee were delighted to receive your letter containing a brief genealogical outline of your ancestry. We wonder whether you will be
good enough to make it formal and official by tracing the descent on one of our regular
forms, which is enclosed. It is not necessary, in our organization, to indicate in any
way race or color.

We are sending you herewith, so that you may have an idea of what we are doing
where we are numerous enough to hold public meetings, an announcement of our
public meeting in honor of Washington's Birthday and to observe National Brotherhood Week. We know all four speakers are excellently qualified. We are giving the
event a great deal of advance publicity and expect a fine audience.

Our Independence Chapter in Philadelphia celebrated the birthday of Robert
Morris by placing a wreath on his grave, the ceremony in Christ Church yard being
doubly impressive because of the colors of some of the local military units and the
presence of the Christ Church congregation. The difference between such a memorial
as staged by our organization and one under the auspices of the Sons of the American
Revolution is that we make use of the occasion to stress our democratic heritage of
liberty and justice for all.

Our Samuel Adams Chapter in Boston will hold a dinner on Washington's Birthday. Our District of Columbia Chapter gives valuable advice as to the status of
pending legislation and the most effective means of making our position known with
regard to it. A Chapter is in the process of formation in Chicago.

Our honored member, Mrs. Henry Holdship Ware, recalls agreeably her acquaintance with you at Atlanta University. We do hope you will soon be a member in full
standing.[1]

Sincerely yours,
Sylvia Wilcox Razey
Executive Secretary

---

* See above, p. 190. In 1928 Du Bois was among the people condemned as subversive by the
Daughters of the American Revolution. He thanked the DAR for this honor in the *Crisis*, May
1928 (35:169).

1. Mrs. Ware, wife of the second president of Atlanta University, was a very active member of
the campus community during Du Bois's first tenure there. I have not been able to further
identify Sylvia Wilcox Razey.

22 April 1940

Mrs. Sylvia Wilcox Razey
My dear Madam:

In accordance with your letter of February 12, I am enclosing my genealogical chart filled in to the best of my knowledge.

Very sincerely yours,
W. E. B. Du Bois

[Enclosure]

GENEALOGY CHART

Descendants of the American Revolution

Name—Du Bois, W. E. Burghardt

Address—Atlanta University, Atlanta, Georgia

Descendant of (American Revolutionary Ancestor)

Tom Burghardt

1. I am the son of Alfred Du Bois, born in 1825 in Haiti, died in (about) 1870 in New Milford, Connecticut, married on February 5, 1867 in————to Mary Burghardt, born on January 14, 1831 in Great Barrington, Massachusetts, died on March 23, 1885, in Great Barrington, Massachusetts.

2. The said Mary Burghardt was the child of Othello Burghardt, born on November 18, 1791, in Great Barrington, Massachusetts, died on September 19, 1872 in Great Barrington, married on September 19, 1811 in Great Barrington to Sarah Lampman, born on July 7, 1793 in Hillsdale, New York, died on January 19, 1879 in Great Barrington.

3. The said Othello Burghardt was the child of Jacob Burghardt born on November 13, 1791, died in Great Barrington, married to Violet, died in Great Barrington.

4. The said Jacob Burghardt was the child of Tom Burghardt born about 1725 in Africa, died about 1797 in Great Barrington, married to Betsy Vosburg.

DETAILS SHOWING THE FAMILY DESCENT: Give reference to a recognized authority for the above statement of birth, marriage and death. Statements based upon TRADITION alone cannot be considered.

1st Gen.—Tom Burghardt (see Service Record)
2nd Gen.—Jacob Burghardt (see Census of 1790)
3rd Gen.—Othello Burghardt See Vital Records of Great Barrington, Mass.
4th Gen.—Mary   "   "   "   "   "   "   "
5th. Gen.—William E. Burghardt   See Vital Records of Great Barrington, Mass.
6th Gen.—Yolande Du Bois Williams "   "   "   "   "   "   "
7th Gen.—DuBois Williams—(born in Philadelphia)

State authority for Service claimed by Volume and page—Record Index to the Military Archives of Massachusetts, Volume 23, p. 2.

Tom (who afterwards assumed the surname of Burghardt, after the family in which he was previously held to service) "Appears with the rank of Private on the Muster and Payroll of Capt. John Spoor's Co., Col. John Ashley's (Berkshire Co.) regt. *Engaged* Oct. 15, 1780. *Discharged* Oct. 17, 1780.

Time of service, 4 days. Company marched northward by order of Brig. Gen. Fellows on an alarm when Fort Ann and Fort George were taken by the enemy. Reported a Negro."

Du Bois called his Dusk of Dawn, *in its subtitle,* An Essay toward an Autobiography of a Race Concept; *its publication date was 6 September 1940. He meant the subtitle to indicate that the work was not intended as an autobiography in the conventional sense, where the individual involved was described in detail with emphasis upon personal matters. The work was read in manuscript by Du Bois's colleague at Atlanta Ira Reid, and Reid's comments upon it were exceedingly probing. There is no response to Reid's questions in the Du Bois papers—perhaps the two men discussed the matter in person; and if so, one regrets deeply that the conversation was not recorded. In many ways, the questions Reid here poses make up the body of writings in Afro-American history since 1940; Du Bois paid some degree of attention to certain among them in his posthumously published* Autobiography *(1968).*

Atlanta, Ga., February 15, 1940

Dear Doctor Du Bois:

I have been thinking very seriously about the matter of your autobiography, and the more I do so the more I regret that so many things are left unsaid. It seems to me that the history of the Negro in the United States, apart from the mass aspect of slavery, is largely a matter of biography. All that has been momentous in our life has been built around the activity and thinking of a few men who have dared to do, dared to think. Such may not be true of our future—and I hope it will not—but it is certainly true of our past and present.

Nothing would please us more, would reveal more than a fuller elaboration of those affairs, movements, ideas, successes and failures, personalities and misunder-standings that you have seen in the picture for more than half a century. Washington, Douglass, Moton, Johnson have all failed us on this point. Your essay rends part of the veil, but we still see too dimly.

[William Monroe] Trotter has been given too little attention in history. You knew him well and long. What did he mean to the progressive elements of the race in those early days? What type of person was he? What of Washington? What did he want to know of you during that first conference when you did all of the talking? What of Douglass? Moton? Dunbar? Chesnutt? the Grimkés? What of Villard? [John R.] Shillady? the Spingarns? Others? When I say "what of" I mean what of their racial and social points of view? Many a time you disagreed with one or the other of them. Why?

Why did Hope call that Harpers Ferry meeting "radical"? Wht has happened to those things we called "radical" in those days? You have seen the label change. In what way? What of that setting up of the General Education Board—the ride from Hampton south? You only whet our appetites with what you say. Whence the Pan-African Conference idea? Did you alone conceive it? Why? Why was there so much

Du Bois at Fisk University, probably at the time of receiving an honorary Doctor of Letters (1938). Photograph from the New York Public Library.

Du Bois's seventieth birthday party, February 1938. Standing, left to right, are Charles S. Johnson, Yolande Du Bois Williams, James Weldon Johnson, Ira De A. Reid, Rufus Clement, and William Stanley Braithwaite; Du Bois and Mrs. Du Bois are seated, center, with Joel Spingarn at the right. The woman seated left has not been identified. Photograph courtesy of the University of Massachusetts Library.

trouble getting it started? And why did it cease? I mean did you really get tired of the "awfulness" of some of these discussions in the United States? Did you really believe that we were still too "preliterate" to discuss world problems?

What of the person side of WEBD? He has notes that were made in grade school! His work was always organized—calendars for the whole week, for years! Do you realize how few of us work that way? You remember the introduction of Teddy Roosevelt—why do you remember it so well? What struck you as so significant about it?

What attended the rise of the Urban League? The Commission on Interracial Cooperation? (I understand that W. W. Alexander has now told the Commission that its work was all wrong, and that it is time to stop this "good-will mess" and go to work.) What are your reactions and your evaluations of the Washington speech in Atlanta? Not as you saw them in *Souls of Black Folk* (THEN), but NOW. What of the struggles in those first Atlanta studies? How does it happen that they can still be cited with scientific respect? What of the Negro Academy? That seemed such a promising movement. What of the jobs you turned down and did not get—Washington, for example, and Tuskegee?

These are parts of your life. I believe that you can tell the story better than anyone else. And I do wish that you and your publishers could see a way in which it could be done. Personally and economically you and they have nothing to lose, while posterity and history have everything to gain thereby.

Cordially yours,
Ira De A Reid

Du Bois's wife was born Nina Gomer and was originally from Iowa. Du Bois met her as a student when he taught at Wilberforce; the two were married in May 1896. There is a glowing description of her and of their marriage in Du Bois's Autobiography *(1968; pp. 187–88). Of course, the young couple lived together in Philadelphia while Du Bois did his research for the University of Pennsylvania, 1897–98, and they established a home together when he began teaching in Atlanta. Their firstborn child, Burghardt, died in Atlanta as an infant—the parents were convinced because of foul water and other deprivations characteristic of the ghetto. The boy was buried in Massachusetts, away from jim-crow, and Mrs. Du Bois soon thereafter made it clear she would no longer live in the South. The Du Boises lived in New York City (both in Brooklyn and in Manhattan) while Du Bois worked for the NAACP (1910–34), but when he went back to teach at Atlanta, Mrs. Du Bois decided to live either in New York or Baltimore with their daughter, Yolande, then a teacher of French in high school. This arrangement endured until Mrs. Du Bois died in 1950; Du Bois spent holidays and weekends, whenever possible, with them.*

The Du Boises shared interests; Mrs. Du Bois was herself active in NAACP work and in anti-war efforts. A characteristic letter is one Du Bois wrote her soon after returning from one of his frequent lecture tours.

Atlanta, Ga., February 21, 1940

My dear Nina:

I have been meaning to send you some books for reading according to your request but have neglected them until now. I am sending three books, one I am sure you will like, *Indians of the Americas* by Edwin R. Embree. The others may also interest you although they are rather long; John Gunther's *Inside Europe* which has been regarded as one of the best of recent books and Carlson and Bates' biography of William Randolph Hearst.[1] I will send you some others as I come across them.

I have just returned from a pleasant trip to the Middlewest: Cleveland, Chicago, Detroit, Dayton, Frankfort, Kentucky. I delivered eight lectures and one or two other talks and had an interesting luncheon with Embree of the Rosenwald Fund. There were present among others: Langston Hughes, Arna Bontemps and Richard Wright, the new young Negro author.

I succeeded in getting a cold at last from the change and snow of the North but I think I have gotten it in hand now. I hope you got through the extraordinary weather without harm and that you and the baby were warm enough. I am glad you got the flowers.

Thank DuBois for her Valentine and birthday greeting.

Yours with love,

Will

In February 1940, Alexander Alland, whose distinction as a photographer was already consider-able, proposed to Du Bois (who did not know him) that they collaborate on a photographic-text volume marking the seventy-fifth anniversary of the adoption of the Thirteenth Amendment to the Constitution. Du Bois asked for details concerning the proposal. The exchange that followed contains significant indications of Du Bois's estimates of his Black contemporaries; the papers of Du Bois do not reveal why the project never was realized and the final letter available there is that of 26 April 1940, published here.

New York, N. Y., March 5, 1940

Dear Dr. Du Bois:

It gives me great pleasure to elaborate more on the plan for a book designed to commemorate the 75th anniversary of the abolition of slavery in the United States.

As I mentioned in my previous lettter, I visualize this volume as a pictorial document, graphically describing the cultural activities taking place throughout the country, as well as the individual achievements of outstanding leaders among the Negro people. To my estimation, the pictorial content should be combined with 25–30,000 words.

---

1. The books he mentions are: Edwin R. Embree, *Indians of the Americas: Historical Pageant* (Boston: Houghton Mifflin Co., 1939); John Gunther, *Inside Europe* (New York: Harper and Bros., 1936); Oliver Carlson and Ernest Sutherland Bates, *Hearst: Lord of San Simeon* (New York: Viking Press, 1936).

I have no doubt, that my work, meeting the highest standards of photography, if combined with your inspired and authoritative literary work, will find a ready publisher. Lately books comprised of full page photographic reproductions with correlated text, are coming into favor. I am convinced that our joint efforts on such an original and timely subject will not only meet with great success, but act as a contributing factor toward better race relationship.

I am sure you have a clear idea as to what form a book of this nature should take, and will leave it entirely to you, as you are best qualified to judge. I will need your guidance in selecting the subject matter, and your introduction to the individuals whose cooperation it will be necessary to secure.

May I suggest that the book be titled "75 Years" and include several forewords by some well known people who have been instrumental in fostering better race relationship, among them, Mrs. Franklin D. Roosevelt, Harold Ickes, Mayors Maury Maverick and [Fiorello] La Guardia, and others.

My original intention, was to secure funds for this work, from the Julius Rosenwald Foundation, and so approach you with the necessary financial backing. Unfortunately, since I wrote you last, I received a reply from them expressing interest, but that my request came too late for this year's consideration.

After discussing this problem with my literary agent, he pointed out that if we could prepare a few chapters and a general outline he might be able to secure a publisher's contract with an advance. I am in a position to prepare photographs of some people living in the metropolitan area. Richard Wright, Augusta Savage, Paul Robeson and Countee Cullen, I am sure will cooperate with me. I already have interesting photographs of the activities in the library of Sandy Springs, Maryland, which was established by the James Weldon Johnson Literary Group, and the induction of Judge Herman E. Moore as District Judge for the Virgin Islands.[1]

Recently I spent four months in the Virgin Islands, where I worked on material for a forthcoming book. The photographs I took there, will soon be exhibited in the New School for Social Research and the 135th Street Library.

So that you can see how my work has been received, I am enclosing excerpts from some of the reviews on the book, "Portrait of New York," published last year.[2]

Hoping that you will agree to our collaboration, I am most anxious to hear from you as soon as possible.

Sincerely yours,
Alexander Alland

1. Herman E. Moore, educated at Howard University and in law at Boston University, practiced law in Massachusetts and Illinois and in 1939 was appointed judge of the United States District Court in the Virgin Islands.

2. In addition to *Portrait of New York*, with Felix Riesenberg (New York: Macmillan Co., 1939), Alland produced *American Counterpoint*, with an introduction by Pearl Buck (New York: John Day, 1943); and contributed the photographs to James W. Wise, *The Springfield Plan* (New York: Viking Press, 1945).

Atlanta, Ga., 14 March 1940

Mr. Alexander Alland
My dear Sir:

I am interested in your letter of March 5 and I shall be glad to cooperate with you if I can. Chiefly, of course, there will come so far as my part of the work is concerned a matter of critical judgment as to just who should be included. To illustrate what I mean: you mention Richard Wright, Augusta Savage, Paul Robeson and Countee Cullen. They represent widely different degrees of accomplishment. Richard Wright has done a first-class job and should be included. Augusta Savage is a hard working artisan but scarcely a first class sculptor.[1] Our greatest Negro sculptor is Elizabeth Prophet who has work in the Rhode Island Museum and New York Museum of Modern Art. Paul Robeson and Countee Cullen in quite different ways should be included. I think you see what I mean. I suppose the next thing would be for us to decide upon just who and what should be included and as that would be largely a matter of the photographs you could have available the initiative would be with you. Suppose, therefore, you send me a list of photographs that you have and propose to get and that I criticize by suggesting some omissions and some other inclusions. If you have any other methods of procedure in mind, I should be glad to hear from you.

I shall probably not be in New York before summer although I might be called there this spring. I shall be glad to hear from you at your convenience.

Very sincerely yours,
W. E. B. Du Bois

New York, N.Y., March 20, 1940

Dear Dr. Du Bois:

Thank you very much for the interest you expressed in your letter of March 14.

I appreciate the reason for your exclusion of Augusta Savage, as it was my original intention that only people of outstanding achievement on a national scale should be represented in the proposed book. There should not be any room in it for apologies, substituting quantity for quality. That is why I look forward to your collaboration.

Feeling deeply the sentiment you expressed in the beautiful lines of dedication to your grand-daughter, in your latest book,[2] be assured of my determination that our

1. Augusta Savage (1900–62) exhibited at the New York World's Fair in 1939–40 and there gained considerable renown. She was born in Florida, and studied at Cooper Union in New York and in Paris with grants from the Rosenwald and Carnegie foundations. Her work won awards in France and is exhibited in leading galleries. The head of Du Bois in the 135th Street branch of the New York Public Library is by Augusta Savage and is called "truly masterful" by the late James A. Porter in his *Modern Negro Art* (New York: Dryden Press, 1943), p. 138. Porter tends to agree with Du Bois's estimate of Augusta Savage as compared with Elizabeth Prophet—he describes Prophet as "a sculptor of firmer concentration and more fluent temperament" (p. 139).

2. He refers to Du Bois's *Black Folk Then and Now*, which states: "This book is dedicated to my grand-daughter, DuBois Williams on her sixth birthday in the hope that her bright eyes may one day see some of the things I dream."

work should be one of the outstanding contributions of 1940. But, feeling as I do, I do not believe I am competent to judge the content, nor capable of preparing the necessary text.

I am not sure that I stated clearly in my previous letters to what extent your participation in this work is needed. Your work would necessarily consist of the preparation of a historical background on the part the Negro plays in the cultural life of America, today; to compile a list of names from various fields of endeavor; to write or edit biographies on those of your selection. My proposition is, that we do this book as partners, you the writing, and I the photography and layout. Of course all benefits are to be shared equally on a fifty percent basis.

In the last two weeks I have been making contacts with some people located in the metropolitan area, and soon will proceed with the photography of Marian Anderson, Countee Cullen, Katherine Dunham, Langston Hughes, Paul Robeson and Ethel Waters. I already have taken an interesting photograph of Richard Wright, who is shortly leaving for Mexico. There are some others about whom I would like your advice. Would you include any of the following names: Rosamond Johnson, Claude McKay, Walter White, James H. Hubert, Roland Hayes, Harry T. Burleigh, James Ford, and Judges, Hubert Delany, Myles Paige, Jane Bolin?

Having a great deal of experience in designing books, I will see to it that our book will be an exceptionally handsome volume. As the occasion demands, I visualize it as a rather large format, measuring about nine by twelve inches, with full page reproductions of each photograph printed on the side of the page, with short biographies of about 500 words facing each. Of course the book should be divided into chapters, each covering a specific field preceded by an introductory foreword to each chapter. I feel it is essential to include a short chapter reflecting on the work of various Negro organizations promoting culture among the young. To keep this book within the reach of the general public, the price should not exceed $3.50.

Please let me know if you are under option to any publisher and whether you would prefer to have your own literary agent handle this book. It would be splendid if it could be ready for fall or early winter publication, to co-incide with the anniversary which, I feel, must be celebrated.

Since we are located far apart and correspondence is not the best avenue for collaboration, I will try to visit you as soon as possible, as I am also anxious to photograph you at the University. Of course for the sake of economy, my trip to Atlanta must take in as many visits as necessary. Preliminary arrangements, with those you choose to include, must be made before hand, notifying them of our aims and requesting their cooperation.

If you would be kind enough to send me a letter at your earliest convenience, acknowledging our collaboration—a letter that I could show to other people, it would be of great help to my preliminary work.

Hoping to hear from you soon, I am,

Very sincerely yours,
Alexander Alland

Atlanta, Ga., 4 April 1940

My dear Mr. Alland:

I have been in a push since January getting out two copies of our quarterly, *Phylon*, and doing some work on the Encyclopaedia of the Negro. During the spring and summer, however, I shall have more time to devote to your proposition.

I suggest that our basis of selection be a matter of types rather than exhaustive inclusion. This will save me some difficulties of temperament and psychology. For instance, suppose the book was provisionally called *Types Of American Negroes Seventy-Five Years After* and that from the following short list of persons we make a preliminary write-up of twelve people to show to the publishers. Eventually I think all of these should be included and several others. I should want to be as catholic as possible and at the same time careful to avoid undeserved praise and unworthy publicity. Mordecai Johnson, President of Howard University; Channing Tobias, senior secretary of the colored YMCA; Charles Wesley, professor of history, Howard University; E. Franklin Frazier, head of the department of sociology, Howard; Ernest Just, biologist at Howard; Charles H. Thompson, editor of the *Journal of Negro Education;* Sterling Brown, poet; W. L. Dawson, head of the music department at Tuskegee; H. M. Bond, president of Fort Valley State College; Aaron Douglas, artist; Elizabeth Prophet, sculptor; Countee Cullen, poet; Richard Wright, novelist; Marian Anderson, singer; William Grant Still, composer; Ira De A. Reid, sociologist at Atlanta University; Charles S. Johnson, sociologist, Fisk University; W. R. Banks, president of Prairie View State College; Paul Williams, architect in Los Angeles; Paul Robeson, Katherine Dunham, Rosamond Johnson, Roland Hayes, Harry T. Burleigh, Myles Paige, Jane Bolin, Carter Woodson.

Perhaps the best way to begin would be for you to let me know which twelve persons among the above you already have photographs of or could easily get them. Then I will prepare a general outline of fields of activity and special short biographies of the twelve persons whom you have. I could probably finish this sometime in May.

I am under no option to any publisher and have never had a literary agent.

I should be glad to have your reaction to this proposal at your convenience.

Very sincerely yours,
W. E. B. Du Bois

New York, N.Y., April 16, 1940

Dear Dr. Du Bois:

Just a short note to let you know that I am busy preparing action portraits of people included in your preliminary list. From the list of names you sent me in your last letter, there are only ten that live in New York City. I have already photographed Richard Wright and Countee Cullen, and am in touch with the other eight whose photographs I will soon be making. I could now very conveniently secure photographs of: W. C. Handy—composer, Ethel Waters and Langston Hughes as well, should you wish to include them in our volume.

I will send you the prints for criticism as soon as they are ready. Please let me know, at your convenience if you have made any more selections of people living in, or about, N.Y.C.

Very sincerely yours,
Alexander Alland

Atlanta, Ga., 26 April 1940

My dear Mr. Alland:

I think it would be quite all right to add to the persons mentioned in my last list: W. C. Handy, Ethel Waters and Langston Hughes. They all deserve inclusion. E. Franklin Frazier and Charles Wesley, both of Washington, are apt to be pretty often in New York. Ira Reid will be there this summer. I do not at present think of any other persons living in and near New York that I should like to include but I will think the matter over.

Very sincerely yours,
W. E. B. Du Bois

Rufus E. Clement (1900–67), born in Atlanta, was educated at Livingstone College in North Carolina, the Garrett Biblical Institute in Illinois (from which he received a divinity degree), and Northwestern University. He served in the ministry and as a teacher; from 1931 to 1936 he was a guiding spirit at the newly founded Louisville (Kentucky) Municipal College for Negroes. Upon the death of John Hope, he was selected—with Du Bois's support—as president of Atlanta University, which position he held from 1937 until his death.

Clement and Du Bois did not get along well; by 1940 the edginess between them was clear.* The communications that follow came in the midst of several memoranda exchanged by the two men, but they are self-explanatory.

1 March 1940

Memorandum to President Clement:

I am disappointed that you have not answered to date my second memorandum of January 31.

May I review the facts? On May 19, 1939, we had an interview in your office in which I told you that the appropriation made by the Phelps Stokes Fund to supplement Miss [Irene] Diggs' salary would probably terminate December, 1939 and that there ought to be some clear understanding as to her future connection with this institution. You promised that beginning with the month of January, 1940 and continuing to the close of the academic year, July 1, the University would pay Miss Diggs at the rate of $150 a month.

You did not say then or at any other time (until your memorandum of January 31, 1940) that after July, 1940 Miss Diggs would be permanently hired on a nine

---

* Du Bois discusses his relationship with Clement in his posthumously published *Autobiography* (pp. 322–23).

months basis at $150 a month. This may have been in your mind but you did not mention it to me. If you had, I should have immediately pointed out that this was a serious reduction in Miss Diggs' annual salary which she could hardly be expected to accept. I assumed that you planned subsequent consultation would be had with me as to Miss Diggs' status after July 1, 1940. This was the message I gave Miss Diggs.

Meantime the appropriation of the Phelps Stokes Fund [for the encyclopedia project] was renewed; but it was renewed of course on the understanding that Miss Diggs would still be able to give service in return. Because of the establishment of *Phylon*, however, Miss Diggs has had no time either in December, January or February to do any work upon the Encyclopaedia except a half dozen letters. What little work has been otherwise done, has been done by me personally. I have already written Mr. Stokes concerning this situation and I assume of course that you do not suggest that I use trust funds for university work.

The reason for this is clear: when I proposed to you undertaking the publication of a quarterly magazine for $2,000 it was on the assumption that part of Miss Diggs' time would be available and that her salary would not be a part of the *Phylon* budget. If I had not assumed this, it would have been impossible to plan the magazine for $2,000.

You propose now that I should have the services of a clerk for only nine months of the year. You have surely forgotten to take into account the third and fourth editions of *Phylon*. The publication of *Phylon* for the third quarter will take place between July 1 and July 15. It will require clerical aid for practically the whole of the month of July to distribute this copy. Moreover, the fourth copy of *Phylon* must appear in October and must be prepared in the month of September which means that the *Phylon* office must be operated during July and during September; and of course during August there must be someone to attend to mailing and incoming subscriptions. It would be quite impossible to dispense with clerical aid at this time.

We have no prospect of any sum from *Phylon* available for a secretary's salary. We may take in this year $500 or more in subscriptions; but out of this must be paid all costs of enlarging the magazine, all payments for articles, all costs of printing and postage for circulation drives, all extra engraving, the costs of expert printing advice, copyright, patent registry and correspondence. These costs cannot for the four issues of the magazine amount to less than $400 or $500. In setting the cost of *Phylon* at $2,000, I had counted upon the revenue from subscriptions to carry these extra expenses. In other words, it was easy to know that the total cost of the magazine would be between three and four thousand dollars; that a part of this would be met by subscriptions and part by use of the clerical force in my office leaving a balance of about $2,000 to be paid by the University appropriation. This whole calculation is now upset if the University requires *Phylon* to support in part the cost of a secretary.

I am, therefore, asking specifically: first, will the University fulfill its promise to me to pay Miss Diggs $150 a month for January through June, 1940; provided that if any part of her services in this period are used for Encyclopaedia work, the University be reimbursed for this time by Phelps Stokes Funds? Secondly: will the University guarantee the sum of $1,500 for the fiscal year 1940 (July 1, 1940–June 30, 1941), for clerical assistance in this department, one-half for secretarial aid for me in my writing in accordance with past arrangements; and one-half for clerical services in connection with *Phylon?*

W. E. B. Du Bois

6 March 1940

Memo to President Clement:

I am enclosing a memorandum which I dictated covering our conference yesterday. I should be glad to have my attention called to any misapprehension in this statement.

We have pressing need for a file case for letters and manuscripts in connection with *Phylon*. I hesitate to purchase it because a new one would cost about $30. Is it possible that you have in the office of the Administration Building a file which we could at least borrow for the year with the idea of returning it and buying a new one next year if necessary?

Will you kindly return to me the statement as to the mailing machine together with any comment which you may have?

W. E. B. Du Bois

[Enclosure]

5 March 1940

On March 5, Mr. Du Bois had a conference with President Clement with regard to the future employment of Miss Diggs and of clerical help for *Phylon*. The President stated that at the time of the interview, May 19, he had agreed that the University would pay Miss Diggs at the rate of $150 a month from January 1 to the end of the fiscal year July 1, if the Phelps Stokes appropriation was not forthcoming. When he did not hear further from Mr. Du Bois he assumed that the appropriation had been renewed and that the University was obligated to the extent of only $100 a month.

Mr. Du Bois pointed out that at the time he was very busy getting the new magazine started and that he ought to have reminded the President that while the Phelps Stokes appropriation was renewed, that Miss Diggs had been unable to give time during December, January and February to that work. The President agreed that considering these facts the University would see that Miss Diggs received her full salary of $150 a month from January 1 to the end of the fiscal year. Mr. Du Bois agreed to reimburse the University for any time which Miss Diggs was able to give the Encyclopaedia during March, April, May and June.

The President also said that he planned to have the University employ Miss Diggs at the rate of $150 a month for nine months of the fiscal year 1940–41. Mr. Du Bois brought to his attention that this would be a serious decrease in Miss Diggs' salary; that if this had been mentioned before he would have discussed it at length. The President thought that this had been specifically mentioned in May but agreed that there was necessity for Miss Diggs' work as Mr. Du Bois' secretary and in connection with *Phylon* for twelve months in the year with one month's vacation. The President, however, disliked to ask the trustees that the current appropriation for *Phylon* be increased since with Mr. Du Bois' consent, he had promised to publish the magazine for $2,000. Mr. Du Bois acknowledged that it would have been better to have made it clear to the board that this appropriation would only be sufficient in case the University furnished him a secretary for twelve months and that he had assumed this was understood. The figure of $2,000 was thus left partially unexplained because of this assumption and because of his anxiety to get the magazine started after six years of waiting.

The President finally agreed to leave the matter at present hoping that between now and July 1, some way would be found of supplying the necessary $450 which would make Miss Diggs' salary of $1,800 for the year without appeal to the trustees; and that in future years this salary for the service of the secretary for Mr. Du Bois and clerical aid for *Phylon* would be paid jointly out of the budget of the University and the University appropriation for *Phylon*.

In the 1930s there was founded by F. H. Hammurabi in Chicago the organization World Wide Friends of Africa; its headquarters was called House of Knowledge. Its founder affirmed that "a race without knowledge of its history is like a tree without roots," and his organization sponsored weekly meetings, lectures, and films on Africa's past; this work continued for a generation. *

An exchange between the director of Friends of Africa and Du Bois occurred early in 1940.

Chicago, Ill., March 2, 1940

Dear Sir:

We are gathering together a list of books on Africa for those who are interested, for our many lecturers and our own collection. We note your very excellent contribution in your last book, *Africa, Then and Now [Black Folk Then and Now*, 1939], that you too are aiding in restoring the heritage of the black man.

We would like to have your opinion and a list of the best books for high school and college students about Africa written by any Africans or Americans or Europeans who have gone to Africa.

Do you have any African collections at Atlanta University?

What would you consider the oldest African collections and best in the States?

But in particular to your knowledge as a scholar what would you consider the oldest written African cultures on the East and West Coasts or any other sections in ancient Ethiopia, Cushite, Zimbabwe, etc., and how far back do you say they go from your researches?

May we thank you for a prompt reply.

Dasipe or Thank you.

F. H. Hammurabi

---

* See E. U. Essien-Udom, *Black Nationalism: A Search for Identity in America* (Chicago: University of Chicago Press, 1962), pp. 50, 162.

Atlanta, Ga., March 14, 1940

Mr. F. H. Hammurabi
My dear Sir:

There are not many available general books on Africa and its history. There are innumerable books on certain phases of African life: discovery, travel, description of various parts. The best recent general book is Lord Hailey's *An African Survey* published by the Oxford University Press, 1938. Another good book for general reading is Miss Gollock's *Sons of Africa* and a later one on *African Women*. Readable also is Lord Olivier, *The Anatomy of African Misery* and Middleton, *The Rape of Africa*. [1]

We have no notable collections on Africa at Atlanta University. The best collections of Africana are in the British Museum, London; the Museum of Anthropology in Berlin; and other collections in Vienna and Paris.

The oldest African cultures are those of Zimbabwe, Ethiopia and on the West Coast like Yoruba. They date back some one to three thousand or four thousand years before Christ.

Very sincerely yours,
W. E. B. Du Bois

One of the significant struggles in the 1930s and early 1940s was against peonage, which then was the condition of labor for millions of Black—and white—sharecroppers and tenant farmers in the South. It is with this effort that a letter from the Reverend Donald L. West—a white man born and raised in Georgia and a well-known poet and fighter against racism—is concerned. At this time, West was minister for the Christian Fellowship Parish in rural Ohio, having been driven out of Georgia earlier by threats upon his life.

Bethel, Ohio, March 23, 1940

Dear Mr. Du Bois:

You may recall that I visited you something like a year or two ago with Dr. Hedwig Kuhn. I'm writing you at this time because the recent issue of peonage in Georgia, and the struggle around it, has interested me deeply. In April I am scheduled to speak at a number of church conferences in the south, including one state conference of young people of the Congregational-Christian churches of Georgia near Buford. And I also hope, during the time down there, to spend several days in Oglethorpe County investigating, interviewing and talking with all classes of people from the preachers, court-house officials, to the sharecroppers of both races as well as the chief "boss man," Mr. [Will] Cunningham. It is my hope also that, in coming through Atlanta, I may have the pleasure of a visit with you, particularly to discuss this situation and get any helpful suggestions you may have.

1. The books not fully identified by Du Bois are: Georgina A. Gollock, *Sons of Africa* (New York: Friendship Press, 1928); Gollock, *Daughters of Africa* (London: Longmans, Green, 1932); Sydney H. (Lord) Olivier, *The Anatomy of African Misery* (London: Leonard and Virginia Woolf, 1927); Lamar Middleton, *The Rape of Africa* (New York: Random House, 1936).

Out of the investigation I hope, of course, to get ample materials for news stories and some feature articles, as well as a first-hand touch that will make it possible to better aid the efforts being made around Cincinnati. I was in Cincinnati interviewing some of the refugees from Mr. Cunningham's plantation recently, and their tales are surely blood-curdling.[1]

Would you tell me, please, whether you expect to be at home during the period of April 5 to 15th?

With good wishes and kind regards, I remain

Sincerely,

(Rev.) Donald L. West

Atlanta, Ga., 12 April 1940

Reverend Donald L. West
My dear Sir:

You must forgive my delay in answering your letter of March 23. I have been out of town and returned with a bad cold. I am afraid this letter may be too late for you but I shall be in town nearly all the time this spring and will be glad to have you call at any time.

Very sincerely yours,

W. E. B. Du Bois

John Hope Franklin (b. 1915), now professor of history at the University of Chicago and in the 1950s chairman of the history department at Brooklyn College, was at the early stage of his distinguished career, teaching at St. Augustine's College in Raleigh, North Carolina, when he wrote to Du Bois for information.

Raleigh, N. C., March 26, 1940

Dr. W. E. B. Du Bois
Dear Sir:

I am, at present, preparing a paper entitled "Courses concerning the Negro in Negro Colleges."[2] In trying to give a historical introduction to the courses offered at present, I find it difficult to ascertain just what courses, if any, were offered concerning the Negro in the period before 1914.

1. Details concerning peonage at this period and the struggle against it especially in Ogle-thorpe County, Ga., will be found in Herbert Aptheker, *Afro-American History: The Modern Era* (Secaucus, New Jersey: Citadel Press, 1971), pp. 191–201. Escaped peons were sent, by bus, from Lexington, Georgia, to New Orleans and from there to Cincinnati and then to Chicago, where a Black attorney, William Henry Huff (originally from Oglethorpe County, Georgia), was in charge of assisting the fugitives.

2. In a letter to the present editor, dated 14 November 1973, Professor Franklin stated that this paper was prepared for and delivered in 1940 at the annual meeting of the Association for Social Science Teachers. It was published under the title given in the letter in the *Quarterly Review of Higher Education Among Negroes* 8 (July 1940): 138–44.

It occurs to me that perhaps you had the opportunity to offer some formal courses concerning the Negro either at Wilberforce or during your first years of teaching at Atlanta University. If such was the case, I should appreciate any information which you may care to give concerning them. The difficulty of ascertaining information about courses offered in that early period is intensified by the fact that the college records are, in many instances, obviously incomplete. So, in a few cases of importance, I have sought to find out what was happening directly from the persons who may have had something to do with teaching courses concerning the Negro.

   Any information that you may give will, I assure you, be greatly appreciated.

Sincerely yours,
John Hope Franklin

11 April 1940

Mr. John Hope Franklin
My dear Sir:
   While I was at Wilberforce, '94–95 and '95–96, I gave no course on the Negro. I offered a course in sociology which would have touched the race problem but the University did not accept it. At the University of Pennsylvania as assistant instructor I was in charge of a special study of the Negro in the Seventh Ward, historically and sociologically. This became the basis of my studies afterwards at Atlanta University. They were outlined in the *Annals of the American Academy* in 1898.[1] At Atlanta University the studies instituted in 1896 and carried on until 1914 were done through a conference, that is, a meeting of persons interested from various parts of the United States and included university teachers and students. There were, however, no special undergraduate courses which touched the Negro except incidentally. In teaching United States history we gave attention to the Negro but there was no course in the history of the Negro in the United States. Also there were no courses on Africa or African history.

   I trust this information may be what you want.

Very sincerely yours,
W. E. B. Du Bois

Frank J. Klingberg (1883–1968), born in Kansas, was educated there and at Yale. He participated in several organizations seeking disarmament and was at various points a feature writer for the Los Angeles Times, *but his major occupation was as professor of history at the University of California in Los Angeles. His main historical interests were Anglo-American relations, British reform movements, and—an early concern for a white scholar—Afro-American history, especially in the colonial period.*

1. Du Bois, "The Study of the Negro Problems," *Annals of the American Academy of Political and Social Science* 11 (January 1898): 1–23.

Los Angeles, Calif., April 1, 1940

Dear Professor Du Bois:

May I trouble you about a citation which I wish to find in your works? Although I have most of your volumes in my library and also in the University Library for the use of my students, I do not recall just where I read that you point out that up to the year 1890, the migration of Negroes from Africa to the New World was as great as the migration of white immigrants from Europe. I wish to refer to this in a paper I am writing on South Carolina.

I am just reading your *Black Folk*, with much profit. May I send you with my compliments a copy of a recent monograph that may be of some interest to you? It is part of a volume, *Anglican Humanitarianism in Colonial New York*, which is now in the press.[1]

With thanks for any trouble my query may cause,

Sincerely yours,
Frank J. Klingberg

Atlanta, Ga., 4 April 1940

My dear Mr. Klingberg:

I do not remember making the statement to which you refer nor if I made it but I think it may be approximately true. On page 142 of my *Black Folk: Then and Now* you will see that I refer to [Edward E.] Dunbar's estimate that the total immigration of Negroes to the New World was about fifteen million. Of course this is partially guesswork but I do not know any better way to check it. It is estimated that about fifteen million came to the United States from Europe between 1821 and 1892 and to this would have to be added the white immigration to South and Central America. There must have been, therefore, a point somewhere between 1850 and 1890 when the immigration of whites and blacks to America was approximately equal. I am sorry that I cannot give you more explicit information.

Very sincerely yours,
W. E. B. Du Bois

The Fisk News, *a student newspaper of the university, published an article early in 1940 treating in part of Du Bois's days at Fisk. It contained some inaccuracies, and these evoked a letter from Du Bois to the* News's *editor that contained reminiscenses about his college years.*

Atlanta, Ga., April 11, 1940

My dear Sir:

I thank Mr. William Baxter Collier for his kindly reference concerning me but want to make some corrections: my only connection with athletics at Fisk was through

---

1. (Philadelphia: Church Historical Society, 1940). In 1941, Klingberg published *An Appraisal of the Negro in Colonial South Carolina* (Washington: Associated Publishers). There is a selected bibliography of his writings in *Negro History Bulletin*, December 1957, pp. 52–57.

helping to raise money to start the first gymnasium. Tom Calloway and myself and others raised an initial sum of seven hundred dollars. Football, however, was not started as a collegiate sport until after I had left college. I was not the first editor of the *Fisk Herald*. The *Fisk Herald* was in my day carried on entirely by students through three literary societies. The costs were defrayed entirely by subscriptions and advertisements. I do not know who the first editor was but when I arrived at Fisk in the fall of '85, A. O. Coffin of Texas was editor and I was made exchange editor. In '86–87, I served as literary editor and '87–88, as editor-in-chief. It should not be forgotten that the *Fisk Herald* was later revived under my editorship. The Associated Fisk Clubs reestablished the *Fisk Herald* in 1924 and issued two numbers of vol. 33 in 1924 and 1925. This was during the fight for reorganizing Fisk University. I think that a search through the library would reveal the name of the first editor of the *Herald*. [1]

Very sincerely yours,

W. E. B. Du Bois

After a lapse of over two decades, Du Bois sought to reinstitute the studies of the conditions and prospects of Afro-American people that had made the Atlanta University Studies of the late nineteenth and early twentieth centuries world-famous. He did manage, after great effort, to make a start in this direction with what was called the First Phylon Institute and the Twenty-Fifth Atlanta University Conference, held 17–19 April 1941. This effort, which Du Bois charateristically projected as a ten-year one, was thwarted by the Second World War, just as the first studies had been terminated largely because of World War I.

Part of the funds for the Phylon Institute came from the Carnegie Corporation; this entailed considerable correspondence between Du Bois and F. P. Keppel, its executive officer. The two letters that follow convey the essence of Du Bois's ideas on the subject.

New York City, April 17, 1940

Dear Dr. Du Bois:

I have your note of April 4th, and I'm authorizing the Treasurer to send you a check for $1,000. I am also noting on our records that a similar sum is to be earmarked for you in the grants-in-aid budget for 1940–41.

As this whole program of ours is experimental, we are watching the details carefully for their experience value, and it would therefore be helpful if we could have a statement of the studies for which our money will be used, and occasional reports on your progress as the work proceeds.

Sincerely yours,

F. P. Keppel

1. The first editor of the *Fisk Herald* was T. F. Sublett. On the struggle at Fisk in 1924–25, involving students and alumni, see Du Bois's "Opinion" in the April 1925 *Crisis* (29: 247–52), and his "Negroes in College," *Nation* 122 (3 March 1926): 228–30. Du Bois was responding to the article "The History of Athletics at Fisk," by William Baxter Collier, Jr., in the *Fisk News*, 11 April 1940, pp. 12–14. The information on the first editor of the *Fisk Herald* was obtained through the courtesy of Johnny J. Wheelbarger, of the Fisk University Library.

Atlanta, Ga., 26 April 1940

My dear Mr. Keppel:

I want to express my very deep appreciation of your check for one thousand [dollars] recently received and the promise of a similar check for 1940–41.

I propose to use this money as follows: my growing conviction has been since the depression that the fundamental problem facing American Negroes is securing a place in American industrial life. I am certain that if they simply wait to get their share in any change of plan and reorganization of economic life in America the so-called race problem will show itself by making their entrance into this economy late and uncertain and in this time of waiting and adjustment they will contribute to the national life a disproportionate amount of poverty, crime and disease. I am terribly afraid of the results of the depression on American Negroes already discernible and yet to be faced in the next generation. For that reason I want Negroes to begin intelligent planning for themselves, not of course for a separate economy but for the purpose of seeing how far their own efforts can help them toward economic security and toward ability to cooperate on an intelligent level with such economic planning as is going on in the world.

For that purpose I am going to use your first thousand dollars for assembling at Atlanta University early in the fall a Phylon Institute for economic study and planning among American Negroes. I am going to try to get about a dozen key men here, more if possible, but as I shall have to pay a considerable part of their traveling expenses the number must of necessity be limited. I want to get well-trained students of economics as well as practical observers and men of affairs. I am going to ask the University to entertain with board and lodging for a week and then I want to sit down and ask the question first: what do we know of the present economic conditions of the Negroes; what studies have been made or are in making; and what information can we begin to gather. Perhaps something can also be said in this meeting of possible future planning.

In the second meeting, 1940–41, I want to have reports from those who attended the first meeting and from others, published books and pamphlets and such preliminary matter as the Census may by that time have gotten out and then go further into the matter of asking what we know, what can we find out and what we can plan for betterment in the economic development of American Negroes.

I hope that by these two meetings and by publication of at least some of their findings in *Phylon* that sufficient interest may be aroused to make the Phylon Institute an annual meeting at Atlanta University and a seat of continuous planning of the human uplift of American Negroes.[1] On this economic foundation I hope we can expand and spread to other cultural accomplishments.

1. See on the Phylon Institute two pieces, unsigned but by Du Bois, in *Phylon* (Second Quarter 1941; 2: 146 and Third Quarter 1941; 2: 275–80); and Frank G. Davis, "The Nature, Scope, and Significance of the First Phylon Institute," *Phylon* 2 (Third Quarter 1941): 280–87. See also, by Du Bois, "The Twenty-Fifth Atlanta Conference," *Unity* 127 (November 1941): 145–46.

I should be very glad to have your comments and criticism of these plans and I shall from time to time keep you informed of their progress.

Again thanking you for your interest, I am

> Very sincerely yours,
> W. E. B. Du Bois

As editor of the newly founded Phylon, *Du Bois wrote to prospective contributors. One such exchange involved Langston Hughes.*

> New York City, May 1, 1940

My dear Dr. Du Bois:

Your letter of April 4th was waiting here when I ran into town for just a few days between lectures. I appreciate the request from *Phylon*; I liked the first issue of the magazine. Along with this letter I am sending an article on the "Blues" which you may be able to use. If you do not publish it, please return it to me.

> Sincerely yours,
> Langston Hughes

> Atlanta, Ga., May 24, 1940

My dear Mr. Hughes:

We shall be glad to use your article on the blues in the October number of *Phylon*[1] and at that time I shall send you a small check. When you have anything else, please let me know.

> Very sincerely yours,
> W. E. B. Du Bois

Unfortunate for Du Bois was the fact that the presidency of Spelman College of Atlanta University was held by Florence M. Read (1886–1973). Miss Read was born in Delevan, New York, and graduated from Mount Holyoke College in 1909. She served as Mount Holyoke's alumnae secretary for two years and served also, for a time, as secretary of Reed College in Oregon. From 1920 to 1927 she worked for the International Board of the Rockefeller Foundation; in 1927 she was appointed president of Spelman College in Atlanta (Laura Spelman was a member of the Rockefeller family, which endowed the college). She served as Spelman's president for twenty-six years, retiring as emeritus in 1953.*

After John Hope's death in 1936 and before the appointment in 1937 of Rufus Clement as his successor, Miss Read served as acting president of the university. There was some movement to appoint her president, but this idea was opposed by Du Bois. She was a devoutly religious woman

---

1. "Songs Called the Blues," *Phylon* 2 (Second Quarter 1941): 143–45.

* Miss Read died in April 1973 in California. There is an account of her life in the *Spelman Messenger*, May 1973, pp. 26–29. A memorial service for her was held at Spelman College on 30 May 1973.

and very conservative politically. Du Bois believed—and wrote—that she delayed his own appointment to Atlanta and was basically responsible for the six-year delay in the establishment of Phylon and the Phylon Institute idea. It was Miss Read who moved, at a meeting of Atlanta's trustees in 1944, the dismissal of Du Bois. †

Because of this relationship, and because they shared the same campus, the two exchanged few letters. One from Du Bois came in response to an invitation to speak at Spelman; another, from Miss Read, was written the next day but was devoted to another matter entirely and contained not a word in response to Du Bois's very pointed and characteristically frank letter.

Atlanta, Ga., May 6, 1940

My dear President Read:

I appreciate your invitation to speak at Spelman chapel this month, and I am sorry to have to decline.

It is now six years since you have extended me such an invitation. During this time I have spoken annually at Morehouse at its urgent request. One reason for your silence may have been, as you intimate, a desire not to overtax my strength; but the interval is too long for me to regard this as the real explanation. The reason is, I believe, that you do not agree in general with my ideas and are unwilling to have me express them. The number of Spelman students in my classes has always been very small and I have repeatedly been told how difficult it is to obtain your consent for a student to major in sociology. I recall how your determined opposition to any university periodical has cut five irreplaceable years from my creative life, despite John Hope's previous promises and his repeatedly expressed desire to have such a journal.

I am not questioning your motives in these decisions and attitudes. But I think you will admit that I am justified in the face of them in concluding that you do not regard my teaching of Spelman students as essential or desirable; or my ideas in general as deserving publicity.

For these reasons, Miss Read, I am with deep regret declining your kind invitation.

Very sincerely yours,
W. E. B. Du Bois

Atlanta, Georgia, May 7, 1940

To Dr. Du Bois

A group consisting of officers and trustees of the Rockefeller Foundation and General Education Board are expected on our campus Wednesday evening, May 8th. The party will consist of: Mr. Walter W. Stewart, Chairman of the Board of Trustees of the Rockefeller Foundation, Mr. Raymond B. Fosdick, President of the Rockefeller Foundation and the General Education Board, Dr. A. R. Mann, vice-president of the General Education Board and director of the southern program, Jackson Davis, associate director of the southern program of the General Education Board, Stacy

† See Du Bois's *Autobiography* (1968), pp. 301–2, 322–23.

May, Assistant Director for the Social Sciences of RF and GEB. Whether or not Mr. John D. Rockefeller, III, will be with the group I do not yet know.

I am asking several members of the Faculty to come to my house about 9:30 pm to meet these gentlemen informally. President Clement and I expect to take them to the play and will return to the house immediately after the play. If you do not go to the play, there will be someone at the house to admit you at 9:30.

Will you please leave word at my office during the day on Wednesday whether or not we may count on your coming?

Sincerely yours,
Florence M. Read

8 May 1940
Mr. Du Bois will be glad to come to Miss Read's house at 9:30 pm tonight.[1]

Robert R. Moton, the successor to Booker T. Washington as head of Tuskegee, was not one of the Black leaders Du Bois looked upon with favor, and, particularly in the period just after World War I, there had been sharp exchanges between the two men. Years mellowed the bitterness, and when Moton died in 1940 Du Bois published a moving, though not uncritical, tribute to him in his Amsterdam News *column (8 June 1940). He prepared a fuller evaluation of Moton's life for publication in* Phylon 1 *(Fourth Quarter 1940): 344–51, meant to be included eventually in the projected Encyclopedia of the Negro.*

Dr. Anson Phelps Stokes (1874–1958), a main supporter, as we have seen, of the encyclopedia idea, had been a trustee for many years of Tuskegee and had known both Washington and Moton very well. Hence, Du Bois sent the manuscript of the essay meant for Phylon *to Stokes for criticism; this inviting of criticism from people whose opinions he respected—and perhaps especially if they differed from his—was habitual with Du Bois. The result was a meaningful exchange.*

New York City, October 8, 1940
My dear Dr. Du Bois:

I took the first opportunity this morning on the train ride down from Lenox [Mass.] to look over your draft of a biography of Major Moton. I read it with the deepest interest. May I make the following comments:

1. I think that under all the circumstances you have done a difficult task extremely well.

2. General Armstrong's successor at Hampton was, as you probably know, Dr. Hollis B. Frissell. You will probably notice that his name has been misspelled throughout.

1. On 4 June 1940, Florence Read wrote inviting Du Bois to speak at the Spelman College chapel service some morning in October; his papers contain no written response to this request.

3. There were a few positions which Major Moton held in addition to those named that are perhaps worthy of mention. He was for many years, I think, President of the Negro Business Men's Association in which he took a deep interest. He was also a member of the Board of Directors of the Encyclopedia of the Negro.

4. It was he who secured the gift of several million dollars for the Hampton-Tuskegee Fund from Mr. George Eastman.

5. I think he was the speaker representing the colored people at the dedication of the Lincoln Memorial in Washington.

6. I have heard him say, I think, that his forebears were of the Mandingo Tribe on his father's side.

7. I think that more can be said of his exceptional administrative capacity as head of Tuskegee. The fact that there was no white man on the staff and that everything went like clock work with admirable discipline and order is worth recording. Tuskegee was, I think, one of the few higher educational institutions for the Negro that did not pass through a crisis after the World War. This was mainly due to Major Moton's wisdom and tact.

8. If I remember rightly, there was one intermediate step not mentioned in the Tuberculosis Hospital matter. The proposal of the Government was for an entire white staff. Negro public opinion was for an entire Negro staff. Major Moton suggested that they start with a compromise, namely, a white officer in charge, with Negro physicians, nurses and other assistants, with the definite idea that after the institution was well started it should go on an all Negro basis. This was, I think, the plan adopted.

9. Your little postscript is fine and moving. I have suggested the possible modification of two words, especially the changing of the word "always" to the word "often."

You speak of his life being "crowded with disappointments and increasing sorrow." This may have been true but I was not aware that the situation was as serious as the words would indicate, except insofar as his health and some financial difficulties were concerned. As I retired from the Tuskegee Trustees a few years before his resignation, I was not however in intimate touch with the situation.

I greatly appreciate your sending me the sketch and the postscript. I repeat that I think you have done an excellent piece of work and I know that for many reasons it must have been a difficult one. Possibly some of the minor suggestions that I have made may be worthy of consideration.

Major Moton always impressed me as a man of remarkably fine spirit. He was sincere, fair, and on the whole wise, and he did a great piece of work for the colored people and for the whole cause of education and interrracial adjustments in this country.

With kindest regards, I am

Very sincerely yours,
Anson Phelps Stokes

Atlanta, Ga., 17 October 1940

My dear Mr. Stokes:

Your letter was a bit too late to make many changes in the Moton biography but I did change that "always" to "often" which seemed to me important. The spelling of Dr. Frissell's name had already been attended to and I had noted that Dr. Moton was President of the Negro Business League. A few other matters I could not change but they ought to be changed in a final biography. I think of special interest is note of his administrative capacity.

Thank you very much for the $300 which you offer to put at my disposal during the coming winter. I shall see that it is carefully spent and let you have details.

I think Dr. [Rayford W.] Logan has the only copy of the bibliography of bibliographies. As I remember he compiled that. I have written to him for a copy and hope to receive it soon.

Very sincerely yours
W. E. B. Du Bois

In a typically forceful address at Wilberforce University in June 1940, Du Bois argued for scientific and secular education of the highest quality and suggested that church and factional interests, then hindering Wilberforce, might well kill higher education in general and that provided Black people in particular. He added that the work going forward at Virginia State College reflected what was positive and hopeful.

One result of this address was a letter from John Manuel Gandy (1870–1947), president of Virginia State (since 1914). Gandy, born in Mississippi, was educated at Fisk and was a teacher for some fifteen years before his appointment at Virginia State. In 1929 he received the Harmon Award for distinguished service in education.

Petersburg, Va., October 16, 1940

Dear Dr. Du Bois:

I have just read with much interest your article on "The Future of Wilberforce University"[1] and found in that article a statement regarding the Virginia State College at Petersburg.

This letter is to extend to you my profound thanks for your evaluation of the achievement of this institution to which you referred. Your language is not by any means too strong. Being close to the problem here, I feel you have spoken both courageously and accurately.

Come to see us when you are traveling this way again.

Very sincerely yours,
John M. Gandy, President

1. *Journal of Negro Education* 9 (October 1940): 553–70.

In addition to normal filing of his letters—chronological and alphabetical—Du Bois maintained two files marked "curious" and "sick." In the latter were placed letters filled with obscenities and threats upon his life or the lives of his family; such letters any Black person of prominence, especially if known to be what is usually called "militant," received in abundance. Letters marked "curious" were sometimes, however, of general interest, inducing replies from Du Bois that were quite consequential. One such is offered below; it came from a white woman in rural Texas who knew less than nothing about "the Negro question" and—one would almost add, therefore—was to report on it at an impending meeting of the American Association of University Women.

La Feria, Texas, November 10, 1940

Dear Dr. Du Bois:

I may be very presumptuous in asking you to help me in getting information on the subject of "The Negro in the U.S.A." or "The Negro Problem." If you think I am presumptuous you probably will not answer this letter. But if you do wish to take the time to answer I shall be very grateful to you.

The subject will have to be a rather superficial study compared to the way you would go into it. However I have become very much interested by what I have read so far. I don't agree with one statement I read in your article in June 1935 *Current History*: "Today there can be no doubt that Americans know the facts about the American Negroes."[1] I feel that there are many like me who know very little of the facts, but perhaps you referred only to the industrial world.

My study of the subject is for preparation of a program to be given at a meeting of the American Association of University Women. Could you tell me what I ought to read to get the most *up-to-date* information on the subject? For instance I'd like so very much to know whether your ideas have changed on the subjects which you wrote of in the June 1935 *Current History*—5 years ago—about a Negro cooperative State— about segregation—whether industrial treatment of the Negro is better or worse than in 1935—etc. etc. etc.—

I'd like to know how many Negro colleges there are. I read 100 somewhere else. I read Howard U. is considered the best scholastically. Is that correct today? Where is Howard? Excuse my ignorance.

I'd like very much to see a copy of *Crisis* and of *Opportunity* and know whether you approve of their present policies—I'd like to know something about the work and present policies of the N.A.A.C.P. and who is at the head of it. Whether the organization favoring a return of Negroes to Africa is still active and what you think of it. I'd

---

1. "A Negro Nation within the Nation," *Current History* 42 (June 1935): 265–70. Note in Du Bois's reply to this letter his statement that the essay's title was chosen by the magazine's editor and that he thought it misleading. The *New York Times*, 21 May 1935, p.9, quoted a few lines from this essay under the headline, "Advocates 'Negro Nation.' "

like to know what you think of the novel *The Flaming Sword* by Dixon?[2] I'd like to know how true the picture of Harlem Negro life is—I'd like to know something of Atlanta University—I'm glad to pay postage both ways on any reading material you send and *thank* you if you answer at all.

Sincerely,

Mrs. J. G. Cockrane

Atlanta, Ga., 18 November 1940

Mrs. J. G. Cockrane

My dear Madam:

I agree with you that my assumption expressed at various times that Americans in general know the facts about Negroes is an overstatement. What I should have said, to be correct, is that the knowledge which is available to the average American is so much larger today than what it was twenty years ago that it is not necessary to concentrate as much today upon giving this factual information but rather on ways and methods of bettering relations and conditions. I think perhaps with some lack of personal modesty, that the most up-to-date information on the subject of the Negro and his relation to the modern world will be found in my *Dusk of Dawn*, an autobiography published by Harcourt, Brace and Company, New York City, this year. You will be able to find it in most of the larger libraries or you can order it through any bookstore. This explains the development and change of thought especially in the last few years.

The article in *Current History* was given a false over-emphasis by the editor in his caption. Even that article did not contemplate a separate cooperative state for Negroes. Such complete separation would be impracticable. What I wanted and still want is such a degree of inner economic cooperation among colored folk as would enable them to support themselves in the face of the large, and in some cases increasing, economic discrimination.

The best Negro periodicals of which you could easily get copies are: *Phylon*, Atlanta University, Atlanta, Georgia; *Opportunity*, 1133 Broadway, New York City; and the *Crisis*, 69 Fifth Avenue, New York City. Howard University is in Washington and can be reached by addressing a letter to the President of Howard Uni-

2. Thomas E. Dixon, *The Flaming Sword* (Atlanta: Monarch Publishing Co., 1939), was the final book from the pen of probably the most rabidly racist author in United States history. He wrote *The Leopard's Spots* (1902), but his most widely known work was *The Clansman*, published in 1905 by Doubleday, Page and a best seller for years; the latter was the basis of the film, *Birth of a Nation*, first released in 1915. *The Flaming Sword* (whose title, according to Dixon, came from Du Bois!) is a five hundred-page novel depicting, Dixon indicates, "the Conflict of Color in America from 1900 to 1938." Du Bois, by name, is a major character in the book—that is, a major villain. The theme of the book is the destruction of democracy in the United States largely through "Communistic corruption of the black race"—to quote Stanley J. Kunitz and Howard Haycroft, in *Twentieth Century Authors* (New York: H. W. Wilson Co., 1942), p. 387. Du Bois made no reply to the correspondent's inquiry about this book; his papers and published work do not refer to it.

versity, Washington, D. C. The leading Negro Universities are: Fisk University, Nashville, Tennessee; Atlanta University; Howard University, Washington, D. C. You can get a complete list of Negro educational institutions from the annual reports of the United States Commission of Education, Washington, D. C. They will send you pamphlets containing this information on request.

I trust these notes will help you.

Very sincerely yours,
W. E. B. Du Bois

As previous correspondence in this volume has shown, there were signs by 1939 and 1940 of significant differences between Du Bois and President Clement of Atlanta University and between Du Bois and President Read of Spelman College. These differences reached a critical point late in 1940 and induced long letters from Du Bois to several people, in particular to his friend W. R. Banks, head of Prairie View State College in Texas and a member of the board of trustees of Atlanta University, and to Dean Sage (1875–1943), a wealthy Wall Street attorney and director of several philanthropic enterprises, and since 1929 president of the board of trustees of Atlanta.

Two of Du Bois's letters to these men are published below; these offer details of the differences mentioned above, as Du Bois saw them. To publish the full correspondence about this episode would require nearly as many pages as this volume; the exhibits mentioned in Du Bois's letter to Banks are summarized by him therein and have been elucidated in earlier letters. Following these letters of 1940 to Banks and Sage, there are published memoranda made by Du Bois in the 1930s concerning his agreements with President John Hope of Atlanta University. The final item from this correspondence given here is a letter from President Clement to Du Bois in December 1940, which indicates the nature of the partial resolution of that particular difficulty; the relationship between the two men —and that between Du Bois and Miss Read—remained strained and eventually produced the explosion of 1944 and Du Bois's dismissal.

Atlanta, Ga., 14 November 1940

My dear Mr. Banks:

I have been wanting to see you and talk with you during the whole fall and at several times determined to write but am glad that I put if off because the urgency of the message has passed in part.

I have been having a perfect hell of a time here this fall and for the first time have felt my age distinctly. Beginning last year I have had a controversy with the President over *Phylon* which grew in intensity until at the first meeting of the board in September I had to tell him in plain English that I regarded his decisions "as arbitrary, unjust and as contradicting his written word." I said I would not voluntarily accept them and that "I am going to appeal over the President's decision to the Board of trustees," etc. Suddenly now at the last moment the President has changed his decision and appears in the guise of a cooing dove. What in the devil is the matter with the man I really don't know.

As the whole thing may come up before the board of trustees, I want to put the facts in your hands so that you will know them in detail. I think I had better put it down chronologically. I knew in 1938 that the appropriation made by the Phelps Stokes Fund by means of which I was supplementing Miss Diggs' salary would cease and I wanted to know what if any chances there were of keeping her services. A year ahead of time I sent the President the letter marked 1. President Clement did not acknowledge or reply to this communication. One month later, January 5, 1939, I again brought his attention to the matter—attachment 2. Five days later President Clement wrote me assuring me of adequate secretarial help for my work—attachment 3. On April 24, 1939, as Miss Diggs did not get the Rosenwald fellowship, I wrote again to the President and asked for a conference on the matter of her retention. There was no reply to this. Twenty days later on May 15, I began to get worried. If Miss Diggs was not to return she ought to have at least a month's notice. I, therefore, wrote the President, May 15: "I am anxious about Miss Diggs and her position next year. May I ask if any decision has been reached and if not when the matter will be taken up?" On May 19, the President asked me to come to his office. He assured me that the University appreciated the services of Miss Diggs and proposed to retain them. He promised specifically that when in 1939 the Phelps Stokes appropriation ended, the University would supplement Miss Diggs' salary so that she would receive $150 a month until the end of the fiscal year. He did not say anything concerning the next year except his statement that the University wished to retain Miss Diggs' services. I was so pleased with this interview that I went immediately to my office and assured Miss Diggs that she was certain of continued employment. This happened you will note before *Phylon* had been established or before anyone had any assurance that it would be established.

I had asked the President, March 29, 1939, to recommend a periodical to the board of trustees and he had promised that he would. In the middle of August the President informed me that permission for a magazine had been given by the trustees and that I could go ahead and make plans. Nothing more was said either as to the magazine or as to my future connection with it until November 21, 1939, when I was asked to act as editor-in-chief and as you know *Phylon* appeared January 25, 1940. I immediately put all my energy and practically all of Miss Diggs' time into this project; so that from December 1 until the middle of February all of my time and all of that of Miss Diggs was given to *Phylon* and from January 25, 1940 until today at least one-half of Miss Diggs' time has been given to *Phylon* magazine.

It happened that the Phelps Stokes appropriation was extended until June in order that my office should complete for the Phelps Stokes Fund a bibliography of all the books published on Africa and the Negro race in Africa, the United States, the West Indies and South America from 1927 when Work's bibliography was finished to 1940.

It went without saying that it was impossible for Miss Diggs to do this work. I had it done finally by using one or two stenographers whom I hired in the city and in paying A. C. Logan, a bibliographical expert in Washington, about $200 to complete the work. I also hired other clerical help in New York and Baltimore during the summer. It was necessary, therefore, for me to remind the President that in spite of the fact that the Phelps Stokes appropriation did not stop until June, 1940 that nevertheless it could not be used to supplement Miss Diggs' salary as formerly, since her services were now engaged with *Phylon*.

In bringing this matter to the attention of the President, January 31, I received a reply the same day. This reply and my answer to it appear as attachments 4 and 5. I was frankly flabbergasted by the President's attitude but I received no acknowledgement or answer to my reply for a month. On March 1, I wrote again—attachment 6. On March 5, the President asked me to come to his office. We had a conference which was pleasant and in which as I thought we found ourselves in substantial agreement; but because of the clear apprehension which had arisen in our conference on May 19, I went immediately to my office and wrote down the facts of the conference, as I understood them, and sent a copy on the next day to the President telling him I should like to know if there were any mistakes. He replied a week later—attachment 7. You will note that twice: January 31, 1940 and March 12, 1940, the President explicitly said that whatever extra salary Miss Diggs was to receive outside the $1,350 must be paid from *Phylon* funds and at the decision of the *Phylon* board and that there was no objection to having Miss Diggs' salary supplemented through outside funds. I did not see any way out of this difficulty and was discouraged because unwittingly I had promised Miss Diggs a continuation of her work for the year with the same salary. I therefore felt in honor bound to see that she was paid.

Now if Miss Diggs was to be paid what I had promised her either it must come out of my own pocket or the income of *Phylon*. The income of *Phylon* proved larger than I thought and the expenses smaller. I, therefore, found to my satisfaction that the deficit in salary could probably be made up from the *Phylon* funds. But I also realized that even if that were done that the matter must be settled for another year and that it must be made clear to the trustees that when I said that *Phylon* could be published for $2,000, I assumed that I had a secretary paid by the University for twelve months in the year who could be used at my discretion not only on my work but on that for *Phylon*. I not only assumed this but I assumed that we were to have rental space free; that we were to have light, etc. And I meant that the $2,000 would suffice for expenses outside of these fundamental items.

I called a meeting of the board, May 20. I had talked the matter over with several members and we had agreed that if there was a sufficient surplus we would pay Miss Diggs' salary for the summer months out of this money. Of course this did not mean that the payment was simply for her summer work. She had given or was to give one-half her time for nine months to *Phylon*, which at her rate of pay would have amounted to over $600. When I laid this before the board I did not for a moment dream that there was any difference of opinion and least of all did I think that after the explicit statements that I had received, that there was any objection on the part of the President. The President, however, did object strongly, first, because he doubted if there was going to be sufficient surplus to pay Miss Diggs and secondly, he intimated that this would make her salary too high in accordance with University standards. The board, therefore, took no action but appointed a committee which consisted of the President and myself to iron out the difficulties which did not seem to me insuperable. I waited a week for the President to call the committee together. It did not seem to be proper for me to summon the President to a committee meeting and I knew of course that he was busy with commencement matters. Therefore, on May 27, I wrote him suggesting as you know that we pay Miss Diggs the full amount which I had promised her but, and I quote from a note, "that *Phylon* should be responsible for the balance of $450 provided the funds permit this expenditure without incurring a deficit for the year and without lowering the quality of the magazine." Voted that, therefore, during the summer that such payments be made as we seem able to afford and that the board at its September meeting take up the matter of paying the balance. This was written May 27. For the next ten days, that is, until commencement, I received no acknowledgment of this note, no request for a meeting of the committee of two and no decision as to his opinion. Meantime the members of the board, except the President, signed a petition to the board of trustees which read as follows—attachment 8.

It was not until nearly a month later on the 19 of June, after I had left the University on my vacation, that the President sent me this letter—attachment 9. You will notice in this letter not only does the President refuse to allow Miss Diggs to be paid $150 even if the magazine had sufficient surplus funds; but in addition to that he so changes the fiscal year that her work begins the first of September and ends the first of June which would leave the magazine even more helpless for the preparation and distribution of the third number which is issued in July. I did not acknowledge this letter but when I returned to the University at the first meeting of the board, September 20, I put before them an estimate balance sheet for the whole year showing that we would probably have enough to pay the $300 which we owed Miss Diggs. I told them that fearing some outcome of this sort, I had, before I left the University, placed in Miss Diggs' hands two personal checks for $150 payable August 1 and September 1 so that the obligation to her had been settled but on the other hand I considered that *Phylon* owed me $300; that the magazine had expended so far less than $50 for clerical aid; and that the President's decision was not an agreement between myself and him and he had not conferred with me. I then read a written statement—attachment 10.

The President and the board were naturally very much upset and adjourned without action. I then determined to take the matter to President Read as treasurer of the University. I was certain in my own mind that she was responsible for much of the attitude of the decisions of the President. I think both of these executives are coming to a working understanding and as a concession to that the President was more or less consciously yielding to her determined opposition to *Phylon*. I think she and perhaps others had been especially disappointed: first, that *Phylon* was a respectable magazine worthy of the University and so far as I know not a single complaint had come against its contents. Second, instead of exceeding our appropriation which everybody knew was very small, we actually were going to be able to complete a year's publication with a small surplus. I may say incidentally that the Howard University *Journal of [Negro] Education* receives $3,000 from the University and a secretary who serves the dean who is editor both in his office work and in his editorial work. I wrote Miss Read, September 27, and sent the budget and my written declaration and asked her for an interview at her convenience. No reply came until October 23. An interview was arranged October 26. I sat down and for two hours had a very plain talk with Miss Read. I went over the reasons for my coming to Atlanta University and the reiterated desire of John Hope that I should come. I reminded her of certain conditions of my coming that I had made and had been assented to: first, that I should have a secretary; later that I should teach only two semesters or if I was called upon to teach summer school I was to have one semester free. I told her of Hope's desire for me to do literary work and reminded her of the work that I had done. I told her that since John Hope's death I did not feel that I had any cordial cooperation in my work and that I felt that the University spirit was getting worse. I reminded her that four productive scholars, [Rayford W.] Logan, [Luella F.] Norwood, [Frank M.] Snowden and [Richard A.] Schermerhorn, had left the University since Hope's death; that Dr. [Otis W.] Caldwell had decided that he could be of no use here; that Ira Reid had to hand in his resignation before he could get satisfactory conditions of teaching. I expressed gratification that we had added one scholar, Dr. Coulborn, an Englishman, but reminded her that Dr. Coulborn was the only person in the University set-up who had received up to that time a written contract and with whom she had cooperated in arranging adjustment between the Spelman College courses and the University courses. I told her that John Hope had wanted a journal like *Phylon* but that her opposition had delayed it. I then went over the whole controversy concerning my secretary and the clerical services for *Phylon*. I told her frankly that I had concluded that the President's decisions were instigated by her but that I did not want to do her injustice and wanted to ask her frankly if she had concurred in this last decision of June 19. Miss Read was very cordial and sympathetic. She declared that she had not known of this decision and had only known of the controversy indirectly and lately. She, however, asked me twice not to take the matter before the trustees. She intimated that if I did I would probably not be supported. I told her that that was quite possible but that the government of Atlanta University was not an absolute monarchy and that I had a right to take this matter to the board and the board had a duty to hear me.

Meantime the members of the board got together and talked separately with both myself and the President. I assured them that the controversy was not of my making; and that I would pursue it no further than necessary; that as a matter of fact I had not taken it to a single member of the board; but that I was going to unless the matter was settled. At last Mr. Reid came to me and asked if we could not first settle some of the general principles, that is, after this year how was the matter going to be carried on and what provisions were going to be made for clerical services. I told him that I was quite willing to divide the question into such two parts. I then suggested that a meeting be called of the board and that he be asked to preside. He did not quite like this and at the same time he saw some advantages. When, therefore, I was asked to go to Chicago and speak at International House, I called the meeting for the night of my departure, asking Mr. Reid to preside because I was absent.

The board at first was unwilling to discuss the matter in my absence but nevertheless did. They said nothing about the $300 debt except that they would concur in anything that the President and myself agreed upon. They laid down certain rules and regulations for the future conduct of *Phylon* and suggested an increased appropriation from the University so as to cover part-time employment of a clerk. They asked for another meeting when I returned November 11. This meeting was held and I spoke very frankly: first, about the budget of 1940 saying that again it seemed that we would have a surplus from which what I considered a debt of $300 to me could be paid. I brought to their notice the two statements of the President saying that such use of funds was not only allowable but necessary if we were to pay any part of the clerical service. The President reminded me that afterward I had limited this decision which, of course, was true. Then he said that he did not want to be stubborn and if there was surplus enough from the income of 1940 that he would consent to it. He pointed out, however, that in the income of 1940 there must not be included any subscriptions for 1941 or later. I immediately assented to this and that part of the controversy was settled as suddenly as it began. Why on earth it ever began I am still wondering.

I next took up with the board the future conduct of the magazine. I told them that under the circumstances it seemed to me as it must seem to them quite possible that the President and I could not work in close harmony and cooperation for which such an enterprise called. I told them that I did not think that the trouble would come from my side. I had always been willing to cooperate with the President. I then went on to reject a proposal which they had made which substituted two executive heads for the magazine instead of one. They were proposing to have not only an editor-in-chief but a business manager appointed. I told them if the business manager was appointed by the administration and worked in his own office, separate from mine, I would be willing to assent; that the business management of the magazine perhaps did belong logically directly under the supervision of the President. But I said if they proposed to appoint a second executive who was to work in my office or use my office force at his discretion that would, of course, be impossible and I would not assent to it.

I therefore suggested that since I had succeeded in bringing out a volume of the magazine that it might be the best thing for me to retire from further connection with *Phylon*; that I would not, of course, say that this was my desire but nevertheless it might be the wisest thing to do. The board and the President both declared that this was not necessary, and therefore, appointed another committee with power to make another set of proposals as to the operating principles of *Phylon*. I wrote proposals of the kind of set-up under which I was willing to continue work and presented them to Mr. Reid and the President for their approval. With a few verbal changes it was approved and is annexed—attachment 11.

I am sorry to bother you with all this. I do not know why on earth it had to come up. If the President had simply said to me frankly, we cannot afford to pay Miss Diggs, $1,800 a year, I should have taken his decision as unquestionably within his power but consciously or carelessly he entirely deceived me with the idea that I had a secretary for twelve months, adequately paid. I promised to publish *Phylon* for $2,000 and then found out to my surprise that I had a secretary for only nine months. But said the President you can pay her the extra amount from *Phylon* funds if you have them. Very well, said I, I will. And then when the funds were apparently available the President turns about again and says you can't do it. Of course, this still leaves the future in doubt. If the President sticks to his statement that administrative officials in Atlanta University are not to be paid as much as $1,800 there again the matter is settled. Of course this is not true. Mrs. Nabrit, the President's secretary, gets $2,100 and Miss Read has had a secretary paid as much or more. In fact one of them now is getting more than that although Miss Read says that she is hired only temporarily. It may, of course, be answered that Mrs. Nabrit is not simply a secretary. She is not. She is assistant treasurer because Miss Read wanted to plant a stool pigeon in the President's office and raised her salary in order to do it. Moreover, it can be said that Miss Diggs is by no means simply a stenographer. She has been business manager, bookkeeper, and in fact the whole business establishment of *Phylon*. Just what we are going to be able to do, therefore, after June 1, I do not know. Much will depend on the appropriation from the Board. If the board gives us $2,500 instead of $2,000, we can allocate $500 of this for clerical services and carry on. If not, we will be in a jam. I do not know where I can get a clerk for a thousand dollars or even twelve hundred that can fill Miss Diggs' place. I have a right to demand from the University at least a thousand dollars for a secretary. If separate and aside from this *Phylon* has to hire its clerical work done it cannot do it for less than another $1,000 which will be more than we are paying now.

I put these facts in your hands for your use in any way you see fit. Two other things I want to bring to your attention: first, I want you to allow Miss Diggs to refer to you for a recommendation in case she applies again to the Rosenwald Fund. I am sure you know enough about her and her work to be able to do this. I am enclosing a letter from Anson Phelps Stokes concerning her work for the Encyclopaedia of the Negro—attachment 13. Second, I have a plan afoot for reviving the Atlanta Conference in a little different form. The *Phylon* board has already voted to promote the "First *Phylon* Institute and Twenty-Fifth Atlanta University Conference." I am attaching—No. 14—a statement concerning this conference which I am sending the President. I hope he will present it and the board of trustees will take some action.

Finally, I hope for you good health and for Pete's sake stop by when you come back from the meeting. Oh yes, I am planning to be with you in January if the plans for your agricultural conference go through.

Very sincerely yours,
W. E. B. Du Bois

Atlanta, Ga., 16 November 1940

My dear Mr. Sage:

I have sent you the first volume of *Phylon* which we have published within the appropriation furnished by the University and the income from sales. We have no debts. Our circulation is about six hundred fifty in thirty-nine states and Europe, Asia, Africa and the West Indies. We have on our list fifty libraries including many of the leading institutions of learning. We have received unsolicited commendation from persons of distinction in many parts of the country.

Despite this and to my great distress, a controversy between myself and the President over *Phylon* has been simmering since last May. I have hoped to settle it amicably. I gave up that hope in September and was about to write you or come and see you when again matters settled down and smooth sailing seemed to be ahead. The final agreement and arrangements were to be consummated Friday by a special committee of the President, Dr. Ira Reid and myself who were to meet in my office at two p.m. The President did not appear, nor were we able to locate his whereabouts either by telephoning his home or his offices. I sent a reminder to his desk but although he is not leaving the city until Sunday, I have had no word.

To my great regret, therefore, I have got to bother you with certain information in sheer self defense. I have been connected with institutions of learning for twenty-three years and this is the first time that I have appealed to the board of trustees over the president's head. Whether in this case such appeal is necessary I leave entirely to your discretion after a recital of the following facts.

When I offered in 1939 to publish *Phylon* within a University appropriation of $2,000 I did so because I thought at the time that I would have the services of my own secretary paid by the University for twelve months; and that by offering at least one-half her time to *Phylon* without charge we would need to spend little or nothing for clerical help. However, after the publication of the first number of *Phylon*, the President astonished me by saying that the University had promised to pay my secretary only for nine months in the year and that he had told me this before *Phylon* was authorized. The President may have meant to tell me but I did not so understand and I certainly never would have undertaken to publish a quarterly magazine if I had thought that I would have no clerical help for the fourth quarter.

Before I came to Atlanta University, I had a clear and definite understanding with John Hope that I was to have a secretary for my literary work. I explained that on account of writer's cramp I was helpless without a stenographer. He promised to furnish me one and since I have been here the university had paid $100 a month for ten months in a year for a secretary. I succeeded in 1936 in getting the Phelps Stokes Fund to supplement this because of work that I was doing for them so that since 1936 my secretary has received $150 a month for twelve months with one month's vacation. The Phelps Stokes appropriation ceased in 1939 and a year before its stoppage I sought an interview with the President to determine whether I could keep my secretary at her present wage or would have to let her go. I reminded the President that my secretary was a graduate of the University of Minnesota and the first master of arts in sociology of Atlanta University; that she had been chosen by John Hope for service with the administration; had worked three years in the office of President Read; and finally four years for me; that she was, as he knew, a woman of intelligence, education and character, independent in thought and action but well-liked by everybody. The President was slow in answering my query but finally May 19, 1939, before *Phylon* was definitely planned or authorized, he assured me that the University appreciated the services of Miss Diggs and that she would be retained at her present salary. Later, in March, 1940, he told me, as I have said, that I had misunderstood his promise and that what he had promised was $1350 a year for nine months and not $1800 a year for twelve months.

Misunderstandings are always possible and while I felt pretty strongly on the point, I nevertheless admitted to him that possibly I had misunderstood him but at any rate we were now faced by a critical situation and I asked if he could not allocate other University funds to this purpose. He said finally that he could not and if my secretary was to be paid for the fourth quarter, the payment must come from *Phylon* funds and by vote of the *Phylon* board. He said this in writing over his own signature on two different occasions. I thought this decision unfair but, of course, under the circumstances I could not back out of my promise to edit and publish *Phylon*. The *Phylon* board of editors, my secretary and myself worked very hard and ended the year with a surplus large enough to pay my secretary her full salary.

However, because our ability could not be settled until near the end of the calendar year, I paid Miss Diggs two months salary, $300 in all, with my own checks, August 1 and September 1. Meantime, however, the President changed his mind and finally, June 19, 1940, forbade the use of *Phylon* funds for supplementing the secretary's salary either from the University appropriation or the sale of the magazine "or from any other source." The ground for this was that a salary of $1800 was higher than the University was paying other secretaries. This was not true because his own secretary was getting $2100 and secretaries in Miss Read's office at various times have received as much or more, but, of course, that was no business of mine. I, however, protested vehemently against his continual shifting of positions and against a final position which I regarded as "unjust and arbitrary" and I threatened to take the matter to the board of trustees. However, I did not hurry about this and members of the board and I went into consultation and I also communicated the facts to the treasurer, Miss Read. I did this latter because I suspected that the President's attitude was in some way a prolongation of her opposition to *Phylon*. This she verbally denied. After six weeks the President yielded and said he would approve the payment of the deficit in salary if *Phylon* funds were available. The board of editors, thereupon, appointed a committee of three with power consisting of the President, Dr. Ira Reid and myself, to ascertain if there was a sufficient surplus to repay me and also to draw up a proposed budget for 1941 and a more definite statement of the general principles according to which hereafter *Phylon* was to be conducted. This committee met Tuesday, November 12, 1940 and agreed upon a set of principles for operating *Phylon* in 1941. I am appending this agreement. We also decided to adjourn and have a later meeting, Friday,

November 15, at which time we could have the report of the auditor and be certain that in the surplus of expense of operation there should not be included any commitments, that is, prepaid subscriptions for 1941. The auditor's report came in and I am appending that. It showed a surplus of $290.96 not including segregated funds amounting to $76.75 which were pre-payments for 1941 subscriptions.

With this auditor's report in hand I prepared a statement completing the budget of 1940 and suggesting a refund to me of $275 and offering to forget the balance of $25. I also added to this a plan to avoid any recurrence of trouble about clerical help in 1941. It seemed to me that we ought to face this matter and have no further misunderstanding. If the President was willing to approve a budget which would provide for Miss Diggs' salary of $1800 paid partially by the University and partially by *Phylon* funds I would be satisfied. On the other hand, if the President decided that this was not feasible I thought that Miss Diggs ought to be given sufficient notice before June 1 when her present contract expires to seek other work.

I also went on to say that in the event of her leaving, then according to the expressed wish of the board, all connection between the payment of my secretary and funds allocated for clerical services to *Phylon* should be separate. I added that I did not see how a full time secretary or part time service capable of doing the work that Miss Diggs had done could be secured and that unless they could be found, I would not be willing to have further connection with the magazine. I append this statement.

Frankly, Mr. Sage, I am not at all clear as to what I ought to do. I am putting these facts before you and Mr. Banks. As you know, I was one of the persons who advocated the election of Mr. Clement as president. Since he has been here I have tried to cooperate with him in every way possible although my cooperation has not often been asked. I am not conscious of any action on my part that could have led to this extraordinary situation over a comparatively small matter. If Mr. Clement had been clear and definite at the end of 1938 that Miss Diggs' services could not be retained at her present salary, the matter could have been settled then and there and although I would have hated to lose her the final word was with the President and that I have not for a moment questioned.

There are two matters which I think have irritated the President more or less: first, that I have a secretary. But this, as I have said, was by arrangement before I came here from a permanent job and I should not have come unless that had been assented to. Second, there was another matter which John Hope and I agreed to after I came. I told him frankly that I could not teach the whole year and then teach summer school. I tried summer school twice. It requires five hours continual lecturing, five days a week for six weeks. Teachers are not allowed to occupy their regular rooms in the dormitory but have to occupy during the hottest part of the summer, small single rooms in the Spelman dormitories. The food furnished is not good. I told Mr. Hope that I could not teach but two semesters in the year, and that if I were asked to teach summer school I should expect one of the semesters free. This he assented to and this has been carried out. In 1936, for instance, I took a semester off to go to Europe and on my return taught in the summer school. These are the only two matters on which I can imagine there is difference of opinion between myself and the President and I am not sure that there is any difference here. He intimated once that I was serving for only nine months in the year. I am on a twelve months' basis and paid on that basis. During the summer I have three times hired an office in the North and worked with my secretary there for a month or more. At other times she has taken home with her work which I was engaged upon.

My first secretary was paid $100 a month for ten months in a year. Mr. Clement has changed this and announced that he was going to pay Miss Diggs for nine months in a year and also changed the fiscal year in which she was to be paid so that her services begin in September this year and will end June 1. The fourth number of *Phylon* comes out July 15. All June is required to prepare it for the printer and all of July to read the proof and distribute the copy. August should be a well-earned vacation.

I am perfectly willing to withdraw entirely from the editorship of *Phylon*. I offered to do this at the November 11 meeting of the board in the presence of the President. Both he and other members of the board vehemently protested and I do not want to run out on them or seem to break my word with the University. At the same time I must have clerical help. I cannot do my work without it.

As I have said before, I am sorry to trouble you with this and you can make such disposition of this letter or of its information as you think best. The documentary proof with letters, reports, etc., are in this office and can be sent to you. Mr. Banks has copies of them. I hope that no decision of the board will be made without these facts being known. If you should wish, I could come to New York and be at the service of the board, but I presume this is not necessary. Another suggestion would be that a committee of the trustees visit the institution and go thoroughly into this matter. Something, at any rate, ought to be done.

Very sincerely yours,
W. E. B. Du Bois

[Copies of memoranda from the 1930s, concerning Du Bois's employment at Atlanta University]

June 25, 1934

The understanding with President Hope was as follows:
Memorandum to President Hope:

On June 15, I sent you a memorandum which we discussed together at length Friday, June 22. I am herein setting down my understanding of the main results of that conference, and would be glad to have this memorandum confirmed or corrected:

1. That I am to receive $300 extra recompense for my work in the Summer School.

2. That I occupy the position of professor of sociology in Atlanta University, on the usual permanent basis of university professor; that is, tenure during good behavior, and during my ability to perform the services expected of me satisfactorily.

3. That it is understood that usually I am to teach the two semesters of the main term, but if at any time the President should wish me to teach during the Summer

School, then equitable allowance for absence during one or the other semesters will be arranged.

4. That the President will try, if financial conditions allow, to meet my request for a salary of $5,000, but that this he cannot at present definitely promise.

5. That while, naturally, it is impossible that every professor or even head of the department, as I have been designated at present, should be furnished a secretary, yet the President will try to see that I receive a secretary at a salary of $1,200 a year, and that I have as now two rooms for offices.

6. That my duties will be writing and teaching and lecturing, with the emphasis in that order, provided that the lecturing outside the school shall be for limited periods and not interfere with my regular work, and that in all cases, I shall consult with the President with regard to such engagements.

The above is my understanding of the results of our conference, and I shall be glad to know if it is yours. I want to thank you for the careful and understanding way in which the matter was discussed, as indeed I knew it would be from what I have always known of you.

July 18, 1934

Memorandum to President Hope:

In our interview yesterday, my understanding was as follows:

1. That my salary for the ensuing year was to be $4,500.

2. That I am to teach two semesters, or one semester and the summer school.

3. That Miss Wilson is to be retained as my secretary, and that her salary is to be paid at the rate of $100.00 a month. That payment at present can only be guaranteed for ten months; that is, beginning with August and through the payment of May 1. That the payment for the other two months of the fiscal year will depend upon the availability of university funds.

W. E. B. Du Bois

Mr. Hope confirmed this understanding later in 1936 when the Oberlaendar Trust of Philadelphia asked me to travel in Germany for observation. Mr. Hope granted me leave at full salary for one semester. On return I taught summer school in 1937.

In the case of another professor, while leave from semester work with pay is not granted, President Clement pays him $500 extra for teaching summer school.

W. E. B. Du Bois

Atlanta University, December 13, 1940

Dear Doctor Du Bois:

I am willing to make the following provision for secretarial services for you and for *Phylon*.

1. The university will pay your secretary, $1,350, at the rate of $150 per month for nine months, beginning September first and extending to June first.

2. I am approving the minimum *Phylon* budget as submitted, including the item of

$450 for clerical assistance. I have done this with the understanding that it may be necessary to revise the *Phylon* budget as we go along, which will certainly be the case should our anticipated income from subscriptions and sales fall below the budget figure. The figure for clerical assistance is therefore not inviolate, and, like any other *Phylon* budget figure, would be subject to revision.

The $1,350 out of the University budget is being paid with the understanding that Miss Diggs will be your personal secretary and will at the same time assume a definite obligation for secretarial work in connection with the publication, *Phylon*.

As I said to you in our conference today, I still feel that we are not justified in making this much of a financial contribution for clerical and secretarial work on *Phylon*. I have agreed to do this, however, out of respect for you and for your contributions to Atlanta University and to the journal.

> Yours very truly
> Rufus E. Clement

An exchange with H. A. Noyes—not otherwise identified—is brief but meaty; Du Bois's reply has his sharpness. His reference to the present "time" is of course to World War II, then at its early stages.

> Walla Walla, Washington,
> November 14, 1940

Dear Sir:

I have just read with interest your monumental work *Black Folk*. It shows infinite research and patient toil and is a valuable contribution to knowledge on the subject.

In my judgment the work is marred by your apparent slavery to the dictums of Carl Marx—which are rarely more than half truths.

Also it seems to me you overestimate the ability of colored races. While there are exceptions, the average black will require several centuries to attain the mental capacity which it has taken a thousand years for the best European and Asiatic races to reach.

With you I want vast improvement in the treatment of the backward races while they are evolving.

> Sincerely yours
> H. A. Noyes

> Atlanta, Ga., 29 November 1940

Mr. H. A. Noyes
My dear Sir:

Karl Marx has repeatedly been refuted by persons who have not read his works. As to the "ability of the colored races" I think I am possibly in better position to judge that. I have been in Europe, Asia and Africa and have sat in the school room with representatives of nearly all the principal races. Moreover, just now is hardly a time to boast of the mental capacity of Europeans.

Very sincerely yours,
W. E. B. Du Bois

Another exchange with F. P. Keppel of the Carnegie Corporation contains details of the plans and views of Du Bois.

New York City, November 27, 1940

Dear Professor Du Bois:.

We've begun the difficult job of parceling out the modest grant-in-aid fund which the Trustees have allotted to us for the current year, and if you're planning to take me up on my offer of last April, I'd be glad to have a brief report on your activities so that I can make the necessary overtures to the Committee.

Sincerely yours,
F. P. Keppel

Atlanta, Ga., 2 December 1940

My dear Mr. Keppel:

Answering your letter of November 27, I beg to say that my general plan is to attack with as much scientific accuracy as possible and also with certain practical objects in view the problem of The Economic Condition of the American Negro and his future possibilities. I believe that basically at present the problem of the Negro in America is that of earning a living of a standard sufficient to repel crime and disease and give opportunity for steady social uplift. I am convinced that the possibility of guiding the future of the Negro in America and integrating his efforts with those of the nation begins, therefore, with the scientific background of carefully presented facts. I am then first of all seeking to assemble in logical order and in easily understandable form the facts of the Negro's economic history. Once before in 1900 I made such an exhibit for the Paris Exposition which gained for me and my colleagues a grand prize. Such an exhibit I have under way at Atlanta University.

As adjunct to this I shall be able to use *Phylon*, the Atlanta University Review of Race and Culture, which after seven years of effort I finally succeeded in having established in 1940. I am editor-in-chief and thus will have a vehicle for publishing results. I am sending you herewith a copy of the first volume. Beyond this I plan to hold April 10, 11 and 12, 1941, a conference which I have outlined to the administration here as follows: It will be called the first *Phylon* Institute and Twenty-fifth Atlanta University Conference. I thus plan to bind up with my present effort the fact that from 1896 to 1919, twenty-four Atlanta University conferences were held and twenty publications issued. Nineteen of these were under my editorship and largely of my own authorship. The conferences and publications lapsed between 1919 and 1940 when I was not connected with the University. I think it, therefore, an opportune time in 1941 to begin again keeping in memory the first establishment of these conferences forty-five years ago.

This conference, however, I want to be on different basis. I want to assemble a comparatively small number of people, somewhere between twenty-five and fifty. I want them to come mainly from the South and to be colored men trained in economics and expert in social investigation. In addition I want a few white men. I think I have in mind a man at the University of Georgia who is at the head of some new social investigation and, of course, somebody from the University of North Carolina and from Emory University. I want these men to stay in conference for about three days and to talk seriously about the economic plight of the Negro, about possible investigations and studies, about the correct interpretation of the past. To some of the meetings I want the public invited but only such ones as are really interested and who show their interest by asking for tickets of admission after having been apprised of what we are trying to do. Out of the conference I want two sets of things to emerge: first, a series of detailed studies either voluntarily taken up by certain of the conferees or suggested and assigned by the conference. Secondly, I should like to have a concrete effort emerge. What I have in mind is the establishment of a consumers cooperative in connection with the University affiliation and the neighborhood. We have a university book store with two branches carried on with the usual profit and loss procedure. I think there is an opportunity with these four institutions and their more than two thousand students in addition to two housing projects right in the neighborhood with over a thousand families to start a practical cooperative effort which should not only put in practice well-known principles of consumers cooperation but be a laboratory for teaching this technique to colored people in the South.

For the work which I have in mind you have already contributed, April 17, 1940, one thousand dollars. That I have budgeted and am in process of spending as follows:

Expenses:

Books and materials	$100
Secretarial aid	250
Draftsmen	250
aid in travel expense	250
miscellaneous	150
	$1,000

In 1942, I want to follow this with a second conference keeping to the same general subject and with the same objectives but with the additional facts which publication of some of the earlier reports of the 1940 census with regard to the Negro will give us and perhaps with the beginning of realizing the cooperative project. The proposed budget for 1942 is as follows:

Research and compilation	$500
Secretarial aid	250
Travel	250
	$1,000

I should be glad if you can see your way clear to recommend a second grant of

$1,000 for this work. Up to this writing I have told no one the exact source of the funds which I am using. I have simply said that I have been promised a little financial help. Eventually, of course, I shall reveal its source and amount. May I thank you very much for your interest in this work.

Very sincerely yours,
W. E. B. Du Bois

New York City, December 5, 1940

Dear Dr. Du Bois:

Many thanks for your good letter of December 2nd, which brings me up to date on your activities. I am keeping my promise of last April by asking the Treasurer to send you a check for $1000 on or about March 15th.

Thanks, also, for the bound copies of *Phylon*, which I am very glad to have for my personal library.

Sincerely yours,
F. P. Keppel

During World War I, Du Bois fought fiercely against the atrocious discriminatory practices that marked the United States military effort—despite his then favoring United States participation in the war. With war again a fact in Europe and Asia, with United States participation quite likely, and with the draft instituted, Du Bois began a new effort to minimize racist practices in the armed forces. Reflecting this activity is an exchange with Clarence A. Dykstra, who became director of the Selective Service System on 17 October 1940 and held this post until June 1941, when he resigned it to give full time to his position as chairman of the Defense Mediation Board.

Clarence Dykstra (1883–1950), born in Cleveland, specialized in the study of municipal administration. He held significant positions in Los Angeles, taught at the University of California in that city in the 1920s, and in the 1930s was city manager of Cincinnati. From 1937 until President Roosevelt selected him to head the draft, he served as president of the University of Wisconsin. After the war and until his death, Dykstra was provost of the University of California in Los Angeles.

Atlanta, Ga., 19 November 1940

Personal

My dear Mr. Dykstra:

I trust you have not forgotten me from your days in Los Angeles and Cincinnati.

You will remember that in the World War, fifty-one per cent of the Negro draftees were put in class one and only thirty-two per cent of whites. The discrimination in one draft board in Atlanta compelled the dismissal of the whole board. I hope that the same thing is not going to happen this time but I have just seen in a Georgia paper that in Stewart County where seventy-one per cent of the population was Negro in 1930, 296 whites and 826 Negro draftees were registered this year which [means] unless population changes have taken place in the last ten years, the Negroes are furnishing seventy-four and a half per cent of the draftees. May I ask if there are figures concerning the Negro and white draftees and if a report of them with the census figures for 1940, which must be nearly ready, could be made public? I am afraid both in the draft and in the selected classes there is going to be color discrimination and if so we ought to know about it as early as possible. I should be very glad if you could get me any information or take steps for securing it.

I wish you the greatest success in your new opportunity for service.

Very sincerely yours,
W. E. B. Du Bois

Washington, D. C., December 7, 1940.

Dear Mr. Du Bois:

I was pleased to hear from you again and particularly interested in your comments in connection with the question of white and Negro selectees.

As you know, the present law specifically provides that there shall be no discrimination on account of race or color in the interpretation and execution of the Selective Service Act. I understand from the General Staff Officers of the War Department that it is the intention of the Army to provide organizations and facilities for the proper percentage of colored trainees and white trainees from each of the states based on the proportion in these states. This will not mean that during any one month the proportions can be accurate. The present quota of 800,000 trainees is to be filled between now and the end of next June. During that period that state quotas will be adjusted from time to time as more definite figures become available.

For the country as a whole I understand that the 1930 census shows approximately 9.7 of the population to be colored, but that the 1940 census figures are not yet available. The Army intends to provide for the correct percentage and to call for the proper numbers in each state based on the proportion of Class I-A men as between the races in the particular state. For the immediate present, however, the percentage of colored trainees called will be considerably less than the proper proportion because of lack of facilities. This comes primarily from the fact that there are now only two or three per cent of Negroes in the Regular Army and National Guard, and, while new organizations are being activated and others are being planned, it is impossible overnight to produce the non-commissioned officers and training cadres necessary to properly care for the trainees. For this reason, the January call for Negroes will be small, but in February this will be increased rapidly and shortly after that the proper percentage of colored and white will have been inducted.

I have tried to explain this in some detail so that you would realize that in a particular county or state a particular call during any one month would not necessarily follow the proper percentages. The surprising thing concerning the instance you cite where the respective percentages were 71% and 74½% is that they were so close. Of course, the time of induction represents no discrimination, since the selectees will probably serve the same twelve months' period no matter whether they start in January or in March. It would be a very real discrimination if equal facilities, which include not only barracks, hospitals, and other physical facilities, but also the necessary organization, including supply sergeants, cooks, training cadres, and other personnel were not available when either white or colored selectees are inducted. As you are doubtless aware, the law requires that men not be inducted until necessary facilities and equipment are available for their reception, and, regardless of the law, this is the only proper policy.

I note you suggest that the census figures for 1940 be made public as early as possible, and I will do what is possible to have this published as promptly as practicable.

Selective Service, both as a matter of law and as a general policy based on the need for national unity under existing conditions, is based on fair and equal treatment for the races in this most important phase of national defense, and I can assure you that everything possible will be done to see that this policy is carried out.[1]

Appreciating your good wishes for my work here in Selective Service, I am

Yours very sincerely,
C. A. Dykstra

A leader in the African independence movement was Archie Casely-Hayford, born in Axim in 1898 in what is today Ghana. Educated in England and trained as a barrister, he became district magistrate in the (then) Gold Coast in 1936, retired in 1948, was elected to the legislature, and served in cabinet positions when the Republic of Ghana came into being.

An exchange of letters, from late in 1940, has survived; the letter Casely-Hayford mentions from Du Bois has not been found.

Koforidua, Gold Coast, West Africa,
November 31, 1940

Dear Professor Du Bois,

I fear I have been a very long time answering your letter.

As you can well imagine, my work keeps me pretty occupied, and leaves me very little leisure for my private correspondence.

I happen to be in bed with malaria, and so take the opportunity of writing to you. I regret the rules and regulations of the service make it impossible for me to contribute any article to your magazine.

I tried very hard to reach the States on holiday about the time of the Sept. '38 Munich crisis, but it was not possible then. I should so much have liked to make personal contact with you, as my late father The Honorable Casely Hayford often spoke about you. But for the present war, I might have visited the States this fall. It

---

1. The racism in the armed forces during World War II—with rare exceptions—was blatant. There is some evidence that Dykstra, during his brief tenure in charge of the draft, did try to keep discriminatory practices down: *The United States in World War II* (Washington: Office of the Chief of Military History, 1966), vol. 8, *The Employment of Negro Troops*, Ulysses Lee.

was such a pleasure meeting the Ira de Reids here. I do wish they could visit us again. I have not heard from him lately. Please tell him to write.

I shall appreciate at any time a copy of "Atlanta,"[1] as I found that which you sent me extremely interesting.

It seems as if War preparations are pretty active your end. I at times hear from Dr. [Philip M.] Savory of the *Amsterdam News* as also the Hon. Lester A. Walton.

I am wondering very much if he is still at Liberia. I have been trying very hard to get a copy of the American rose annual, and would greatly appreciate a copy if you can send me one. I do hope your good work continues to flourish. There is so much to be done.

With every good wish for Xmas and the New Year

Yours very sincerely,

A. Casely-Hayford

Atlanta, Ga., 21 February 1941

My dear Mr. Hayford:

I was very glad indeed to get your letter of November 31 and sorry that the situation in the world makes the transportation of both news and persons rather difficult.

The Reids speak of you with pleasant memories and I hope that after the war we shall see you in America.

Very sincerely yours,

W. E. B. Du Bois

Du Bois tried every form of writing—poetry, plays, short stories, novels, journalism, and scholarly books. A letter exists showing that he submitted a volume of short stories for publication; it was rejected but among his papers the manuscript has not been found. The rejection came from William Sloane, then manager of the trade department of Henry Holt and Company,* publishers of two of Du Bois's books, The Negro *(1915) and* Black Folk Then and Now *(1939).*

New York, N. Y. December 9, 1940

Dear Professor Du Bois:

Your manuscript, *The Sorcery of Color*, has come to my desk and I have considered it with all the judgment at my command. The writing is as fine as anything you have

---

1. The reference to "Atlanta" is obscure; perhaps what is meant is *Phylon*, published by Atlanta University.

* William M. Sloane (1906–74) went on from Holt in 1945 to found his own publishing firm, which was sold to Morrow in 1952. Thereafter he was editorial director for Funk and Wagnalls and in 1955 became director of Rutgers University Press, a position he held until his death in September 1974. Sloane served (1969–70) as president of the American Association of University Presses.

ever done, I believe, and there's a real freshness and originality in the concepts which lie back of these dramatized stories. On the other hand I must tell you frankly that I can't believe there's any market for what you have written. The dramatic dialogue form in which much of it is cast would stop the ordinary book purchaser right in his tracks. And there are many other aspects of your stories which would make them difficult to present. One of the most serious of these is that it is almost impossible to sell any collection of short stories in sufficient quantities to pay back the manufacturing costs.

There is nothing I enjoy less than saying that we can't do a manuscript submitted by one of our own authors, especially so distinguished a one as yourself, but I can only say about this book that it's not down our alley. If we were to publish it I would not know how to handle it and our salesmen feel that they could not sell it.

Sincerely and regretfully,
William Sloane

Kenneth Wiggins Porter (b. 1905), author of a two-volume biography of John Jacob Astor (1931) and other books, has published most recently The Negro on the American Frontier *(New York: Arno Press, 1971). He is now professor of history at the University of Oregon. Late in 1940 he sent to Du Bois a letter of great interest treating of Black-Indian relations in the pre–Civil War South. Professor Porter was one of the earliest among white scholars in the United States to write in Afro-American history, and his work in the particular field of Black-Indian history has been especially pioneering. At the time of writing this letter, Porter was teaching history at Vassar College.*

Poughkeepsie, N.Y., December 23, 1940

Dear Dr. Du Bois:

I hope the project of a *Dictionary of Negro Biography*, suggested by you in a recent number of *Phylon*, will go through. Ever since the early days of the DAB [*Dictionary of American Biography*] I have felt that some such dictionary would be required as a supplement—though I should like to see it a dictionary of American Indian *and* American Negro biography, since I believe that both those minority racial groups have suffered, not wantonly but nonetheless actually, at the hands of the DAB editors.

I first realized what was happening when I wrote to the editors suggesting the inclusion of some characters whom I had encountered in the course of some special studies I had made in the history of the fur-trade and in Negro-Indian relations—two subjects not so widely separated as they might seem at first thought. My suggestions were five in number—and all were of Negro or Indian blood, or both. 1. Coacoochee (Wild Cat) was the greatest Seminole Indian in the Florida War, with the possible exception of Osceola, and after removal to the Indian Territory planned a great southwestern confederacy of Indians and Negroes, with headquarters on the Mexican side of the Rio Grande and including, if possible, all the Indian tribes of Texas and the Indian Territory, together with Negroes belonging to some of these tribes or who should run away from white planters or from Indians failing to co-operate. Of course he did not succeed in his vast design, but did establish a colony of Seminoles, Seminole Negroes and runaway slaves, Kickapoos, Pootawattomies, Delawares, Shawnees, based on friendship toward Mexico and calm determined watchfulness toward the U.S.A., which might have meant a great difference in the history of the Indians of that region had not his premature death by small-pox prevented his carrying his plans nearer fruition. His colony was a beacon light for runaway slaves and I am informed that their descendants still live in Mexico on the Rio Grande and recently received from the Cardenas government land taken from their ancestors by the Diaz dictatorship. 2. Abraham, a runaway slave from Pensacola, became chief counsellor to the head-chief of the Seminoles and was a leader in the military actions and peace negotiations of the Seminole War during its most important period. Next to Osceola, Coacoochee, and possibly Sam Jones (Arpeika), he was most prominent in the accounts from the scene of action. His later life was obscure (see enclosed ms.) but his activity in the most severe and protracted 'Indian' War in U.S. history would seem to entitle him to biographical mention. 3. Louis Pacheco, an educated slave who could speak, read, and write English, French, and Spanish, and speak Seminole, was hired as a guide to Maj. Dade, who was to strike the first blow against those Seminoles who refused to leave Florida for the Indian Territory. He revealed the plans of campaign to the Seminoles, led the troops into an ambush, joined the hostiles, fought through the war with them, accompanied them to the Indian Territory, assisted Coacoochee in his Mexican plans, and returned at the age of 90 to Florida where he died in the home of the family to which he formerly belonged. 4. Gopher John was Abraham's successor as chief interpreter to the Seminoles. He is a mysterious character and I am still investigating his career. He was Coacoochee's principal Negro aide and apparently died in Mexico. 5. Edward Rose, son of a white trader and a Cherokee-Negro woman, was a guide and interpreter to fur-trading and military parties on the Upper Missouri, became a Crow chief, and was killed by Arikaras.

I sent in all these suggestions for biographical sketches and *one* was accepted—the last, of course, for Edward Rose, though a surly ruffian, suspected of being a pirate in his earlier days, is not usually thought of as being a Negro—the color-line on the frontier being drawn between white and *Indian*—and never associated with Negroes. The careers of Abraham, Louis Pacheco, Gopher John, as historically important as Edward Rose's and much more unusual and interesting, were, in my opinion, considered unsuitable for use in the DAB, principally because they were leaders in what the officers who participated in it called a Negro War—but which American schoolchildren are taught was merely another Indian war! Coacoochee, I believe, was excluded—while dozens of chiefs of minor importance were written up—because he was always a leader in the Negro party among the Seminoles, though himself of pure Muskhogean blood, and because he lived long enough to make his affiliations unmistakable. Osceola, the great popular hero of the Seminole War, had the good fortune from a biographical viewpoint to die romantically in prison; Coacoochee escaped and carried on the war and continued it even in the western country to which he was eventually transported. I don't believe this is the result of any conscious race-prejudice—merely the product of an unconscious feeling that Negroes operating on their own, without white leadership or guidance, *can't* be important—and that therefore Negroes co-operating on an equality with Indians in fighting against U.S. troops are an aberration of nature to be passed over in brief silence.

If your projected *Dictionary of Negro Biography* ever gets under way I should like to do the biographies of Abraham, Louis Pacheco, Gopher John, and any other of the Seminole Negro leaders—such as John Caesar, Inos, Ben, Garcon, Nero, et al.—who are considered of sufficient importance and for whom adequate material may be available. For some of them a few lines, embodying two or three episodes, would be all that could be expected, from what my researches indicate.

I enclose a sketch of Abraham, for consideration for use in *Phylon*, since I have read that you plan including in that publication sketches preliminary to the DNB. I have given more background than might be required for a dictionary but which I thought advisable in an article. Should you wish a portrait of Abraham I can furnish one—though I wouldn't vouch for its being more than an ideal likeness.[1]

Very truly yours,
Kenneth Wiggins Porter

In 1939, Missouri was the center of a significant struggle to change the jim-crow character of professional and higher education that characterized the state. Accordingly, the effort of Lloyd L. Gaines, beginning in 1935, to enter the law school of the University of Missouri received statewide (and even nationwide) attention late in 1939 and into 1940; in the same period Miss Lucile Bluford applied for admission to the School of Journalism of the University of Missouri. Various impeding expedients were then attempted by the legislature and by Governor L. C. Stark, and these were countered by demonstrations of young Black—and some white—people in Saint Louis and in Jefferson City.*

In the midst of all this turmoil came plans to celebrate the seventy-fifth anniversary of the founding of Lincoln University in Jefferson City. Lincoln's president, Sherman Dana Scruggs (b. 1894), had come to this position in 1938 (he held it until 1956) after having been supervisor of

1. Professor Porter, in a letter to the present editor dated 28 June 1973, offered some corrections to his 1940 letter to Du Bois: land was not taken by the Diaz dictatorship from the ancestors of the people he described in the letter; Louis Pacheco was less historically important than he then thought, for Porter had been misled by the historical writing of Joshua Giddings, a good and even noble politician but a better novelist than historian; Gopher John was more important than his letter suggested; and Porter wished to "apologize for calling Edward Rose a 'surly ruffian,'" for he came to think of Rose as "the victim of a great deal of prejudiced testimony." The "sketch" he sent to Du Bois was published with the title "Abraham," in *Phylon* 2 (Second Quarter 1941): 105–16.

* For a contemporary study, see N. P. Barksdale, "The Gaines Case and Its Effect on Negro Education in Missouri," *School and Society* 51 (9 March 1940): 309–13; see also Jessie P. Guzman, *Twenty Years of Court Decisions Affecting Higher Education in the South, 1938–1958* (Tuskegee, Ala.: Tuskegee Institute, 1960).

instruction in the (segregated) public schools of Kansas City, Kansas, for twenty-four years. The
governor was to speak briefly at the celebration, but as the main speaker President Scruggs
invited Du Bois. After Du Bois accepted the initial and formal request, he received a long and
illuminating letter from President Scruggs.

Jefferson City, Missouri,
December 26, 1940

Dear Dr. Du Bois:

We are pleased that you have consented to accept our invitation.

I write you again, however, because there are two aspects in the situation which
will require your cooperation with us to make the affair the success which we wish for
it.

One has reference to the date. Upon further consideration it has been decided that
we shall hold the Founders' Day exercises on the date of Sunday nearest the
fourteenth day of January each year instead of the day on which it comes, unless it is a
Sunday. In this coming year the date and hour has been set for Sunday afternoon,
January 12, at three o'clock. It is our request of you then that you be with us on
Sunday afternoon, January 12, instead of Tuesday, January 14, if this is at all
convenient for you.

The other matter concerns your acquaintance with our situation, that is, the program of development and expansion which is now under way at Lincoln University
and for which on January 8, 1941, we are asking the General Assembly, the state
legislature, to grant an appropriation of approximately three and one-half millions for
its promotion. Enclosed herewith is a clipping of an article written by one of our men
and published in *School and Society*, March 9, 1940. This article may give you a more
complete picture of the educational situation in Missouri and how the Administration
of this Institution is attempting to do its job of educational service.

At present we believe that there is generally a good feeling among legislators
toward our Institution. We are approaching the General Assembly respectfully and
with every courtesy. On the date of its convention, January 8, we are presenting our
estimated budget and requesting what we consider a reasonable appropriation grant.
What we are asking for is based upon a careful study of needs and our figures are
conservative.

We are inviting the members of the Assembly to our Seventy-fifth Anniversary
services on the Sunday afternoon on which day you are invited to be our speaker.
What you shall say on that occasion may improve our relations with the legislature
and enhance our chances to get the appropriation grant. It is our belief that a knowledge and acquaintance with the situation will be a sufficient guide for you in the
preparation of the message you shall bring to us which may strengthen the good will
already developing, and at the same time it can possess an appeal for the reasonableness of adequate support of higher education for its Negro people.

What we mean in the foregoing statements is to make clear to you our position
before the legislators of our State, and to avoid what can be an easily mistaken attitude

by those who hold the legislative "purse strings" should our guest speaker's message include statements which may affect the situation undesirably through lack of acquaintance and understanding of our problem.

Dear Dr. Du Bois, you will pardon me if what I am saying here reflects excessive caution. It is not with an attempt to censor your speech that I write you, but I do hasten to give you the picture of our situation that you may be in the better position to deal with it in your message and thereby win our guests, the legislators, over to the reasonableness of our request for adequate appropriation for an educational program which we are mandated to provide.

We are most happy over the title of your message. The terms of your engagement are quite satisfactory. We eagerly await your word that the change in date from Tuesday, January 14, to Sunday afternoon, January 12, will be satisfactory to you.[1]

Sincerely yours,
Sherman D. Scruggs
President

P. S. A train over the Missouri Pacific Railway leaves St. Louis at 8:45 am and arrives at Jefferson City at 10:50. We shall meet you at the station.

S. D. S.

Late in 1940 and early in 1941 correspondence was exchanged among the widow of the great attorney Clarence Darrow, his biographer-to-be Irving Stone, and Du Bois.

Irving Stone (b. 1903) was at this time at the beginning of his remarkably successful career as novelist and biographer. He had already published Pageant of Youth *(1933); his works on Van Gogh,* Lust for Life *(1934), and on Jack London,* Sailor on Horseback *(1938); and a novel,* False Witness *(1940). His* Clarence Darrow for the Defense *was first published in 1941 by Doubleday.*

Chicago, Ill., December 14, 1940

Dear Friend of *Ours:*

Long before this I should have sent word about the life of Clarence Darrow being written by Irving Stone, author of *The Lust for Life,* portraying Van Gogh, and the life-story of Jack London, *Sailor on Horseback,* and other books, as is rather well-known; and, to save Mr. Stone's time, I have been commissioned to invite certain ones to please send him their recollections of Mr. Darrow, personal associations and impressions, etc. your name among them. Illnesses, deaths, responsibilities and family-concerns have prevented promptly attending to my share of the fostering of

---

1. Du Bois's address, delivered 12 January 1941, was entitled, "The Future of the Negro State University." It was published in the *Wilberforce University Quarterly* 2 (April 1941): 53–60. It appears in Du Bois's *Education of Black People: Ten Critiques, 1906–1960*, pp. 129–38. Readers may examine it to see if they think President Scruggs's letter had any moderating impact upon Du Bois.

friends furnishing suitable material to be woven into the biography, but—here I am asking you to send Mr. Stone whatever you feel may enhance and warm the tenor of his production. Once you were our dinner guest, and many times in our zig-zaggings we were almost, but not quite, able to meet you in places, but it is not necessary for me to tell you of the admiration and esteem Mr. Darrow entertained for you, whether vis a vis or long distance, of course. I find that biographers are hungry as octopi for the "human interest" element, and maybe you might make a neat incident of that evening at our home, if you will, in connection with other close links in your acquaintance, by way of indicating how together you had in common causes and activities that drew you into a fine friendship. We lived a square east of this number, but it was necessary for me to bid farewell to the beloved rooftree where we dwelt for more than thirty years, and I am now on "the other side of the tracks"—(the Ill. Cent.) Clarence would want you to add your quota, as you know, and so do I, always yours with sincere and cordial well-wishing,

Ruby H. Darrow (Mrs. Clarence)

Atlanta, Ga., 31 January 1941

My dear Mrs. Darrow:

Your letter of December 14, has been awaiting an answer while I finished some hectic traveling and speaking: before the American Historical Association in New York at Christmas time; at the Lincoln University, Missouri and finally I went to a Federal Government agricultural conference in Texas.

I wish I could set down definitely and with real emphasis and detail some of the many impressions which Clarence Darrow made upon me, but that would be hard to do at this distance and time. However, I am writing a short note to Mr. Irving Stone.

I trust this will find you in good health and may I send my best wishes.

Very sincerely yours,
W. E. B. Du Bois

Atlanta, Ga., 31 January 1941

My dear Mr. Stone:

Mrs. Clarence Darrow has written me asking me to send some of my impressions of Clarence Darrow. It is difficult to be very definite and to convey the strong impression which he always made upon me. I saw him casually and for short bits of time over a period of a number of years between 1900 and 1925 or so. I have been a dinner guest at his home and he visited me in my New York office.

First of all, as a Negro and rather tense in my feelings, I was drawn to him because he was absolutely lacking in racial consciousness and because of the broad catholicity of his knowledge and tastes. He was one of the few white folk with whom I felt quite free to discuss matters of race and class which usually I would not bring up. Darrow was a close friend of Dr. Bentley of Chicago, a colored dentist whom I know for many years and who together with his wife was very close to me. I think they first introduced me to Darrow and I met him often at their home. There is one story that sticks in my mind because I heard Darrow tell it several times and it is rather characteristic of his social ideas. We were talking about freedom and slavery and he said that he had heard about a freedman in the South, a sort of happy-go-lucky derelict. Some one questioned him "Sam, how are you getting on?" "Well, not doing so well." "Don't get food so regular as you used to?" "No, suh!" "Don't have nobody to look after you?" "No suh, that is a fact." "Well Sam, weren't you better off in slavery?" "Well, I tells you suh, it's like this: there's a sort of looseness about this here freedom that I likes!"

I can see Darrow in his loose fitting clothes chuckling over this story. The "looseness" of freedom was something that appealed to him.

I wish I could think of more to tell you. Something may occur to me and if it does, I will write you later.

> Very sincerely yours,
> W. E. B. Du Bois

Encino, Calif., February 6, 1941

Dear Mr. Du Bois:

Your letter arrived at a very timely moment, for I was just writing about the Sweet case and Mr. Darrow's life-long friendship for the Negro. I have used your comments about the matter and I think I shall also use the amusing anecdote.[1]

I think that you will like the work I have done in relation to the problems between the white and the colored people in America.

> Sincerely yours,
> Irving Stone

Merle Curti (1897), educated at Harvard, was a professor at Smith College (1925–37), at Teachers College of Columbia University (1937–42), and at the University of Wisconsin (1942–68), where he is now emeritus. His writings include The American Peace Crusade *(1929),* Social Ideas of American Educators *(1935), and* The Growth of American Thought *(1943), which was awarded the Pulitzer Prize. While at Smith he had invited Du Bois to lecture to his classes and had corresponded with him concerning his research for what became the second of the books named above.* Curti was the program chairman for the 1940 American Historical Association convention, at one session of which—as noted earlier in this work—Du Bois presided. A result was a kind of "courtesy" letter from Curti of more substance than usual for that genre.*

1. Stone quoted from Du Bois on page 471 of *Clarence Darrow:* "Being a Negro and rather tense in my feelings, I was drawn to Clarence Darrow because he was absolutely lacking in racial consciousness and because of the broad catholicity of his knowledge and tastes. He was one of the few white folk with whom I felt quite free to discuss matters of race and class which usually I would not bring up."

* The 1934 Curti–Du Bois letters are published in H. Aptheker, "Some Unpublished Writings of Du Bois," *Freedomways* 5 (Winter 1965): 127–28.

New York City, December 31, 1940

Dear Dr. Du Bois:

I was very sorry I did not get a chance to speak to you again and to thank you for coming to the meetings of the American Historical Association. It was a great compliment to us and we all appreciated it. The meeting as far as I was able to attend seemed to me to go very well on the whole. What I had hoped was that scholars, regardless of color, might discuss the Negro in American history as any scholars would do. I thought that this was largely accomplished and I hope I am right in so thinking.

With best personal regards.

Sincerely yours,
Merle Curti

1941

Other than the biographical remarks in his letter to Du Bois, given below, further information on William C. Ewing has not been found. The exchange captures a widespread mood of the period.

Williamsburg, Va., January 9, 1941

Dear Dr. Du Bois:

Here's hoping that you will not have entirely forgotten the last secretary of the New York Civic Club.[1] I am writing to congratulate you most heartily on your book which I have just read, "Black Folk." I discovered it in the library of The College of William and Mary, here in Williamsburg, and have read every word with the greatest of satisfaction. I was not surprised at the excellent arrangement and organization of your material—and of course I should not have expected anything but good style of writing from you—but what amazed me very greatly was that any man, in a single lifetime, could acquire so vast a knowledge of so complicated and extensive a subject. The grand-daughter to whom you dedicate the book will surely have something to boast of in her ancestry.

After reading the last chapter, I have kept thinking that I would like her opportunity of reading a corresponding chapter in such a book that may be written thirty years from now. With all the thought you have put on this subject, you must be continually wondering what effect the present war will have on the development of Africa and on the entire subject of racial prejudice. I confess that I anticipate very little good to come out of warfare; yet, its aftereffects may be beneficial even as the horrors of the French Revolution eventually resulted in a better society than seemed otherwise possible.

Your book is the clearest example I ever saw of the soundness of the economic interpretation of history. I must say that, while I appreciate the evils of capitalism as much as I ever did, I am not so pleased as I once was with any propect of socialism as it is usually conceived in America. I am becoming increasingly suspicious of any form

---

1. The New York Civic Club, organized in 1916, was a radical organization for fellowship, debate, and consultation. It lasted until the early 1930s, when William C. Ewing was its secretary. It was remarkable not only in its radical and yet broad quality but also in the fact that men and women and Black and white participated equally. Du Bois was a member of the original executive committee; other leaders in its effort included Frederic C. Howe, Freda Kirchwey, Inez Milholland, Mary White Ovington, George Gordon Battle, Winthrop D. Lane, Henrietta Rodman, John Reed, Alexander Trachtenberg, Rose Pastor Stokes, Ida Tarbell, and Arthur Spingarn. For years it maintained its own headquarters and restaurant in the downtown section of New York City. A history of this club is needed.

of monopoly, even state capitalism; if the means of production are owned by "all the people" I am not at all sure that the minorities (which let us hope will always exist) will be any freer than now. There is no doubt that English (and perhaps American) social and economic life have reached the end of an era, and our desires will probably have little influence on changes which will be little short of "the course of nature"; but so far as I am able to form ideals for the future they are more along the lines of a cooperative commonwealth in which those who so desire shall be free not to cooperate. I have recently read a book by Granville Hicks entitled "The First To Awake"[2] which, though sketchy, is nevertheless very suggestive and worthwhile.

If ever you come to Williamsburg you must let me know so that I may have the pleasure of renewing our acquaintance. After leaving New York I came here for a small community organization undertaking, since which I have continued as a delightful home; and now I have taken over a small shop for my old age. If our spare-room is not rented when you come, it will be a pleasure indeed to entertain you as our guest. Meanwhile, accept my best wishes for your welfare and again my compliments on your wonderful book.

Sincerely,
William C. Ewing

Atlanta, Ga., 6 February 1941

My dear Mr. Ewing:

I thank you very much for your kind words concerning my book *Black Folk: Then and Now*. I share in your difficulties of trying to evaluate the future. The present mess is certainly terrifying. I should be glad to look you up if I come near Williamsburg. I remember driving through some years ago.

Very sincerely yours,
W. E. B. Du Bois

An exchange between Andrew J. Allison (b. 1892), the alumni secretary of Fisk University, and Du Bois permitted the latter to express at some length his views concerning the Second World War and the United States relationship thereto and, particularly, an appropriate attitude of Black people toward the war at the time. Allison, a graduate of Fisk, studied law at both Harvard and Yale, served the National Urban League in the 1920s, and helped organize Black workers in several industries in New York City during the same period. In 1927, he accepted appointment as alumni secretary of Fisk, and held this position through World War II.

Nashville, Tenn., January 13, 1941

My dear Dr. Du Bois:

The matter of Fisk University in the scheme of National Defense has been on my mind for some time. Fisk men have always rallied to the colors as far as I have been

---

2. The reference is to Granville Hicks and Richard M. Bennett, *The First to Awaken* (New York: Modern Age Books, 1940).

able to learn from records and stories handed down. Certainly Fisk men achieved outstanding success in the last World War and Fisk women performed nobly here at home. Through shortsighted leadership at Fisk during the last World War, Fisk men never received full credit for their heroism in fighting for the flag. Our present leadership is that of pacifism, which has meant no encouragement has been given toward bringing military records up to date nor playing them up.

I have known all along President [Thomas E.] Jones' philosophy of education. I have known very intimately his convictions regarding war and peace. I respect his convictions as I admire and respect him as a man of great leadership qualities who has meant so much to Fisk. I take it, in his present pronouncement, that he is living up to and has the courage of his conviction because he believes thoroughly in America, is a patriot, and accepted the position at Fisk as being one of the ways in which he might make his contribution for a pure Democracy. Therefore, in his periodic absences from the campus at Fisk for the next year, he is being fair to himself and to Fisk, as I see it, because if war does come to these shores in a more definite form than is now present, Fisk will have to declare itself, or, probably before that time the Government will force its hand or take over the plant. I take it that President Jones does not wish to be placed in a position of challenging the Government's right to do this on account of his personal conviction and is, therefore, more or less freeing his hands at present.

It does seem to me, however, that at this time Fisk should take some position regarding National Defense, or make suggestions which could be later moulded into a statement or policy and that alumni opinion should share in moulding that policy. We owe this to our young people here at Fisk and to friends of Fisk who, at this time, have seen only one side of the picture. Almost every educational institution of note in the country has either offered its services in one way or the other or made its stand known. President Jones has been kind enough not to make his personal conviction that of Fisk. Therefore, as far as I have been able to learn, Fisk as yet has no position regarding National Defense. Hampton immediately let its position be known with the inauguration [in 1940] of President [Malcolm S.] McLean. Wilberforce University, Tuskegee Institute, West Virginia State College, Howard University, and now Tennessee State College have all stated their positions. President [James B.] Conant of Harvard was one of the recent committee, as you know, who asked the President to tell us in plain language where we were going, how fast or how slowly, as the case may be, and the chances of immediate danger to the United States.

I think every Fisk man is proud that our own Dr. Julian Dawson has recently been promoted to the rank of Colonel in what was formerly the old Eighth Illinois, now the 184th Field Artillery. Several other ranking officers who are Fisk men, notably, Attorney James B. Cashin and Dr. Homer P. Cooper, have also been promoted, as well as other Fisk men of the old 369th, New York. None of us want war. I think even though we may in the future be involved in war, more so than we are at present, the national policy and intent of the United States is good. However, that is purely my own opinion, the future interests of the American Negro are tied up in the security of these shores and the support of our national policy, no matter what it might be. We had our chance at the polls last November. Whether it is war or peace it is going to mean Defense of one kind or another, in which we are already engaged. What shall be Fisk's stand and contribution at this time when the country is being put to a supreme test and when there are greater chances than ever before of grave peril to our people? These are the questions I am asking you and others to answer and place before our constituency immediately in the Fisk News in order that they might be able to think through the channel of Fisk as to what and how we should chart the future. I am sure each Fisk man will have the courage of his conviction, as has President Jones, because, after all, we not only believe in Fisk but have a great stake in it. You may write this article independently or get in touch with other of the Fisk men that I am writing, or that you might suggest, for an article that would represent the composite view of all. However, I would prefer your independent opinion. But whatever you do, please act immediately and let me hear from you at your earliest convenience.

> Sincerely yours,
> Andrew J. Allison
> Alumni Secretary

P. S.—A similar letter is being sent to Rev. William Lloyd Imes, Dr. Charles H. Wesley, Captain M. V. Boutté, Dr. Ernest R. Alexander, Attorney James B. Cashin, Dr. L. D. Reddick, Attorney J. Alston Atkins, and Attorney Carter Wesley.

> Atlanta, Ga., 3 February 1941

My dear Mr. Allison:

Answering your letter of January 13, I beg to say that I am glad that Fisk University up to date has not yielded to War hysteria and tried to capitalize it by beating the tom toms of war. I have lived through one period of deliberate and prolonged propaganda for war and partially succumbed to it *until* I really believed that the first World War was a war to end war and that the interests of colored people in particular were bound up in the defeat of Germany. I have lived to know better and my opposition to war under any circumstances has been immeasurably increased. I still believe that defensive war is justifiable but I utterly refuse to believe that there is any excuse for the United States entering the present world war. We are not being attacked; there is no reasonable possibility of our having to defend ourselves. On the contrary in this war we are trying to attack Japan because of race prejudice and we are defending China not because we love the Chinese but because we want to exploit them. I do not believe that the British Empire stands or has ever stood for democracy. It is idiotic to talk about a people who brought the slave trade to its greatest development, who are the chief exploiters of Africa and who hold four hundred million Indians in subjection, as the great defenders of democracy. The British Empire has caused more human misery than Hitler will cause if he lives a hundred years. I appreciate England's many gifts to civilization and suffer with her suffering but I do not forget nor minimize historic facts.

I know that Fisk University and other colored institutions are being greatly influenced by the example of Hampton. Hampton has as its new president a man who may make, and so far as I know will make, a good president but the mere fact that as a former publicity man he used the present war hysteria to advertise his advent into Hampton, does not mean that all other Negro institutions must fall pell-mell in the same direction. Fisk University as an institution of learning has a right to keep calm and stay aloof from this war insanity. It should attend to its business of education and appeal for support to those who believe in education and not to those who are advocates of organized murder. I, therefore, hope that Fisk University, its officers and students and its alumni will take a firm stand against all participation in the present war and against the present insane rush to overturn civilization in the name of defending it.

Very sincerely yours,
W. E. B. Du Bois

Nashville, Tenn., February 8, 1941

My dear Dr. Du Bois:

Thank you very kindly for sending in your statement and views regarding "Fisk and National Defense."

I am extremely gratified that you took the time from your busy life to do this for Fisk. Every Fisk man and woman will be interested in the position you take on this question.[1] I again thank you for your contribution.

Sincerely yours,
Andrew J. Allison

Something of the realities of basic struggles against discrimination and for human dignity comes out in an exchange between Du Bois and friends in Virginia early in 1941, concerning one of the myriad little-known but decisive fighters in the struggles.

Richmond, Virginia, January 28, 1941

Dear Dr. Du Bois:

The Friends' Appreciation Society with the aid and cooperation of some friends is sponsoring a program in recognition of the pioneering work of Mr. Thomas L. Dabney in the interest of equal salaries for the colored teachers of Virginia. This program will be held at Ebenezer Baptist Church this city Sunday evening, February 16 at eight o'clock. We would like for you to share in this affair.

Mr. Dabney launched the state-wide movement for higher salaries in April, 1931, while he was principal of the Buckingham Training School and president of the Buckingham County Teachers' Association. His organization in that county cooperated with him and gave some financial support. That spring Mr. Dabney circulated petitions and spoke at district teachers' meetings in Bedford, in Chesterfield County and in other localities where the cause was presented and explained. In November he

1. Du Bois's letter was published in full in *Fisk News*, February 1941, p. 5.

spoke to the Executive committee of the Negro Organization Society at West Point at the organization's 1933 annual meeting. On December 7, 1933 he appeared again before the central committee of that body in Richmond with facts on unequal salaries and low per capita cost of instruction for colored children in various sections of the state in comparison with figures for white teachers and white children.

Mr. Dabney kept up a consistent and continual publicity in the white and colored press for five years showing the wide differences in salaries and cost of instruction for colored teachers and colored pupils as compared with figures for whites. His various studies and compilations during these years were sources of many newspaper stories and in several instances data he gathered were released by the Associated Press, Associated Negro Press, Federated Press and other news gathering agencies in articles for their member papers. Within two years he had secured the signature of 2,571 teachers to the petitions for higher salaries. All these facts were presented to Governor Pollard and other state officials. Mr. Dabney secured endorsement of the movement by several district Baptist associations and other meetings and conferences during these years and thereby gave wide publicity to the cause. In one instance at least the [Norfolk] *Journal and Guide* carried an editorial on the salary fight. By this work a foundation was laid for the work of the National Association for the Advancement of Colored People and other organizations within the past two or more years. Public opinion was created favorable to the cause of the teachers and there is no doubt but that Mr. Dabney's work and that of others with him paved the way for better chances of success within the coming years for equal salaries for our teachers in every section of this state.

If you favor this program, send us a list of your friends whom you think will join us in this affair. Also send us your gift in the enclosed envelope and help us make this affair a big and successful one.

> Very sincerely yours,
> Hezekiah Walls, President
> Dabney Apprèciation Committee

P. S. Mr. Dabney met you at home of Dr. J. B. Simpson after your lecture on War and Prejudice about 1915. An active NAACP member, he had led in arranging for that lecture. He lost two principalships in fight in Virginia for equal salaries.

> Atlanta, Ga., 6 February 1941

Mr. Hezekiah Walls
My dear Sir:

I am very glad to join other friends of Mr. Thomas L. Dabney in making tribute to his work in Virginia. I remember when he started the agitation for equal salaries and his great devotion to this task. He ought to be recognized as one of the fathers of the movement.

> Very sincerely yours,
> W. E. B. Du Bois

Richmond, Virginia, February 18, 1941

Dear Dr. Du Bois:

Our committee heartily thanks you for your very fine letter in behalf of Mr. Thomas L. Dabney who was honored at the meeting at Ebenezer Baptist Church Sunday night. I am instructed to tender you Mr. Dabney's thanks also.

We had a very nice program and Mr. Dabney renewed his pledge to continue his efforts in cooperation with others for equal salaries for our teachers and better schools for our children. He mentioned you particularly as one of his spiritual guides in his work explaining that after being schooled by leaders like the late John Mitchell, Jr., Chandler Owen and A. Philip Randolph and Dr. Du Bois he could not refrain from being a fighter for justice and liberty.[1]

Very sincerely yours,
Hezekiah Walls, President

Du Bois's ideas on segregation were misunderstood and distorted while he lived and have been misrepresented frequently in works since his death. Du Bois has been made to say either that he opposed segregation—period—or that he favored segregation—period; of course, neither position was his and at every opportunity he strove with great patience to make his view clear. One such occasion presented itself in the exchange with Sherman Briscoe, director of public relations for the Chicago Defender *newspaper, given here.*

Chicago, Ill., January 30, 1941

Dear Dr. Du Bois:

We are herewith enclosing copy of our this week's National Edition which carries an editorial concerning your attitude on the separate school set-up.[2]

This editorial was written by our chief editorial writer, Dr. Metz T. P. Lochard, a staunch admirer of your work.

Very truly yours,
Sherman Briscoe

Atlanta, Ga., 11 February 1941

My dear Mr. Briscoe:

I thank you for your letter of January 30 and the editorial by Dr. Lochard. I appreciate Dr. Lochard's statement but he doesn't give the whole of my argument and consequently might lead the reader into a false conclusion as to my beliefs. At the

1. Thomas L. Dabney was among the first of the Black students at the Brookwood Labor College in Katonah, New York. He published articles on Black people and the labor movement in the *Messenger*, November 1926, and in *Opportunity*, March 1926, November 1929, and September 1930. He also published frequently on aspects of education in *Southern Workman:* November 1927, January 1928, April 1929, and January 1930. A biographical study of Dabney is badly needed.

2. The editorial, entitled, "Dr. Du Bois and Separate Schools," appeared in the issue dated 23–30 January 1941.

Seventy-Fifth Anniversary of Lincoln University of Missouri, a separate Negro state institution, I was correctly quoted as saying that segregated schools are "extravagant and idiotic and in direct contravention to that democratic equality toward which all education in the end must strive." But my argument did not stop there. I said "you have here a segregated institution and two-thirds of the Negroes in the United States are being educated in segregated schools; there will be no change in this principle of segregation during our lifetime because it is engrafted in the customs and mores of the nation and these change slowly. Therefore, you must go to work to make your segregated institutions the very best schools possible; make the institution not equal to but superior to the University of Missouri and make the public schools and other insitutions of the South the best of their kind."

I might have gone on to say that even in the North in a city like Chicago, you have segregated schools, Du Sable High School, for example. Instead of neglecting or criticizing such a school because it is separate, make it the best high school in Chicago. That is the only practical way to attack segregation in education today. Attack it by accepting it and making the best of it and at the same time stating the fact that the principle underlying such segregation is idiotic.

I will be glad to have you bring this to the attention of Mr. Lochard.

Very sincerely yours,

W. E. B. Du Bois

In response to a request for data on the Pan-African movement, Du Bois offered some remarks on its past and its probable future. George A. Finch (1884–1958), educated in the law at Georgetown University, served the State Department in various technical capacities through 1919, became editor of the American Journal of International Law, *and for many years was associated with the Carnegie Endowment for International Peace, of which he was from 1940 through 1943 associate director, and from 1943 through 1947 director.*

Washington, D. C., February 4, 1941

Dear Professor Burghardt Du Bois:

The attached inquiry is designed to fill gaps in the information available in this office relative to various governmental and non-governmental international organizations. In a volume which we have just published under the title, *The International Conferences of American States*, there were included some details on organizations of this type. We hope that in subsequent volumes it may be possible to include more information which will be of value to the organizations themselves, to persons having contact with them, and to students of administration.

Enclosed is a self-addressed stamped envelope for the return of the form. Your cooperation in the compilation of this information will be greatly appreciated.

Sincerely yours,

Geo. A. Finch

Atlanta, Ga., 11 February 1941

My dear Mr. Finch:

I am not sure whether the Pan-African [Congress] ought to be regarded as an existing institution or not. It was planned as a conference without specific organization. I acted as organizer at its first meeting and as secretary at subsequent meetings. For a while we had a permanent paid secretary in Paris but that lasted for only a year. I am still permanent secretary but there has been no meeting of the Congress since 1927.

The Pan-African Congress has held the following meetings: Paris, France, 1919; Paris, Brussels and London, 1921; Paris, London and Lisbon, 1923; New York, 1927. Further meetings were planned for later years for Tunis, Africa but permission was refused by the French Government; also in the West Indies but proper transportation could not be secured.

The ideas back of the Congress are still alive and discussed and if the world ever settles down to peace again, there will be another meeting of the Congress. At present, however, it is only an idea on paper and in the memory of a considerable number of former participants in America, the West Indies and Africa.

Very sincerely yours,
W. E. B. Du Bois

An amusing exchange involving Du Bois, Countee Cullen, and Ira Reid occurred early in 1941; the letters show also Du Bois's concern with the work of others and the care he exercised in his duties as editor-in-chief of Phylon.

Atlanta, Ga., February 12, 1941

My dear Countee:

Will you read the enclosed and tell me what you think of it? I want to publish it in *Phylon*. I am for the time being concealing the authorship.

I enjoyed *The Lost Zoo*.[1] Do not forget us if you have something you want published.

Very sincerely yours,
W. E. B. Du Bois

New York, New York, February 20, 1941

My dear Dr. Du Bois:

Thank you for letting me see the poem which I am returning to you, and thank you even more for asking me my opinion of it. I like it and feel that it would not be out of place if published in *Phylon*. I am not an ardent admirer of the freer forms of verse, but this has rhythm, imagery and language of an arresting order, and if I were an editor I should be happy to publish it. I might single out for especial praise such

1. Countee Cullen, *The Lost Zoo: A Rhyme for the Young, But Not Too Young* (New York: Harper and Bros., 1940).

expressions as: "In each hand a bucketful of glory," and "the fecund-mellow beauty of momentary forgetfulness in silver laughter." But perhaps it is enough to say that I like the poem.

I have not forgotten my promise to send you something for consideration for the pages of *Phylon*, but when I do send something, I want to be fairly hopeful that it will please you.

> Very sincerely yours,
> Countee Cullen[1]

Atlanta, Ga., 6 March 1941

Memo to Mr. Reid:

Braithwaite recommended Miss Holmes' poem and I heartily concurred.[2] When I received your dissent, I concealed the authorship and sent the poem to Countee Cullen. Enclosed is the answer. As a poet you are a great sociologist.

A long letter—that seems not to have been answered—was sent by Du Bois to the Twentieth Century Fund in the hope that the fund might be persuaded to help his projects for the study of economics with regard to the Afro-American people, and especially with regard to cooperative enterprises. While this letter repeats some details appearing in earlier letters, it adds significant material concerning Du Bois's great interest in the cooperative movement.

Atlanta, Ga., February 13, 1941

Gentlemen:

I have long been interested in the promotion of consumers cooperation especially among American Negroes and I understand that your organization is interested in promoting such cooperation.[3]

I believe that the economic future of the American Negro has reached a critical stage. In the expanding industry of the South the Negro has found no adequate entrance as a worker and in the declining state of agriculture he is one of the most unfortunate of the victims. I think it, therefore, necessary particularly today when we must forecast the disarrangement of industry after the present war to begin a serious study and planning for the economic future of the Negro in America; and that this is necessary not simply for him but in order to avoid the catastrophe of having a tenth of our population retrograde into poverty with its resultant disease and crime.

1. Copyright © 1976 by Ida M. Cullen.
2. The reference is to William S. Braithwaite, the poet and a member of *Phylon's* editorial board. The poem in question was "Flower Vendors," by Ethlynne E. Holmes; it was published in *Phylon* 2 (Second Quarter 1941): 117–18.
3. The Twentieth Century Fund has existed since its founding in 1919 by Edward A. Filene. Among those active in its work through the years were Adolf A. Berle, Jr., Francis Biddle, Robert S. Lynd, and Charles P. Taft. Only white men have constituted its officers and board of trustees. It considers itself "an operating research institution conducting its own work"—not funding others; the quotation is from page 2 of its 1953 publication, *The Work of the Twentieth Century Fund*.

I began urging the attention of Negroes to consumers cooperation as a method of beginning to solve their economic problems in August, 1917.[2] On August 26, 27, I called a conference in the office of the *Crisis*, 70 Fifth Avenue, New York City. Twelve representatives came from seven states and adopted a tentative program. Out of this came the establishment of several local efforts of cooperation of which the most important was a cooperative store at the colored Bluefield Institute, West Virginia and the Roddy cooperative grocery stores in Memphis. The West Virginia experiment was very successful and lasted for about ten years. It was especially commended by officials of the Harvard business school but the state administration finally ruled that the store was in competition with private business and could not be allowed to continue in a state school. The Roddy stores were very successful for a period but soon failed when they were changed from a cooperative to a stock investing enterprise. Since that time I have written considerable in Negro papers about a more carefully planned start in cooperation preceded by a careful survey on economic conditions among Negroes. One rather elaborate plan of this sort was worked out here at Atlanta university in 1933 but funds for its support were not obtained.

Last year I obtained a small grant of a thousand dollars from the Carnegie Foundation to finance a meeting here which would take up the general question of the economic condition of the Negro, the present trends and the possibility of future planning. This is to be called *The First Phylon Institute*, being named after the quarterly review of race and culture which Atlanta University is publishing and of which I am editor-in-chief. It is also to be called the *Twenty-Fifth Atlanta University Conference*, thus linking it to the well-known studies of the Negro problem held at Atlanta University between 1897 and 1914. These conferences made twenty publications on conditions among Negroes which were widely circulated and read.

I want the present meeting which will take place April 17, 18 and 19 of this year to consist of some twenty-five experts chiefly from the colored land grant colleges of the South and I want to present to them carefully prepared statitistics, charts and statements covering the economic condition of the Negro. I have been promised a second appropriation of a thousand dollars for a similar conference next year in which we could use the returns of the Census of 1940 and face more carefully the problem of future economic planning. In this planning I want the matter of consumers' cooperation among Negroes to take a prominent part. At present there are in the United States perhaps a half dozen local efforts: one in Chicago, one in Gary, Indiana, one in Philadelphia, and one just started at Tuskegee. With the new federal housing experiments further local efforts may be expected but they need careful guidance and long term planning.

I am writing to ask if your Foundation would be interested in helping this enterprise in any lines and could perhaps arrange to give such help beginning with the third year of these meetings in 1943. Meantime I suggest that you might send an observer to the meeting this year to attend the session and to confer with me and other

2. Actually Du Bois wrote on cooperation in the *Crisis*, April 1915 (9: 310–12) and devoted an editorial to it in the issue of November 1917.

persons, in this way making up his mind as to the advisability and feasibility of help to this enterprise. Personally, I think it is the most important movement for the future uplift of the Negro race in America and consequently for the social security of America that could possibly be undertaken.

May I hear from you at your convenience?

Very sincerely yours,
W. E. B. Du Bois

Early in 1941 Du Bois thought of reconstituting the American Negro Academy founded in 1897. Its first president had been Alexander Crummell, its secoond, Du Bois himself, and Du Bois was succeeded by Archibald H. Grimké. In 1919, John W. Cromwell of Washington, D. C., its secretary at the academy's founding, was elected president, but the academy functioned only until 1924. At about the same time that the idea of reviving the academy occurred to Du Bois, similar thoughts were expressed by Charles H. Wesley and by Rayford W. Logan, the historians at Howard, and by William P. Dabney, author and newspaper publisher in Cincinnati.

In this connection, Du Bois wrote to Dr. Otelia Cromwell,* daughter of John W. Cromwell, seeking information about the academy. She wrote in response to his inquiry.

Washington, D. C., February 24, 1941

My dear Dr. Du Bois:

My failure to send you material from my father's papers relative to the Negro Academy was due not to indifference, negligence, or lack of time but simply to the fact that when you wrote me our home was undergoing structural changes involving an upset condition that persisted for four full months. To make the premises convenient for the workmen, we had to pack and store away into the few unused spaces of the house everything movable, and of course these boxes became and continued inaccessible. When the house was finally turned over to us in the middle of the winter, the task of making a habitable home engrossed us so relentlessly that there was just no time for anything else except routine demands. You can see now that it was quite impossible for me then to go over my father's papers.

After your letter last week, plus the one to Mary [her sister] who began to look over the papers herself and then gave me unequivocal orders, I went down to the storage case this morning. As a result of our searchings one or two things which may be of help to you have been discovered.

There are individual membership cards endorsed as follows:

* Otelia Cromwell (1873–1972) was the first Black graduate of Smith College and received a doctorate from Yale in 1926. She taught in high school in Washington, D. C., in the 1920s and in 1930 became professor of English and chairman of the English department at Miner Teachers' College in Washington. She was co-editor (with Lorenzo D. Turner and Eva B. Dykes) of *Readings from Negro Authors for Schools and Colleges* (New York: Harcourt, Brace and Co., 1931). In 1950 she received an honorary doctor of laws from Smith College. Upon her death, an account of her life appeared in *Jet*, 1 June 1972, p. 27. The *Smith Alumnae Quarterly* of August 1972 and of February 1973 also contain information on Dr. Cromwell.

"I hereby indorse this Constitution of the American Negro Academy, as a member thereof."

Individual cards thus signed are here for thirteen of the members.

Matthew Anderson	S. G. Atkins	J. W. E. Bowen
L. J. Coppin	J. W. Cromwell	W. E. Burghardt Du Bois
G. N. Gresham	Wm. H. Ferris	C. W. Mossell
C. H. Parrish	Benjamin Tucker Tanner	C. H. Turner
Booker T. Washington		

Cards for the others known to be members, as the Grimkés, and Professor Miller, for instance, are lacking.

There are program cards of the meetings for 1897, 1898, 1899, 1901, 1903, 1906, 1907, 1908, 1910, 1911, 1913, 1914, 1918, 1919, 1920. (I enclose one or two duplicates.) The 1897 program is entitled "The First Annual Meeting of the Negro American Academy."

There is a copy of the consitution "Incorporated under the general laws of the District of Columbia." (Since this may be of much importance to you I am enclosing it, but please return it.)[1]

An excerpt from my father's diary of December 31, 1919 reads:

". . . The 23rd anniversary of the American Negro Academy was held at the Y.M.C.A. (12th St. Branch) and at the Lincoln Memorial Church . . . But the outcome of the session of the Academy and to me the most personal was my election as president of the Negro Academy, third in succession from Alexander Crummell, the order being Crummell, Du Bois, Grimké."

I hope you will find this material useful.

Very sincerely yours,
Otelia Cromwell

Atlanta, Ga., 6 May 1941

My dear Dr. Cromwell:

Thank you very much for your kind help with information on the American Negro Academy. I am returning the copy of the constitution.

I hope this will find you and your sister in good health.

Very sincerely yours,
W. E. B. Du Bois

---

1. The constitution stated that the academy should "endeavor with care and diligence" to promote publication of scholarly works; to encourage "youths of genius"; to establish an archive relevant to the interests of the academy; to aid in "the dissemination of the truth and the vindication of the Negro race from vicious assaults"; and, "if possible," to publish an *annual* "designed to raise the standard of intellectual endeavor among American Negroes." For the text of an early address to this academy by Alexander Crummell, see *A Documentary History of the Negro People in the United States*, ed. H. Aptheker (New York: Citadel Press, 1951), 1: 771–74. The academy published twenty-two occasional papers from 1897 to 1924. They were republished in one volume by Arno Press, New York City, in 1969, as *The American Negro Academy Occasional Papers, 1–22*, with an introduction by Ernest Kaiser.

Du Bois gave some details of what he thought was the success of the First Phylon Institute in a letter to his close friend W. R. Banks of Prairie View State College in Texas. In this letter, again, are references to his difficulties with President Rufus Clement of Atlanta University. The letter was marked Personal.

Atlanta, Ga., April 18, 1941

My dear Mr. Banks:

I was sorry you could not be here. The President ran out on me and Mr. Reid did not come. Notwithstanding these three blows we had a very fine session. There were 51 representatives from 35 institutions here and the proceedings were interesting and informative. I had made under Mr. Dean's direction eighty of the best charts illustrating our economic situation that I have ever seen. I hope to publish them at least in part. President [Benjamin E.] Mays [of Morehouse College] gave us a tea, otherwise there were no social activities. The delegates boarded at the dormitory and were charged the regular fee of $1.50 per day which I paid to the University.

I invited the President to say a few words of welcome but he said he had another engagement out of town and was also inclined at the meeting of the *Phylon* board to criticize the general scheme of the meeting and to criticize me for not having consulted him more as to the objects and procedures. He furnished the library exhibition room for the meetings but asked us to furnish one hundred chairs at our own expense.

During the year I have had as I anticipated a rather difficult time with Mr. Clement but I have been determined not to get into open controversy. First, we have needed an extra room for *Phylon*. It is overflowing my offices. He has promised to get us such a room repeatedly but finally said he could not and offered us open storage space in the tower. I said we could use this if one of the rooms at the side of the tower could be locked and an electric light put in. He said he could not afford this expense. Then came the matter of New York University.[1] He was, of course, quite within his rights to decide that he could not spare me during the semester but he wasn't right in intimating that I did not consult him concerning arrangements. As I wrote him, there were no arrangements. I was asked and I told him exactly what I had said to the University authorities before a definite offer was made. I think it would have been an excellent thing for Atlanta University to have made some sacrifice in order that we be represented on the university faculty. But, as I said, it was in his province to decide this and when he did, I said nothing further.

He has not been cooperative at all concerning this Institute.

I shall be away when you come, to attend my annual lecture tour which I put off from February to April this year. I am filling the following engagements: Macalester College, Saint Paul; University of Minnesota; Saturday Lunch Club; Northwestern

---

1. He refers to an inquiry from New York University asking if Du Bois would be interested in serving one semester as a visiting professor. Du Bois was interested—and at that time such an appointment would have been an important breakthrough against jim-crow—but his presence in New York would have required release from President Clement of Atlanta University. The release was not forthcoming.

University; Chicago City-Wide Forum; and forums in Cleveland, Ohio and Springfield, Illinois. I thought I would let you know about this in case any question came up in the board. I secured the President's consent to fill these dates before I went. Also I am speaking one night in May at the Seventy-Fifth Anniversary of Fisk.

I hope this will find you well and so sorry that I will not be here when you come. Greet Mrs. Banks and Elizabeth when you go back and give them my love.

Very sincerely yours,
W. E. B. Du Bois

On 8 April 1941 Professor Rayford W. Logan of Howard University, in his capacity as general president of the Alpha Phi Alpha fraternity—of which Du Bois was a member—issued a press release which, among other matters, proposed that consideration should be given by Black scholars to plans for African-derived peoples in the post-war world. In urging this consideration, Logan recalled the Pan-African movement, headed by Du Bois and participated in by himself. The press release produced an exchange between Du Bois and Logan.

Atlanta, Ga., April 19, 1941
My dear Mr. Logan:

I am very much interested in your release to the Alpha Phi Alpha of April 8. I agree with you and make the following proposal: suppose that in my capacity as Permanent Secretary of the Pan-African Congress, I announce through you a Fifth Pan-African Congress to be held in Port-au-Prince as soon as it is practical after the close of the present war with the understanding that such congress should immediately appoint delegates to wait upon the peace conference or any organization which is re-arranging the world to put before them the demands of the peoples of African descent. If you will look after this and work out a plan of the sort, I shall be very glad to sign it and ask you to act again as my chief assistant.

Very sincerely yours,
W. E. B. Du Bois

Washington, D. C., April 26, 1941
My dear Dr. Du Bois:

Thank you very much for your good letter of April 19 about the Pan-African Congress. My suggestion would be to ascertain first of all from Bellegarde whether President [Elie] Lescot would take kindly to the idea. In the meanwhile, we can be working on the details.

We are trying especially to have various white groups examine the question of the Negro. It would be better for us to be integrated into one or more of the twenty-odd organizations that are working on the problem. I am endeavoring to do this and will keep you informed.

In brief, affairs are still in a nebulous state. The first thing to do is to find out whether Haiti will receive us.

I very much wanted to come down for the conference, and am eager to hear about it.
Many thanks for your note about my book.[1] I am elated to have your commendation.

> Very sincerely,
> Rayford W. Logan

> 8 May 1941

My dear Mr. Logan:
One matter with reference to your last letter: do you not think that the matter of participation of the Negro in the defense program and the Pan-African Congress ought to be kept entirely separate? I am glad to see you concentrating on the matter of defense opportunities but on the other hand I want to concentrate on conditions after the war. That was the main purpose of the *Phylon Institute* and I think that should be the main purpose of the Pan-African Congress. After the war what we want to do is to get a large and representative assembly of colored people together and ask "Where do we go from here?"

I just gave a card of introduction to you to Mr. Grant, a colored British official from British Honduras. He is interested in Pan-Africa.

> Very sincerely yours,
> W. E. B. Du Bois

Du Bois, along with Alain Locke, was a main inspiration for what became known as the Harlem Renaissance of the 1920s. An early and historic herald of that renaissance was Langston Hughes's work; his first published poem appeared in 1921, and this letter to Du Bois recollects that moment.

> Hollow Hills Farm, Monterey, Calif.,
> May 17, 1941

Dear Dr. Du Bois,
This June marks for me twenty years of publication, my first poem having appeared in *The Crisis* under your editorship in June, 1921. I send you my gratitude and continued admiration.[2]

> Sincerely,
> Langston Hughes

The superintendent of the Sunday school in Great Barrington, Massachusetts, attended by Du Bois when a youngster, was Edward J. Van Lennep. When Du Bois was in Germany as a

1. This was Logan's *Diplomatic Relations of the United States with Haiti* (Chapel Hill: University of North Carolina Press, 1941), praised by Du Bois in an earlier letter and recommended in his *Amsterdam News* column of 10 January 1942.
2. This handwritten note appears on the reverse side of a printed version of the cited poem; the poem itself is signed by Hughes and dated 1941.

student in the 1890s, he wrote to Van Lennep and enclosed a long letter, meant for the school, describing the land he was visiting (this correspondence is published in volume one, pp. 18–20). Almost fifty years later it came to the attention of Van Lennep—by then in his eighty-fifth year—and the result was a fascinating exchange.

Great Barrington, Mass., May 21, 1941

Dr. W. E. B. Du Bois

My dear Doctor:

Looking over letter files of years gone by, I find a very interesting account of what you wrote me to be read to our Sunday School, Sept. 29, 1892, from Eisenach, S.W. Germany.

I have in mind turning it over to our Committee that is getting together material of interest to the general Church activities, all to be preserved as we approach the anniversary of its 200 years since it was organized in 1743. Several have been much interested in reading over what you sent to the home Sunday School 49 yrs. ago.

It occurs to me that you may like to see it, while it is still in my hands. A word by the inclosed card will bring it to you.

Our dear Walter Scott in the rapid movement of one of his absorbing, great, historic poems, pauses again and again, to repeat, "Time rolls his ceaseless course!" and certainly it does![1] Here I am 85 years young! Not quite able to do hand stands on the bars, or tramp off to Mt. Everett on snow shoes, but still something of a youngster! And You! Well, I won't even [one illegible word] the age of such a youngster—some might say "kid"! Old time greetings from Alice Shedd that was, and

Yours very Cordially

E. J. Van Lennep

Atlanta, Ga., May 26, 1941

My dear Mr. Van Lennep:

I am delighted to hear from you and should be so glad to see that letter of 1892. If you send it to me, I will see that it gets back to you quickly and safely.

It is fine to know that you are well and evidently in good health. On the other hand, I think that the argument in "That Leveling Process" is all wet.[2] If the income of most men depended directly upon their effort and desert that would be splendid. The marks of men studying for examination do depend upon their effort and desert; but for most men and especially for the richest men, money income depends upon monopoly, privilege, chance and is seldom measured by their labor and effort. A man gets what he earns in case in intellectual effort, e.g. knowledge and power. In the case of money income a man needs three meals a day, clothes and shelter and something but

1. The quoted words appear twice in the third canto of Walter Scott's *Lady of the Lake*.

2. Du Bois's reference is obscure. Presumably an enclosure from Van Lennep stimulated the discussion.

not much more; but despite effort he gets starvation in some cases or in others fifty thousand dollars a year more than he can spend. Equality of income is rational and based on essential equality of human needs. There is no equality of human accomplishment and no demand for it and no need for it.

With best regards to you and all friends in town who remember me, I am

Very sincerely yours,
W. E. B. Du Bois

Gt. Barrington, Mass., May 28, 1941

Dr. W. E. B. Du Bois
My dear Doctor:

We connected promptly and yet a thousand and one things, each quite natural, might have happened to interfere with our connection.

Now I am mailing that old letter to you. In all probability it will reach you safe and it will be back here without anything happening. At a railroad crossing just a few hundred feet from this desk on which I am writing, thousands upon thousands have crossed without thought of accident, and yet three men were instantly killed not so long ago.

Suppose we level off, in all fairness to all. Every human being has the same to a cent. How will it be at the end of the first week? So infinite and varied are the influences affecting these complex lives of ours, argument and discussion and the laying down of rules all seem useless.

Your old friends often speak of you. We wish you could be up here for the gathering of High School Alumni.

Our younger daughter with her husband was away for about three months, the early spring and most of the winter. They motored down just leisurely, the two of them thro' southern coast states down into Florida, and took their time on the way home.

As to the letter, there is no special hurry about its return. It will find its place eventually with material being kept as of interest among our Church activities.

You would hardly know the group of School Buildings. Classes run way over 100. As elsewhere 75% and more of teachers are Catholic and Irish. When it comes to the general help, hardly a single one not Irish. For years an Irish doctor has been chairman of the School Board and he is a typical Boss! The same of all town works. Hardly a dollar paid out to help not Irish. If one wants old New England or real old stock now, one must go west!

Best wishes to you

Cordially yours,
E. J. Van Lennep

Atlanta, Ga., 7 July 1941

My dear Mr. Van Lennep:

Thank you very much for letting me see this letter. I am returning it herewith. I realize that Great Barrington has changed. It would be pretty difficult for me to feel at home there now.

Very sincerely yours,
W. E. B. Du Bois

Exchanges between Lester A. Walton and Du Bois were usually significant; another such occurred in the summer of 1941, addressed to Walton as the United States minister to Liberia.

Atlanta, Ga., July 8, 1941

My dear Walton:

I want to congratulate you upon the new Legation Building and your generally successful work in Liberia. I was sorry to have missed you on your last visit. If I mistake not, you owe me a dinner or do I owe you? Let me know certainly when you come again.

There is one matter which I have been going to take up with you when I saw you but time is flying. A way back in 1908, under the presidency I think of Arthur Barclay, the Liberian Government nominated Booker Washington and myself to the Order of African Redemption. I forget who the American minister [was] who pushed the matter of the medals through without any knowledge of his action on my part or any suggestion.[1] I understand that the medals were actually struck. Afterwards mine was withdrawn and eventually, I am told, was bestowed upon Bishop [Alexander] Walters. The alleged reason for this was a criticism of Liberia that appeared in the *Horizon* of which I was one of the editors. The real reason [was] that Ernest Lyon and some other friends of Mr. Washington did not want me honored at the same time that he was. I said nothing at the time although I had a perfectly legitimate defense. I did not write the criticism on Liberia which appeared in the *Horizon*. The *Horizon* was a little magazine divided into three parts. These three parts were independently edited by F. H. A. Murray, L. M. Hershaw and myself. Each part was independent and I did not write the criticism of Liberia nor did I see it until afterwards. Moreover, the criticism was not bitter nor unfair but was directed at the committee of Liberians headed by Vice-President Dossen who had just visited the United States.[2] In any event it was not my criticism and I was in no way responsible for it.

1. The United States minister to Liberia from 1903 to 1910 was Ernest Lyon, mentioned later in this same letter.

2. In June 1908 a delegation from Liberia, headed by Vice-President James J. Dossen, visited Washington and conferred with the president and state department officials. France and Britain were threatening the integrity and existence of Liberia and Washington's assistance was sought—and obtained. Prior to the visit Dossen published an essay, "Past, Present and Future of Liberia," in the *Independent* 64 (2 January 1908): 21–26. *The Tuskegee Student*, 20 June 1908, published an account of the visit. See also the *Outlook* 91 (13 March 1909): 575. Booker T. Washington was of course consulted by President Roosevelt on this matter.

What I ought to have done was immediately to have made these facts known to the Liberian Government but I had the confidence of young manhood that the truth would eventually come out of its own accord. When, however, I went to Liberia and was given the temporary title of Minister Plenipotentiary to represent President Coolidge at the inauguration of President King, I secretly hoped that the injustice which had been done me would be repaired and that the Order which had been voted me would be given. I have reason to think that the matter did come up but nothing was done and I said nothing.

I write to you to make you cognizant with the facts and to ask that if you think it would be wise or worthwhile to bring the matter to the attention of President [Edwin] Barclay. I shall enter my seventy-fifth year in February, 1942 and I should like, as a matter of justice, to have the Order which was at one time given me. I should never of my own initiative ask for the decoration but it rather goes against my grain to have been unfairly deprived of it.

I am glad to see that you have successfully withstood the climate of Liberia and kept in good health. The tropics are much maligned. I have just been on a month's visit through Cuba and had a splendid rest.

My best regards to yourself and family and to anyone in Liberia who may remember me.

Very sincerely yours,
W. E. B. Du Bois

Monrovia, Liberia, August 12, 1941

My dear Dr. Du Bois:

I was pleased to receive your letter of July 8, and I wish to thank you for your complimentary reference made in the first paragraph of your communication. While in the United States last summer on leave of absence, I had looked forward to seeing you and must confess that I was greatly disappointed when the opportunity did not present itself for us to get together for an oldtime "eatfest" and "talkfest." I agree that I owe you a dinner which I shall gladly pay whenever conditions permit. I presume Lüchows is still doing business at the old stand.

I shall look into the matter as regards the medal conferred on you by the Liberian Government some years ago. You have a warm admirer in President Barclay and it will be a pleasure for me to do whatever I can to secure for you the recognition which you justly merit.

Judging from your writings, which I take pleasure in reading, you are as militant as ever in the advocacy of a square deal for all citizens. It is my sincere wish that in your 85th year you will be as actively engaged in the good work which has brought you distinction at home and abroad.

Liberia is very much in the international picture these days and I should not be surprised that it were not more so the time this letter reaches you. Judging from figures I saw today, giving customs collections and internal revenues for the first seven months of 1941, Liberia will again balance its budget. It is one of the few countries operating on a balanced budget. However, when you give out such constructive information very little or no attention is paid to same. But some reference to the "Leopard Society" or one case of yellow fever will make the headlines.

I am happy to state that Mrs. Walton and I are enjoying good health and are enjoying the comforts of the new American Legation, which is the most modernly constructed building on the West African Coast.

Mrs. Walton joins in best wishes to Mrs. Du Bois and you.

With every good wish,

Cordially yours,
Lester A. Walton

Monrovia, Liberia Ocotober 20, 1941

Confidential.

Dear Dr. Du Bois:

On October 7, Secretary of State Simpson called the Legation to inform me that President Barclay had given instructions that the decoration—Knight Commander of the Order of African Redemption—be turned over to me for transmission to you. However, a mistake had been made as the decoration had been sent to Mr. Walter F. Walker, Liberian Consul General at New York, who, I presume by this time, has delivered decoration to you.

I wish to take this opportunity to congratulate you on the deserved consideration shown you by the Liberian Government.

I transmit herewith a copy of a letter which I wrote Mr. Irving Dilliard, of the St. Louis *Post-Dispatch*, on August 24, 1940, while I was home on leave of absence. For several years we have exchanged correspondence and he has always accorded me a hearty welcome when I visited the *Post-Dispatch* to say "howdy" to my old friends. Mr. Dilliard has never answered my letter and I have been puzzled regarding his silence. Please inform me if, from your point of view, anything objectionable was stated.

I note with great misgivings the growing tendency in the United States to put into the mouths of our people Negro dialect. In every advertisement I have seen in magazines or daily newspapers wherein the Negro appearing in the advertisement is quoted, it has been "dis," "dat," "sho," "dese," etc.

I should like to see the colored American make an organized protest against making our people speak other than the plain "United States." Moreover, I should like to see an organized campaign waged against the presentation on the screen of but one type of Negro, that is, the subservient, bowing and scraping servant; and usually both men and women must put on cork. I feel confident if a united protest is made some favorable results can be obtained.

I shall appreciate hearing from you in the near future.

Very sincerely yours,
Lester A. Walton

P. S. Mr. Dilliard is a comparatively young man who is one of the paper's chief editorial writers.

Atlanta, Ga., 2 December 1941

My dear Mr. Walton:

You are surely a wizard. I had just returned from Cuba, having to my great surprise been selected by the Council of Learned Societies to be one of about fifty scholars from the various American republics to take part in an intercultural conference at Havana. The Government kindly paid my expenses and I flew down and back and had a gorgeous time spending money right and left and getting acquainted with a number of interesting people from all over the world. Then when I landed here at the airport, Miss Diggs, my secretary, drew out the decoration and handed it to me. My cup was full and running over. I am deeply obliged for your good offices. When we meet next time it will be an extra lunch; in fact, here is a promise of champagne unless it goes a good deal higher than it already has.

I know Mr. Dilliard of the St. Louis *Dispatch*. He visited here a year or so ago and we had a nice visit and corresponded afterwards. I think your letter to him was all right and if you do not mind I shall be glad to publish it.[1]

My best regards to you and Mrs. Walton. I am writing to the President.

Very sincerely yours,
W. E. B. Du Bois

William Alfred Fountain, Jr. (b. 1895), whose father was a bishop of the AME *church and president of Morris Brown College in Atlanta (1911–20), himself became president of that college in 1928 and held the position until 1950. The letter to him from Du Bois reveals with clarity features of the latter's plans.*

Atlanta, Ga., July 15, 1941

My dear President Fountain:

I presume you have already heard something of the *First Phylon Institute* and Twenty-Fifth Atlanta University Conference. I am going to send you later reports and reprints of some of the papers read. There were fifty-one delegates present representing thirty-five institutions. Several other institutions were unable to be represented but expressed sympathy with the idea.

I am writing to ask you to give some thought during the spring and summer to the future of these conferences and the cooperation involved. Nearly every one of our institutions has a section devoted to vocational guidance. Sometimes it is un-

1. Irving Dilliard (b. 1904) began working for the *Saint Louis Post-Dispatch* in 1923; he was editorial writer from 1930 to 1949, and editor of the editorial page from 1949 to 1957. He has produced books on two justices of the United States Supreme Court (Louis D. Brandeis and Hugo L. Black) and on Judge Learned Hand. Walton's letter to him was not found and Du Bois seems not to have published it.

organized, but the distinct burden of finding employment for the men and women we are educating has been laid upon us. My idea which is tentatively illustrated by the First Phylon Institute is through cooperative effort among the land-grant colleges, the private colleges and other organizations, to make regular and repeated surveys of the economic possibilities lying before American Negroes. There is a good deal of work of this sort done by individual colleges and organizations and if every college had a separate field and problem this might suffice. But for the most part we are all studying the same field and the same problems with minor local differences.

Is not this a chance for cooperation; for cooperation in the collecting of materials, the laying down of research programs; the interpretation of proposed helps and remedies? If one college, for instance, or one study group should appropriate five hundred dollars for investigation into economic conditions and should give a competent scholar some relief from his teaching so that he could undertake this work, something but not very much would be accomplished. If, on the other hand, fifty institutions and groups should appropriate five hundred dollars a piece and if the field of work was so planned and laid out that it could be covered by twenty or thirty professors or students giving part time, we would have a research budget of twenty-five thousand dollars and personnel among the best in the United States. What we would need then would be guidance and coordination of this work and publication of results.

I want you to think of how this can be best brought about. I have in mind a sort of federation of the colleges and groups for this limited economic purpose, leaving full autonomy and financial control to each institution, and yet having enough of coordination so that one unified study would result. The publication of results could be done in part through periodicals like *Phylon*; in part by spcial publications issued by individual institutions and in part possibly by some scheme of joint publication.

Will you think this matter over and write me sometime in the next few months any proposal which you have for the carrying out of a plan of cooperation something like this which I have outlined? I have come to no fixed conclusions myself. I started the movement at Atlanta University because I happened to be myself situated here and because it is a central place and an institution with traditions along this line; but it is quite possible that you will prefer some other center of effort. The only thing that I am certain of is that the greatest problem before the American Negro today is a plan for such economic organization of his life that he can earn an income suitable for a person who is to take part in civilization. Such planning I believe to be possible by united effort. The only question is: how can such union of effort be obtained?

Very sincerely yours,
W. E. B. Du Bois

Pedro Albizu Campos (1891–1965) received his bachelor's degree from Harvard in 1916 and his law degree from that university in 1921. He was the leader of the Puerto Rican Independence movement and was convicted of the charge of seeking to overthrow the United States govern-

Ira De A. Reid. Photograph from the
New York Public Library.

Walter White. Photograph from the
New York Public Library.

Du Bois with Sterling A. Brown and Dorothy Maynard at Fisk University in 1941. Photograph courtesy of the University of Massachusetts Library.

ment; he was imprisoned in the Atlanta Penitentiary from 1937 through 1943 and then hospitalized in New York City. He returned to Puerto Rico in 1947 and was again jailed in the 1950s. He died in prison 21 April 1965.

Du Bois's letter to the warden in Atlanta Penitentiary was not answered.

Atlanta, Ga., July 7, 1941

My dear Sir:

During a recent trip to Cuba I heard of Pedro Albizu Campos of Puerto Rico who I believe is incarcerated in your institution. I should like very much to have permission to talk with him under such regulations as are usual. He is, I understand, a colored man and a graduate of Harvard, which is my alma mater. I should be glad to hear from you at your convenience.

Very sincerely yours,
W. E. B. Du Bois
Head, Department of Sociology

Most of the time, for most people, living is not especially easy; but Black people in the United States have found normal existence particularly onerous. The problems include the so-called little things—like locations of mailboxes and the collection of garbage and the provision of street lighting, and so on—as well as such major questions as unemployment and housing and institutionalized racism. Du Bois fought on all fronts all the time. Two examples of his efforts in "little things" follow; in neither case do the Du Bois papers show a reply.

Atlanta, Ga., July 16, 1941

Stoddard's
Atlanta, Ga.
Gentlemen:

During the last few years I have been spending about twelve or fifteen dollars a year with you for cleaning and pressing of clothes. I find this year that apparently you no longer hire colored helpers on your delivery wagons. I think that it is only fair that in the future I confine my patronage to those who reciprocate by hiring colored people.

Very sincerely yours,
W. E. B. Du Bois

Atlanta, Ga., July 18, 1941

The Mayor
City of Atlanta
Atlanta, Ga.
Sir:

There is a stretch of street on Beckwith Street Southwest between Chestnut Street Southwest and Raymond Street that is unpaved and that has long been a source of great inconvenience and danger to travelers. I have parked my car in a garage on this street for five years and sometimes it has been almost impossible to get in and out. Cars coming along Beckwith Street and striking this spot are seriously liable to accident.

I am writing to ask if the city cannot arrange for the pavement of this block?

I am, Sir,

> Very sincerely yours,
> W. E. B. Du Bois

A long letter of beauty and significance came to Du Bois from a woman in California; it is apparent that neither knew the other and efforts at learning more about the writer have not been successful.

Berkeley, Calif., September 10, 1941

My dear Dr. Du Bois:

I would greatly appreciate your courtesy in giving me the benefit of your opinion in regard to a matter that has increasingly seemed to several others as well as myself to be worthy of effort—possibly, indeed, of some constructive and lasting value, undertaken at a time like this.

For some years, many years ago, I lived in the bayou section of the "piney woods" north of Lake Pontchartrain in Louisiana, before there was any railroad connection with that region, and "sand-schooners," etc., crossing the lake from New Orleans, were rowed or poled up and down the Bogue of Falaya and other rivers by Negroes who sang a number of songs and spirituals which, so far, I have been unable to find in any anthology or anywhere in print. Some of them were quite unusual, some really very beautiful, and recently, in talking over with others the possibility of preserving them, the thought occurred that it might be practicable to plan a uniquely different radio program by using these in a series that would include actual incidents and experiences with which they were contemporary, also some particularly picturesque bits of history re that whole region, intimate sympathetic delineation of some of the outstanding Negro personalities there—plenty of humor (in no way derogatory, including no slur or slight), an occasional delectable recipe such as the French Negro element delighted in, and that I have never found anywhere else (as bait later on, perhaps, for some food sponsor?)—an appealing word—fabric of the daily background out of which these particular songs and hymns were, literally, woven. Early morning sun, and the jolly songs and rousing versions of bible-stories that matched those buoyant hours; and then others, that seemed part of the moonlight nights drenched with the fragrance of magnolia and jasmine and all the forest scents of the riverlands—mellow rhythmed music of haunting cadences, and again the searching appeal of upwelling prayer that must have first been born of depths of need we all have sometimes known—a unison of some of the finest voices I have ever heard, with the beat of the oars far in the distance at first, then nearby for a few moments, then fading into the night again as another bend was rounded—

An unforgettable word-picture in the mood of a single hour of the twenty-four could be made a two-minute introduction to eight or ten minutes of the singing-sequence belonging to that hour's incidents and work; then a half dozen sentences of further background description perhaps, preparatory to a closing and particularly effective number?—roughly, that would give a general slant, though always different in content, of course.

A mature, even elderly, voice—cultured, capable of sensitive modulation—would carry the script; preferably a man, to minimize any tendency toward *mere* sentiment; in the first person, as having himself witnessed the incidents related, or having heard them at first hand—"One night we were out under the live oaks when a schooner was snagged on a submerged tree in the river just below us—" and then the songs the polers and rowers sang as they tried to keep it from shunting over on a sandbar, etc.; or "my father told me when he was a boy—" and the singing-sequence belonging to that, etc.

There is a point I am particularly desirous to "get over" gradually in the course of such a series—the utterly unselfish devotion (and occasionally very real heroism) of all those to whom the care of young children was entrusted; and the inescapable fact that all of us whose early lives were conditioned by those times are, literally, under lifelong obligation for that conditioning—for health, for the education and breadth of experience made possible by a financial competence based upon the labor of others who are *still* unrequited for what was then forcibly taken from them. It should not of course be "preached," or "rubbed in," but just a sentence or two once in a while apropos of some particular incident, the speaker's own depth of feeling and sincerity evident in the tones of his voice.

Psychologically, this *is* a "time of reckoning" all over the world, both inwardly and outwardly—some such realization as this must have come to many others besides those whom I know personally! If "the note is struck," possibly it would find echo in the understanding of an increasing number, and could perhaps eventuate in some unison of constructive action?

There is a Negro church here (with a fairly good choir) whose minister is interested in such a project as this could, I feel sure, be made to develop into, but no practical step to this end has yet been taken, for lack of means. This minister (really a fine character) was sent here some years ago by a Central Board (I can not at the moment recall its exact designation) to build up a small church that had practically fallen to pieces—in regard to its congregation. My original contact was through tickets sold for Christmas and other entertainments, to help pay off the heavy indebtedness of the church—it is well on the upgrade now, though there is still a considerable financial burden.

There are good voices in the church. It is thought that considerable local publicity (and additional self-confidence and experience) could be gained by gratis programs given to the institutions for the Blind here, hospitals, etc., if radio connection could be obtained for the church, and this would gradually lead to special requests for their services, elsewhere, when payment could be asked.

None of us to whom this idea occurred, is capable of taking any part in any radio work (other than preparing the script which, I should have said, would not of course be used in any *gratis* programs—only the choir-singing). Nor, equally, do we want, or would under any circumstances accept any part in any financial returns that might later accrue. It is wholly to "get over" the *idea* referred to above, and the unknown spirituals, that we are eager to do whatever may be in our power to this end.

I do not belong to any church, nor attend any (I happened to have been born into a Quaker family, but in recent years have not kept up my connection with any such group). I do not want even to try to get any support for this idea from any "religious" organization, and I am quite sure in advance that no such effort would be successful— many of them are complaining that their own resources are shrinking. I have no means whatever of my own. Do you think a very modest sum could possibly be obtained from the Rosenwald Fund, just to start such an enterprise? I am convinced it can speedily stand on its own feet, and its income increase on its own merits and hard work. If you think this appeal to the Fund feasible, who would properly make the approach? Have you by any chance a personal friend in this locality whose point of view is, by and large, the same as your own as to the matter of *not* making *everything* a vehicle for some political propaganda—I mean the unwisdom of trying to saddle such propaganda on everything—several good enterprises in this part of the country have been wrecked because of the determination of their personnel to make them serve the ends of a political organization—you referred to the same sort of thing re Scottsboro, in *Dusk of Dawn*. It is not unlikely that good voices outside of this church would volunteer to help, and then dissension would begin. I am too advanced in years to be of any effective use in "managing" anything, and I have not that sort of personality. The minister of this church of course has his hands more than full with his regular work. I hoped you might know someone of the West Coast with whom I could confer, consult, as to the feasibility of this idea, and who—if he approved of it, considered its prospects sound business—could also attend to the business manage-ment of it, making the appeal to the Rosenwald Fund also?

I would indeed greatly appreciate your kindness in giving me whatever advice and assistance you can, regarding any and all points that may occur to you.

Glancing back over this letter, I realize its shortcomings and inadequacy, but I hope it will at least serve to convey someting of my intent? And that the matter as a whole will seem to you worth consideration, and whatever effort may be necessary for its development.

Very truly yours,

Mrs. Esther Harlan

Atlanta, Ga., 25 September 1941

Mrs. Esther Harlan

My dear Madam:

Your letter of September 10 is very interesting and I wish that some action could be taken. My advice to you would be to approach Mr. Edwin R. Embree of the

Rosenwald Fund and also Mr. F. P. Keppel of the Carnegie Foundation. Of course, both of these foundations have numerous applications, only a few of which they can take up; but I think it would be worthwhile to put this matter before them. There is also, of course, the bare possibility that some commercial organization might be interested but probably it would not be as well nor as artistically done as it might be through philanthropic help. I am glad to have had your letter and I think it indicates possibilities.

Very sincerely yours,
W. E. B. Du Bois

By the end of the 1930s, certain state and city educational bodies had been pushed to agreement with at least tentative steps in the direction of improving textbooks by ridding them of naked racism. Indicative is an exchange between a Black woman schoolteacher in Chicago and Du Bois; Madeline Morgan at this time was a member of the bureau of curriculum of the board of education in Chicago.

Chicago, Ill., September 10, 1941

Dr. William B. Du Bois
My dear Sir:

Dr. William H. Johnson, Superintendent of Chicago Public Schools, is making it possible for Negro achievements to be blended into the elementary school curriculum of the Chicago Public Schools. This is a city-wide project and we are anxious to have our manuscript accurate. Therefore we beg of you to allow us to submit our material for criticism, accuracy, and for suggestions of improvement.

If you will honor us by reading our manuscript we will forward it as soon as it is completed.

May I ask that no paper publicity be given to this project? Thank You.

Yours truly,
Madeline Morgan.

Atlanta, Ga., 23 September 1941

Miss Madeline Morgan
Dear Madam:

Answering your letter of September 10, I shall be glad to examine your manuscript on Negro achievement.

Very sincerely yours,
W. E. B. Du Bois

Helen Boardman was one of several white women—Martha Gruening and Elizabeth Lawson are other examples—who, beginning in the 1920s and continuing for a generation, devoted their energies effectively and with courage to the struggle against racism. Helen Boardman helped expose the peonage and brutality in Mississippi and Louisiana in the 1920s, was prominent in many cases involving unjust imprisonment of Black people, and pioneered in efforts aimed at improving textbooks in the school systems of the United States. Her quite militant and left views brought her into frequent conflict with much of the leadership of the NAACP.

Indicative is a letter concerning William Pickens; the reply from Du Bois contains important information. A later letter from Pickens to Du Bois (on pp. 318–19) also deals with the subject mentioned by Du Bois.

New York, N. Y. September 10, 1941

Dear Dr. Du Bois:

I have a story to tell you, and I may as well plunge right in. Some time after I had heard of Mr. Pickens' appointment in the Treasury I wanted to get the facts about it and turned to the *Crisis* as a logical source. After looking through several numbers I found that the only reference to it was one sentence in an editorial paragraph, which stated that a year's leave of absence had been granted to Mr. Pickens so that he could assist in the sale of defense bonds.

This deliberate belittlement of a very important appointment annoyed me. I got an order for an article on the subject from *Opportunity*, and then went to see Mr. Paul U. Kellogg at the *Survey*. He said he would use 300 words and a photograph if I would get them in within ten days—which I did.

I went to Washington, where I interviewed Mr. Pickens, Mr. [Lorimer D.] Milton, Mr. [Harold] Graves, Mr. Stephen Spingarn, Mr. Robert Weaver and others. *Opportunity* carried my article in August.[1] I enclose a copy of an article I sent to the Associated Negro Press. My only copy of the *Survey* article I have sent to Mr. Pickens, but I will ask him to send it to you.

Anyway, the *Survey* cut the large photograph I had sent them of Mr. Pickens at his desk, and instead of the brief paragraphs I sent used three sentences, one of which was a repetition of the erroneous and derogatory statement made in the *Crisis*. I enclose a copy of a letter I sent Mr. Kellogg. In reply Katherine Close, assistant editor, called me up and said I was mistaken, because her statement came from Mr. White of the N.A.A.C.P. When I asked why she consulted him rather than me in regard to my copy she had nothing to say.

Obviously, White used this occasion to add to the campaign of defamation he has carried on for years against Mr. Pickens. (Not to mention what he doubtless said about me.)

What I am hoping is that you will publish the photograph I am sending of Mr. Pickens and Mr. Milton in conference, and also some appreciative remarks about Mr. Pickens and this appointment, in the October *Phylon*. If it is not too late you might ask

1. Helen Boardman, "The U. S. Treasury Takes a Step," *Opportunity* 19 (August 1941): 238–39. Pickens was named staff assistant in the treasury defense savings division. The photograph to which Helen Boardman refers is published in this issue of *Opportunity*, p. 239. A photograph of Pickens and a brief announcement of his Washington appointment are in *Survey* 77 (August 1941): 246.

Mr. Harold Graves, head of the Defense Savings Division, for some comment. I am sure you intended to make adequate reference to the appointment anyway, but Mr. White's action seems to me to make it more important.

Sincerely yours,
Helen Boardman

Atlanta, Ga., 25 September 1941

My dear Miss Boardman:

There are two reasons that keep me from using your matter concerning Pickens: in the first place I think the significance of his appointment has been over-emphasized. It means something but it does not mean as much as he seems to think. But secondly, and more important, you probably do not know that when I was still connected with the National Association for the Advancement of Colored People and wanted to reform it and re-organize it and curb the power of Walter White, I undertook at the direct request of Pickens, [Robert] Bagnall, [Herbert] Seligmann and Wilkins to write a statement and complaint to the board of trustees. They read and discussed the complaint and signed it. I put it before the board. The board was very much upset and then without giving me any notice at all everyone of these men withdrew their signature and left me standing alone. Joel Spingarn tried to get me to withdraw my signature and I refused absolutely to budge. The result is that I have had just as little to do with this group of people as possible and I withdrew from the NAACP because I saw it was impossible to reform it from the inside and I was not willing to lead a national fight against an insitution which still was of use to the world.

For these reasons I am not going to print Pickens' picture and I am returning it to you. I do appreciate your kind interest.

Very sincerely yours,
W. E. B. Du Bois

New York, N. Y., October 3, 1941

Dear Dr. Du Bois,

Thank you for your explanation. I am astonished and shocked. I can't help feeling that as far as Pickens is concerned there must be some explanation of his action. I do believe in his honesty and integrity, although not in that of the other members of that group. I often disagree with Mr. Pickens but I have always respected him. But what a terrible mistake! It must have been about that time that Walter called me into his office and said he thought it was time "we young people" took over control of the Association. As I was past forty and he nearly my age it struck me as funny. I think I said "we old people" might step aside and let younger ones in, or something equally tactless. But I never took him as seriously as I should have. I have never understood how such an inferior person ever got so much power. It was chiefly, I think, through the backing of the Spingarns and Miss Ovington, who should have known better. At the time your resignation was coming up Miss Ovington dined with me one night and spent the evening "pumping" me on the question. I said your loss would be an irreparable injury to the Association. The following Monday I was fired. Well, I was right. It has been an irreparable injury and I think even Ovington knows it now.

I understand your position but I think a piece of the puzzle is missing. Pickens would not double-cross you. I know he has a high regard for you. Recently I asked him for names of men who had come to position and prominence as a result of their own ability without political or other influence. He put you first on the list. I believe your account of that incident absolutely, but I am perplexed because that does not represent the man I know.

Last August I spent some weeks at Henrietta Buckmaster's cottage in the country. I wrote nearly all of the first draft of an article on Brazil and the American colonies, intending to submit it to *Phylon*. Suddenly my lame arm got worse and I couldn't finish it. I have been five days writing this letter because I can only do a few words at a time. I will have to have an operation on it (the arm!) and hope to do so next month. It will be several months before I am over it which is disappointing to me. I did want to send you something.

Thank you again for your letter.

Sincerely yours,
Helen Boardman

A Black postal worker's letter was thought-provoking and, according to his custom, Du Bois sent a prompt and substantive reply.

Chicago, Ill., September 16, 1941

Dear Mr. Du Bois:

While discussing the movie industry as a propaganda agency to maintain the concept of Negro inferiority by always portraying Negroes in the movies as domestics or clowns I met with such a united protest of this belief of mine that I am writing to you to give your opinion of the matter, namely, that the movie industry is guilty of using the movies to maintain the theory of white superiority among the whites as well as among Negroes.

I was so shocked that so many Negroes were willing to defend the movie industry that if you agree with me, I should like to see some effort made to acquaint the American Negro of this insidious propaganda.

These individuals who disagreed with me are all postal employees in the Chicago Post Office and since federal civil servants are generally considered to represent the more intelligent Negro, it is not surprising to me that little has been done to curb the social forces that tend to poison American minds about Negroes.

I would greatly appreciate an answer to this letter because if I can do anything to cause my fellow workers to consider such things more seriously I will feel that I am contributing something to a better Negro.

Yours truly,
Marshall Gray

Atlanta, Ga., 26 September 1941

Mr. Marshall Gray
My dear Sir:

The attitude of the Negro toward the movie industry is something like this: Negroes have received some recognition and employment; the roles which they portray have improved somewhat in character during the last twenty years, that is, the Negro appears now not simply as clown and fool but now and then in more human and natural roles. On the other hand, all Negroes are quite aware that anti-Negro propaganda still goes on through the films; that in every scene that brings in a jail there will be Negro prisoners prominently displayed; that the Negro clown is still frequently used; and that almost never can a Negro take a role which involves real manhood. The result of this is that Negroes are afraid to protest too much against this propaganda for fear that those Negroes who are employed regularly by the Movie industry like Louise Beavers, Clarence Muse, Rex Ingram, and others might lose their jobs.

Personally, I think that a determined fight against propaganda with regard to Negroes might be made but should be done carefully so that distinction is made between hurtful propaganda and the beginnings of real recognition of Negro manhood.[1]

Very sincerely yours,
W. E. B. Du Bois

Although Edward A. Weeks (b. 1898), the editor of the Atlantic Monthly *from 1938 through 1966, decided against publishing the articles Du Bois suggested late in 1941, the outlines of those articles are themselves very much worth publishing. The first article by Du Bois to appear in a nationally circulating magazine was his "Strivings of the Negro People," in the* Atlantic Monthly *back in August 1897. Thereafter, he published at intervals in that magazine, and his notable essay "The African Roots of the War" was published in its May 1915 issue. No doubt it was the memory of this past that suggested to Du Bois that he try again to publish an analysis of Black people in the world as a whole in the* Atlantic, *but this time he was refused.*

Atlanta, Ga., October 2, 1941

Mr. Edward Weeks
Dear Sir:

I want to suggest to you in outline two articles concerning the relations of the Negro peoples to the modern world. I think that the time has come for a complete restatement of the so-called Negro problems and I should like to submit these articles to you, if their consideration is in line with your editorial plans.

The *first article* would be entitled "The Future of Europe in Africa." It would stress the fact that in the various peace proposals which envisage the end of this war, there is

---

1. A vigorous attack upon Hollywood's depiction of Black people, Loren Miller's "Uncle Tom in Hollywood," was published in the *Crisis* 41 (November 1934): 329, 336.

no coming to grips with the problem of the future relations of Africa and Europe. One can see in these proposals the persistence of old patterns: the need of raw material from Africa; and the assumption that this raw material must be made cheap by land monopoly and low wage; and that the object of the whole African economy must remain primarily the economic advantage of Europe. These old patterns of thought and action will be almost entirely swept away by the two world wars. First of all "Africa" as an entity is a myth. There are a multitude of Africas both in the thought of the inhabitants of the continent themselves and in the thought of the various European and American nations who own and exploit Africa. The seven character- istic Africas have different potentialities and demands; face different situations; and different paths to the future. Above all the plight of Africa must be made logically clear and not be subject to the kind of deliberate contradiction and misapprehension so long current. For instance, when we say that African colonies are not profitable it is meant that government expenditure is not balanced by government income. But this does not deny the fact that individual enterprise investing in African labor and material has in the past reaped increasing profit and is doing so today.

The question as to what we want the future of the African people to be and what they themselves want, must be clearly envisaged. Do we want them simply for their use to Europe or do we look forward to a time when they are to be deliberately trained for their use to themselves and their own development? The academic discussion as to the capabilities of Africans for receiving education is no longer of interest. Judging from the experience of missionaries, travelers and government schools, it would be possible at the four present centers of African education, to train an intelligentsia which could eventually take complete charge of the social development of the conti- nent. Such development of Africa for the Welfare of the Africans would interfere certainly at first with the private profit of foreign investment and change totally the relation of Africa to the modern world. The question is, do we really want this? Or, desiring a world dominated by Anglo-Saxons or at least by white Europe, do we want to keep Africa in subjection just as long as it is possible? If we do are we not planting right here inevitable seeds of future hatred, struggle and war? This is not denying that in the education of an African intelligentsia we face difficult problems: the problem of preserving rather than violently destroying the native culture patterns; all the prob- lems of new, untried social and educational leadership. But the decision in these matters must not be left to profiteers, to colonial imperialists, or to white persons alone. It must become an international mandate with the intelligence of Africa repre- sented on the guiding boards and the half-dead conscience of Europe in cooperation. It will mean a new scientific and cultural crusade which might be the greatest result of the two world wars. Even if this problem is not frankly faced the African is bound to be trained as a fighter and modern soldier. That was true in the first World War. It is true in this. But there is no more dangerous thing in the world than thus setting fire to this potential dynamite. Moreover, to the trite truths that a nation cannot exist half- slave and half-free and a culture cannot survive half democratic and half totalitarian, we must add the much more practical dictum that the modern world cannot survive with democracy among white Europeans and colonial imperialism rampant in Asia and Africa; and that this is true not simply from the point of view of the good of the colored people, but from the fact that any attempt at democracy among Europeans will be overthrown if the more powerful classes within the democracy are supported by streams of wealth which come from low wages and cheap materials over more than half the earth. This war cannot end without wide economic revolution in the leading nations of the world. Such revolution can never be satisfactory or complete if the new economy rests on African poverty and Asiatic subjugation.

Of course this outline does not bring in all the points I should like to make. I should like, for instance, to go into more detail concerning the seven Africas, their situations, demands, etc.

The *second article* would be "The Future of Africa in America." Here again there is needed a complete re-statement of the so-called American Negro problems with a frank facing of the methods in which they must be faced and the decisions that must be made. We know that there are some fourteen million persons in the United States of acknowledged Negro descent. We are quite aware that the population of the West Indies is overwhelmingly Negroid. In Latin-America there are one hundred thirty million inhabitants of whom twenty million, at least, are of Negro descent. Now what is to be the future of these peoples and their relations to each other?

In the United States we have gone far enough to know that the ability which can be developed among persons of Negro descent, is of the widest range; that in physical, intellectual and artistic lines, the Negro is not only in evidence but if it were not for deliberate hindrances set-up to his development he would make even better showing. We know that his health and crime can be adequately explained by his poverty, and that increased income and education can without reasonable doubt raise the mass of the Negro people to or above the average level of their white neighbors.

But these very facts disclose a problem which the nation and the white world is unwilling to face. Even with present barriers, if the Negro continues to develop at the present rate in the United States and Latin America, there is not a single door of human progress and of social recognition at which he is not going to knock with increasingly bitter violence. On the other hand, if the barriers are done away with, the Negro race in America is going to reach within a calculable time a high level of efficiency which will challenge the whole assumption of the natural superiority of the white race. It will take more and more deliberate effort on the part of whites to enforce caste restrictions. What now is going to be our policy?

In order to preserve our intellectual honesty and ethical pretensions this question must come in for frank discussion and decision. We cannot permit the Southern United States to be a social back-water in order to hold the Negro in his place. Neither can we allow the West Indies and Central America to be made deliberate slums for the profit and vacation activities of the whites. In South America we have long pretended to see a possible solution in the gradual amalgamation of whites, Indians and blacks. But this amalgamation does not envisage any decrease of power and prestige among whites as compared with Indians, Negroes and mixed bloods; but rather an inclusion within the so-called white group of a considerable infiltration of dark blood, while at the same time maintaining the social bar, economic exploitation and political disfranchisement of dark blood as such. We have thus the spectacle of Santo Domingo, Cuba, Puerto Rico and even Jamaica trying desperately and dog-gedly to be "white" in spite of the fact that the majority of the white group is of Negro or Indian descent. And despite facts, no Brazilian nor Venezuelan dare boast of his black fathers. Thus racial amalgamation in Latin-America does not always or even usually carry with it social uplift and planned effort to raise the mulatto and mestizoes to freedom in a democratic polity.

This problem of the African in America cannot be avoided. He is not dying out; and he is not likely to die out. His sudden physical absorption without planned social effort would result in a distinct lowering of the level of culture over wide areas. On the other hand, the attempt to raise the culture among the whites and lower or even retard it among the Negroes and mulattoes, is a task inexcusable if not impossible.

There is needed, therefore, in the Western world widespread consultation and planning, backed by united effort first to decide just how far we are willing to treat Negroes and mulattoes as human beings, and if not what open and tenable justification we have for denying it. If we are going to break down the barriers and at great cost in wealth and effort gradually raise this depressed class to the level of the culture of which they are capable, we must frankly understand that this does not mean the domination of a white world in the future; in fact, it is the beginning of the end of such domination. There is no moral question facing the Americas of greater and more pressing importance than this question of racial tolerance in the Western Hemisphere.

I should be glad to know if you would be willing to consider two articles on the lines of the above outline? Of course, they would be much more carefully integrated and logically arranged than in these hasty and tentative forecasts.[1]

Very sincerely yours,
W. E. B. Du Bois

Atlanta, Ga., 20 November 1941

My dear Mr. Weeks:
I am sending you herewith a rough outline of the kind of article which I should like to write for the *Atlantic*. You will understand that it is still not in finished form nor as carefully arranged and thought out as I can eventually make it; but it will give you an idea of my thesis.

Very sincerely yours,
W. E. B. Du Bois

1. Several of the columns Du Bois published at this time in the *Amsterdam News* treated of the ideas in this letter; see especially the issues dated 4 October 1941, 29 November 1941, 3 January 1942. The ideas, so far as foreign policy is concerned, were elaborated in his book *Color and Democracy: Colonies and Peace*, written in 1944 and published the next year by Harcourt, Brace and Co.

Two months later, Weeks's letter of rejection was mailed; its last sentence suggests that
Du Bois had more to contend with, in this rejection, than differences of opinion on the substance
of the essay projected.

Boston, Mass., January 26, 1942

Dear Dr. Du Bois:

You will, I trust appreciate the reason why we have had to deliberate so long over this revised prospectus of yours. The world has been altered very radically for all Americans since December 7th, and statements which could have been contemplated with relative objectivity before that date now take on an emotional content which may be very explosive indeed. Even your second outline, which reached us in mid-December, suffers from this change of atmospheric pressure.

You have attempted to give a bird's-eye view of the race problem as it exists on this hemisphere, and I intend it as a compliment when I say that I know of no other man who would have the courage to attempt so broad a sweep. Your writing is courageous. It strikes me as deeply penetrating in certain passages and equally intemperate in others. But what seems to me the greatest drawback is that by distributing your force over such a vast panorama you have left us with less than enough conviction in any single area. In short, you have bitten off more than you—or any reader—can chew at one session. Let me give you two brief illustrations of what I mean:

When you say that "Hitler's race philosophy and methods are exactly the same as ours," you make an assertion which will antagonize literally forty-nine out of fifty readers. To my Northern eyes, it simply isn't true, for I know of no sections in the South which have had to submit to what the Jews in Germany and Poland are going through today. Nor does it defend your position to say that this is a question of degree only. Your purpose in writing such an article is to make people aware of an injustice existing between citizens of a democratic state. But you won't gain a single convert if you say that we are part and parcel of Hitler's gang.

Again, it seems to me that your criticism of the British Empire is so sweeping that you will lose rather than gain by it. They are our Allies in a fight for survival, and it ill befits us at this time to try to reform their internal organization. We have got enough to do on our own domestic front.

Whether you can adjust your sights to a more limited field and consider the part which the Negro is playing in our defense effort and the part which he ought to share in our labor organization, is a question which I have asked myself as I have mulled over your prospectus. Again, I would ask for more temperance and a clearer recognition that changes come slowly—yet come they do. I would ask you to consider whether it is strictly true that all barriers to the Negro's advancement are social and political or whether we have not a biological handicap to contend with which can only be overcome by painstaking education.

Yours sincerely,
Edward Weeks

One of the best-known and most widely respected American historians of this century was the late Howard K. Beale (1899–1959), whose writings on Charles Beard, Andrew Johnson, and Theodore Roosevelt, and in the field of intellectual freedom, remain consequential. From 1935 to 1948, Beale was a professor at the University of North Carolina; thereafter, until his sudden death, he was at the University of Wisconsin. His letter reflects the kind of crossing of racist barriers that was in its fairly early stages prior to the Second World War; if Du Bois sensed sincerity and respect, he encouraged the process.

Chapel Hill, N. C., November 14, 1941

Dear Mr. Du Bois:

I want to thank you for your courtesy while I was in Atlanta. It was a great pleasure being in your home and having a chance to talk to you at length. I particularly appreciated your letting me bring Vernon Wharton to meet you.

I have another student near Atlanta who is very anxious to meet you. I wish I had thought to ask to bring him along too. He asked me afterward if I would mind giving him an introduction to you so that he could call and meet you some time. May I do so? He is William Geer of Charleston, S. C., at present teaching history at Fort McPherson to aspirants to West Point. If you could drop either him or me a note saying that you would be willing to talk with him sometime, he could make an appointment. He is Lieutenant William Geer, Fort McPherson, Georgia.[1]

Again let me tell you how much I enjoyed the talk with you and how much I appreciate your hospitality.

Yours cordially
Howard K. Beale

Atlanta, Ga., 18 November 1941

My dear Mr. Beale:

It was very nice of you to come out to the University and I certainly enjoyed the evening. Tell Mr. Geer that I shall be glad to see him if he will call and make an appointment—Walnut 7956. I am going to be in Havana next week but shall be back within a week.

Very sincerely yours,
W. E. B. Du Bois

An exchange with an author from Panama reflects the sweep of Du Bois's influence; it contains, too, an observation upon his own habits of writing.

1. Vernon L. Wharton (1907–64) was on the faculty of Millsaps College from 1935 through 1952; in his last years he was dean at the College of Liberal Arts of the University of Southwestern Louisiana. His book, *The Negro in Mississippi, 1865–1890* (1947), was remarkable in its time and remains a standard work.

William M. Geer (b. 1915) went on to teach at West Point (1942–45); he holds the rank of colonel in the army reserves and teaches at the University of North Carolina.

Cristobal, Canal Zone, November 18, 1941

Dr. W. E. Du Bois,

Four years ago—on December 1, 1937—in reply to an inquiry of mine you wrote me to the effect that I should continue writing and submit my work to the best markets. This bit of professional advice has brought me much happiness of soul and encouraging success as a writer. Today I again ask of you a few paragraphs of advice on a subject close to my heart.

Over the span of those years I have come quite a way along the road to literary recognition. I have acquired and held down since that time a job as reporter of West Indian news on a local white daily, and seen a number of my pieces printed in the Urban League's *Opportunity* Magazine.[1] These pieces, especially, attracted comment from New York circles, and during the recent racial pogrom here W. A. Domingo wrote me of his own accord from that metropolis on the subject of the local situation and my own work.

Recently I began recording my observations as a preliminary to doing a study of the Isthmian Negro scene. I feel that this is a book that must be written. This phase of the Negro's struggle toward justice and progress in the New World must be made intelligently vocal, if his entire case is to be aired. It is my belief that although it would of necessity be proved sensational in material, the book would meet an urgent demand and realize results worthy of the effort.

Do you think that North American publishers would be sympathetic toward such a manuscript? Do you think they would consider accepting it for reading with a view to publishing should it meet requirements? Of course I could have inquired this much of the Viking Press, Knopf, or any publishing house, but I do not think that they would give me the frank personal reply that you might.

I trust that you may find the time to again write me a few lines. Please accept in anticipation my thanks for these; also my appreciation for the wealth of ideas, the spiritual fortitude and professional guidance I gleaned from reading *Dusk of Dawn*.

Respectfully yours,
José J. Smith

Atlanta, Ga., 20 January 1942

My dear Mr. Smith:

Answering your letter of November 18, I think there is no doubt of the need of a study of the Negro on the Isthmus. Eric Walrond once planned and partially finished a study called *The Big Ditch* which treated the Panama Canal and the various West Indian Negroes who worked upon it. I have often wondered what became of that manuscript.[2] I hope you will do the study. Of course nothing can be said definitely

1. Smith's articles included "Black Panama," *Opportunity* 18 (August 1940): 234–35 and "The C.I.O.-Canal Zone Episode," *Opportunity* 19 (May 1941): 135–37. Smith worked on the *Panama American*, a daily newspaper.

2. The editor wonders, also. Perhaps some reader knows the answer? Walrond, born in British Guiana in 1898, spent much of his youth in Panama, studied in New York colleges, was

now as to whether a publisher would accept it or not—the war throws all plans awry. But in any case, my method has always been first, to write the book and afterwards to get it published. Of course if you can get an order from a publisher and an advance of royalties, it is helpful; but I don't think that could be considered at this time. If I were you, I would go to work, get a rich and wide collection of data and write the kind of book that ought to be written and then trust to the Good Lord to get it published sometime.

Very sincerely yours,
W. E. B. Du Bois

---

on the staff of *Opportunity*, and published widely in such periodicals as *Vanity Fair*, *Saturday Review*, and Mencken's *Smart Set*. He was a significant figure of the Harlem Renaissance; in 1926 a collection of his short stories, called *Tropic Death* and set in the islands of the Caribbean, was published by Boni and Liveright in New York City. Walrond lived in France for some years and died in London in 1966. It is said he then was working on a book dealing with the Panama Canal—perhaps this was "The Big Ditch" study that Du Bois wondered about. See the entry on Walrond in R. K. Barsdale and K. Kinnaomn, *Black Writers of America* (New York: Macmillan Co., 1972).

1942

Earlier letters have shown the rising interest in the 1930s in what is called today Black Studies; a spurt of such interest and the beginnings of actual courses appeared in the 1940s. Illustrative is a letter from a student at Chapman College in California.

Los Angeles, Calif., January 8, 1942

Dr. William E. Burghardt Du Bois
Dear Sir:

For the past several years it has been the effort of many leading educators and citizens in this state to institute a course in Negro History throughout our schools and colleges. Such attempts thus far have been unsuccessful. Recently however, the Wesley Methodist Club of the Los Angeles City College began a series of Survey lectures in Negro History in the hope of stimulating progressive action for the institution of such course in its curricula.

The source material that the lecturer has used for these lectures has been your book "Black Folk Then and Now." The students have found this book of great value in their study of Negro History. As the lecturer in this course, I would greatly appreciate it if you could give me any further reference readings which would enlarge the course using your publication as the textbook.

I sincerely hope that we may become friends by correspondence, for I feel that any advice or suggestions that may come from you will lead to the success of our purpose.

I trust that I may hear from you as soon as possible.

Yours sincerely,
Reverend James Grant

Atlanta, Ga., 14 January 1942

Reverend James Grant
My dear Sir:

I think the bibliographical references to my *Black Folk: Then and Now* ought to help you. In addition to that you should get a copy of the latest edition of Woodson, *The Negro in Our History.*

Very sincerely yours,
W. E. B. Du Bois

Du Bois never let pass an opportunity to rebuke manifestations of racism; he gave public and private reprimands for over eighty years. One instance is a letter of resignation addressed to the Southern Historical Association.

Plaster bust of Du Bois by Alexander
Portnoff. Photograph courtesy of the
Crisis.

The Liberian Order of African
Redemption. Photograph by Griffith
J. Davis. Photograph courtesy of the
University of Massachusetts Library.

W. E. B. Du Bois. Photograph courtesy of the *Crisis*.

Atlanta, Ga., January 14, 1942

Sirs:

I do not care for further membership in the Southern Historical Association after the revelation of your attitude toward colored members in your Atlanta meeting.[1]

Very sincerely yours,

W. E. B. Du Bois

As already noted, the Carnegie Corporation made two grants of one thousand dollars each 1940–41 and 1941–42 to assist Du Bois in his plans for an educational collective of scholars to investigate the economic present and future of Afro-American people. He sent two letters in 1942 reporting on the use of these funds and projecting plans for the future. These were addressed to Charles Dollard (b. 1907), who had been associated with the University of Wisconsin from 1928 to 1936 and then in 1938 became assistant to F. P. Keppel, president of Carnegie; after leave during the war late in 1942, he became vice-president and then in 1948 president of the Carnegie Corporation, a position he held until 1954.

Atlanta, Ga., January 14, 1942

My dear Mr. Dollard:

Following my report of May 29, I want to give you some further information as to the proposed expenditure of the $1,000 which the Foundation gave me. I started the first Institute with the idea that Atlanta University might be induced to take the matter up and make Atlanta a center for publications of a new set of Atlanta University studies. We had an interesting conference but the University had taken no subsequent action. I, therefore, determined to carry the movement before the Presidents of the Land-Grant Colleges. On November 12, 1941, I spoke at their meeting in Chicago and I am enclosing a copy of the speech which I made there.[2] It was favorably received and a committee appointed to carry the program out. I am a member of this committee and President McLean of Hampton is its chairman.

I propose this spring to hold instead of a single institute a series of local conferences. I have already been to the West Virginia State College where I spoke to the faculty and heads of the departments and held conferences with the president and other officials. I am next going to Hampton where the committee of the Land-Grant Colleges will meet. Subsequently I hope to hold similar conferences in North Carolina, South Carolina, Georgia, Florida and Louisiana and I think that in this way a program of social investigation on a wide scale aimed toward the economic guidance

1. Du Bois wrote of the incident in his "Chronicle of Race Relations" section of *Phylon* 3 (First Quarter 1942): 83. Involved was the suggestion by professors in charge of local arrangements for the annual meeting of the association—held at the Biltmore Hotel in Atlanta, 6–8 November 1941—that Negro members not attend luncheon and dinner meetings.

2. "A Program for the Land-Grant Colleges," *Proceedings of the Nineteenth Annual Conference of the Presidents of Negro Land Grant Colleges, November 11–13, 1941, Chicago, Illinois* (n.p.,n.d.) pp. 42–56.

of the Negro after the war can be inaugurated. I will make a final report to you when this program is finished.

I can, of course, hardly hope that your commitments will allow any further extension of this aid but if there is any possibility I should be glad if you would let me lay before you the further possible development of my idea of social studies.

Very sincerely yours,
W. E. B. Du Bois

Atlanta, Ga., 6 November 1942

My dear Mr. Dollard:

I want to make a further statement concerning the movement which the Carnegie Corporation helped by two appropriations of a thousand dollars. As you know with the first thousand I had a very successful conference. Then to my disappointment I found that the administration of the University was not taking hold of the matter in the way in which I hoped. Therefore I used the second thousand in trying to initiate another movement which I hope eventually the University will support. This movement is an attempt to unite first the seventeen Negro Land Grant Colleges of the South and afterward some of the private colleges in a cooperative study of the social problems of this section. All of these institutions have departments of social science and practically all of them some social study on the race problem.

My idea was that by strengthening the social science departments of these state institutions and by getting them to work in unison, we could make a cooperative study on a broad, continuous and intensive scale. Such an effort, however, would need the guidance and advice of the best sociological thought of the country and for that reason I wanted to inaugurate a series of conferences which would be attended by representatives of the departments of social sciences in these colleges, by representatives of the administration and also of sociologists of national repute.

I put this scheme before the meeting of the presidents of the Negro Land Grant Colleges in Chicago in November, 1941. They were very much interested and appointed a committee on the subject. That committee met at Hampton Institute in June, 1942, and in consultation with government officials, representatives of the American Council on Education and others voted to enter upon this program. In a second meeting of the Land Grant Colleges held in October, 1942, I was appointed Coordinator of this cooperative effort and the college presidents agreed to put it into immediate operation.

I have begun correspondence looking forward to a choice of subjects for beginning these studies. On the other hand, what is needed is a central fund to promote the conferences and the office expense and some preliminary publication. In time the colleges will be able to contribute to such a fund but at present there are certain legal technicalities in the way. It would be a question in the case of many of the boards of trustees as to whether they could contribute to an activity which was outside the state. Nevertheless the colleges promise to pay the expenses of their delegates to the conferences and do as much as is possible.

On the other hand, I have asked the trustees of Atlanta University to make an annual appropriation of a thousand dollars to defray the expenses of the conferences, the clerical expense and the traveling expense of certain nationally known sociologists. The board of trustees will consider this matter at its November meeting. In case I get this appropriation and whether I get it or not, I propose to go forward in what the *Journal of Higher Education* published by Ohio State University has called the "making of educational history."[1]

It may be that I shall have to make some appeal to organizations like yours for help but if I can get the movement on its feet without such an appeal I shall do so and then perhaps ask for aid in insuring its growth and expansion.

I am taking the liberty to give you this information to let you know what your aid has succeeded in starting.

Very sincerely yours,
W. E. B. Du Bois

Moss Hyles Kendrix, born in Atlanta in 1917, was a co-founder, in 1937, of the Delta Phi Delta Journalism Society and originator, in 1939, of the National Negro Newspaper Week, which he directed until 1943. In the latter capacity he asked Du Bois for commentary on the Black press.

Atlanta, Ga., February 11, 1942

Dear Dr. Du Bois:

The week of March 1–7, 1942, has been set for the observance of National Negro Newspaper Week and the 115th anniversary of the American Negro Press.

If it is possible, we would appreciate your writing an article relative to the Negro press which we would release to the Negro newspapers of the nation. The subject and nature of such an article we should like to leave entirely to your judgment.

If it is possible for you to assist us in this matter, we would appreciate receiving your article as soon as possible in order that we may have adequate time to mimeograph it and get it to the newspapers in time for their press week editions.

I am enclosing the outline for the Week which will give you some idea as to our program and objectives.

Sincerely yours,
Moss Hyles Kendrix

Du Bois's response to this request was undated; it contains important biographical information.

About 1882 when I was a school boy in Massachusetts I became local correspondent for the New York *Globe* which was the first colored paper that I had ever seen. I used to sell about ten copies to the small group of colored people in my home, Great

1. October 1942; 13: 392. A fuller report appeared in *School and Society* 56 (25 June 1942): 77–78.

Barrington, and wrote from time to time little news notes which T. Thomas Fortune published to my intense gratification and delight. I continued as agent and correspondent of the paper when it became the New York *Age* and until I left home to go to college.

From that time until this I have followed with great interest the development of the Negro press and especially its enormous expansion in circulation and interest during the last fifteen years. When I established *The Crisis* in 1910, I could make it a "news monthly," because the colored papers of that day carried so little real news. Their interest was in editorials and in local correspondence. Afterward at a meeting in Baltimore I took occasion to criticize the Negro press for its lack of enterprise in the systematic gathering of news concerning the Negro. The speech aroused a great deal of sharp criticism but it was true.

It is no longer true, however, today. The news gathering of the Negro press is upon an extraordinary and ever increasing plane. The next step, however, is already indicated, and that is more careful selection and thoughtful emphasis in the presentation of news. The old insistence of the Hearst newspapers on crime and scandal has naturally had large vogue with our weekly papers and without doubt has helped sell them. I think, however, that now the time has come when at least some of the papers should so temper, explain and sift the news that we would have a better presentation of news according to its real and lasting value; and especially there should be a more careful follow-up of real interest stories which become lost after their initial flare-up in the daily news.

The issuing of newspapers more frequently than once a week has not been very successful as yet among Negroes. Nevertheless, we have here in Atlanta, the *Daily World* which is quite indispensable for those who would follow local news. A daily Negro newspaper in certain localities is a possibility today. High power presses running an evening newspaper from New York could reach a Negro population from Boston to Washington and easily have a large subscription list and paying advertisements. It would, however, call for capital and skill. Here, however, is a future for some real journalist.[1]

W. E. B. Du Bois

A letter of biographical interest was written to Du Bois from a person who indicated he was a doctor of jurisprudence, but who has not otherwise been identified.

Chicago, Ill., March 26, 1942

Dr. W. E. Burghardt Du Bois
Dear Sir:
    When I was a student in Berlin I met in the office of "Das Kleine Journal" in Berlin

1. Du Bois' communication was published, in part, in the *Baltimore Afro-American*, 7 March 1942. A similar statement by Du Bois was published in the *New York Age*, 4 November 1935. Twenty-seven of Du Bois's contributions to the early newspapers prior to his going to Fisk are summarized in Aptheker, *Annotated Bibliography*, pp. 1–4.

(Germany) between April 1892 and April 1894 an American student. I believe I had advertised at the University that I would like to exchange German lessons against English lessons and that it was from that motive that the American student visisted me (The office we met was Jerusalemerstr. 54/55 near Jerusalemer Kirche in Berlin). The exchange of languages took not place I guess because the American student would have liked to discuss at once the German law and I was at that time only in the beginning of my study. But I remember the conversation we had. He spoke about the treatment of the Negroes in the U.S. He showed me that he himself what I never would have thought of was considered to belong to the Negro race and that even small stripes of black colour on the fingernails would be sufficient to classify a person as Negro throughout the United States. Then I was so deeply touched by his description of the Negro-Problem, that even today I remember these facts. Your photograph in Brawley's Short History of the American Negro shows up about the shape of the face of that American I mentioned above who was some years older than I. (I was born at Berlin in 1874).

I learned with great satisfaction that most successfully you devoted your work to the bettering of the standard of life and of the situation of the Negro-population. So I would be very interested to find out whether you have been that American student at Berlin I mentioned above.

Very sincerely Yours
Alfred Eisenstaedt

Atlanta, Ga., 31 March 1942

My dear Sir:

Answering your letter of March 26, I beg to say I was a student in Berlin from 1892 to 1894 and at one time was seeking to exchange English for German with a German student. It is quite possible that I talked with you at the time although I do not happen to remember the incident. I thank you for your kind words.

Very sincerely yours,
W. E. B. Du Bois

William Pickens, born in South Carolina in 1881, was educated at Talladega, Yale, and Fisk. He then was a teacher at Talladega College and at Wiley University in Texas and a dean at Morgan State College in Baltimore. Beginning in 1920 he served the NAACP as a field secretary, until accepting the appointment from the United States treasury in 1941 mentioned in the correspondence published below. Pickens was always very outspoken and tended to take positions on imperialism and the Soviet Union quite to the left of the NAACP board; in particular, he and Walter White often clashed. A letter from Pickens to Du Bois treats of this difference as well as of the earlier matter where Pickens had joined Du Bois and others in censuring White (see above, pp. 299–301). Du Bois does not seem to have replied to this letter.

Washington, D. C., April 29, 1942

Dear Dr. Du Bois:

Seeing you for a minute in the hallways of Atlanta University the other day reminds me that I had thought often that you might like to see the enclosures, if you have time to look them over. Especially, there is my statement to the Board of the N.A.A.C.P., made on April 13, more than two months *after* they had sent out their ridiculous press release through their Secretary. I had refrained from sending anything to newspapers and from answering their requests and telegram, "Until after I see the N.A.A.C.P. Board." And I found out at the Board meeting that some of them, the opposition in particular, did not want me to send out this statement after I had waited and presented it to them first. At first I was inclined to accede to that, but a few hours later I wrote them that I would not withhold my statement, since they could not recall their publicity.[1]

By the way, last fall Miss Helen Boardman told me that she had, on her own initiative, sent you some material of hers concerning my work, and that incidentally you had mentioned how the rest of us had abandoned the position which you had taken to try to rectify things in the Association just before you left it. In my own case that is a statement of apparent fact, but there is another part of the whole truth which perhaps you never have known: I never abandoned the position which had been taken by all of us, but when I saw that some of the others had asked that their names be taken off the list after the fight had been made and lost, and that Roy Wilkins, who had wired me for the use of my name, had taken off his own name with this group, I as a matter of course, took my name off, but told Miss Ovington, on her inquiry, that we had all acted on our own responsibilities, and that you and the others were not more nor less responsible than was I, but that if the movement was not carried forward as started (100% of those who had signed up), it was already abandoned by some of the others (Wilkins, Seligmann, et al.)—[Robert] Bagnall and I knew that you would leave the Association under the circumstances, and he and I conferred together and decided that there would be no further need for him and me to carry on a fight as matters stood. Neither of us two spoke to Walter White or any others about it at the time, but in a telephone conversation with Dr. John Haynes Holmes, we mentioned the fact that Wilkins and Seligmann had already broken up the movement, and that we were off the list. I am sending Bagnall a copy of this letter.

Very best wishes, and highest regards, always—

William Pickens

1. The board of the NAACP met on 9 February 1942 and formally censured Pickens for his article dealing with the establishment of a training base for pilots at Tuskegee, published in the *Amsterdam Star-News*, 31 January 1942. The board read this article as support for segregation; the censure reminds one of similar action taken by the board against Du Bois, ostensibly on the same question, which was the occasion of his resignation in 1934. The press release of the NAACP mentioned by Pickens was sent out on 10 February 1942; Pickens sent out his own release on 13 April 1942 after the board had met and upheld its February action.

The momentous plan that Walter White describes in letters to Du Bois in the spring of 1942 remained only a plan; its importance, nevertheless, was great, and that White put forward the name of Du Bois—under all the circumstances—certainly speaks well for White.

New York, N. Y., April 28, 1942

Very confidential

Dear Dr. Du Bois:

At his invitation I had a long talk last week with Lord Halifax[1] who asked me a number of questions regarding the race problem in the United States and regarding the effect on Negro morale of the situation in the Far East, Africa and the West Indies. During the course of our conversation I told Lord Halifax of an idea which had occurred to me which might be of some value to the cause of the United Nations in assuring to colored peoples throughout the world that in the post war world they would share in the benefits of the struggle now being made. The idea, briefly, is this:

That President Roosevelt be asked to appoint immediately a commission of from three to five persons who would go to India immediately. As a preliminary to their departure and as proof of the sincerity of the United States on the matter of color, President Roosevelt would take a sweeping and unequivocal stand against discrimination on the basis of color in the United States. The commission I had in mind was one made up of three persons, as follows: Wendell Willkie, Mr. Justice [Felix] Frankfurter, and a distinguished American Negro who is unmistakably Negro. This commission would talk with Nehru, Gandhi and other Indian leaders and attempt to work out a formula for independence which would be acceptable to India and to Great Britain.

By implication, the sending of such a commission by President Roosevelt would cause the United States to serve as guarantor of the carrying out of whatever pledges Great Britain may make to India, concerning which pledges there is, as you of course know, great skepticism among the leaders of India.

Lord Halifax informed me, in confidence, that he and the government of Great Britain had had a somewhat similar idea—for a delegation of distinguished American college presidents and educators to make an objective, factual study of the situation. When he asked me for comment on this plan I told him that I believed the situation was too dangerous and immediate for a study of this sort and that it would be preferable during this crisis for the commission to be made up of men of affairs as well as those connected with education. He, therefore, proposed the enlarging of the commission from three to four or five, the added persons to be distinguished educators. He further stated that the situation is so critical that he hoped I would make this proposal to the President as soon as possible. I have requested an appointment with the President for this purpose.

My purpose in writing to you is three-fold: First, I would like to have your

1. Lord Halifax (1881–1959) at this time was British ambassador at Washington; he had been foreign minister (1938–40) and viceroy of India (1926–31). He held his appointment in Washington throughout the war.

comments about the wisdom and feasibility of this plan. What in your opinion would be the position such a commission could take, if you believe that the sending of such a commission would be desirable?

Second: What form and what details would you suggest from the sweeping and dramatic action with respect to the Negro-white situation in the United States the President could take as a preliminary to the sending of such a commission to India?

Third: Should I be asked by the President to suggest a list of Negroes from which he could select one to be invited, may I include your name in the list?

As I may see the President at almost any time, would you be good enough to let me hear from you by return air mail? Will you be good enough to mark the envelope "Personal." And may I very strongly urge that this be treated with the strictest confidence as any preliminary publicity might be most unfortunate?

Ever sincerely,
Walter White

Atlanta, Ga., May 2, 1942

Mr. Walter White
My dear Sir:

Any duty which the President of the United States may lay upon me, I will be glad to perform to the best of my ability.

Very respectfully yours,
W. E. B. Du Bois

New York, N. Y., May 12, 1942

Confidential

Dear Dr. Du Bois:

For your confidential information I wish you to see the enclosed copy of letter to the President and of supplemental letter which I presented last Wednesday through Mr. Sumner Welles along with a list of American Negroes, in which your name was included, from which a selection might be made of a member of a commission to India.[1]

You will doubtless be interested in knowing that Mr. Welles characterized the suggestion as being "of the highest significance" and as possibly being the step which

---

1. Enclosed were carbons of two letters. One, dated 4 May 1942, was from Walter White to President Roosevelt. This touched on the seriousness of Japan's approach to India, mentioned a discussion of the mission to India of Wendell Willkie, Felix Frankfurter, "and a distinguished American Negro whose complexion unmistakeably identifies him as being a colored man" "whose aim would be to help work out a modus vivendi between India and Great Britain." It added "an even bolder proposal" of an Asian conference which would clearly put the United Nations in opposition to colonialism. Finally, it suggested a forthright stand publicly taken by FDR against discrimination and segregation in the United States. Another, briefer letter dated 6 May 1942 was to Sumner Welles, undersecretary of state, suggesting that President Manuel Quezon of the Philippines be among those invited to draft a Pacific charter, if the Asian conference suggested in the letter of 4 May was held.

might be the turning point in the war. He stated that the proposal was of such importance that he would take it up immediately with the President and would as soon as possible advise me of the decision made. As soon as I have further information I will advise you.

Cordially,
Walter White

New York, N. Y., June 5, 1942

Personal and confidential
My dear Dr. Du Bois:

I talked with Mr. Sumner Welles in Washington Tuesday. He told me that the President was enthusiastic about the proposal to send a commission to India and believed it would be of very real value. But the President thinks it unwise to act now until the situation in India changes somewhat, which may take place within the next two to four weeks.[1]

The situation to which the President refers is the effect of Mr. Gandhi's assertion that the chief interest of the United States in India is that of preserving and perpetuating "British imperialism." The President feels that any action by the United States right now would be interpreted by Mr. Gandhi and would be utilized by the Japanese as proof of this.

Should any change in the situation or any new developments occur I will advise you.

Let me again urge that this be kept in the strictest confidence.

Ever sincerely,
Walter White

Howard W. Odum (1884–1954) was born in Georgia and educated at Emory College, the University of Mississippi, Clark University in Massachusetts, and Columbia University. He taught briefly at the University of Mississippi, but most of his academic life was spent at the University of North Carolina as professor of sociology (1920–54). His early writings were conventionally—even vehemently—racist,* but his attitude changed as he matured. From

1. The mission of Sir Stafford Cripps from Britain to India early in 1942 was not successful. The proposals made by Walter White did not reach fruition, but in the spring of 1942, FDR did send a mission, headed by Louis Johnson, former assistant secretary of war, and Henry F. Grady, former assistant secretary of state in charge of trade relations, and some industrialists, to India to study what that country was doing in terms of war production and how this production might be increased. Colonel Johnson while in India made a speech affirming the desire of the United States that the war end with China and India part of the community of free nations; that speech was never reported in the newspapers of the United States. See *Amerasia* 6 (25 October 1942): 397–408; Kate L. Mitchell, "U. S. Technical Mission to India," *Far Eastern Survey* 11 (23 March 1942): 71–72; and *Far Eastern Survey* 11 (1 June 1942): 122.

* In the *Crisis* 7 (February 1914): 202, Du Bois attacked this feature of Odum's work, calling it "most indefensible."

1937 to 1944 he served as president of the Commission on Interracial Cooperation. His greatest distinction was won as an early advocate of regionalism, and his two books, Southern Regions of the United States *(1936) and* American Regionalism *(1938) made great impact in their time.*

Chapel Hill, N.C., May 20, 1942

Dear Professor Du Bois:

I am sending you herewith a little reprint of what I have called "A Sociological Approach to the Study and Practice of American Regionalism."[1]

This follows the pattern of our factorial syllabus and is set up as a sort of teaching method. I am sending copies around to several of my friends and especially to some of the younger sociologists to ask whether they consider this realistic sociology. I have the impression that in the past most of my sociological friends have thought that regionalism was getting out of the field of sociology into the borderline of public administration, political science, and geography. It is my own conviction, however, that in our search for something to make sociology more realistic and rigorously scientific, enabling us to make systematizations and real theory from empirical studies, regionalism offers a first-rate area and tool.

I shall appreciate it very much if you care to write me a little on the following three points:

1. Is it sociology?

2. What special criticism of definitions, premises, assumptions, postulates?

3. In particular, I would appreciate your giving close scrutiny to the problem of delineation of regions, district, states, subregions, etc. We are undertaking about six months of statistical exploration of indices of regional and subregional delineation with a view to having an extensive agenda for a very small, but all-week, working conference in August. I shall appreciate more than I can say any help you will give us on these points.

Cordially yours,
Howard W. Odum

[P. S.] Don't take too much time if you are not in a mood! Thought you might like to see what I am sending out.

Atlanta, Ga., 23 June 1942

My dear Dr. Odum:

I have your letter of May twentieth and it reminds me that I have been going to write to you for some time. I have a feeling that it will be possible at Atlanta University to make an application of your general idea of regionalism with a modification which seems to me vital. You, of course, remember our old studies of the Negro problems. They petered out with the First World War for lack of support. In 1933, I

1. The essay was published in *Social Forces* 20 (May 1942): 425–36.

returned here with the idea of reviving in some way our studies of the American Negro. I finally succeeded in 1940 in starting a quarterly magazine, *Phylon*, the Atlanta University Review of Race and Culture, which is succeeding fairly well. Next I wanted to reestablish the conferences and studies. Here I met difficulties mostly through academic inertia. In 1941, I held a conference here with help of the Carnegie Fund to interest teachers of economics in the various Negro schools in a South-wide cooperative study of the American Negro especially from the economic point of view. The conference was successful but the University was unwilling to follow it up.

I then turned to the Land Grant Colleges and after meeting with the presidents in November, 1941 and at Hampton last week succeeded in getting them to endorse the enclosed resolution. Next I want to get the University to respond with a small appropriation and see if possibly I can not get the American Council on Education to help us.

What I have in mind is that your regional interpretation of human action must be modified in some cases but especially calling attention to so powerful a force as cultural antagonism, cultural lag and group segregation. I can see where you might very easily say that this would not modify your general thesis but exemplify it, but at any rate I want to emphasize this element by having the Land Grant Colleges in a series of state-wide studies of increasing intensity to fix by as accurate a measurement as possible the place of the Negro in modern culture.

I want to begin this by holding another conference in the fall of 1942 or spring of 1943, where in consultation with experts in the social sciences, we can work out a comprehensive method of approach to this cooperation. I should like very much to have your reaction to this plan and to know if it would be possible for you to meet with us provided we get the thing going. Of course, I would expect to pay your expenses.

Very sincerely yours,
W. E. B. Du Bois

Fortune magazine showed no interest in an article proposed by Du Bois, but the proposal itself is sufficiently interesting to merit publication. At this time Henry R. Luce was Fortune's editor; its managing editor was Ralph Delahaye Paine, Jr. The June 1942 issue of Fortune had a feature story, "The Negro and the War"; it is likely that Du Bois had seen this article by the time he wrote the letter below and perhaps that explains his choice of Fortune.*

---

* In his signed "Chronicle of Race Relations" section, *Phylon* 3 (Third Quarter 1942): 320–34, Du Bois attacked the *Fortune-Time-Life* program that envisaged "the present war as a chance for America to supplant England as the greatest nation on earth and to see the domination of the world after the war by an American-British police force on sea, land and in the air."

Atlanta, Ga., May 21, 1942

The Editor
Fortune
My dear Sir:

I should like to write for *Fortune* an article with the following thesis: the present war is a war for racial equality; not consciously but more and more unconsciously. It may end before essential racial equality is achieved, in which case, it will be historically the first phase of this inevitable struggle.

One sees easily the steps by which we have come to this outcome. First, we were fighting dictators. Then we tried to make it a war for democracy but, of course, we meant democracy in Europe and North America. At last we have come to the place where no real settlement of the issues raised by the war can be made without extending democracy to Asia and back of Asiatic autonomy lies the shadow of Africa. Just as the Civil War in the United States began as a war for federal union and became a war against slavery, which gave it the necessary ethical slogan, so the present war which began as a struggle against Germany changed to a plea for the domination of the world by English-speaking nations but cannot achieve ethical sanctions without becoming a war for the political and social equality for the great races of man.

This is the central idea of the article I should like to write. I can, if you are willing, give you a more carefully organized outline; or send you a finished article. Would you be willing to consider such an essay?

Very sincerely yours,
W. E. B. Du Bois

James Edward Shepard (1875–1947) was born in Raleigh, North Carolina, and educated at North Carolina's Shaw University and at Muskingum College in Ohio, from which he received a D.D. in 1910. He was employed by the Internal Revenue Service in Raleigh (1899–1905) and by the International Sunday School Service (1905–9). In 1910 he was pastor of a Baptist Church in Durham, and he founded in that city that year a National Training School, which became in 1923 the Durham State Normal School under his presidency. This in turn became in 1925 the North Carolina College for Negroes, with Shepard as president, a position he held until his death.

An exchange between Shepard and Du Bois in the spring of 1942 reflects the latter's growing plans for the future.

Durham, N.C., May 25, 1942

Dear Dr. Du Bois:

You will recall that in 1927 we held in Durham a Fact-Finding Conference.[1] There

---

1. Du Bois commented favorably on this conference in the *Crisis* 34 (December 1927): 347–48.

seems to be a desire on the part of many that we hold this Conference again in April 1943, and that we take up where we left off at the last meeting.

It is desired that we especially plan for post-war conditions. I am writing to ask your reaction to this matter. Do you think it should be composed of a limited number of white and colored leaders, or simply confined to our own group? Do you think that a particular study of the divisions which we had at the previous conference should be made; namely, Education, Church and Religion, Civic and Political, Labor, Business, Health and Sanitation?

What suggestions can you offer that will aid us in reaching a definite decision as to this matter? Can you recommend experts in these various fields who would conduct these surveys if necessary and the money can be found?

With every good wish, I am

Sincerely yours,
James E. Shepard

Atlanta, Ga., 28 May 1942

My dear Mr. Shepard:

I believe very strongly that the day for the general conference covering all phases of the Negro problem is past. The advance of the Negro has been so great and with this advance has come all sorts of complications so that I think now in our meetings we will have to concentrate on particular subjects.

I am especially interested in the economic condition of the Negro now and after the war. In the first Phylon Institute and at the meeting of the colored Land-Grant College presidents last November, I laid down a broad program of economic research. I wanted to enlist the service of these colleges, each for his own state, as centers of intensive and continuous study of the social and economic conditions of Negroes in that state so that gradually we would build up an unrivaled body of knowledge accurately and carefully done which would cover the Negro in the South. The presidents expressed enthusiasm for this program and appointed a committee of which MacLean of Hampton is chairman to carry this out. We are in process of implementing this program. Now in addition to that there is the problem of the final study and integration and interpretation of the vast amount of data which will eventually be gathered. Also there will be the problem of uniformity of method, etc. I plan to get together a national committee of the best sociologists to plan methods and help in interpretation and after that there ought to be published at least one authoritative volume a year with the results of these studies.

Now in addition to this there is the matter of the careful study of the Northern Negro and there I am hoping that I can eventually get into cooperation and organize the work in colleges like yours, Howard, Lincoln in Missouri and Lincoln in Pennsylvania, Fisk, Wilberforce, Talladega, etc., that is, the leading private institutions together with the one federal institution and the one state institution devoted to higher training. Such an organization working with the departments of sociology in several of the larger colleges of the North might complement the work of the Land-

Grant Colleges in the South and thus by the end of the war we would have a set-up for the study of a group of thirteen million human beings which for completeness and scientific accuracy would be unrivaled in the world.

Now could your proposed meeting in any way work in with this plan? Think it over and let me hear from you.

Very sincerely yours,

W. E. B. Du Bois

Thomas Sancton, born in Louisiana in 1916, was educated at Tulane University and then was a reporter for the New Orleans Times-Picayune. *He later served as* AP *correspondent in Mississippi and then went to Harvard as a Nieman Fellow (1941–42). Early in 1942, leaving Harvard, he became the* Nation's *Washington correspondent, but soon he turned to novel writing; Doubleday published his* Count Roller Skates *(1956) and* By Starlight *(1960). In the 1940s he published regularly not only in the* New Republic *and* Nation, *but also in* Harper's, *the* American Scholar, *and* Survey Graphic.

As managing editor of the New Republic, *Sancton wrote to Du Bois—misspelling his name.*

New York, N.Y., June 11, 1942

Dear Dr. Du Boise:

We would like very much to print a special supplement to *The New Republic* which would be written by Negro writers and which shall not be limited in subject matter. I have been reading for a number of years with special interest the writings of many Negro writers and scholars, but your own books have left the greatest impression upon me. I am wondering, therefore, if you couldn't suggest to me the names of about three Negro writers, professors or literary men who might, in your opinion, be best qualified to edit this supplement, and also the names of about ten others whom we might ask for contributions. We are only seeking for the best possible writing, whether it be essay, short stories or poetry.

I am personally interested in getting a number of strongly written essays on vital subjects which are now of deepest interest to the tenth of this nation which is Negro. I feel sure you will understand the kind of supplement we hope to publish and I hope that you will have the opportunity to suggest a number of names to me. Incidentally, I have had occasion to discuss briefly some of your views in an article to appear in the fall number of *The American Scholar,* which deals with some of the things that sincere Southern liberals must realize and do.[1] I hope you will have a chance to read it.

After your long career of magnificent scholarship I do not know whether you would have an interest in contributing to this supplement, but we should certainly be delighted to have you do so.

Sincerely,

Thomas Sancton

1. "The South and the North: A Southern View," *American Scholar* 12 (January 1943): 105–17.

Atlanta, Ga., 23 June 1942

My dear Mr. Sancton:

Answering your letter of June eleventh, I beg to say that I would recommend the following persons for your proposed Negro supplement: as editors I suggest, Allison Davis, recently appointed Assistant Professor of Education in the University of Chicago. First he specialized in English, leading his class at Williams College and making Phi Beta Kappa. Then after teaching a while he changed to anthropology, studying at Oxford and Harvard. This spring he took his Ph.D. in anthropology in the University of Chicago and received his appointment. Sterling Brown, Professor of English at Howard University and joint author of *Negro Caravan*, an anthology recently published by the Dryden Press. Brown is himself a poet and has wide knowledge of modern literature. Charles Thompson, Ph.D. of the University of Chicago and Dean of the College of Liberal Arts at Howard University. He has edited the very important *Journal of Negro Education* since about 1931 [actually 1932].

Of course, I have not spoken to these men but so far as ability and experience is concerned they ought to do a fine piece of editorial work.

As to the ten persons, I make the following recommendations: Langston Hughes, poet; Rayford Logan, Ph.D., Harvard, Professor of History, Howard; Mercer Cook, Ph.D., Brown, Professor of Romance Languages, Atlanta University; Countee Cullen, poet; Horace R. Cayton, economist; Arna Bontemps, poet and writer of fiction; E. Franklin Frazier, head of the Department of Sociology, Howard University; Richard Wright, novelist; Howard W. Long, research expert in psychology, Washington Public Schools; Doxey A. Wilkerson, Department of Education, Howard University.

Personally, I should like to lay before any such board for its acceptance an essay in poetic fiction which might suit your purposes.

Very sincerely yours,
W. E. B. Du Bois

New York, N.Y., July 10, 1942

Dear Dr. Du Bois,

I want to thank you for the helpful suggestions in your letter of June 23, which I have taken long to answer. The list of names which you suggested in connection with our intention to produce, rather to publish, a supplement written and edited by Negroes seems a good one and we shall certainly draw heavily from it. I am very hopeful that you will submit to the editors the essay in poetic fiction. I read "Litany of Atlanta" long ago and phrases still stick in my memory, and still color my thoughts upon the place and the fate of the Negro. Phrases like the twin hate and murder, and clank, crash and crack in the streets; and surely Thou too oh Lord are not white, a pale and bloodless thing. I know I quote these far from accurately, but the spirit of the prose I shall never forget.[1] I know Atlanta. I know New Orleans. I know Mississippi, and twice I went, as a reporter, with the Mississippi National Guard down into a little dead, forgotten lumber town in the cutover pinelands to prevent a brewing lynching. In my childhood I have loved two Negro women who were close to me with a love that seeps into one's blood and soul, and can never be forgotten. Sometime if you can take time out from your studies for a few idle moments, you might look up two stories I wrote about this: "The Dirty Way," *Harper's*, about April, 1938, and "The Parting," *Harper's*, July 1941.[2]

I have enclosed something that I have written about Odell Waller.[3] Perhaps it will be of interest. Even though I am white, I don't think any thought I have ever had about the Negro has been pale and bloodless, or that anything I shall write will ever be. But perhaps even I too will seem to a Negro philosopher to be half-hearted and ameliorating. That is not the way I feel.

The Negro supplement project goes slowly, but we should be ready to start it in a few weeks. I have not yet written to any of the men you suggested, but shall write to at least a number of them, perhaps all, when we are ready to go ahead.

Sometime, if you have the time, I wonder if you would satisfy my curiosity on a matter: and that is, what white men now alive or in recent years, either writers or doers, do you think have really understood, have really felt, have really helped the progress of Negroes to the decent things of life?[4]

Sincerely,
Thomas Sancton

New York City, Sept. 30, 1942

Dear Dr. Du Bois:

This is just to tell you that our plan for a Negro supplement has been somewhat delayed but that we hope to go ahead with it in the next few months. I shall hold your manuscript to submit it to the supplement's editors unless you are anxious to place it somewhere else in the meantime, and instruct me to return it to you.

I enjoyed the poetry of it and I hope that the editors of the supplement will enjoy it likewise. You need not reply to this letter, merely informative, unless you want me to

---

1. "A Litany of Atlanta" was written by Du Bois on a train in 1906 while hurrying home to Georgia from Alabama to discover the fate of his family after the pogrom of that year. It was first published in the *Independent*, 11 October 1906, and often reprinted. Sancton's recall of some of its lines and phrases was good.

2. "The Dirty Way," *Harper's Magazine* 176 (May 1938): 571–80; "The Parting," *Harper's Magazine* 183 (July 1941): 146–55.

3. "The Waller Case," *New Republic*, 13 July 1942. Odell Waller, a twenty-five-year-old sharecropper, was executed on 2 July 1943 in Virginia for having killed his landlord. The case was widely reported at the time and symbolized the intensity of Black oppression and the reality of resistance.

4. One deeply regrets that Du Bois did not find the time or have the inclination to answer this inquiry.

send the manuscript back to you since the supplement has still not progressed to a definite stage.[1]

Sincerely,
Thomas Sancton

Theodore M. Berry, born in Maysville, Kentucky, in 1908, received a law degree in 1931 from the University of Cincinnati and practiced in Cincinnati for a decade. In 1941 Archibald MacLeish, the poet, who then headed the Office of War Information, asked Berry to serve as a liaison officer, charged in particular with improving the morale of the Black soldier. In 1943 Berry returned to his Cincinnati practice, where, beginning in 1949, he was elected a member of the city council. In 1965 he became an official of the Lyndon Johnson administration in Washington in the Office of Economic Opportunity. From the Office of War Information he wrote to Du Bois.

Washington, D.C., June 18, 1942

Dear Dr. Du Bois:

It was a privilege to participate in the discussion of your social research plan presented to the Land Grant College Presidents last week end. I believe all agreed that yours was the most significant contribution of the Conference, and it is hoped that the several colleges will give it positive activation.

One particular thought suggested at the conference prompts this letter. You may recall at the last session Dean [Charles] Thompson of Howard raised a question regarding treatment of morale of college students. You suggested one approach of comparing situations existent during the last war with the progress realized thus far in the present war. I have thought that this could well serve to hearten our people as a whole.

Because of your intimate knowledge and experience with conditions during the 1st World War and appreciation of present trends, I am prompted to ask if you would be willing to write an article along the line you suggested. My idea is that the article would be published and widely distributed either by this agency or an appropriate private organization.

Please let me have your reactions to this request, and I hope you may have the time to help us in this important task of morale building.

Very sincerely yours,
Theodore M. Berry

1. The *New Republic* of 18 October 1943 devoted fifteen pages to "The Negro: His Future in America" under "Race and Science"; "The Negro in Industry"; "Negroes in the Armed Forces"; "The Negro and Politics"; and "Negro Progress." What became of the Du Bois manuscript mentioned here is not known.

Atlanta, Ga., June 23, 1942

My dear Mr. Berry:

Answering your letter of June 18, I beg to say that I would be glad to write for your office a statement on the following thesis: that despite the amount of discrimination and segregation which today faces the Negro American, he can by comparing his condition now and that at the time of the First World War take great courage. In the first World War there was a movement to keep him out of the draft on the ground that he was not really an American. There was not only no effort of the Federal Government to incorporate him into industry but on the contrary there was a series of riots unpunished to force him out of industry by brute force. These riots were caused not only by the strong opposition of unions but also by lack of housing and lack of effort to furnish housing. There was determination to train no Negro officers and especially to refuse to allow them to be trained with white officers. Finally a segregated camp was established and then hesitation at commissioning the graduates at this camp. The officers finally inducted into the army were treated with discrimination and suffered great injustice especially in the A.E.F. in France. There was curious discrimination in the draft and Negroes were inducted, especially in the South, in considerably larger proportion than whites even though cantonments were not ready for them.

Finally, there was no official action of the Federal Government which could possibly be construed into a basic attack upon racial discrimination as an hindrance to war effort. The present situation is a great improvement upon that of 1917 to 1920. It leaves numbers of things undone and untouched but if we recognize that cultural change is slow, so long as change is evident we ought to be not satisfied but encouraged. Then certainly the recent meeting of the FEPC in Birmingham should be an encouragement to all Americans.   If your office wishes me to write something of this sort and will let me know the length of the article,[1] I should be glad to do it providing, of course, I receive reasonable compensation for my time and effort.

Very sincerely yours,
W. E. B. Du Bois

There was an especially voluminous correspondence between Anson Phelps Stokes and Du Bois in 1942. This dealt particularly with work on the Encyclopedia of the Negro and Stokes's efforts in connection with a Committee on Africa, the War, and Peace Aims. Representative portions of this exchange will convey its essential content.

Lenox, Mass., March 4, 1942

Dear Dr. Du Bois:

I wonder if you would be willing to look over the enclosed very tentative list of

---

1. Berry left Washington in 1943; the essay proposed by Du Bois was not done. But Du Bois did write an essay called "The Negro Soldier in Service Abroad During the First World War," which appeared in the *Journal of Negro Education* 12 (Summer 1943): 324–34.

African Dates for purposes of correction and enlargement. It is just a tentative beginning of an appendix for our report on Africa. I want specially to have events which
have significance from the standpoint of Africa's relations to the outside world. Please
see that this is returned to me at the Phelps-Stokes Fund office within a couple of
weeks.

Sincerely yours,
Anson Phelps Stokes

*The manuscript of a study by the Committee on Africa was sent to Du Bois for criticism. He
responded on 28 April 1942 with a long and detailed and frank critique. Stokes's response gives
the content of that critique as well as Stokes's own decisions on the matters in question.*

New York, N.Y., April 29, 1942

Dear Dr. Du Bois:

I am under more obligations than I can tell you for your frank and full letter of
April 28th. I have spent a couple of hours this morning studying it carefully and
incorporating in one way or another its suggestions in our Report. I have not the time
to take up your questions in detail, but one or two things I want to assure you of:

1. That I think the lack of more than passing reference to the horrors of British and
American slave trade in Africa was a very serious omission in the first report. It will
be corrected.

2. The element of exploitation will be duly stressed.

3. The Liberian matter is difficult. The Liberian Consul General, meeting with
our Committee, said that in his judgment the Republic would not have survived if it
had not been for the Firestone Agreement.

4. The balance sheet certainly needs revision and I have incorporated most of your
suggestions. I am quoting a statement of Dr. [Edwin W.] Smith's on this subject
which ends up by saying, "As regards our interim balance sheet, it must be confessed
that were any one to say that the account is against Europe it would be difficult to
contradict his statement." This was written in 1926.

5. As to Ethiopia, I have studied the documents and think you are right that the
Agreement carries with it many features of a British military and political protectorate, and have so stated.

6. As to South Africa, our theory has been that, although not flinching from telling
the essential facts, we can accomplish more by praising those in South Africa who are
trying to remedy the situation than by extreme criticism.

7. Due reference is being made to the large American interests and investments in
Africa; also to the part that the desire for profits has played in European control.

8. As to Colonial troops, you will remember that I said when presenting this
matter that it is the most difficult one on which to reach a clear conclusion, and that
our consultants showed very different opinions. I have looked up the French attitude
further and the clause as it now stands reads as follows:

The Committee being opposed to the imperialistic use of the troops of any race anywhere is naturally especially opposed to the use of conscripted troops from African colonies in Europe, or of similar troops from Europe in African colonies—except as they may be members of an international police force. In this connection Africa might well make its contribution to the attempt to prevent future wars by endeavoring to restrict its troops to policing and the maintenance of order. The large use in Europe and elsewhere of native conscripted troops from North Africa (Algeria) and Senegal has been open to criticism both on the part of Africans and Europeans. It should, however, be remembered in fairness to the French that these Negro soldiers are French citizens from the "Colony" area and that this conscription does not apply to the ordinary "unassimilated" native population.

9. As to indirect rule, the section where we refer to its liabilities after mentioning its assets will be developed.

10. As to the French attitude, we certainly did not have the slightest idea of implying any support of the color-bar. To make this perfectly clear I have introduced a strong clause saying that the French are to be commended for having less race prejudice than any other group and showing that Latins are less open to this than Anglo-Saxons.

11. As to the British, I cannot go the whole way with you in your pretty near indiscriminate criticism of their political and educational attitude. I frankly do not think you do them justice, although fully recognizing their serious limitations.

12. As to Belgium, I will call attention more clearly to its lack of providing higher educational facilities.

I think when you see the revised Report you will realize that we have gone far toward meeting your various criticisms, although in a public document of the type we are planning, which must secure the support of our Committee and we hope have some influence abroad, it would not, I think, be wise to indulge in such extreme criticisms as one can put in a letter.

Again, many, many thanks for attending the meeting. I am gladly enclosing herewith our cheque for $38, covering your expenses over and above what was paid by Yale and Vassar.[1]

We met until a quarter to five, and went over all of the document. Professor [Ralph J.] Bunche made many excellent minor suggestions of phraseology and some of policy, and has forwarded his copy of the preliminary Report with a good many suggested additions in Chapter IV. They almost seem to me admirable.

> Very sincerely yours,
> Anson Phelps Stokes

P. S. As to the comparison of the merits of the French and English systems on the middle of page 67 to which you raised objection, I have omitted it, merely leaving in the first sentence to the effect that "each policy has its own advantages and disadvantages".

1. Du Bois lectured at Yale and Vassar; in addition he attended a meeting of the Committee on Africa in New York City; it is for this attendance that the travel expenses were paid.

P. S. No. 2. I wonder whether the rumor is true that I have from my private detective force that you left the important Africa Committee meeting to attend the Circus!![2] I confess that I have similar likings.

A.P.S.

P. S. No. 3. I have complied with the suggestion of you and Professor Bunche in modifying the Free French statement as being probably less significant than I had originally thought.

A.P.S.

Atlanta, Ga., 15 May 1942

My dear Mr. Stokes:

The work on the Encyclopaedia is getting on well but involves an amount of detail which cannot be hurried. I have had to personally go through each one of the more than two thousand subjects and see that a bibliographical entry of one or two books is made in accordance with my best knowledge. In some cases I have had to resort to correspondence with experts. Dr. [Rayford W.] Logan's excellent notes referred to the smaller list of subjects and mainly to American and West Indian subjects. To these I am adding the references to the new literature on Africa, especially that which has been issued in the last ten or fifteen years.

Miss Diggs and I are now combining the new subjects with the old in alphabetical order and I have still about five hundred entries to be checked. After this the whole list must be re-checked and made ready for copying. As it is copied I am going to send it to Mr. Logan, who by the way has just returned from the West Indies, and ask him finally to check it. I had hoped to have it in your hands by June first, but I think it would be wiser to say July first.

I hope this progress is in accordance with your wish. By July first I shall put in your hands a final typewritten copy of something in the neighborhood of 2,500 subjects which an Encyclopaedia of the Negro might treat with at least one bibliographical reference where further information on the subject may be obtained. Of course this will mean that in hundreds of cases the scholar and especially an expert would know of either a better reference or one which he would prefer but I think in all cases my references will be fairly recent and authoritative.

Very sincerely yours,
W. E. B. Du Bois

Lenox, Mass., July 9, 1942

Dear Dr. Du Bois:

Thank you so much for your letter of July 2nd. I really think you are doing a very useful work through *Phylon*, and have spoken of it to several of my friends. The

---

2. One may be sure the rumor was true; circuses were very nearly a passion with Du Bois and until well into his eighties he attended whenever possible.

biographical articles of persons with Negro blood have been particularly worth while, and the Atlanta University Supplement was excellent.

As for the Encyclopedia of the Negro, your arrangement with Dr. Logan by which the bibliographical material will be revised and sent me in the fall is entirely satisfactory.

I want you to know of one or two very encouraging things with regard to the Committee on Africa, the War, and Peace Aims. The Conference on Africa, under the auspices of the Foreign Missions Conference of North America held at Otterbein College June 19 to 25, was a very successful one. I was very glad to have Professor Logan present the day that I presented the Africa Report,[1] although he arrived too late to hear the introductory statement. They gave me six hours, and at the close the recommendations of the Report were approved in principle without a dissenting note, although one Southern Baptist said that he did not see that the Christian Church had anything to do with the Mandates!

I have had a perfectly splendid letter from President Nicholas Murray Butler strongly indorsing the Report, and the Carnegie Endowment ordered 18 copies presumably at his suggestion with the idea, I imagine, of sending them to the Board of Directors. We had excellent statements in the *Times* and the *Tribune*, which have resulted in a large correspondence, and over 200 copies of the Report have already been sold. It is, of course, too early to get reviews. I am confidently hoping that you will have a good one in *Phylon* and can perhaps stimulate others in other papers. I have seen practically no reference as yet to the Report in the Negro Press, although Mr. [Claude A.] Barnett was greatly interested. If you think of any persons in the field of Negro public opinion who would be likely to review the Report, and would give me the names, I would be glad to send them copies.

With kind regards, I am

> Always sincerely yours,
> Anson Phelps Stokes

Atlanta, Ga., 1 October 1942

My dear Mr. Stokes:

The work which Mr. Logan and his brother did on the final bibliography of the Encyclopaedia of the Negro was not finished until September 15. I had hoped to have it a month earlier. They have done some very interesting research but it is alas in the form of several hundred card entries of the latest books on various subjects. That means that I must now go over these cards and insert them in their proper places in my finished bibliography or at least see if they ought to be inserted. It makes me

---

1. *The Atlantic Charter and Africa from an American Standpoint: A Study by the Committee on Africa, the War and Peace Aims*, New York, 1942. This was a 164-page work and with it was published *Events in African History*, compiled by Edwin W. Smith, a 67-page supplement to the main work.

pretty sick to start at this again after I finished it in the spring but I shall go right at it and send it to you at the first opportunity.

I trust you had a pleasant summer as I did.

Very sincerely yours,
W. E. B. Du Bois

5 October 1942

My dear Mr. Stokes:

Answering your letter of September 30: One hundred dollars is due Mr. Logan's brother eventually and this finishes the appropriation for the Encyclopaedia so far as I am concerned. However, the remittance to Mr. [A. C.] Logan should not go to him until I have finished checking his work. There is no hurry. The work ought to have been finished in August and did not come to me until the middle of September.

I have selected from the cards sent in by Mr. Logan several hundred new entries for the bibliography as I had finished it last June. I will have these copied and put with the original bibliography as inserts and then send it to you I hope within considerably less time than a month.

We will certainly note the African report in *Phylon*.

I trust this will find you in good health.

Very sincerely yours,
W. E. B. Du Bois

Lenox, Mass., November 9, 1942

Dear Dr. Du Bois:

I want my first letter to you this morning to be a letter of thanks for your fine review of our African Report in *Phylon*. Up to this time the reviews of Negro American writers have been rather disappointing. Mr. [Eric] Williams in *The Journal of Negro Education*—an admirable Journal—gives a fairly good summary, although quite inaccurate in places, but ends up by referring to the Report with some such phrase as that the recommendations are merely mild palliatives; while *Opportunity*, although more favorable, does not realize the extent to which the Report emphasizes freedom.[1] Mr. Barnett of the Negro Press has been most helpful and constructive and has sent out quotations from the Report quite largely to the Negro papers, but otherwise it has not received as much attention from the Negro group in America as I expected.

Most of the comments, as you know from letters that I have sent you, have been over-kind. I was particularly pleased with the statements by Abraham Flexner, Felix Morley, and others.

I shall call Dr. Smith's attention to the omission in the *Events in African History* of

---

1. Du Bois's review is in *Phylon* 3 (Fourth Quarter 1942): 435–37, and Eric Williams's is in the *Journal of Negro Education* 11 (October 1942): 535–36; that in *Opportunity* 20 (September 1942): 283–84 was by L. D. Reddick.

the Fanti Confederation, the Congress of West Africa, and the Pan African Congresses. I am particularly surprised at the omission of the last named. Dr. Smith will appreciate these or any other suggestions that you may have for additions. He told me that he had prepared an inter-leafed copy of the *Events* so that he could insert additions and possible criticism that might come in.

We have not yet had an opportunity to hear from Africa, except from the Governor of the Gambia, who wrote that he had read the Report through with great interest, and from General Smuts, who wrote a two-page letter in his own hand expressing appreciation of our continued interest in Africa. He had not, apparently, read the report.

I shall be particularly interested to get the Reports from the African Press of the West Coast and from Dr. [D. D.] Jabavu, who was one of the first to whom a copy was sent.

Again many thanks.

Sincerely yours,
Anson Phelps Stokes

P. S. A strange little error slipped us all in the reading, namely, the reference in the passage you quote to "animal husbandry." It was duly corrected in the second printing and I must hold myself responsible for the error.

We are continuing the $100 to *Phylon*.

Atlanta, Ga., November 13, 1942

My dear Mr. Stokes:

Thank you very much for continuing the one hundred dollars for *Phylon*. I am glad you liked my review of the African report. I think it was an excellent step and significant now that Africa becomes the great center of war. Of course, I am still suspicious of the Union of South Africa and of Smuts.

If you find that only one "little error" has crept into your report you will be much more fortunate than most of us.

Very sincerely yours,
W. E. B. Du Bois

Lenox, Mass., November 9, 1942

Dear Dr. Du Bois:

A very thoughtful friend of mine whom I am sure you know and honor has written to me with great distress because of the following quotation which he has taken from your book entitled: *Dusk of Dawn*, page 41.

"Only two years before, in 1885, Stanley, the travelling reporter, became a hero and symbol of white world leadership in Africa. The wild, fierce fight of the Mahdi and the driving of the English out of the Sudan did not reveal its inner truth to me. I heard only of the martyrdom of the drunken Bible-reader and freebooter, Gordon."

I am not an authority on Gordon but my friend, who has made a special study of African history, tells me that he is confident that there is no justification for your charge with reference to Gordon's excessive drinking. I have made no special study of Gordon's life for many years, but I have always supposed that he was a man of very high ideals of character and it would amaze me if your statement was justified. Furthermore, the whole implication in the sentence is extremely critical of Gordon. I know, of course, that he was somewhat emotional and probably evangelically narrow in his theology, but I can hardly think that he would be held up by thoughtful people so much as an exemplar of Christian character if your charge is true. My friend has asked me to bring this matter to your attention. I shall be glad to get your reactions and to know on what you base such a very serious charge.

Always sincerely yours,

Anson Phelps Stokes

Atlanta, Ga., November 13, 1942

My dear Mr. Stokes:

Answering your letter of November 9, concerning [Charles George] Gordon, my main authority in my statement in *Dusk of Dawn* is Lytton Strachey's *Eminent Victorians* published by Putnams in 1918 and reprinted a number of times. His last chapter is "The End of General Gordon" and in that he speaks twice, page 264 and page 298, of Gordon's drinking.

But beyond these specific references to drinking, Lord Cromer (*Modern Egypt*, Volume I) and Lord Morley (*Life of Gladstone*, Volume III) adduce severe criticism to overthrow the hero which British imperialism had made of Gordon.[1] No one can follow Gordon's career carefully and not be convinced that he was either crazy or periodically drunk. He was willing to sell his services anywhere for the sake of carrying on organized murder on either side. When he went to the Sudan he was about to sell his services to Leopold of Belgium. Of his personal courage, or rather recklessness, there is no question: but on the other hand, he was no knight in shining armour; although held up as the great opponent of slavery he issued a proclamation sanctioning slavery in the Sudan to the deep distress of the Anti-Slavery Society. Even further than that there are intimations of other irregularities. In his own words after he had boxed the ears of a telegraph clerk "and then as my conscience pricked me I gave him five pounds. He said he did not mind if I killed him—I was his father (a chocolate-colored youth of twenty)." Strachey, page 334.

The fact of the matter is that at this time in the fight between the "Little Englanders" and the new imperialists, a national hero was needed. This the protagonist of the new journalism, [William T.] Stead, furnished by grooming Gordon. Gordon became, therefore, and remains in the minds of many sincere persons, the embodiment

1. Evelyn Baring (Lord Cromer), *Modern Egypt*, 2 vols. (New York: Macmillan Co., 1908); John Morley, *The Life of William Ewart Gladstone*, 3 vols. (New York: Macmillan Co. 1903). Relevant data on Gordon will be found in Cromer, 1:75, 423, 426 n, 429 ff., 458 ff.; Morley, 3: 151–52.

of the knight errantry which made the present British Empire. But to my mind the present British Empire with its methods and ambitions is the main cause of the current debacle of civilization.

Very sincerely yours,

W. E. B. Du Bois

Atlanta, Ga., 11 November 1942

My dear Mr. Stokes:

I hope you will not think that I am forgetting the bibliography but war difficulties about hiring typing machines and getting hold of extra help have delayed the work; but it is going forward now with considerable rapidity and I hope to have the final bibliography in your hands in a few weeks. As I go over it again and again I am convinced that it is going to be something of a great deal of value.

Before paying Mr. Logan I had wanted to wait until I had had him check some of the entries but I think it is unfair to ask him to wait any longer so I should be glad if you would send a check for one hundred dollars to Dr. Logan's brother, Mr. A. C. Logan, 1101 "O" Street Northwest, Washington, D. C.

One additional piece of work which has delayed me is my plan to unite the Negro Land Grant Colleges in a continuous and intensive study of the social conditions of Negroes state by state. My program has been adopted by the conference of presidents of the Land Grant Colleges and you can read accounts of their action in *School and Society* and the *Journal of Higher Education* published by Ohio State University. I shall write you further about this and hope you will be interested.

Very sincerely yours,

W. E. B. Du Bois

Lenox, Mass., November 16, 1942

Dear Dr. Du Bois:

Let me thank you for your three good letters, one of November 11th and two of November 13th.

(1) I am to be in New York tomorrow and I shall arrange with Mr. Roy to send $100 to Dr. Logan's brother, Mr. A. C. Logan, 1101 O. Street, N. W., Washington, D. C. I am particularly pleased that you think that the bibliography that he has been helping you with is going to prove so useful. That gives me great satisfaction.

Your plan to unite the Negro Land Grant Colleges in a continuous and intensive study of social conditions of Negroes, state by state, sounds promising.

Your comments about my inquiry regarding Gordon are very interesting. My guess is that the truth is somewhere about midway between the popular idea of him as a great Christian hero and your own comments on him in your book. Strachey loved to "debunk" people and in the process did both some good and some harm. I am sending a resume of your letter, except for the last paragraph, to my friend. I thought your comments on the policy of the British Empire would upset him so much that they would prejudice him against your comments on the other matter. Furthermore, although I do not hold the British Empire entirely innocent in the matter of our present troubles I cannot agree that its shortcomings even compare as a factor in being really responsible for the present debacle with the terrible totalitarian views of the Nazis. Great Britain would have been willing to hand back almost all of Tanganyika to the Germans had it not been for the outrageous views of race developed by the Nazi leaders, which made it, in my judgment, impossible for it to be returned, while a handing over directly to the League, which would have had many advantages, would, of course, not have satisfied Germany an atom. I think that we will have to agree to disagree about Great Britain. I oppose many of the features of past imperialism as much as you do, but I think the Commonwealth of Nations idea is a very heartening one and am truly encouraged at recent progress in the Colonies.

As to the Union of South Africa, I of course agree with you that its extreme segregation views are entirely impossible and wrong. Just how far General Smuts can and will go to correct them, I do not know, but Rheinallt Jones is of the opinion that as long as Smuts remains in office there will be progress in the matter.[1]

Please do not misunderstand me about the one "little error" that I referred to. There are undoubtedly many others. In fact, some have been brought to my attention, such as the misspelling of Professor Hambly's name. I mentioned it merely because it was in your quotation.

Always sincerely yours,
Anson Phelps Stokes

Atlanta, Ga., December 17, 1942

Dear Mr. Stokes:

At long last I am sending you this bibliography.[2] I am very sorry to be so late with it but the difficulties of getting clerical help under present circumstances and the accumulation of other work has hindered its completion. It has now 1,917 subjects and 4,240 bibliographical notes. These notes are in unsatisfactory shape and if they were published in any final form would have to be checked by a skilled bibliographer. With the many hands who have handled this manuscript, misspellings and wrong dates are bound to have crept in. I wish I could have made another fair copy of the whole manuscript but I could not afford it. As it is this must not lie too long before being copied as the paste is unreliable and slips may get misplaced.

I thank you very much for your help in this matter and appreciate your forebearance in waiting for the final report.

Very sincerely yours,
W. E. B. Du Bois

1. John David Rheinallt Jones (1884–1953) was editor of *Bantu Studies* (1921–41) and the author of many studies on South Africa; he represented "native interests" in the South African senate from 1937 to 1942.

2. This was the earliest draft of what became *Encyclopedia of the Negro: Preparatory Volume with Reference Lists and Reports*, by W. E. B. Du Bois and Guy B. Johnson, introduction by Anson Phelps Stokes (New York: Phelps-Stokes Fund). It was issued in March 1945.

P. S. If this is mimeographed and distributed it ought to be with the request and understanding that the recipients will send back criticisms in writing noting subjects omitted and better bibliographical references and also noting typographical errors.

Expressions of mounting discontent and militancy evoked responses of concern from some of the relatively older and more moderate of the Black leadership, especially in the South. Significant in this connection is an article, "Interracial Hypertension," written in 1941 by Dr. Gordon Blaine Hancock, professor of sociology at Virginia Union University in Richmond, and widely reprinted throughout the Black press. It caught the attention of Mrs. Jessie Daniel Ames, a liberal white woman of Texas and Georgia, who was a member of the Commission on Interracial Cooperation. There followed a meeting between Mrs. Ames and Dr. Hancock; it was then agreed that if prominent southern Black figures would confer and draw up a statement of concern and intent, an analogous group of southern whites would respond favorably and quickly.

The result was a meeting in Durham, North Carolina, in October 1942 with Professor Hancock, Dr. P. B. Young, editor and publisher of the Norfolk Journal and Guide, *and Dr. Benjamin E. Mays, then president of Morehouse College of Atlanta University, and fifty-six other Southern Black people—but not including Du Bois, who only sent a general message of support. From this meeting came the Durham Statement,* then a meeting of southern white people in Atlanta in April 1943, and then a joint meeting of Black and white Southerners in Richmond in June 1943, and from that the birth in 1944 of the Southern Regional Council.*

The two following letters to Du Bois relate to these developments.

Benjamin E. Mays (b. 1895) was born in South Carolina and educated at Bates College and the University of Chicago. He was a pastor of a Baptist church in Atlanta, dean of the School of Religion at Howard University (1934–40), president of Morehouse (1940–67), and presently is president of the board of education in Atlanta.

While Mays and Du Bois were colleagues at Atlanta University, at the time of the letter that follows Du Bois was at his Baltimore home, to which Mays wrote.

Atlanta, Ga., August 22, 1942

Dear Doctor Du Bois:

Professor Gordon B. Hancock of Virginia Union, Mr. P. B. Young of the Norfolk *Journal and Guide*, and President J. M. Ellison of Virginia Union are interested in calling a conference to meet in Durham, North Carolina on October 20 for the express purpose of considering some articles of cooperation necessary to better race relations here in the South during the present conflict and after the war is over. I do not know the details of the proposal but I think they are anticipating what might happen in the area of race relations as a result of the present world conflict and if possible to prevent unnecessary race riots and conflicts after the war. This is what I gather from what little communication I have had.

---

* The text of the statement, and sources for other documents, are in Aptheker, *Documentary History*, 3: 421–22.

I am being asked to suggest two or three more persons. I would like for you to be one of the persons to attend this conference. We need all points of view and certainly need a person of your wisdom and experience in a conference of that kind. As I see it any statement coming from any group of Negro leaders must be a sane, straightforward, courageous statement with no element of retreat but at the same time recognizing the stubborn fact that we are dealing with an evil situation here in the South when any kind of advance is attempted in the area of race. I have agreed to attend this meeting and would like very much to have you go. I would like to suggest to the Committee that they send you further details if you are interested.

I hope you are having a good summer. Mrs. Mays joins me in sending best regards to you.

Sincerely yours,
Benjamin E. Mays

Gordon Blaine Hancock (1884–1970) was born in South Carolina and educated at Colgate, Harvard, and Benedict College in Orangeburg, South Carolina, and at Oxford and Cambridge in England. He wrote a syndicated column that appeared in scores of Black newspapers for a generation, was a pastor of a Baptist church in Richmond, and was on the faculty of Virginia Union University continually from 1921 until his death.

Richmond, Va., September 12, 1942

Dear Dr. Du Bois:

About three months ago a letter came to me from a white Southerner whose integrity there was no reason to question. The suggestion was made that something tangible be done to offset the probable anti-Negro reaction in the South that might follow the current war even as there was such reaction at the close of World War I. This Southerner thought that if a few representative Negroes could come together and formulate a statement setting forth what they wanted in the post-war South, there were in the South whites who would work with them in the realization of their desires. It was thought best to have the move for better understanding made by Negroes themselves.

The matter was taken up with Dr. P. B. Young, Editor, *Journal and Guide*, Norfolk, Virginia. He thought much of the suggestion. Later I went over the matter with Dr. [John M.] Ellison, President of Virginia Union. He too, felt that the suggestion has great possibilities. We decided to sound out the Negro South on the matter by writing a few influential men throughout the South and from the forty "feelers" sent out replies came from thirty-eight and without exception all felt that much good would come from a meeting of the kind suggested. It was then decided to call a preliminary meeting at Virginia Union which meeting was to be composed of ten prominent Negro leaders of the state. In this meeting it was decided that we go into organization and Dr. Young was elected Chairman, Dr. Ellison, Vice-Chairman, Dr. L. P. Jackson, Secretary-Treasurer and Gordon Hancock, Director. The main object of this meeting was chiefly to take the matter off the personal basis and put it on an organizational one. We voted to expedite matters by having the Virginia conference act as sponsor for the South-wide meeting and decided that October 20th was a good date with Durham as the place. I was the only one who thought Atlanta would be a good place even though in the original feeler we mentioned Atlanta.

The Virginia conference drew up what we called Articles of Cooperation in which we set forth under six categories just what we wanted. We wanted to make ourselves specific and attempted to do so by setting forth under each category five specific things we wanted. The categories were civic, educational, economic, industrial, social welfare and domestic. In our invitations we enclosed a sheet form upon which the invitees, some fifty or sixty, might send in advance what they thought the essentials of interracial cooperation. Already the response has been fine and these returned lists are coming in daily from every quarter of the South. We deem it better to confine our invitations to Negroes of the South whom we thought quite able to present their own case effectively; then too, it could not be said that our meeting was packed with "northern radicals" a name too often given any Negroes who want their rights and justice. We were trying to see to it that when our statement went out to the South that it could not be said that it was the work of "subversive elements, etc."

When the lists will have been returned, they will be sent to Dr. Chas. Johnson of Fisk University where a digest will be made of them and what he finds will be presented as agenda at the Durham Conference for us to ratify, reject or modify. Dr. Johnson is therefore heading what we call the Presentation Committee who upon arrival at Durham will furnish the agenda. This will I think save much waste motion and reduce we hope oratory to a desirable minimum. Dr. [Horace Mann] Bond of Fort Valley will head a Findings Committee that will make a digest and summary of the Durham Conference and this will in turn be turned over to a Collaboration Committee whose duties it will be to meet a like Committee of whites where the final discussions will take place and final agreements arrived at.

It was at first thought best to have the white conference to meet in the same city with us and perhaps open their meeting at the close of ours. Then we thought it might be said that we were their "stooges" or their rubber stamps; so we thought best to hold meetings at different times and in different places.

We sent out some rather informal invitations and asked that each invited person invite such other persons as he deemed interested. In some cases their names were sent in and from here we sent invitations. Dr. Mays and all of us thought that it would be fine for me to acquaint you in detail about what we are trying to accomplish and that your willingness to join us would be highly gratifying. In addition then to the invitation that he has extended as he was authorized to do, we are expressing our deep appreciation of your support and shall lean heavily upon your wisdom to help us accomplish something worth while. *The main objective is for Negroes of the South to set forth in specific statements just what they regard as the essentials of interracial amity and concord in the post-war world*. It will make I believe the first time that the Negroes of the South have spoken in concert "touching and agreeing on one thing."

With the fervent hope that things go well with you and yours, I am, Honorable Sir,
                                                Yours very faithfully,
                                                Gordon B. Hancock

                                                Richmond, Va., November 2, 1942
Dear Dr. Du Bois:

The Durham conference was gratifying. With a list of less than eighty invitees and with sixty present and the rest heard from by telegrams pledging their support and cooperation, we seem headed somewhere. Attorney [J. A.] Booker of Little Rock, Ark., wired pledges not only of moral support but financial support and legal assistance as did Attorney [E. M.] Lewis of Jacksonville, Fla. Best of all the men and women who came seemed serious and determined to make our forthcoming statement one of the outstanding documents of the Twentieth Century.

The Sponsoring committee is deeply grateful for your expression; for even in your absence you were strengthening our hearts. The presence of so many fine men and women and expressions from others helped to make our conference among the most noteworthy of history. The outstanding feature of the Durham Conference was its adherence to the original purpose of drawing up Articles of Cooperation to be submitted to the white South. Our very adherence to this original purpose allayed any doubts as to our righteous motives. There were no political axes to grind and there was no glory-seeking. The conferees seemed bent on finding some way out of a dangerously developing situation in the South. It cannot be said of us that we sat supinely by and wished instead of coming to grips with a strained and ominous situation. Thanks for your cooperation and pledge of support.
                                                Yours very faithfully,
                                                Gordon B.Hancock

An exchange with a professor at Haverford has intrinsic interest; it illustrates, also, Du Bois's great respect for fact and the trouble to which he normally went in an effort to satisfy inquiries from other scholars.

Thomas Edward Drake, born in Indianapolis in 1907, was educated at Stanford, the University of Michigan, and Yale, as well as in European universities. He taught at Yale and the University of Minnesota, but in 1936 joined Haverford College as a professor of history and curator of the Quaker Collection there. In 1962 he retired. Drake is the author of Quakers and Slavery *in America (New Haven: Yale University Press, 1950), a book in creation as he wrote to Du Bois.*

                                                Haverford, Pa., September 19, 1942
Dear Dr. Du Bois:

It is almost too much to ask a man for his sources on a book written forty-three years ago, but I very much wish to find out a little more about a statement which you made on page 360 of the *Philadelphia Negro*. In your discussion of intermarriage, you stated:

"Some marriages with Quakers took place, one especially in 1825, when a Quaker-ess married a Negro, created much comment. Descendants of this couple still survive."

This interests me greatly, for I am in the process of completing a book on Quakers and Slavery, and the question of Quaker race attitudes naturally comes into the picture. If you can give me any further information about Quaker-Negro marriages, particularly the one in 1825, I should appreciate it very much. I can assure you that I will keep anything in confidence which you so desire.

In my study I have run across no such incidents as you mention. And, as President Emeritus [W. W.] Comfort here at Haverford says, "Hardly a man is now alive who can remember the days of '25." I should deeply appreciate any enlightenment you can give me on the subject.

Very sincerely yours,
Thomas E. Drake

Atlanta, Ga., September 30, 1942

Mr. Thomas E. Drake
My dear Sir:

I have your letter of September 19, but as you suggest I haven't the slightest idea where I got the information which you quote from *Philadelphia Negro*. Of course, you will realize that then and even now statements about unpopular race intermarriages have to be made carefully so as to offend no one's feelings. I am certain, however, that the facts stated in the *Philadelphia Negro* are absolutely true; otherwise I would not have dared even to make an intimation.

Very sincerely yours,
W. E. B. Du Bois

Atlanta, Ga., October 10, 1942

Mr. Thomas E. Drake
My dear Sir:

Following my letter of September 30, I got in touch with one of the leading colored persons of Philadelphia. She is a granddaughter of a bishop of the African Methodist Episcopal Church and a graduate and Ph.D. of the University of Pennsylvania.[1] She writes me a letter from which I am extracting the enclosed note.

Very sincerely yours,
W. E. B. Du Bois

1. This would be Dr. Sadie Tanner Mossell Alexander; for an account of her life see Sylvia G. Dannett, *Profiles of Negro Womanhood: 20th Century* (Yonkers, New York: Educational Heritage, 1966), pp. 268–73.

[Enclosure]

"I have many times heard the same fact that you state on page 360 of your *Philadelphia Negro*. In fact, on numerous occasions when we passed the house located near Twelfth and Walnut Streets, my mother used to tell me that the daughter of the Quaker family that lived in that house married a Negro, but I never knew the name. I telephoned Dr. Henry Minton, who is well informed on Philadelphia Negro history. He too had heard this fact but he could not give me any name. I also went to see my uncle, Dr. N. F. Mossell. He said that he does not know any facts but that he thinks the family name was Maps. The descendants of the marriage, according to his recollection, taught in some of the Quaker schools when they were first established for Negroes, and later their descendants passed over on the white side. He states that he is by no means positive that the Maps are the family to whom you refer. As you know my uncle is eighty-five years of age and has always been interested in Negro affairs. If he does not know, I do not know anyone from whom I can get the information. I asked him if he had any suggestions. He said that the people who would know are dead."

Haverford, Pa., November 6, 1942

Dear Dr. Du Bois:

I am grateful for your second letter dated October 10, with information relative to my inquiry of September 19. The information which your informant in Philadelphia supplied may be correct, that it was the "Maps" family in which the intermarriage occurred. Henry J. Cadbury mentions this family in his "Negro Membership in the Society of Friends," *Journal of Negro History*, Vol. 21, April 1939, pp. 188–190. The spellings are various—Mapes, Mapp, and Maps—but all of Dr. Cadbury's information seems to relate to David Mapp, of New Jersey, who had a son and daughter by his second wife, Anna Douglas Mapp. The daughter was Grace A. Mapp, who graduated from McGrawville College, New York, in 1852, and in 1853 became a member of the Girls Department of the Friends' high school, "The Institute for Colored Youth."

This does not throw any light on my question, but it is the sort of thing which need not be pursued, in any case. I appreciate your helping me in it.

I have just finished the Reconstruction Period in one of my classes in American History, and have put the story to the boys from various angles, including your own as you express it in *Black Reconstruction*. You would be interested, I know, to hear their reactions. Some of the Southern boys are more sympathetic with your point of view than the Northerners, who tend to be "revisionist."

Very sincerely yours,
Thomas E. Drake

Shirley Graham was in charge of USO *for the thirty thousand Black troops at Fort Huachuca in Arizona during the early part of the war. Her militancy on behalf of persecuted Black soldiers made her persona non grata with the* USO *hierarchy, and she faced exile to Oklahoma; rejecting this alternative, she was forced to give up her Arizona position, at which time she came to New York City. From the Hotel Theresa she immediately sent a rather breathless and somewhat disjointed letter to Du Bois, on 30 October 1942, telling something of her experiences and noting her need for a job.*

To this letter, Du Bois replied.

Atlanta, Ga., November 5, 1942

My dear Shirley:

I should like to hear the whole story of your odyssey to Arizona and back. I am not surprised that you could not effect a revolution there and that you are sorely disappointed but I am not sure but what your presence would still be better than your absence. As to that job I think it will be possible for you to land one just because of the scarcity of men. On the other hand you are of course a little late in applying. I would write to Morgan and to Howard.

I am glad to least to get some news of the boys [her two sons]. I asked in vain in my former letters. Let me keep in touch with you and get some coherent information after you get over being excited.

Yours with love,

W. E. B. Du Bois

New York, N. Y., November 9, 1942

My dear Dr. Du Bois,

Someday I'm going to write a play about myself and it will be the season's comedy hit! I did laugh when I read your note this morning. For one brief moment I saw myself through your very wise eyes and the picture was very funny. One impression, however, I must hasten to correct:

I did not leave Fort Huachuca of my own free will. I was literally torn away despite the requests, pleas, and even threats of generals, Commanding Colonels, USO Citizen Committees throughout the state and finally a petition signed by soldiers representing every company in the 93rd Division! The Y.W.C.A.–USO transferred me to *Muskogee, Oklahoma* (say that over with taps!). I wrote first asking if this transfer could not at least be delayed until the 93rd Division left—somewhere around the first of the year. The YWCA–USO refused. When I finally did have to say I was going such a furor arose that it shook the Empire State Building here in New York. The Commanding Colonel of Fort Huachuca, the Commanding General of the 93rd Division wired—wrote and radiographed everybody they could think of. All of which greatly *angered* my ladies at the YWCA–USO. They ordered me to come into New York for a conference. When I got here they coolly informed me that the USO was not interested in some of my activities which were outside the *recreational* program of USO. They could not consider *race problems*, etc., etc. It seems that the F.S.A. [Field Service Administration] man out there had written in that I was "using my position as a USO director to influence military and civic affairs" throughout the state. Which was perfectly true . . . not so much as to the "USO position" but as to the influence. I had things so tied up inside the fort that every time this particular dirty little rat came along with his discriminatory program I was having him thrown off the reservation! Also, following a riot in Tucson (little space in the papers) when a soldier had been given life sentence I myself reached the General and influenced him to reopen the case and by military ruling had the soldier's sentence changed to *ten years*. I had been called in to sit on a court martial case within the Fort—These are a few of my "unprecedented activites."

No, I didn't want to leave Fort Huachuca. I knew I was getting worthwhile things done out there. And I have cried briny tears into my pillow many nights since I've been in New York. But, one must sometimes accept defeat—or, does one? (I don't as long as I can wiggle a toe!) The story is not finished. The Commanding Colonel is now threatening to close the USO out there. He says he wants no part of them. I've asked him not to do so. Even a little USO is better for the soldiers than none at all. The peculiar thing about the entire situation is that I have been wholly backed up by these two military authorities and only the crummy, hypocritical, religiously controlled USO got cold feet! Can you beat that? The General had me go to Washington about the whole matter. He was trying to get for me some sort of special commission through the Special Service Division. Now—the latest is that this Special Service branch of the army is being abolished and this particular General has been transferred to a desk job in Chicago, Illinois![1]

Just Saturday, however, I had a letter from a Captain now stationed in Alaska who said he had just written a letter to Chester Barnard, president of USO. Since I know this Captain very well (he's white) and am familiar with his particular brand of "cussing out" I shouldn't be surprised at anything which happens.

Meanwhile, I'm getting off some steam through *Common Sense*—and its dynamic setup.[2] Collaboration with Selden Rodman on his book *The Revolutionists* is definitely underway. You can read the excellent review copied from the New York *Times* in the copy of *Common Sense* which I sent you. The work as it stands is not stageable—so say all the Broadway producers. I'm doing a piece of craftsmanship and rewriting on it to make it so. We think we'll have a hit!

The rather grubby thought of "making a living" must occupy some of my attention. Were it not for the boys and their schooling I could practically forget that. But, the fact that they are getting along so well is an inspiration to me. A letter from Robert this morning tells me that after all he may be able to finish this year in school. Apparently the University of Indiana is as lukewarm as most institutions towards the

1. The commanding general of the Ninety-third Division at Fort Huachuca at this time was Charles Philip Hall. This command extended from March to October 1942. General Hall then became commander of the XI Corps in Chicago; under his command that corps from 1943 to 1945 saw combat service in the Pacific theater.

2. *Common Sense* was a left-oriented magazine published in New York City. Shirley Graham contributed an essay, "Negroes Are Fighting for Freedom," to its issue dated February 1943; this is in Aptheker, *Documentary History*, 3: 431–39.

entire war effort and if it can keep any of its good students it will do so—in spite of Congress! I realize this isn't a pretty situation, but I'm human enough to hope that Robert will have these next few months.

I realize I've been a frightful correspondent lately. I did think I'd probably see you this summer and I could tell you everything. Then I just made a quick trip back for Graham's high school graduation. The riot occurred and I hurried back.

Life with me seems a series of ups and downs. But, your little note this morning makes me realize that with it all I do have a "roaring" good time!

Lovingly,
Shirley

A long letter to Edwin R. Embree of the Julius Rosenwald Fund describes in some detail Du Bois's thought and work for much of 1941 and 1942. The appeal for funds was not successful.

Atlanta, Ga., November 3, 1942

My dear Mr. Embree:

In accordance with our talk of October 30, I am sending you a statement concerning the project for cooperative effort in social studies which has been launched by the Negro Land Grant Colleges.

When I returned to Atlanta University as head of the Department of Sociology in 1933, one of my first efforts was to restore on some basis the studies of the Negro problem which the University had carried on under my supervision from 1896 to 1917, and which were pioneer efforts in the scientific study of the Negro in America. My first effort was made in 1941, when with the help of the Carnegie Fund, I assembled at Atlanta University the First *Phylon* Institute, named after the Atlanta University Review of Race and Culture of which I am editor. There were present fifty-one delegates representing the Office of Production Management, the British Foreign Office, the Tennessee Valley Authority, Federal Works Agency and thirty-five colleges. Most of those attending were younger professors and instructors in economics and sociology. They reported on the work which they were doing and the prospects of its enlargement. From this I came to the conclusion that cooperation in the efforts of these institutions and particularly of the state-supported Land Grant Colleges was the next step to encourage a study of the condition of the Negro in each of the states with careful general guidance and planning.

In furtherance of this idea I addressed the presidents of Negro Land Grant Colleges in Chicago in November, 1941. In that speech I proposed a planned scientific procedure for the leadership of the American Negro. The problem before us clearly stated is this: to put fourteen million people to work so that they may receive an income which will insure a civilized standard of living; to make it possible for them to preserve their health; to keep crime down to a minimum and to educate their children; with the eventual object of giving this group sufficient leisure to advance by means of talented persons among them in science and art and cultural patterns. And with the further idea that in so far as these objects are successful, the group will become nearer to actual equality with their fellow Americans and to civilized people the world over, and will thus remove from color prejudice every real reason for its perpetuation.

To accomplish this I proposed that each college should make a broad, intense and continuous study of the social and economic set-up of the state in which it is located. We must know as we do not know today the existing occupations of Negroes; not in the vague and general and necessarily inaccurate report of the decennial census, but by minute and complete survey and study of counties, towns and cities where the Negro population is resident. We must take such a beginning as Charles Johnson's regional study of Southern counties,[1] extend the data to 1940 and then complete it and carry it on continuously from year to year. We must have a group-to-group and person-to-person knowledge of the condition of the laboring masses, of their opportunities and hindrances. And this kind of study ought to be made in accordance with the latest scientific techniques and on a national basis.

A national planning institute must annually gather up and compare and interpret this great body of fact. There must be provided for this work sufficient research funds and sufficient time for research. And finally through a central office, there must be wide and carefully edited publications of results. It is not only illogical but it is an indictment of the Negro college that the chief studies of the Negro's condition today are not being done by Negroes and Negro colleges. The center of gravity as well as truth of investigation should be brought back to the control of an association of Negro colleges and this not for the purpose of creating a Negro science of purely racial facts in science but in order to make sure that the whole undistorted picture is there and that the complete interpretation is made by those most competent to do it, through their own lives and training.

It was moved by the organization that a committee be appointed to study the proposals which I suggested and make recommendations to the executive committee. The executive committee asked the president of the conference to appoint a committee to consider these proposals and later a meeting of this committee was called at Hampton Institute in June, 1942. The report of this meeting in *School and Society*, July 25, said:

> In a recent three-day conference at Hampton (Va.) Institute, the presidents of fifteen Negro land-grant colleges approved a proposal of W. E. B. Du Bois, editor of the Atlanta University Studies, to have the colleges conduct a series of co-operative studies on the American Negro's social condition, stressing his economic status during and after World War II.
>
> The plan, which marks a new trend in cooperative ventures by educational institutions, was outlined in detail at the conference, and the college presidents discussed present and post-war problems with a number of widely known au-

---

1. Charles S. Johnson, *Statistical Atlas of Southern Counties* (Chapel Hill: University of North Carolina Press, 1941).

thorties on employment, defense training, the nation's Army and Navy programs, labor unions, and other issues.

In an introductory statement at the conferences, Malcolm S. MacLean, president of Hampton Insitute and of the Association of Presidents of Negro Land-Grant Colleges, pointed out that these developments, arising out of the immediate problem of successfully prosecuting the war and the more remote problem of post-war reconstruction, will deepen and broaden several phases of Dr. Du Bois's proposal.

The cooperative study of socio-economic conditions among Negroes aims to accumulate a body of knowledge, which, when tabulated, interpreted, and integrated, can "be used as the basis of raising the standard of living and cultured patterns of American Negroes through education, work, law, and social action." The study will be financed by the land-grant colleges and conducted by qualified instructors on their staffs. The findings will be brought together periodically, compared, edited, and published annually in convenient form for the use of legislators and students of social problems.

The land-grant colleges also agreed, in adopting the proposal, "to complete a division of the social sciences giving their students unified knowledge of social conditions and modern trends." The subject, method, and scope of the individual studies to be undertaken will be determined after conferences with executives and investigators in other institutions, and with recognized authorities in the social sciences, including students of conditions in the white population.

Fifteen of the seventeen Land Grant Colleges agreed to take part in this cooperative program and the two others will undoubtedly join and in addition to this we may expect cooperation from many of the private colleges. On October 28 and 29, 1942, at the regular annual meeting of the Presidents of Land Grant Colleges it was voted that Dr. Du Bois be made the coordinator of this program of cooperative social studies to be carried on by the Land Grant Colleges; that the colleges would finance the studies in their own states and would pay the expenses of delegates to a general conference on ways and means to be attended by leading sociologists.

In addition to this there would be necessary funds for the following purposes: to pay traveling expenses of visiting sociologists, white and colored, from various parts of the country. Two, for the clerical work of a central office. Three, for some publication of results. So far as possible the several institutions agreed to contribute toward such a central fund although it was recognized that legal technicalities might make it difficult for these institutions to contribute to any activity that was not confined to their own states. It seemed, therefore, necessary that a general promotion and publication fund should be raised. Recognizing the connection of Atlanta University with the work of social investigation in the past, I petitioned the President and Board of Trustees in April, 1942, asking them to make a contribution toward such a fund. This matter is under consideration and will be considered by the Board at its meeting November 19, 1942. Meantime, the work must go on and much depends upon the success of its inception.

At a conference to be held this fall or winter we want to get together not only a representative body of men from the Land Grant Colleges but other institutions together with sociologists of distinction like Professor [Howard W.] Odum, who had already consented to attend, Charles S. Johnson, E. Franklin Frazier and others. In this way we could be sure of adopting the best methods and procedures and give the enterprise the authority of thorough scientific planning. There ought to be also some publication of these plans and provisions made for editorial inspection, supervision and arrangement of results. For this reason funds must be available. I estimate that a thousand dollars would insure the beginning of the program and if by various contributions we could raise this eventually to two thousand dollars the success of the enterprise would be certain; I do not doubt that once it has begun the constituent colleges will be able to take care not only of their own expenses of investigation but of the general fund.

Very sincerely yours,
W. E. B. Du Bois

Toward the end of 1942, Du Bois received a letter from an official of the Harvard Alumni Association, Dwight P. Robinson of Saint Davids, Pennsylvania, inviting him to become a member of the Harvard Club in New York City. A response came from Du Bois.

Atlanta, Ga., December 16, 1942

Mr. Dwight P. Robinson
My dear Sir:

Your letter of November seventeenth rather astonished me. I have been graduated from Harvard College over fifty years and this is the first time during that period that I have been asked to join a Harvard Club.

I have assumed that the reason for this reticence was that I am of Negro descent. Possibly, however, Harvard is learning something from this war for democracy and has changed her attitudes. If this is true, I shall be very glad to hear from you and to become a member of the Harvard Club of New York City.[1]

Very sincerely yours,
W. E. B. Du Bois

Cy W. Record, born in Texas in 1918, was employed early in the 1940s in research work for the Atlanta, Georgia, office of the War Manpower Commission. After conversing with Du Bois concerning assistance, an exchange of interest occurred.

Record, now known as Wilson Record, served in the armed forces shortly after this correspondence with Du Bois, and in 1946 was awarded a Rosenwald Fellowship and went on to graduate work at the University of California. Author of The Negro and the Communist Party

---

1. There was no response.

(1951) and Race and Radicalism: The NAACP and the Communist Party in Conflict
*(1964), he has taught at Sacramento State and Southern Illinois and is now a professor at
Portland State College.*

Atlanta, Ga., December 31, 1942

Dear Dr. Du Bois:

In conformity with your suggestion, I am setting forth in writing and in a bit more
detail, my request for a bibliography on minority group strategies.

1. I am principally concerned with strategies developed and employed by Negro
groups in the South; not only those now being utilized, but those which have been
developed since the Reconstruction Period.

2. I am interested particularly, however, in material on the techniques and strategies which have been developed since the outbreak of the current war.

3. I would also like to have references to material relating to the Negro's growing
conception of himself as a member of a minority group and not as a member of a
stabilized caste system.

4. I would also like to secure references to material relating to the increasing
utilization on the part of the Southern Negro of the Federal authority and cooperation
with the more politically articulate Negro groups in other sections of the country.

I might indicate that my purpose in reviewing the material which you will suggest,
is to prepare for the President's Committee on Fair Employment Practice both background and current information relative to the formulation of policies designed to
more fully utilize the available Negro labor supply in this area; the strategies developed by the Negro minority in this area having significant and direct bearing on the
work of the Committee. I am acquainted directly with the development of certain of
these strategies, but I have not had an opportunity to review what I believe is a
considerable amount of source material on their development. When I have progressed further in the preparation of my report to the Committee, I would like to
discuss it with you.

Thanking you for your cooperation and assistance, I am

Very truly yours,
Cy W. Record.

Atlanta, Ga., January 4, 1943

Mr. Cy W. Record
My dear Sir:

Answering your letter of December 31, I beg to say that historically the strategies
and techniques employed by the Negro minority groups in the United States have
been as follows:—

1. revolt
2. running away to the free North and Canada
3. colonization in Africa
5. emancipation

6. enfranchisement
7. protective laws
8. legal defense
9. agitation
10. pressure group techniques
11. defensive and offensive segregation
12. international Negro organization
13. international cooperation with other colored races
14. cooperation with the white labor movement.

Of the historical sequences of these techniques the best single account would perhaps be chapter ten in my *Black Folk: Then and Now* published by Henry Holt and Company in 1939. With this might be read chapter seven and eight in my *Dusk of Dawn,* Harcourt, Brace and Company, 1940. Chronologically the developments in which you would be interested would be those strategies employed during and since the Reconstruction period. For this you might consult my *Black Reconstruction.* Harcourt, Brace and Company, 1935; also *These United States,* edited by Ernest Gruening, published by Boni and Liveright, Chapter twenty-two.

Since the outbreak of the current war the inner thought and striving of the Negro could be followed by reading *Survey Graphic* for November, 1942, "Color: Unfinished Business of Democracy." Leading up to that you might read *The Negro in American Civilization* by Charles S. Johnson, Henry Holt and Company, 1930 and *American Minority Peoples* by Donald Young, Harper, 1932.

With regard to the cooperation of the Southern Negro with federal authority and Negro groups in the North you could get a good deal of information by talking with W. H. Bell, head of the Urban League in Atlanta and by consulting the *Journal of Negro Education* published at Howard University.

The above references are all very general and I could give you more specific references and acts if you will later indicate more precisely what you want. I shall be glad to consult with you at any time.

Very sincerely yours,
W. E. B. Du Bois

[Du Bois added at the bottom of the letter:]
Black Worker
Black Workers and the New Unions[1]

---

1. The two books added by Du Bois were Sterling D. Spero and Abram L. Harris, *The Black Worker* (New York: Columbia University Press, 1931), and Horace Cayton and George S. Mitchell, *Black Workers and the New Unions* (Chapel Hill: University of North Carolina Press, 1939). The chapter in the book edited by Ernest Gruening was by Du Bois and was entitled, "Georgia: Invisible Empire State"; it appeared in volume two of the cited work, published in New York in 1924 (pp. 322–45).

1943

The Black press during the years of World War II carried on a persistent and powerful campaign against racism in general and jim-crow in the armed forces in particular. One result was a spate of articles in leading commercial publications "discovering" and criticizing that press. This background explains a letter to Du Bois early in 1943 from the editor of the Chicago Defender.

Chicago, Ill., January 18, 1943

Dear Dr. Du Bois:

Since the ribald attack by Westbrook Pegler last Summer, it has become a popular pastime to heap criticism on the Negro press.[1] We have a strong suspicion that these outcries are not born out of honest desire to improve the quality of Negro journalism, but are rather issued from an organized plan to intimidate and eventually silence the Negro Press. This, I believe, is due to our militancy and critical attitude toward certain aspects of the war.

We should like to have you answer our critics and state the case of the Negro Press in your usual spicy and trenchant style. You are the only authority who can answer these arguments with requisite grace and logic. Above all we want you to feel free to say what you please in your examination of the position of the Negro Press in a world at war. We will pay you fifty ($50.00) dollars for a piece of 2,500 words. We should like to have the article within two weeks.

Sincerely yours,

Metz T. P. Lochard

1. Westbrook Pegler—a kind of William F. Buckley of the 1930s and 1940s—had a widely syndicated column. In it in the *New York World Telegram* for 28 April 1942 he began a vicious attack upon the Black press, explicitly because of its anti-racist campaigns. See also his columns of 11 May and 16 June 1942.

Articles critical of the Black press by John Temple Graves appeared in the *Virginia Quarterly* (Fall 1942); Virginius Dabney in *Atlantic Monthly* (January 1943); William A. H. Birnie in *American Magazine* (January 1943); Warren H. Brown in *Saturday Review of Literature* (19 December 1942), reprinted in *Reader's Digest* (January 1943). Du Bois commented on the last-named article—its author was a Black man—in his column in the *Amsterdam News*, 23 January and 13 February 1943.

Atlanta, Ga., 1 February 1943

My dear Mr. Lochard:

Enclosed is the article which you ordered in your letter of January 18. I trust it will prove to be what you want.[1]

Very sincerely yours,
W. E. B. Du Bois

Du Bois throughout his life received letters of appreciation and commendation from rank-and-file Black people; this support was one source of his astonishing strength. Here are two examples.

Fort McClellan, Ala., February 21, 1943

Prof. W. E. B. Du Bois
Dear Sir:

Every man has his ideal. Therefore, I trust that you will not criticize me severely. It has been rumored that one of our greatest generals has a picture of a German General that he treasures, to the extent, that even tho' they face each on the African battle front, he admires this Picture.

In recent years, I have grown to admire you and your work. Not especially because I have read all of your books, nor because I have had one class under you, but moreover because I admire your militant spirit and progressive ideals.

I trust that you will not consider me too forward in asking for a picture of you. I feel that it will mean much to me and my life while in the army. I can assure you that no matter where I go, even if my destiny is trampling through the hot sands of Africa, or fighting my way through the Pacific Islands, I shall treasure it until the end.

Wishing you the best of health, and hoping to receive a line from you when you have the time

Respectfully yours,
Cpl. Robert L. Williams

Atlanta, Ga., 26 March 1943

Cpl. Robert L. Williams
My dear Sir:

I thank you for your kind letter of February 21 and all your good wishes.

Very sincerely yours,
W. E. B. Du Bois

Ft. McClellan, Ala., March 14, 1943

Prof. W. E. B. Du Bois
Dear Sir:

On Sunday of the above date I listen to your broadcast,[2] this is a letter of Sincere

1. The essay appeared in two issues of the *Chicago Defender*, 20 and 27 February 1943; a condensed version appeared in *Negro Digest* 1 (April 1943): 33–36.

2. On a CBS radio program, chaired by Lewis Gannett, and broadcast during the morning of 14 March, Du Bois discussed the life and ideas of Booker T. Washington.

thanks from the Negro's of army forces, for the Point that were brought out in your talk.

As you have discovered I'm sure, I am not a college man but, I am a race man and with all my power I am fighting for the progress of my People, I'm now station at Ft. McClellan have been there for 14 mo. as an instructor if at anytime you need a group of Negros I shall be very happy to assist you in any respect.

Please bear this in mind I am sincere and we as a race need more Du Bois, would like so much to take this up later with you in person, we do have problems.

Respectfully yours,
Sgt. Wm. L. Mitchell

P. S. Please let me hear from you, *Thanks*

Atlanta, Ga., 29 March 1943

My dear Mr. Mitchell:

I thank you for your letter of March 14 and I am glad you liked my broadcast. I am very glad to have your approval and sympathy.

Very sincerely yours,
W. E. B Du Bois

Albon L. Holsey (1883–1950) was born in Athens, Georgia, and educated at Knox Institute in that city and at Atlanta University. In 1911, he became the first advertising manager of the Crisis; his main work, however, was as secretary to the principal at Tuskegee Institute, which position he held from 1917 until his death. Holsey also was prominent in the National Negro Business League and in 1929 organized the Colored Merchants Association, which attempted briefly to function on cooperative principles. The same broadcast that evoked the letter from a soldier in Alabama was the occasion for a letter from Holsey.

Tuskegee Institute, Ala., March 15, 1943

Dear Dr. Du Bois:

Hearing your broadcast yesterday morning reminded me of the article which I wrote about you nearly thirty-three years ago. In that article I related an early impression of you that still remains with me.

I am sure you have forgotten the incident which occurred in Athens, Georgia over forty years ago. You were a guest in our home, and I went to the station with you when you left to help with your luggage.

You made inquiry of the ticket agent concerning a special low rate, and he replied that he knew nothing of it. Unafraid and somewhat impatiently, you said to him: "Look it up." He flushed slightly but did look it up, and found that you were correct.

I do not recall who was the more astonished; the ticket agent or I; for that was the first time in my life I had heard a Colored man give an order to a white man.

I refresh your memory on this, because one of the speakers yesterday contrasted your early background with that of Booker T. Washington.

To me, your experience with that ticket agent is a symbol of your contribution to the advancement of the Negro in America, just as Booker T. Washington's "Let down your buckets where you are" was a symbol of his contribution.

Your distinguished contributions and achievements were exalted yesterday when you gave such a just and impartial appraisal of Dr. Washington's achievements.

Very truly yours,
Albon L. Holsey

Atlanta, Ga., 29 March 1943

My dear Mr. Holsey:

Thank you very much for your letter of March 15. I remember the incident of the ticket office although I had forgotten what it was I asked the man to do. I am glad I wasn't lynched. I am rather hoping to come down when the Moton Gates are dedicated [at Tuskegee] unless there is going to be too big a crowd. Write and tell me about it.

Very sincerely yours,
W. E. B. Du Bois

Ruth Anna Fisher (b. 1886) was educated at Oberlin College and the London School of Economics. She worked for several years in London for the Department of Historical Research of the Carnegie Institution, then headed by Dr. John Franklin Jameson. After the latter became chief of the manuscripts division at the Library of Congress, Ruth Anna Fisher was appointed by him in 1928 to head the manuscripts division's work in the British Museum and British archives. She returned to Washington in 1940 and worked at the Library of Congress until 1949, returning to England then and remaining until 1952, when she retired from her library connection. For a time in the 1930s, a suggestion was pending that Du Bois might join her in research work for some months in England, but this plan did not eventuate. In the light of what was soon to transpire, her reference to a rumor that Du Bois was to leave Atlanta University is especially interesting—as is Du Bois's comment in reply.

Washington, D.C., March 17, 1943

Dear B,

For some time now I have [been] meaning to write you this letter. But on Monday, the 15th, I meant more particularly to take the time to write it because it was my birthday, and I felt that it would come as a message from one centenarian to another, as it were, for I am fast approaching your venerable age. If you will only give me time, and not so long a time at that, I shall soon be caught up with you.

Since the forty-eight hour week has come into effect we have little time for ourselves. I get up at the crack of dawn—six-fifteen to be exact—arrive at work at eight-thirty—leave at five-fifteen and arrive back home just before six. By the time I have got my evening meal, for I hope never to succumb to the spinsterish habit of living off bread and milk, it is nearly time to go to bed.

The government, of course, is being damn silly about the whole thing, for they get much less work out of us than before as everyone is more or less permanently tired, and Sunday does not give one sufficient time to catch up on one's rest. It may come to its senses when the civilian casualties begin to mount up.

I hate Washington with an intense hatred. But I think my attitude to it and America as a whole is rather detached. I see no difference between the Japanese and Prussian military caste and the Southern oligarchy here. They are all convinced of their race superiority, and they control the army and navy. The Klu Klux Klan is like the Storm Troopers. And all of these groups want to make their opinions the predominant and powerful ones in their respective countries and the world with all else subservient to them. It further seems to me as likely for a Hitler to arise here in these circumstances as in Germany.

The other thing which distresses me here is the kind of education we have. There isn't another country in the world which worships information to the extent that we do, unless it was Germany (Note the programs on our radio—Information Please, Quiz Kids and the like). I can understand that this [is] a real problem—to give the kind of education to so many people which makes them think instead of filling their minds with facts which remain in their minds unrelated to anything else.

Did I hear a rumour that you were thinking of leaving Atlanta? If you are, I wish you would find some opportunity of having me invited there before you go. I'd like to get a peep at the South.

Here is my *Phylon* subscription which would have gone sooner, but that I simply don't have the time to write letters.

As Always,
Ruth Anna

Atlanta, Ga., 29 March 1943

Dear Ruth Anna Fisher:

Thank you for your kind letter of March 17 and congratulations on your seventy-fifth birthday.[1] You didn't go into particulars but intimated that we are about the same age which I imagine is not too far from the truth. I am so glad you are having plenty of work to keep you out of mischief. I imagine it is a long time since you became familiar with the look of the world at 6:15 a.m. Personally the world at that hour never attracted me and as a rule I refuse to stir before seven which I regard as quite uncivilized enough.

You would save yourself a lot of time by omitting that evening meal and I don't think you really need it judging from your contours when I saw you last. I am sorry you hate Washington "But I say unto you, love your enemies. Do good to them that hate you," etc., etc. There is no use of your trying to be detached from America; you are permanently attached and you had better learn to like it. There are certain resemblances between America and Germany but perhaps we had best not emphasize

---

1. A touch of Du Boisian humor. He had reached his seventy-fifth year on 23 February 1943.

them just now. At least not too much. The way not to be overwhelmed with the kind of education we have is not to listen to Information Please and Quiz Kids. I don't.

If there is any rumor of my leaving Atlanta, I have not heard it. Of course there is always a possibility of being kicked out but I am not expecting it yet. I wish very much that you would visit us say April nineteenth and twentieth when we have a sociological conference. Get your boss to send you down as an official delegate. I have no strings on the purse here.

I am always glad to hear from you.

Very sincerely yours,
W. E. B. Du Bois

A memorandum from Du Bois to John Phillip Whittaker, who since 1930 had been registrar of Morehouse College and of Atlanta University, reflects the concentration upon the work of his sociology department and his plans for making Atlanta University a national center of learning and scholarship.

March 25, 1943

Memo to Mr. Whittaker:

I have just sent to Mr. Reid the enclosed proposal for changes in our courses in sociology. I hope to hear from him in a day or so. Please return this as it is our only copy.

I also think there should be a short paragraph in the catalogue on the social studies center. I am enclosing a proposed statement. It can, of course, be modified in any way that you and the President may think best.

[Enclosure]

THE ATLANTA UNIVERSITY CENTER FOR SOCIAL STUDIES

The Conference of Presidents of the Negro Land Grant Colleges voted in 1941 and 1942 to inaugurate a series of continuous investigation of the social condition of American Negroes, each college taking its own state as the center of investigation. The Presidents have united in asking Atlanta University to be the coordinating center of this cooperative effort. The Trustees of Atlanta University have appropriated funds for supporting this center and the Land Grant College Presidents have appointed Dr. Du Bois, head of the Department of Sociology, as coordinator for the work. Thus after a lapse of years the annual Atlanta Conferences will be restored and annual reports made of work in social investigation accomplished during the year.

Frank Eugene Taylor (b. 1916), educated at Hamilton College and the University of Minnesota, was advertising manager for Harper and Bros. in 1940–41 and vice president and editor-in-chief of Reynal and Hitchcock from 1941 to 1948; more recently Taylor has been a film producer and has maintained an association with McGraw-Hill Book Company.

Atlanta, Ga., March 29, 1943

Mr. Frank E. Taylor

My dear Sir:

Dr. Ira Reid tells me that you have been in the South scouting for literature with indifferent results. I am sorry you didn't come in and talk with me but I am following the suggestion given Mr. Reid by you and writing of certain literary plans.

Let me say in introduction that I have published thirteen books in addition to a large number of pamphlets and studies. My publishers have been A. C. McClurg, Harcourt, Brace and Company of New York and Henry Holt and Company. I do not think that any of these firms have lost money on my works but my work has not sold largely because I have insisted on writing on a subject which is unpopular: the relation of the Negro to the United States. I have a feeling, however, that this subject is increasing in popularity and that sometime soon a book or books on the subject will sell well.

I have the following literary work in hand: one, a novel stressing and illustrating the leadership of the presidents of Negro Land Colleges. These men are political and social leaders of a new sort. They are manipulators and guiders of the educational power of the Southern states in such a way that a dozen or more Negro colleges have been established and supported by the states and form a new educational development not nearly as well known as the old mission colleges but much more impressive in buildings, equipment and attendance. This has been accomplished by extraordinarily subtle political manipulation and social sacrifice. I have begun this novel but have not finished it.

Two other novels which I wrote: *Quest of the Silver Fleece*, McClurg and Company, and *Dark Princess*, Harcourt, had some success and merit. This will be better.

A book might be written on Negro education in essay form showing the rather extraordinary developments in the last fifty years. It could contain the substance of several criticisms of Negro education which I have written and applied to the educational program at Hampton Institute, Fisk University and at Wilberforce University.[1]

There is a lot of interesting biographical material touching the lives of American Negroes which might make good reading. I have three men in mind: John Hope, late president of Atlanta University; Henry Hunt, late president of Fort Valley State College and Colonel [Charles] Young, lately of the United States Army. This would make an interesting triumvirate. These men were widely known and touched American life at critical times and points.

I prepared and sent to two or three publishers in 1938 a book of poems; all of the

---

1. A manuscript of these essays on education had been accepted for publication in 1940 by the University of North Carolina Press but in fact was not published by that press. Reynal and Hitchcock rejected the same manuscript. With some additions it was published by the University of Massachusetts Press in 1973 as *The Education of Black People: Ten Critiques, 1906–1960*, H. Aptheker, editor. The other writings mentioned by Du Bois in this letter have not yet been published.

publishers said something nice but were scared of poetry. I nevertheless believe that this volume contains some of the best writing that I have done and touches the race problem in unusual ways. There is, for instance, a narrative poem in three parts called *The Christ of the Andes* which studies race strife from the conquest of the Indians to the present World War. It was once adjudged the best play submitted for a prize for a peace society in Boston but they reneged on giving me the prize unless I had the play staged, which was of course impossible. There is another poem on the relations of the three races and their All-Mother and another one on Black Man who married the moon and had seven sons colored like the rainbow.

If any of the above plans interest you for a possible book, I should be glad to hear from you at your convenience.

Very sincerely yours,
W. E. B. Du Bois

New York, N. Y., April 5, 1943

Dear Dr. Du Bois:

Many thanks for your recent letter. I regret that I was unable to look in on you at Atlanta but my hours were numbered because of bad railroad connections and I had to leave Atlanta very abruptly. I should very much like to know more about your novel. By that I mean, if you have a few chapters, rough or otherwise, completed and outlined, you might forward them. I should also be very interested in seeing your book of poems.

I am interested in your ideas on negro education and there may well be a very important book in that field. I suggest that you keep it in mind and develop it a little more fully and, in my next trip to Atlanta which should be in the next two or three months, we can discuss it in some detail.

It might interest you to know that we have just signed a contract with Miss Lillian Smith of Clayton, Georgia and plan to publish her first novel next fall. It is a magnificent job and we are all extremely excited about its prospects.[1]

Again, thanks for your letter and hope to hear from you soon.

Very sincerely yours,
Frank E. Taylor

In 1942 an Inter-Racial Association was formed by students at the University of Michigan, under the immediate impetus of learning that Black people were refused service at a restaurant on the main street of Ann Arbor. Through the association an enhanced awareness of racism developed. Early the next year, Jim Conant, the son of Harvard's president, wrote two articles for the Michigan Daily, *the student paper, 8 April and 9 April 1943, entitled, "Capable Negroes Fail to Get Teaching Jobs"; he reported that after discussion with professors in the*

1. This was Lillian Smith's *Strange Fruit* and Taylor's excitement about it certainly was justified.

mathematics and philosophy departments it was clear that competent prospects had appeared for positions at the university but had been rejected because of their race. Several hundred students were polled and ninety-five percent of them said they would welcome Black professors; the president then asserted that the university did not discriminate in hiring, but had simply never hired any one who was Black!

Out of this background came a letter to Du Bois from a sophomore, Ann Fagan, who was secretary of the Inter-Racial Association. The writer is now Ann Fagan Ginger, an attorney, professor of law at Hastings Law School in California, and president of the Meiklejohn Civil Liberties Institute in Berkeley.

Ann Arbor, Michigan, April 16, 1943

Dear Mr. Du Bois:

I am writing to you with the assumption that you don't have enough problems now to keep you busy. The problem I am laying before you is made clear by the enclosed clippings from last week's "Michigan Daily," the student newspaper at the University of Michigan. At present no Negroes are on the faculty, and none have applied for positions for next year, at least to my knowledge. However, the University will need to add some professors to its faculty, and it has declared, as you can see from the articles, that it will not be prejudiced.

The question is, what to do about it? I thought that perhaps, from your wide experience, you could provide the solution. I know that, whatever is done, it is quite likely that this first fight won't be won. It is possible to win even now, but not extremely likely. The only thing I could think of to solve the problem was for someone like you, in a position to know qualified men who would be willing to take a chance and apply for a position with the University of Michigan, to suggest it to them.

I am no aged strategist in such matters, however. I am a sophomore in the Literary school, and I always have been interested in, and active wherever possible on, the question of racial discrimination; probably I am so interested because I am a mixed breed, half-Jewish and half-Irish. We have an Inter-Racial Association here at the University, but so far it has either been held back by its members' own timidity and lack of knowledge about what practical steps to take, or by the ever-present cry of "red." But I'm sure that, if you found two or three qualified people to apply, both the Inter-Racial Association, and the "Michigan Daily" would back the campaign.

The departments which need men most now are: Mathematics, Physics, Political Science, possibly English or Sociology. Inasmuch as the semester will be over the last of May, and I won't be here after that date, I would very much like to hear from you immediately as to what you think of the matter.

Respectfully yours,
Ann Fagan

[undated]

My dear Miss Fagan:

It has been impossible to answer your letter of April sixteenth before now and even if it had been answered, I do not suppose that I could have helped you much.

It is impossible in cases like this to lay down any general rule of procedure. In some cases political pressure has been used. This has succeeded in New York state in securing the appointment of a Negro instructor and a Negro assistant professor. Determined inside pressure from friends has landed two assistant professors in the University of Chicago. Nothing has been able to stir the conservatism at Harvard University or at Yale while at Princeton not even a Negro student can be enrolled although I believe there have been some partial exceptions in the graduate school.

The thing to be done at Ann Arbor is for a group of interested persons to lay down a program and work at it for about ten years trying to see to it first that the worth of good Negro candidates is known, their eligibility must include not only their intellectual gifts but their characteristics, manners and presentability since they are going to undergo more critical inspection than ordinary candidates. Then a quiet campaign must be carried on among the members of a department where they seek appointment; usually the department has large influence if not final decision in such matters. A continuous, careful, well-equipped campaign of this sort will bring results but it will take time and sometimes a lot of it.

> Very sincerely yours,
> W. E. B. Du Bois

Earlier correspondence has shown the concern in the Black world about the nature of agreements ending the war. Another reflection of this concern appears in the plans of the NAACP, *as conveyed in a letter to Du Bois. If the latter responded, a copy of his letter does not seem to have survived; but, especially in view of the impending resumption of Du Bois's connection with the association, this letter is significant. It was written on* NAACP *stationery and signed by Walter White in his capacity as its secretary.*

New York, N. Y., June 19, 1943

My dear Mr. Du Bois:

In October, 1941, the Board of Directors of the National Association for the Advancement of Colored People authorized the formation of a committee to present the cause of the Negro, not only of America but of the West Indies and Africa, at the next Peace Conference.

Very recently the Board named the personnel of this committee. The enclosed list includes your name and we hope very much that you will be willing to aid in working for integration of the Negro as a full participant in the post-war world.[1]

The work of the committee in its early stage may well be divided into several

---

1. Enclosed was a mimeographed sheet, dated 17 June 1943 and listing sixty-six men and women, Black and white, who had been asked by the NAACP "to serve on a committee to present the cause of the Negro at the next Peace Conference." In addition to Du Bois, the list included Ralph Bunche, Dr. Rufus E. Clement, Pearl S. Buck, Walter Reuther, Paul Robeson, Walter White, Eric Williams, Rayford Logan, Marshall Field, and Mary McLeod Bethune.

projects. The study of individual proposals heretofore advanced in the light of the Negro's interest, the special problems of particular areas such as the Caribbean, the formulation of plans in the fields of health or sociology or some particular social science—any one or more such matters may be of special interest to the individual committee member.

Will you be good enough to let us know in which one of these phases you would be particularly interested? Perhaps there are certain topics which you feel might be assigned to sub-committees. We will heartily welcome any suggestion you may have looking toward the very best presentation—suggestions as to experts who might be available to devote some time on a volunteer or compensation basis to the preparation of data in a particular field; and any others which you think might be helpful.

When we shall have heard from a sufficient number of those who have been invited to serve on this Committee efforts will be made to fix a time and place for a meeting which will be convenient to the greatest number.

Ever sincerely,
Walter White

Once again a direct question put with clarity and sincerity drew from Du Bois a response of substance and consequence. The author of the inquiry is an attorney, now living in Berkeley, California.

Oakland, Calif., June 24, 1943

Dear Mr. Du Bois:

In your article in the July issue of *Foreign Affairs*, "The Realities in Africa," you state at the end of your article as follows—"I would say, finally, that political control must be taken away from commercial and business interests owned and conducted in the foreign nations which dominate the continent and this control be vested provisionally in an international mandates commission."

Mr. Carl Brandt, in the same issue at the end of his article entitled "Invasion and Occupation," states—"It would seem that contracts for reconstruction jobs in occupied territory ought to be awarded to private corporations on condition that they utilize to the maximum the existing local resources and man power."[1]

It appears to me that Mr. Brandt's idea of the needs of Africa are at considerable variance to yours. As one interested in the future problems of the United Nations in the post-war era, could you help me untangle the problem? I am not sure which of the two thoughts produced by you two gentlemen would be the better.

Thanking you very much, I remain

Very truly yours,
Eric Cochrane

1. The articles from the July 1943 *Foreign Affairs* were Karl Brandt (not Carl), "Problems of Invasion and Occupation" (21:699–710), and Du Bois, "The Realities in Africa: European Profit or Negro Development?" (21:721–32).

Baltimore, Md., July 6, 1943

Mr. Eric Cochrane
Dear Sir:

Replying to your letter of June 24, may I say that you are right in assuming a world of difference between the ideas of Mr. Brandt and my own. Mr. Brandt wishes the United States to seize territory and administer it for private profit, and the only conditions he would impose would be to use local materials and local labor. There would be no laws to protect labor in wage nor conditions of work, the native would have no voice in politics or industry, and the object of this "reconstruction" would be profit for American industry and not the well-being of the natives. If Mr. Brandt should assume that this well-being would automatically follow "American Free Enterprise," he surely has not studied European imperialism.

I am convinced that the development of backward races and lands cannot be left in the unguided and uncontrolled power of private investors. Private investment should be welcomed; but it should be under control in Africa even more than it is in England. In England and all civilized countries today wages of labor, conditions of work, the work of women and children, are regulated in the public interest; further then, popular education is required, rules of sanitation and health are enforced and we are about to insist on regular employment and security in sickness and old age. The public cost of this legislation cuts down the profits obtainable by private industry. Private investors seek territory where such costs can be evaded; where, as in Africa, labor works long hours at 30 to 50 cents a day, where the cost of education and public services paid for by the public are negligible. This sort of profit ought to be curbed by international legislation and guardianship. And this not solely for philanthropy, but for insurance against future war and turmoil.

Very sincerely,
W. E. B. Du Bois

A letter reflecting the impact of Du Bois's writings—especially upon white authors "discovering" his work—came from a well-known novelist of the 1930s and 1940s. Mary Schumann was the author of Strong Enchantments *and* Bright Star, *published in Philadelphia in 1933 and 1934 by Macrae Smith Company, and* Strife Before Dawn *and* My Blood and My Treasure, *published in New York City by Dial Press in 1939 and 1941. The novel she projects in her letter to Du Bois seems never to have been published; if Du Bois replied, his response has not survivived.*

Pittsfield, Mass., July 14, 1943

My dear Mr. Du Bois:

I have been very much interested in reading your *Black Reconstruction*. You released some dynamite there that blew my previous ideas to cinders. Some kindly Providence let me find it in the library to keep me from committing grievous errors in a novel I am contemplating. My reading has startled me all along; first I delved into the causes, and I have that picture correctly—the current Hitlers mad for power who forced a ghastly war. The analogy with Hitler is complete, isn't it? The terrorizing at the polls, the persecution of those who didn't follow them, the "race supremacy" sounding off: "We are descendants of Cavaliers, nobility, Jacobins—we welcome disunion which will separate us from Northern serfs, descendants of scum and spittle of Europe. . . ." Yes, my reading on the causes of the Civil War check with yours. But my reading on reconstruction and the ideas I have always held differ from the picture you present, which I can't help feeling is the true one.

Let me introduce myself: I wrote a historical novel of western Penn. during the Revolution, *Strife Before Dawn*, 1939, which won me considerable reputation and which the reviewers acclaimed as the first novel that had given a fair picture of the Indians' side of it. I did not start with a bias for the Indians but the facts were a matter of the white man's record (the Indians kept no record). I could not help presenting the truth of their wrongs. Then *My Blood and My Treasure*, 1941 was a novel of War of 1812 and Perry's victory on Lake Erie, Johnny Appleseed—that great soul! and the Ohio campaigns. In Perry's crew were many negroes who conducted themselves with extraordinary gallantry. Perry depended on them, and at the time of writing that episode I promised myself that [I] would sometime write a novel bringing out some of the intolerable wrongs of the negro.

I have made a start on it. The theme is perhaps trite, but a good one, that this country started so fairly and with such noble hopes for mankind: witness the Pilgrims, Penn's colony, Oglethorpe's, Stephen Austin's. But the despoilers entered in, cheating, murdering, oppressing, while in each generation were a few shining ones, "bright enemies of evil." (Your Lincoln, Sumner and Stevens would be "bright enemies" which I hope will be my title.)

I am working it out through a girl heroine who is unusually clear-minded and visioned. I did think the South had a side during reconstruction and had intended to have the girl marry a *decent* Southerner and live in Georgia during Reconstruction, blaming the North for the ensuing tragedies. But your book knocks that idea galleywest. I am in a dilemma. My agent has warned me that I am handling dynamite and for heaven's sake go slow and light no fuses. Yet, Mr. Du Bois, I cannot write it unless I am truthful. That would be intolerable to me. From the quotes in your book and the carefully gathered records, I can see that the psychological attitude of the south was as arrogant as ever and even more murderous. And if I write that . . . ! Wouldn't I be accused of playing Hitler's game and causing division in our U.S.? The Author's League Bulletin yesterday warned all writers to avoid that. But dear God, how it needs writing—and Mr. Du Bois what a sad sad book you have written! Even I who know more than most of the crimes of our dear country had no idea of the depths of sadism that exist beside our brave talk of democracy.

Did you read Fanny Kemble's life on a Georgia Plantation? She was a great actress, a woman of noble mind and heart, a lover of justice, and one who had a fine literary gift also. It moved me to the depths. Yet even she said that conditions on the Butler plantation were not so bad as others in the vicinity. I wonder how they could be more horrible!

Also—this is scarcely apropos—I had idealized W. Wilson mainly for his idea of the League of Nations. He tumbled from his pedestal when I read his History of U.S. and his glossing over the leaders of the rebellion making them idyllic patriots, "behind the times"—yet truly right according their lights. "Uncle Tom's Cabin was greatly exaggerated." Never a word for negro suffering under the abomination!

Can you help me with any suggestions? Perhaps I should take a trip to Georgia and familiarize myself with the setting, learn more about the people. I was there once but long ago. Yes, I am one who believes negroes are human beings, more than that, we are brothers in God's sight, and any wrong done to the helpless *injures the doer more than the victim.*

Sincerely yours,
Mary Schumann

I note you have written *Darkwater*, and *Dark Princess*. Are they novels? Some gorgeous poetic paragraphs pages 122–126 in *Black Reconstruction!* I am buying the latter.

Have you read *American Saga* by Marjorie Barstow Greenbie? It is charmingly written and I think you would agree with her picture of the south and the southerners.[1]

From at least as early as 1911, Du Bois demanded, by name, "social equality"—which he defined as meaning full equality in every respect for Black people, including quite explicitly the right for them to be married to any persons by mutual choice. He kept at this demand, at intervals, for two generations, and in the midst of World War II he submitted to Harper's Magazine a long essay, still unpublished, on the actual meaning of equality. It was rejected and the editor, Frederick Lewis Allen, explained why in a letter published below.

Allen (1890–1954), educated at Harvard, had been on the editorial staffs of the Atlantic Monthly and Century Magazine before joining, in 1923, the staff at Harper's. He was Harper's editor from 1941 to 1953 and was the author of several best-selling works: Only Yesterday *(1931),* Lords of Creation *(1935),* Since Yesterday *(1940), and* The Big Change *(1952).*

New York, N.Y., August 16, 1943

Dear Mr. Du Bois:

We have all read your manuscript with great interest. We much admire your spirit. But we feel that the manuscript is a good deal too long and in a way too slow-moving for a magazine article; and I must confess that I personally am somewhat uneasy about your most interesting and sober and thoughtful discussion of segregation and

---

1. The Kemble book is Frances A. Kemble, *Journal of a Residence on a Georgian Plantation in 1838–1839*, issued in London in 1863 and many times reprinted. The book by Marjorie Barstow Greenbie is *American Saga: The History and Literature of the American Dream of a Better Life* (New York and London: Whittlesey House and McGraw-Hill Book Co., 1939).

inter-marriage toward the close of the manuscript. This topic does not often get this sort of discussion and ought to have it, and yet I am uneasy about provoking the discussion just now. In a couple of long talks with a group of Negroes and Whites serving as a committee for The Council for Democracy, I have had the feeling that it is in this area that it is hardest to reach any conclusions which would be widely accepted by both elements in our population; and in view of the present tension in many places I have been wondering whether this discussion had not better be adjourned for the time being, while we concentrate on these matters on which men of good will of both races can work together with the least sense that they are playing with dynamite. Maybe this is a timid attitude, especially for a journalist; but I have so strong a feeling that the need of the moment is to concentrate upon the things on which we can agree and to defer wrangles on other points that I am inclined to take this attitude even as an editor.

I am writing in this detail because I want you to know that the declination of your manuscript is not based on indifference or antagonism.[1]

Sincerely yours,

Frederick L. Allen

Will W. Alexander, at that time a special assistant in the office of the War Manpower Commission, wrote Du Bois of an idea that still awaits realization.

Washington, D.C., November 11, 1943

My dear Dr. Du Bois:

There is a small group of scholars here, men of wide experience in international matters, who feel that there is need of a universal history of racism as it has appeared in various places about the world. It is their feeling that we do not know just how often this idea has arisen to plague the world, or how it has been dealt with, whether it is recent or whether its present manifestation is a reappearance of something that has happened before.

Although I am not a historian, the idea appears to me to be sound. I asked Dr. Feilchenfeld, an international lawyer of considerable standing, both here and in Europe, to give me a short memorandum of the idea which he had about it.[2] He has prepared a tentative statement which I am attaching.

I should like to have your reaction to Feilchenfeld's tentative statement regarding

1. Du Bois's column in the *Amsterdam News*, 25 December 1943, was devoted to "social equality" and its horrifying impact upon many white people; he insisted that social equality means human dignity and obviously is just.

2. Ernst H. Feilchenfeld (1898–1956) was born in Berlin, came to the United States in 1924, and was associated with Harvard and its law school from 1924 to 1932 and later in the 1930s with Oxford. During the war he served on the Board of Economic Warfare in Washington and thereafter was connected with Georgetown University. He was the author of several books in areas of international law.

this problem. I am not sure that either the money or the personnel could be found to do it but your judgement would affect any decision that I would make about it.

Sincerely,
Will W. Alexander
Special Assistant

Atlanta, Ga., November 26, 1943

My dear Mr. Alexander:

Your letter on November 11, found me absent in New York. I feel that a Universal history of racism would be an excellent undertaking, but I am afraid that Dr. Feilchenfeld's outline illustrates the difficulties: If you are going to take the wide definition of race including nationalism, minorities, status, slavery, etc., it would be attempting a new universal history on a vast scale.

On the other hand, if you could confine your definition to [the] modern idea of biological race differences and trace it from the eighteenth century down to today, you would have a very excellent field for a limited and valuable study.

Very sincerely yours,
W. E. B. Du Bois

A letter from Dorothy Thompson manifests the great interest displayed by painters and sculptors in the fascinating personality of Du Bois. Dorothy Thompson (1894–1961) was one of the best-known columnists and radio commentators in the United States during the 1930s and 1940s in particular. She was educated at Syracuse University and the University of Vienna. Her column appeared in the New York Herald-Tribune *from 1936 to 1941, and she served as editorial writer for the* Ladies Home Journal *from 1937 until her death.*

New York, N.Y., November 23, 1943

Dear Dr. Du Bois:

I am writing in behalf of my husband, Maxim Kopf, the painter.

To be brief and to the point—he greatly wishes to paint your portrait, as one of a selected number of eminent colored Americans, whose faces, as he has seen them in life or in photographs, awaken in him great interest for their beauty of spirit and talent. This idea has obsessed him since he first came to America.

He has spent much time among colored peoples in Africa and in the South Seas, and perhaps this is one reason he sees in the faces of representative colored Americans something unique and remarkable, which he thinks the American white world passes by as too familiar.

May I say (what he would not say, being the most modest of men) that he is a very fine painter, widely recognized in Europe, from which he is a voluntary refugee and already beginning to be highly esteemed here. His first exhibition has resulted in purchases for several museums of art. In soliciting sitters for this venture he has consulted Mr. Walter White, who has been most interested and cooperative. Insofar

as possible he would like to make these portraits here in his studio but where that is
not possible he will come to his sitter.

May I learn from you whether you are willing to sit for him?

Sincerely yours,
Dorothy Thompson

Atlanta, Ga., November 26, 1943

My dear Miss Thompson:

I shall be glad to sit for a portrait by your husband, Maxim Kopf.[1] As I have no
present plans of being in New York before next fall, I am afraid the work will have to
be done here.

Very sincerely yours,
W. E. B. Du Bois

*In November 1943, Du Bois learned for the first time that he was probably not to be permitted to
remain at Atlanta University. The correspondence concerning his severance from that connection
and his rejoining the NAACP, correspondence which extends from late 1943 through mid-
1944, will appear after letters treating of other matters in this period have been presented.*

*There was some irony in the fact that shortly after Du Bois first learned of what amounted to his
projected dismissal from Atlanta University, he received a telegram and a letter recognizing, if
belatedly, his extraordinary contributions to culture and learning.*

*Henry Seidel Canby, in his capacity as secretary of the National Institute of Arts and Letters,
sent both the telegram and the letter. Canby (1878–1961), born in Delaware, was educated at
Yale and was on the faculty there from 1903 to his death. He was assistant editor of the* Yale
Review *(1911–20) and editor of the* Saturday Review of Literature *(1924–58). He was the
author of several books, notably biographies of Thoreau (1939) and Whitman (1943) and a study
of Henry James and Mark Twain (1951).*

*The National Institute of Arts and Letters was chartered by act of Congress in 1899; Du Bois
was the first Black person elected to membership in it.*

The telegram was dated 14 December 1943; the letter repeated its contents and added details:

New York, N. Y. December 21, 1943

Dear Mr. Du Bois:

I have the honor and pleasure to inform you that at the Annual Meeting of the
National Institute of Arts and Letters held on Wednesday, December 15th in New
York City, announcement was made of your election as a member in the Department

1. Maxim Kopf (1893–1958), born in Vienna, visited the United States in 1923 and then
returned to Prague. He came to the United States again in 1940 and married Dorothy Thompson in June 1943. The planned portrait of Du Bois was not done.

of Literature. Formal induction of new members will take place at our Public Ceremonial to be held in the Spring, at which you will receive the Diploma of the Institute.
Under separate cover I am sending you our Yearbook and Insignia.

Very sincerely yours,
Henry S. Canby

P. S. If you have a photograph available for Press purposes would you send it to me as soon as possible?

Atlanta, Georgia, December 28, 1943
My dear Mr. Canby:
I have received your telegram and letter announcing my election to the Institute of Arts and Letters. This morning the Yearbook and the Insignia came. May I thank you.

Very sincerely yours,
W. E. B. Du Bois

(Frederick) Ridgely Torrence (1875–1950), born in Ohio, was educated at Miami University in Ohio and at Princeton. He was on the faculties of Miami University and Antioch College and was an editor of the Cosmopolitan *and later the* New Republic *(1920–34). He published several volumes of poetry, but he distinguished himself most as a playwright; in particular, he was the first white dramatist to write serious plays of Afro-American life, preceding O'Neill in this effort. At the time of his letter to Du Bois, he was at work on a biography of John Hope, which was published in 1947; it was in this connection that he wished to consult Du Bois.*

New York, N. Y. December 15, 1943
Dear Dr. Du Bois:
Thank you for your explanation of my failure to see you during your recent visit. I can see that it was impossible for you to meet me at that time but I need very much to consult you as soon as may be. Sometime after the first of February I expect to go again to Atlanta. Will you kindly let me know your own schedule, as to whether you will be there during that month or here in New York again before then?
And now, by occasion, let me be the first to congratulate you on your election to the American Institute of Arts and Letters. It is an election absurdly belated, by several decades, but at least it has now occurred.
I don't know whether you approve of such academic bodies and I doubt whether this kind of recognition means much to you personally but—well, there it is to refuse or accept and I hope you'll do the latter.

Sincerely yours
Ridgely Torrence

Atlanta, Ga., December 29, 1943
Dear Mr. Torrence:
Thank you for your congratulations. If I were an individual I might with much joy,

join Upton Sinclair and others and tell the Institute that since we have lived more than seventy years without them,[1] we would tread on the rest of the way alone, but I am not an individual, I am a group; and the group must say yes very humbly.

I may be in New York in February, but I'm not sure. If I am I will let you know. Meantime if you are coming this way in January, that would be a safer time.

Very sincerely yours,
W. E. B. Du Bois

New York, N. Y., December 27, 1943

Dear Dr. Du Bois,

Let me add my word of congratulation to the many you must be receiving on your election to the National Institute of Arts and Letters. In honoring you the Institute has honored itself.

Yours sincerely,
Countee Cullen

1. Upton Sinclair was nominated for the institute at the same time as Du Bois; Sinclair, whose writings began to be published about the same time as Du Bois's, rejected the nomination.

1944

Early in 1944, Du Bois received from Mrs. Amy Jacques Garvey (1899–1974), the widow of Marcus Garvey, a letter which told of plans involving the post-war future of Africa. That first letter seems not to have survived, but Du Bois's response did and several subsequent letters were exchanged between them.

Atlanta, Ga., February 9, 1944

Dear Mrs. Garvey:

I thank you for your letter of January 31, and I am glad to know of Dr. Moody's plans for Africa. I shall be glad to cooperate with him or you in any way possible.[1]

Very sincerely yours,

W. E. B. Du Bois

The reply to Du Bois came on stationery headed "Garvey's African Communities League." And, off to the right: "Amy Jacques Garvey: Widow of Marcus Garvey: Successor and Director of All Allied Garvey Associates and Societies."

Windward Road P. O., Jamaica, B. W. I.

April 4, 1944

Dr. W. E. B. Du Bois

My dear Professor:

Your favor of February 9th received. Our effort to influence the United States to declare for an African Freedom Charter etc., goes on apace. Our world-wide representations to them are having effect, and the questioning of world-leaders regarding the "depth and breadth" of the Atlantic Charter, are soundings that augur of a "something must be done" attitude in our favor.

I know only too well, that it takes continuous and sustained efforts, to bring about such international reforms, when we have no Material Power with which to enforce

1. Harold A. Moody (1882–1947), born in Jamaica, was educated in England and received an M.D. degree there. In 1921 he was the first Black person elected chairman of the board of the Colonial Missionary Society and ten years later the first Black president of the London Christian Endeavor Federation. Also in 1931, partially as the result of a visit from Dr. Charles H. Wesley, the Black historian of the United States, a League of Coloured Peoples was formed with Moody as president. The LCP published a periodical, *The Keys*, with worldwide circulation; its policy was anti-segregationist and pacifist. Moody published several pamphlets during the war attacking Hitlerism as a vile form of racism; he toured the West Indies in 1946, but died in England upon his return the next year. David A. Vaughn has written a biography of him (London, 1950).

our demands. All we have are Righteous Arguments, levered by the exigencies of a world-war; the duration of which creates opportunities, and also prepares us for greater opportunities.

Not being able to get American reading matter here, unless mailed by friends, I only saw your column in "The Amsterdam News" which carried Dr. Moody's letter;[1] but I feel sure that, in view of your interest in Africans (100% and 1%) you, in your own inimitable way, have used many openings—written and spoken—to present the case of Africa *et al.* for a restoration of manhood rights, and a cessation of the ruthless exploitation of lands and labor of Africans.

Our efforts in this grave matter, have reached the stage of progress, where Statesmanship, as also strategy of Leaders at focal points, and an awareness and appreciation of each others' efforts are showing splendid results.

However, our Race, lacking a cultural and ethnic background, is not able to fully appreciate the intrinsic worth of Leadership, when perforce, it moves on and on, without broadcasting its manoeuvres. Bear with us Professsor, we are just emerging.

Enclosed are two clippings that may prove thought-provoking for your articles.

I may mention that Bermuda, although a British Colony, having to exist mainly from tourist revenue, caters to Southern tastes and habits, even to segregated schools.

I recall that in 1929 M.G. was prevented from landing at Hamilton, Bermuda by a detachment of soldiers, who would not even allow a Committee of Bermudians to go on board ship to interview him. Fortunately, I was permitted to land there two weeks before, for health reasons, and was able to make a survey of the unhealthy conditions affecting our people. So I was proxy for M.G. in his scheduled speech. I sailed next morning, before government Reporters could transcribe their notes of my speech.

Did you get a copy of *The West African Memorandum*, for self-government for Gambia, Sierra Leone, Gold Coast and N. and S. Nigeria? I have a copy of same. It is comprehensive in its survey of areas, exports, and imports, suggestions for improvement of all phases of government, finally asks for Self-government within the British Commonwealth, by stages of course, being ten years of Representative government, and five years of Responsible government.

I will be glad to give you excerpts, if you let me know under what heading you want, as the document is long, and I have to combine homework, the support of my boys, and my work for my Race. I am not permitted to even print a circular letter out here, due to war restrictions.

Please instruct your Secretary to send me any used copies of magazines, etc. as I can't get many American magazines, of literary and political worth out here. I have

1. In his column dated 26 February 1944, Du Bois wrote that Mrs. Garvey had recently written him of the election of Moody to the chairmanship of the London Missionary Society. Moody was himself quoted as stating that he meant to place that society at the disposal of the movement to enhance the rights of Africans.

never seen a copy of your University Magazine, please send me a few old ones. I can pass them on to others here, and in Africa.

Best wishes,

Yours very truly,

A. Jacques Garvey

P. S. By the way, I was surprised to hear that M. G.'s Ex-wife "Amy Ashwood" is in America, from 1920 she lost no time in villifying him, and ridiculing his Movement, now blossoms *forth as his widow*, and the *Brains of the Garvey Movement*. Professor now we realize that the dead has no power.!!!

AJG

Please send me any Newspaper, Magazines, or Books about Africa, Africans or peoples of African descent, (commonly called Negroes).

Windward Road P.O., Jamaica, B.W.I.

April 5, 1944

Re: *African Freedom Charter*

Dear Professor:—

Before mailing my previous letter I received this cable from Dr. Moody:—

"Thanks letters, please draft Memorandum acceptable authoritative Negro Organizations, America, West Indies, Africa, for discussion Conference London, July. Moody"

While we will draft our Memorandum, covering the abovementioned areas, and embodying the Six Freedoms:—Economically, educationally, socially, politically, spiritually and morally, I do want *you* to draft one too. Send Dr. Moody a copy direct, he is at:—164 Queens Rd. Peckham, South East 15, London, Eng. Please send me a copy, which I will consider one of your greatest contributions to our people's effort to rise in the might of their Manhood, and to provide for posterity equal opportunities with others.

Your experience, your calm, calculating judgment, your knowledge of international affairs, admirably fits you to send in *a one-man Memorandum*. I wish I knew Mdme Du Bois personally, I would try to get her busy, making you see what a fine opportunity presents itself, for you to serve, those whom you have, all your life served, but who as I explained in my previous letter, are so unmindful of real worth and service.

I know that Mdme Du Bois, has many a times been sacrificed on the altar of *"Service to the Race,"* but still, I feel sure, that she feels that an opportunity like this for *international Service,* may well be given to adorn and cap your long list of Services rendered freely and cheerfuly. Thank you Professor, and don't forget to autograph my copy.

Yours very truly,

A. Jacques Garvey

Atlanta, Ga., April 7, 1944

Mr. Paul Robeson
My dear Mr. Robeson:

I have had within the last month two interesting communications. One was from Amy Jacques Garvey, widow of the late Marcus Garvey living in Jamaica; the other was a telegram from Dr. Harold Moody from London. Dr. Moody as perhaps you know is a black West Indian, long resident in London and recently elected Chairman of the old and celebrated London Missionary Society. Both these communications asked for my cooperation looking toward a post-war conference to consider needs and demands of Negroes.

I am writing the enclosed letter to Dr. Moody and at the same time I am writing to Mr. Max Yergan and Mrs. Garvey asking each if they would join me as conveners of a Fifth Pan-African Congress to meet in London as soon as practical at the end of the war.

I do not insist upon "Pan African" but suggested it merely to indicate a certain continuity in our efforts since the First World War; also for establishing our claim to the name since it is a tendency in certain parts of the world to use this name for an organization dominated by white folk; however, any other name or designation will be acceptable to me.

Will you kindly let me know at your convenience if you are willing to join me and the others named in such a consideration and will you add any suggestions you may have.[1]

Very sincerely yours,
W. E. B. Du Bois

Atlanta, Ga., April 7, 1944

My dear Dr. Moody:

I am enclosing the proposed form of a letter which would call together a Pan-African Congress after the War. I do not insist upon the name "Pan-African" but suggested it as embodying a certain continuity in our efforts and also for establishing our claim to the name, since there is a tendency in certain parts of the world to use this name for an organization dominated by the white folk.

I am writing to the other proposed conveners to get their assent. Just as soon as I hear from them, I will write you again. Meantime let me have your reaction and suggestions.

Very sincerely yours,
W. E. B. Du Bois

Atlanta, Ga., April 8, 1944

My dear Mrs. Garvey:

I am enclosing the proposed form of a letter which would call together a Pan

---

1. There is no record of a written response from Robeson to this letter. He did not participate in the Fifth Pan-African Congress, held in Manchester, England, in October 1945.

African Congress after the War. I do not insist upon the name "Pan-African" but suggested it as embodying a certain continuity in our efforts and also for establishing our claim to the name, since there is a tendency in certain parts of the world to use this name for an organization dominated by white folk.

I am writing to the other proposed conveners to get their assent. Just as soon as I hear from them, I will write you again. Meantime let me have your reaction and suggestions.

Very sincerely yours,
W. E. B. Du Bois

Windward Road P.O., Jamaica, B.W.I.
April 24, 1944

Personal
Dr. W. E. B. Du Bois
My Dear Professor:—

Yours of the 8th inst by air received. I am very busy on a Memorandum correlative of Africa, West Indies and America, as cabled for by Dr. Harold Moody, and mentioned in my previous letter to you. I pause to rush you this letter, hoping it reaches you before you have any printed matter relative to publicity prepared.

There are a few things that you must take into consideration when you read this letter. First this is a war-time letter. Second, I am bottled up here in this small Island with two small boys to support, etc. The sword of Damocles that hung over M.G.'s head is hovering around mine. That, notwithstanding all the attendant disabilities, consequent on the points I have mentioned, I am one hundred per cent African, devoting all the strength of my being, to the end that all Africans and people of African descent (as a whole—a mighty whole too), reach a standard of self-assertion and self-reliance, comparable to other Races.

My preceding paragraph, will enable you to realize that your esteem and confidence in me, asking me to be a Co-convener of the proposed Congress, will be helpful to those whom we serve, and in turn our collaboration will encourage others to submerge personalities and close ranks for the common weal.

I agree with the name "Pan-African," bearing in mind your reasons stated and inferred.

Anent the "proposed form of letter"—my dear Professor, *you must avoid* any reference to the word "Negro." Regardless what white Scientists say, in order to have the hearty co-operation of all, and we will, we must not use the word. To the mind of the African it is synonymous with slavery, serfdom, it is just as if it were spelt with two g's. We must respect the peculiar psychological reaction of our people in all the different parts of the world, where language, etc., tends to divide us, and our opposition used these peculiarities to drive a wedge further between us; thank God I know my people in every nook and corner of the world, and will, from time to time, point out these things to you and others, so as to solidify our Union.

White America has abused the word "Negro," its reference means a low person to be kicked about. No, don't use it. Except where an Organization bears the name. That is why M.G. later organized the African Communities' League.

In the West Indies, many of our people feel insulted to be referred to as a Negro. In Central America the word is tabooed. Even in registering "The Universal Negro Improvement Association," we had to eliminate the word Negro, before many of the governments would consent to registration.

We, in this year 1944, want a direct ethnic affiliation and cultural development, that must have Africa as a background, etc.

The Africans would be horrified to read your reference to "Negro Leaders of Tanganyika." Those brave Bantus are intelligent and dignified, notwithstanding oppression and repression, etc. The African in his hut still feels that he is not "the descendant of slaves," in his mind he is unbent, not broken, he looks over the vastness of his continent, and feels the freedom that one breathes when one is so near to nature. He laughs with the sun, because he knows that God did not make white bodies to do the same and live and procreate his kind in such a climate; so he continues to gather inspiration from the bush, and the heat and broiling sun, these elements are saving tropical Africa for him. We must put ourselves in his place, then, and then only can we interpret his feelings and understand what he understands as the omni-science of his being.

Many thought Gandhi silly, after his experience in South Africa, he discarded European dress forever, and lived as the pariahs of India live. He—Gandhi, the scholar, the brilliant Barrister, accustomed to the amenities of a European gentleman, living like that? But he was right. European dress represented sham and pretence in the eyes of the untouchables. He got others of his kind to follow his example, he became a saint to the masses, who are the ones who needed leadership most. It was a psychological feat, and it had and has tremendous effect on his people for unification. The weaving of home spun was only secondary.

I cite all this, Professor, to prove my points, as I cannot come to America to talk, heart to heart with you. In doing this great work, we must detach ourselves, at times, completely from our surroundings, and feel as Africans in Africa feel. Do you wonder that Paul Robeson can play "Othello" with such realism?

You must try not to be bored with the length of my letters. I want you to thoroughly understand my thinking regarding our people, so that in your plans will be implemented my thoughts, that are worth-while, even if hastily expressed by letter.

Now, here is how I would recast the second paragraph of your "form letter";

The Conveners will seek cooperation from the following sources:—

Africa:

The Emperor of Ethiopia

His Excellency, the President of Liberia

The West African Leaders, that comprised the Press Delegation, the Sponsors of The West African Memorandum for Self-government (I will supply names and addresses if you haven't got them).

Governor-General Felix Sylvester Eboue, of Fr. Equatorial Africa.

African Leaders of:–Senegal, Fr. West Africa, Belgian Congo, Uganda, Kenya, Tanganyika, North and South Rhodesia, the Union of South Africa, The Protectorates of Basutoland, Bechuanaland, and Swaziland in South Africa. The Protectorate of the Sudan, Eritrea, Somaliland; Angola (Port. West Africa), Mozambique (Port. East Africa), etc.

London　The Aborigine Protective Society

George Padmore, African News Service Bureau

African Students Union, known as "Wasu."

America National Association for the Advancement of Colored Peoples; Urban League, March on Washington Movement; [National] Negro Congress, Church Leaders, especially the Baptist Denominations. The Negro Press Association. The African Academy of Arts, etc.

West Indies　Negro Progess Convention of British Guiana, Peoples National Party of Jamaica, West Indies National Committee, Headquarters in N.Y.

Captain Cipriana of Trinidad, etc.

His Excellency the President of Haiti

Central and South America　Representatives of peoples of African descent such as Editor Young of "The Panama Tribune."

British Honduras, Editor of "The Clarion." I am not so certain if the gentleman I have in mind is still Editor. Can let you know later on.

French Islands of Martinique, Guadeloupe, *West Indies*

This only gives you an idea as how it should be set out, in the proper groupings.

As I remember it—please do not refer to Africans or West Indians as "natives," it is just as offensive to them as the word "Negro." White people in Africa are called "White Settlers" or "Alien Settlers," Africans argue, and rightly so, that one does not refer to the natives of England, or the natives of France, why then are they called natives, with the inference of contempt for their condition of handicap and suppression.

In the third par. of your "form letter," you state:—"The object shall be for consultation and information so as to set before the world the needs of African Negroes and of their descendants overseas." Please delete everything after the word African, and substitute—"all Africans and peoples of African descent, the world over."

Further down in the same third par. you state, "a voice in government, education," please delete the balance, the objectionable word "Negro" is again used, further, it is not clear as to what is meant, it is a rather feeble objective, in that if I understand what you mean, the other objectives cover that, and in a more manly fashion.

I feel that the broadest objectives should be stated and nothing more, it is best; I have learned that in my dealings with men of big affairs in Europe, to say little, and do more, in matters of this kind, as the slightest word can be misinterpreted, purposely of course, to upset a magnificent effort for the future of our Race.

I notice the Statesmanship of the United Nations adopt the same policy of having a rather general thin outline, and as they go along they weave in the pattern. This is best, you feel your way, you know what will be accepted, you know what will be opposed, and who will oppose it, you can refer to your thin outline, and say, I never meant that, I meant something else, your thin outline becomes a safety line, it is vague, it is elastic enough to embody any decent, righteous, just effort for all our people everywhere.

In view of the fact that the "Pan-African Congress" will be a culmination of our (I mean the Conveners and other) efforts, and it is regrettable that it could not be held before the war is over, so that United Africa would speak, as never before, I suggest, and strongly so, that our co-ordination of efforts be permanent, and call it a "*Pan-African Union*," so that all the work of the calling of the Congress, would be under the heading of the "*Pan-African Union*."

That, during the war, we continue, under "*The Pan-African Union*," to watch over the interest of our people the world over, and to present Memoranda, as the exigencies of the planning of the United Nations warrant, so that, although our Pan-African Congress will not convene until the war is over, we will not have lost opportunities, we would not anyhow, as individual Organizations, etc., but it is so much more dignified to have a Definite Union. Close your eyes and think, and you will be able to visualize all the benefits to be accrued, now and in the future from such a Union.

I had not planned to write so much today, but since I have said so much, please rush me back a letter letting me know if you concur re the Pan African Union, so that I can use that name in sending my Memorandum to Dr.Moody, and he will then be our accredited Ambassador in London.

Give this matter immediate, and deep thought. We want to lay the foundation of a great World Union of our people, and all of us must be represented. Our children can build and expand on same, as fitting United Nations, comprised of people of African blood.

Let me know if your are free from Atlanta now, etc., as we can better plan, as we must have a central point for you, as your Secretariat, and to continue work, in publicity, and exposé of grievances etc., as also to get all the world-field properly represented, and registered with the Union, as Organizations, Societies, Leagues etc., working for the betterment of our people anywhere, or everywhere. Each to his own form, or locality, but all united toward the one grand aim of Self determination and independence as a Race.

Before closing may I ask you please, to refer to me as "*A. Jacques Garvey*," and omit the Christian name of "Amy," as M.G.'s Ex-wife is in America, impersonating "the widow" and she has a bad rep, for rackets and schemes. I would never like to be further mistaken for her, as unfortunately our christian names are alike; and she purposely misleads the public so as to exploit them with her schemes and rackets. I am very sensitive on this matter, as I have caused my family much pain, by the conduct of this person.

Please read my letter over twice, so that you can catch the unexpressed references, in matters of moment to our people, and the great work that we are carrying out.

Best wishes for good health, and strength in the task that lies ahead.

> Yours fraternally,
> A. Jacques Garvey

> Windward Road P.O., Jamaica, B.W.I.
> April 26, 1944

Personal
Dr. W. E. B. Du Bois
My dear Professor:

In continuation of my letter to you, of the 24th inst., I think it is of vital importance, from all angles, that you include a born African, as one of the Conveners of "The Pan African Congress." I suggest Nmandi Azikiwe, M.A. Editor in Chief of "The West African Pilot," Lagos, Nigeria, West Africa. He is also Editor-in-Chief of three other newspapers, namely:—

"Eastern Nigerian Guardian" of Port Harcourt, Nigeria

"Nigerian Spokesman" of Onitsha, Nigeria

"Southern Nigeria Defender" of Warri, Nigeria

He was the Chairman of the West African Press Delegation that visited England, last year, at the invitation of the British Government, and before leaving presented The West African Memorandum for self-government, by stages. I brought this matter to your attention last month.

Mr. Azikiwe attended Lincoln University, also Howard. If you met him, perhaps you may not like him personally, but we have long ceased to allow personalities to hamper unity of efforts, in this great and wide-spread work. The West African Memorandum is a practical, informative, well-balanced series of reforms leading up to self-government, and bespeaks the minds of Statesmen, worthy of the most progressive Races.

Now my dear Professor, perhaps you may misunderstand the tone of my letters, as I have been so accustomed to talk with M.G. and take part in Conferences with men, as "man to man," that I don't think or act, as if I "were just a woman."

By the way, established governments, such as Liberia and Ethiopia could not send Official Representatives, but their Representatives would be called *"Observers."*

Please send Mr. Azikiwe's letter by Trans-Atlantic Air-express, via Trinidad, and it will reach him quickly, by going across from Trinidad to the mainland of W. Africa.

Best wishes,

> Yours fraternally,
> A. Jacques Garvey

Remaining correspondence with Mrs. Garvey and others relating to the Pan-African movement falls within the province of the third volume of Du Bois's correspondence. It will be continued there.

Coleman Leroy Hacker, born in Florida in 1910, was educated at Benedict College in Columbia, South Carolina, at Howard, and at Oberlin. He taught at Bethune-Cookman College (1939–41), was the principal of Holsey Institute in Georgia (1941–42), and served as a chaplain in the United States Army (1942–45). In the late 1940s and early 1950s, the Reverend Mr. Hacker was active in the anti-peonage struggle.

While serving as chaplain in a Black battalion stationed in Iran, he and his men remembered Du Bois on his birthday.

APO 795, c/o Postmaster, N. Y.
February 23, 1944

My dear Du Bois:

You will not remember me because we met only once and that was at Bethune-Cookman College in Daytona Beach, when you were on a short visit in 1941. You spoke that afternoon and I was chairman of the meeting. However that is not important. The important thing is that today is your birthday and I want you to know that even in far away Persia there are many who are grateful for the day upon which you were born.

Tonight I had a program arranged for the soldiers here (Military Security forbids my telling you how many were present but the number was large). We spoke of Washington, Lincoln, Booker T. Washington, Douglass and of course of you.

Although words are powerful when speaking directly to an individual about himself they can be embarrassing, therefore I shall not repeat to you what I said to the boys tonight. However the thing that I want you to know is that you are appreciated and it is not important that all of us might not agree upon details or even upon big issues but the fact remains that we are all working for the same thing.

I have read many of your books. Just a few nights ago I had the pleasure of reading from the *Negro Digest* words that you had penned about your life and what things you would emphasize if you had it to live again.[1] It is primarily for that reason that I shall never have to reproach myself for not writing you when I had the opportunity to extend greetings of the day and to let you know further that as long as youth can look to the hills for a light your spirit will be a portion of that fuel.

Around me I have gathered ten men who will join me in a cooperative project in Cleveland, Ohio. This will be a furniture factory and it will be owned by ten people. As soon as it is established I will take to the road going from community to community encouraging my people to look to the cooperative movement not as a solution to all problems but as a partial solution on the economic level.

Sir, I wish for you long life. It has been fruitful and will stand as a beacon light for all of us. God's richest blessing upon you sir.

Respectfully,
C. Leroy Hacker

1. "Reading, Writing, and Real Estate," *Negro Digest* 1 (October 1943): 63–65.

Atlanta, Ga., March 7, 1944

Dear Lt. Hacker:

I appreciate your kind letter of February 23 and your reference to my birthday. I hope you will thank the men and wish them all good luck.

Very sincerely yours,

W. E. B. Du Bois

The theme of economic cooperation recurs in a 1944 exchange between a white attorney in New Jersey and Du Bois. Edward Gaulkin (b. 1903) was educated at Columbia and New York University and has practiced law in New Jersey since 1929.

Newark, N. J., March 8, 1944

Dear Professor Du Bois:

It occurred to me that one way that the colored race could help itself, would be to use its collective purchasing power to create a cooperative corporation, for the purpose of buying up existing housing facilities to be operated by them and to be thrown open to colored tenants. Dr. Milton R. Konvitz of the N.A.A.C.P. told me that you have given considerable thought to a project along this line and suggested that I write you.

Can you give me the benefit of your thoughts and experience along this line? Perhaps I should state that I have no personal interest in the matter. I am not seeking to organize such a venture myself, nor do I have any desire for employment by such a corporation if one is organized. The thought came to me as a result of my interest in the welfare of the negro and my experience in the practice of law, through which I discovered that white people were buying up real estate at low prices, for the express purpose of exacting exorbitant rents from colored tenants, giving them a minimum of service for their money. Collective purchasing power would also be effective in breaking down the barriers which confine the negro population to small congested areas in all our cities.

Very truly yours,

Edward Gaulkin

Atlanta, Ga., May 4, 1944

My dear Mr. Gaulkin:

Before answering your letter of March 8, I took the opportunity to write to friends in Newark concerning you and your work. The answer is very encouraging. I have for a long time urged colored people to join cooperative efforts, in Consumers Cooperation, Cooperative Housing and even Cooperative Production. You must realize however that we Negroes have been trained in American individualism in our industries' life and we are rather slow to realize that cooperation is the next step.

I hope that despite any discouragement you may meet, that you will persist in your plan and I rather think that in time you may accomplish something. My friend, Dr. T. B. Bell of 340 Belmont, Newark, will give you valued advice.[1]

> Very sincerely yours,
> W. E. B. Du Bois

A suggestion for the kind of autobiography that Du Bois was not to write until the late 1950s and that would not appear until after his death came to him in 1944 from Joseph A. Brandt (b. 1899), when the latter headed the University of Chicago Press. Brandt, born in Indiana, was educated at the University of Oklahoma and Oxford University in England. After editing periodicals in Oklahoma, he founded the University of Oklahoma Press in 1925 and directed it until 1938, when he became director of the Princeton University Press and later president of the University of Oklahoma (1941–44). The latter year he became director of the University of Chicago Press, leaving that position in 1945 to head Henry Holt and Co. In 1949 he became head of the journalism department in the graduate school at the University of California in Los Angeles.

> Chicago, Ill., March 24, 1944

Dear Mr. Du Bois:

Mr. [Robert] Redfield, Dean of our Division of Social Sciences and one of the world's greatest anthropologists, and I have been discussing a proposed series of books which will have the general title "The Negro in American Life." When we say "Series" we are not thinking of a conventionally numbered series of books edited by a specific individual, but of a program designed to furnish a vehicle through which the status of the Negro as a citizen may be consistently explored.

Mr. Redfield feels, as do I, that you should by all means write your life experience and that this book, if written, should be an early title in this series we hope we can launch. We would hope that you would not do a conventional autobiography but rather the kind of job that Lincoln Steffens did. After all, you have been at the heart of the struggle to make the Negro's place in American life one of dignity and withal you have kept a balanced outlook. We feel that you can perform a pre-eminent service to America were you to undertake such a book. It would be in reality through you the story of the upward struggle of the Negro.

I hope that you will give serious thought to this suggestion and let me know your reaction to it.

> Cordially yours,
> Joseph A. Brandt

> Atlanta, Ga., March 30, 1944

My dear Mr. Brandt:

I have your letter of March 24. I have, as perhaps you know already, written

1. Not otherwise identified.

something of my autobiography in the first chapter of *Darkwater*, published in 1919;[1] and more in detail in *Dusk of Dawn*, published in 1940. The latter however is an "autobiography of a race concept" and naturally there is considerably more autobiographical material which I might collect.

I think I would like to do this but there comes first the question of how you think that what I have already written will provide the matter which you have in mind; and second the question of financial help. I shall probably be retired from my work here in June and further literary work that I undertake would need to be helped by some contribution toward secretarial aid and the like. I should be glad to hear from you at your convenience.

Very sincerely yours,
W. E. B. Du Bois

Chicago, Ill., April 6, 1944

Dear Mr. Du Bois:

We are greatly encouraged here by your gracious letter of March 30. Before replying in greater detail, we are going to study *Darkwater* and *Dusk of Dawn*. I was familiar with *Darkwater* but not with *Dusk of Dawn*. I can say that unless these two books have preempted what we have in mind, I am confident we can work out an arrangement whereby you will have such help as you will require in the writing of the proposed book for us. I shall be out of town from the 6th of this month through the 19th, so it will be later in the month before I can write you.

Cordially yours,
Joseph A. Brandt

Atlanta, Ga., April 10, 1944

My dear Mr. Brandt:

Since writing you, the following considerations have occurred to me. Neither the short biography in *Darkwater* nor the long one in *Dusk of Dawn* touch on the great amount of accumulated matter, letters, documents and other writings, which I have in my files and which date back to the beginning of the century. It would be possible I think to write a book called Memories or Reminiscences, which would be an account of my personal reaction with men of my day as illustrated by these documents and which would begin with my public life after graduation from Harvard and bring the matter down until today. I have long wanted to go through these papers and abstract the meat and meaning but have not gotten to it. Perhaps I could do this if you decided that such a book would meet current demand.

Very sincerely yours,
W. E. B. Du Bois

---

1. *Darkwater's* postscript is dated 1919, but the book was copyrighted in 1920.

Chicago, Ill., April 24, 1944

Dear Mr. Du Bois:

We are greatly encouraged by your gracious letter of April 10 which arrived while I was in the West. I think we are moving in the right direction, although I am delaying fuller comment until we have completed our study of the biographical material contained in *Darkwater* and *Dusk of Dawn*. I am happy that you feel as we do, as indicated by your letter, that your book should be an intellectual history with yourself as the focal point.

Cordially yours,
Joseph A. Brandt

One of the most difficult of all northern lily-white institutions to civilize was Princeton University. By the mid-1940s developments had reached the point where precise information was needed.

Elmer Adler (1884–1962), born in Rochester, New York, was educated at Phillips Academy in Massachusetts, at the University of Rochester, and at Harvard. He was an organizer of Random House in 1927 and served as its vice-president until 1932. In 1928 he founded the Colophon, *editing it until 1940. He was a consultant for Princeton's library and university press from 1940 to 1952 and a member of Princeton's faculty from 1945 to 1952. From 1956 until his death he served as director of La Casa del Libro in San Juan, Puerto Rico.*

Princeton, N. J., April 11, 1944

Dear Mr. Du Bois:

Could you, without too great trouble, refer me to statistics on the Negro in Northern Colleges?

As you know, there has been a sort of underground movement at Princeton which breaks out from time to time, and now there is a demand for more information. So I should like to learn the dates of first admissions, with resulting attendance, and hope you can tell me where these figures may be found.

I am

Cordially yours
Elmer Adler

Atlanta, Ga., May 4, 1944

My dear Mr. Adler:

I am very much ashamed at not having been able to answer earlier your letter of April 11, but I have just been through the ordeal of being retired, somewhat against my will, and that perhaps will explain.

You will get the best and most recent statistics concerning the attendance of Negroes in northern institutions by writing Roy Wilkins, in care of the *Crisis*, 69 Fifth Avenue, New York City and Charles H. Thompson, editor of *Journal of [Negro] Education*, Howard University, Washington, D. C. They are familiar with recent statistics.

I may say in general that Princeton University is the only northern college that has never admitted Negro students; also though repeatedly approached, it has never had the courage to explain its attitude. John Chavis, a North Carolina Negro who became a celebrated teacher of whites, received his education at Princeton but probably did not appear in class. This was back in the Eighteenth Century. As a matter of fact, the attitude was based upon the custom before the Civil War of building up Princeton as a Southern Pro-Slavery institution. The present set of figures concerning attendance of Negroes at Northern Institutions have been published in my *College-bred Negro*, published by Atlanta University in 1900 and 1910. Later figures were collected and published by Charles Johnson in the *Negro College Graduate* published in 1938 by the University of North Carolina Press. The total number of bachelor degrees granted Negroes in Northern colleges from 1914 to 1936 was 3,504. I hope this information will be of some use.

Very sincerely yours,
W. E. B. Du Bois

Princeton, N. J., May 8, 1944

Dear Mr. Du Bois:

Please accept my thanks for your letter of May 4, it gives just the information I hoped to get from you.

Very likely you know that there has always been some movement here at Princeton towards the admission of Negroes. Some day its power will be too great to resist.[1]

Cordially yours,
Elmer Adler

The first edition of the volume Encyclopedia of the Negro: Preparatory Volume with Reference Lists and Reports *came to 208 pages and was published in 1945 in New York City by the Phelps-Stokes Fund. Letters relative to this work appear in preceding pages. The manuscript was ready for the printer in the spring of 1944, at which point Du Bois wrote Anson Phelps Stokes.*

Atlanta, Ga., May 11, 1944

My dear Dr. Stokes:

First of all, let me thank you very much for the abstract from Robert Pleasants. I am going to use it.[2] Secondly, concerning Guy Johnson's proposal: if of course, there

1. Back in 1910 Du Bois had attacked Princeton for its failure to admit Black students in the *Crisis* 1 (December 1910): 5; in his column in the *Chicago Defender*, 10 May 1947, he called attention to "the first Negro college graduate of Princeton University"—John Howard had received his bachelor's degree that year. (Two Black men were graduated much earlier from Princeton's theological seminary.)

2. The life and work of the eighteenth-century anti-slavery figure in Virginia, Robert Pleasants, are summarized in Du Bois's *Chicago Defender* column, 5 August 1944. Stokes had sent Du Bois a copy of Pleasant's letter to Patrick Henry, written in 1777 and proposing the emancipation of slaves.

is no very substantial difference between the cost of printing and mimeographing, I think he is right; but otherwise not. I would be quite willing to agree to his proposal in the second paragraph "Dictionary of Negro History, Preface to an Encyclopedia" etc.

I have thought several times over the title page but it is not perhaps of enough importance to hesitate about. As a matter of fact, in terms of actual work, this manuscript was due to the work of the following persons in the order named: W. E. B. Du Bois, Rayford Logan, Irene Diggs, Guion Johnson and Guy Johnson. Strictly speaking, the authorship should be "by W. E. B. Du Bois with the assistance of" these other persons in the order named. On the other hand, since this is really a part of the Encyclopedia project, it is perhaps best to have the names of the editors of the Encyclopedia appear as joint authors of this first part of the work, with the other persons named as assistants. In that case the title should be "by W. E. B. Du Bois and Guy Johnson, with the assistance of Rayford Logan, Irene Diggs and Guion Johnson."[2] I have no particular preference in the matter and will leave it to your judgment.

I wrote you that I would be in New York on the morning of the 19th and 20th. I might make an appointment early on the morning of the 20th, say at 9 A. M. I leave here the 17th and can be reached at the [Hotel] Theresa.

Very sincerely yours,
W. E. B. Du Bois

While Du Bois was in the midst of his departmental work, his plans for the Phylon Institute and Phylon *itself, his books, his newspaper and magazine writings, and his concern with the nature of the post-war world, a shocking communication came to him late in November 1943. The decision reported in the letter published below was taken by a board which assumed—naturally, but erroneously—that Du Bois had been prepared for the action it was taking.*

Atlanta, Ga., November 23, 1943

Dear Doctor Du Bois:

Pursuant to the action of the Board of Trustees of Atlanta University at the meeting in New York on November 16, 1943, and in accordance with the tenure and retirement provisions which the Board has adopted, I wish to inform you that you will be retired from the active faculty of Atlanta University when your present contract expires on June 30, 1944.

The Board wishes you to know that it has appreciated your services to Atlanta University, and as a token of this appreciation you are to be retired as Professor Emeritus.

A committee is to be appointed by the Acting Chairman of the Board with instruc-

2. The credits on the title page of the volume read: "by W. E. B. Du Bois and Guy B. Johnson, prepared with the cooperation of E. Irene Diggs, Agnes C.L. Donohugh, Guion Johnson, Rayford W. Logan, and L. D. Reddick, introduction by Anson Phelps Stokes."

tions to consider what, if any, financial provisions will be made for you upon your retirement.

Meanwhile, we shall be glad to have you think about this matter and I shall appreciate having any suggestions you may care to make.

> Yours very truly,
> Rufus E. Clement
> President

Du Bois was stunned by this letter and the action reported; he did nothing about it for some weeks. * *Then, early in January 1944, he received a letter from his friend W. R. Banks of Texas, a member of Atlanta's board of trustees, asking for Du Bois's reaction to the November 1943 notice from that board. Du Bois sent what he called a "Memorandum to Mr. Banks."*

> Atlanta, Ga., January 11, 1944

In answer to your letter of January 7, 1944, may I say how I dislike to burden you with complaint. On the other hand, you must realize how difficult it is for one in my position to have no avenue of protest or complaint, when I feel myself unjustly treated. I venture therefore at your request to state plainly my reaction to the action of the Board of Trustees, November 18, 1943. I think that my services to Atlanta University over more than twenty-five years, entitled me to at least consultation and hearing before drastic action was taken severing my connection with the institution and so interfering with my life work as virtually to end it.

The age limit often laid down in universities has reference to normal conditions when a number of young and gifted scholars are awaiting advancement and their way is clogged by ageing and ineffective men. Today at Atlanta University in a faculty of eight, there are only six productive scholars. Three of these are on leave and two are now being retired. In Sociology, there are but two men, myself and Mr. Reid. Mr. Reid, beside teaching and lecturing, is assisting Charles Johnson of Fisk in his race relations work under the American Missionary Society and the Rosenwald Fund; he is assistant director of the newly organized Southern Regional organization; he is Director of the People's College.[1] The President informs me that after my retirement, Mr. Reid will edit *Phylon*. As Mr. Reid is the only other member of the Department of

---

* Of course, the news of his dismissal filled the Black press. Joseph D. Bibb in his influential column in the Baltimore *Afro-American*, 11 March 1944, denounced the dismissal and insisted that Du Bois "richly deserves the opportunity to continue his sociological pursuits, writings and editing." Ralph Matthews also vigorously attacked Du Bois's dismissal in the same paper, 13 May 1944.

1. Soon after Du Bois joined Atlanta University in the 1930s, he and Ira Reid instituted what was called a People's College open to any resident in Atlanta who could read; it was taught gratis by a few faculty members of the university. The tuition was ten cents a course; classes were held in the evening and attended by Black working people. Du Bois had written about a projected people's college as early as January 1930, while he was in New York City; see volume one of this work, p. 415.

William Pickens. Photograph from
the New York Public Library.

Rufus E. Clement. Photograph from the
New York Public Library.

Sociology beside myself, he will also presumably become Co-ordinator of the social study program of the Land-Grant Colleges. It took the President six years to find a chairman of the department of Education. Even if he appointed a professor of sociology next year to succeed me, he would be a man with no acquaintanceship with the plans and procedure I have been building for ten years. Would it not have been wisdom as well as courtesy to have brought in a man a year or more ago to work with me?

I am not the one to decide as to whether or not I am still capable of productive work; but certainly no one in this institution today has done or is doing the work that I am. It happens too that against many obstacles, I have just brought into active being a scheme of co-operation in social studies between Atlanta University and twenty Negro Land-Grant Colleges. It is regarded by experts as the most promising movement in Negro education and social study since the Atlanta studies which I carried on thirty-five years ago. It certainly would have been wisdom if not courtesy, at least to have consulted with me and the Presidents of the Negro Land-Grant Colleges before taking this drastic step which neither I nor they dreamed of.

If I had been consulted I would have asked the Board to take this action: To retain me at Atlanta University.

A. Without teaching assignment since we have only three graduate students in sociology, and are not likely to have more until the Department is integrated with the School of Social Work.

B. To let me continue to edit *Phylon*.

C. To let me act as Co-ordinator of the social studies program of the Negro Land-Grant Colleges.

D. To provide me with a secretary as at present; and to appoint an assistant in sociology as my understudy.

E. To retain this arrangement until June 30, 1946, unless I should become incapacitated before that date.

F. To retire me June 30, 1946 with a salary sufficient for me to live on. If the above plan is not followed, not only will Atlanta University cripple this department at a time when competent young scholars are very difficult to obtain, but my own work will be ruined; my library for working consists of 2500 selected volumes; I could not remove it to my home without building a room for it; this war priorities would not permit. I am engaged on two important books; without my library and a secretary they will probably never be finished.

I am especially amazed that the trustees express doubts as to my need of a pension. I worked 13 years for Atlanta University for $1200 a year. The most I could do was to keep out of debt. I worked 23 years in New York at an average salary of $4325 a year. With this I supported my family; sent my daughter through school and college and saved about $15,000 in life insurance and real estate. All of this I lost in the collapse of Standard Life, and in the real estate slump in New York in 1929. During my ten years back in Atlanta, I have built a home in Baltimore on which I owe $3000. I have myself and wife to support and no insurance. I ought to help my daughter put my grand-daughter through college.

W. E. B. Du Bois

P. S. Although I had [no] and did not think of asking [for] any written guarantees, the Board should know that I left a permanent job to come to Atlanta in 1933; that there was a clear understanding between myself and John Hope that I was coming here with a life tenure as long as I was able to work and a pension on retirement. Under no [other] circumstances would I have thought of changing work at the age of sixty-five.

Overcoming the sense of pain that must have been very intense, Du Bois soon was fighting back, not only with the letter to his friend Banks, but with the kind of letter that follows, written to another Black memb. of Atlanta's board, the Reverend James B. Adams (1892–1946). Adams, born in Georgia, educated at Morehouse and the University of Chicago, was pastor of the Concord Baptist Church in Brooklyn, New York, from 1921 until his death. At the time Du Bois wrote him, Adams also was moderator of the Long Island Baptist Association, president of the Brooklyn Interdenominational Ministers Alliance, and a director of the Protestant Council of New York.

Atlanta, Ga., April 13, 1944

My dear Dr. Adams:

When I was informed November 23, of my retirement by the trustees, I was so stunned that I determined to take no action. Finally I felt compelled to write W. R. Banks, of Prairie View, because at his request and after three years of work, I had just launched the social study program of the Negro Land-Grant Colleges and Atlanta University had been designated the center of this work under my direction. Although President Clement was present and went directly from that meeting to recommend my retirement, he did not then mention the matter nor has he at any time informed me of his plans for my retirement nor consulted with me in any way about it until his note of November 23.

Despite this he has in public statement and written communication, insisted

1. That I had been officially informed of the time of my retirement.
2. That I had not communicated with the committee on retirement.
3. That I have always been "difficult" to consult or work with.

I have served this institution long and faithfully. I do not deserve this treatment at the hands of the authorities. In a career of over fifty years I have never been dismissed from a position. I have never left a position without being urged to remain. I worked 13 years at Atlanta University in my young manhood. I kept in close touch with it during the next 23 years and visited and lectured. I returned to Atlanta at the reiterated solicitation of John Hope. I gave up a life position which I might have held to this day and returned here. I came with the clear understanding that I would finish my life work here and be pensioned when I could no longer work. No contract was drawn nor thought of because John Hope was my life-long friend and a gentleman of honor. For no other living person would I have returned.

I write to declare that I never have in any way been notified of my retirement or consulted about it until November 23, 1943 by written note. The adoption of a pension and retirement system at 65 was publicly announced but it certainly did not apply to me since I was 65 when I returned here.

I think therefore I have a right to request from the trustees a careful investigation as to the following facts; and a postponement of my retirement until facts have been ascertained.

1. When did President Clement announce the terms of my tenure to me? If it was written, he must have a carbon of the letter. If it was announced in a meeting of which I was a member, there must be minutes; if it was oral, when and where did it take place?

2. When did he announce to me the names of the retirement committee with whom I could discuss the matter?

3. What arrangements have been made to edit *Phylon* and to carry on the Land Grant College social program; when this was discussed in Chicago, with Mr. Clement present, why did he not then tell me or the 17 Presidents of my imminent retirement, especially when that possibility at some future time was discussed?

4. When, where and in what respects have I failed to cooperate with President Clement or been "difficult" of approach?

I have a right to ask thorough investigation of these matters. If it is proven to the satisfaction of the trustees that I was notified; and that I have not cooperated with the president, I will bow to dismissal without protest.

Sincerely yours,

W. E. B. Du Bois

In addition to newspaper attacks on the firing of Du Bois, such distinguished scholars as Professor Melville J. Herskovits, the anthropologist of Northwestern University, sent sharp letters of protest to members of the board of trustees, with copies to Du Bois. A meeting of the board to consider further action in connection with Du Bois was scheduled to be held at Atlanta University on 28 April 1944. Again, the members received letters and wires of protest. One such protest, addressed to Dr. Trevor Arnett, acting chairman of the board of trustees, came from Walter White in the form of a telegram, dated 28 April. A copy of that wire was in Du Bois's papers.

April 28, 1944

On return to country have learned with sadness of difficulties between Atlanta University and Dr. Du Bois. Am informed his services have been terminated as of June 30 without adequate provision for retirement. As alumnus of Atlanta University I most vigorously and sincerely urge reconsideration by board of trustees. Although I have not always agreed with Dr. Du Bois nor he with myself there is no doubt that his intellectual leadership has done more than that of any other individual towards enlightening thought on the race question. It would be tragic to accord him cavalier treatment after a lifetime of service.

Walter White

The action of the university's board of trustees at its meeting was conveyed to Du Bois by President Clement.

Atlanta, Ga., May 1, 1944

Dear Dr. Du Bois:

In recognition of your distinguished career as a scholar and teacher and of your services to the University, the Board of Trustees of Atlanta University at the annual meeting on April 28, 1944, unanimously adopted the recommendation of the special committee as follows:

That beginning with your retirement on July 1, 1944, you be paid your full salary of $4,500, divided into twelve equal monthly installments for one year;

That beginning July 1, 1945, you be paid $1,800 per year divided into twelve equal monthly installments for a period of five years; and further

That after July 1, 1950, you be paid $1,200 per year divided into twelve equal monthly installments.

Payments will be continued through your lifetime but will not be continued beyond that.

Beginning July 1, 1944, your active service with the University will end and you will have no further responsibilities to the University. The trustees, however, have been pleased to confer upon you the rank of Professor Emeritus.

Yours very truly,

Rufus E. Clement

Among the papers of Du Bois is a copy of a press notice marked "for immediate release." It is undated, but "(from W. E. B. Du Bois)" appears at the top margin; though not in the form of a letter it was sent to the editors of many Black periodicals. It is given here in its entirety.

At its meeting Friday April 28, the Board of Trustees of Atlanta University retired from active service as of June 30, Dr. W. E. B. Du Bois, Head of the Department of Sociology. In view of the fact that Dr. Du Bois had been given no prior notice of his proposed retirement before the action was decided upon, he was voted a full year's salary for next year without duties. He was also granted a pension which will amount to a little over one third of his present salary for five years and after that to something over one fourth of his present income. Dr. Du Bois has served Atlanta University for more than 25 years and this pension is less than his normal expense of living. The action was taken against wide protest on the part of the Alumni Association and persons of prominence throughout the United States.

During the past year, Dr. Du Bois has lectured at Cooper Union and Town Hall, New York City; before the City Club of Cleveland and at Howard University Forum, and in Detroit, Indianapolis and Austin, Texas. He will deliver the commencement address at Talladega College this year. He has founded and edited *Phylon* for now the fifth year, with a circulation that includes every great library in the United States. He has also just initiated a cooperative social study to be carried on continuously by nineteen Negro Land Grant Colleges. This project according to the *Journal of Higher Education* of Ohio State University "has made educational history," and its program has the approval of professors in sociology at Harvard, Yale, Bennington College, the University of Chicago, the University of North Carolina, the University of Iowa, Duke University and others.

On May 19, Dr. Du Bois will be inducted into the National Institute of Arts and Letters at the annual ceremony in the Academy Auditorium, New York City. At the same time, special awards will be presented by the Institute to Willa Cather, Theodore Dreiser and Paul Robeson.

With the announcement of the termination of his employment at Atlanta, several institutions offered positions to Du Bois. Among these were the North Carolina College for Negroes, Fisk University, and Howard University. Correspondence in this connection follows.

Atlanta, Ga., May 2, 1944

President James E. Shepard
North Carolina College for Negroes
My dear President Shepard:

I was retired from Atlanta University in accordance with the enclosed slip.[1]

I am unable at present to make a definite proposition to you because I feel bound to see my project with regard to the Land Grant Colleges go through if possible. I have been working for four years to get [it] started and just as it gets on its feet there comes this serious interruption.

Fisk University has offered me office facilities and secretarial aid for this work if I will to carry on the project from that center; but in that case the Land Grant Colleges would have to furnish me part salary to piece out my small pension. I am not sure whether they could or would do this, but I am writing them about it. As soon as I have heard from them, I will write you.

Meantime, you might be considering these matters: A graduate journal of the sort which you have in mind ought to cost $2000 a year for manufacturing, postage and incidentals, outside of salary and clerical assistance. *Phylon* has been published for $1550 a year because the President compelled me to take $450 from the appropriated $2000 to supplement my secretary's salary, after he had promised to furnish it from the University funds. In addition to the appropriation of $2000 you could expect at least $500 or perhaps $750 from the sale of the magazine after it was once started. This would allow enough to pay the contributors small sums, and it is only in this way that you can get the best contributions. It is impossible today to secure contributors who pay for paper, ink, postage and copying, in order to get matter printed.

In addition to this cost, there would of course be office space, heat and light, which probably would be furnished without charge. There should be a managing editor. I

---

1. The enclosure was a copy of President Clement's letter to Du Bois of 1 May 1944.

have carried Mr. Reid as Managing Editor for five years on our title page but as a matter of fact he has done nothing but read a little proof. A real managing editor would take a good deal more responsibility for the magazine by editing and proof reading and leaving the Editor time to outline a general policy. The subscription to your magazine probably ought to be $2.00 a year, not more than that. I think we made our subscription too low, in putting it at $1.00. Most of our subscribers can easily pay double the price and with the $2.00 subscription the magazine could be handled on the news-stands; that is impossible with the $1.00 magazine because we have no room for rebates.

So far as contributing and associated editors are concerned, there should, if possible, be one editorial board and that local, consisting of four to six persons in addition to the editor-in-chief and managing editor. They should come mainly from your faculty, although they might be from adjoining parts of the state and they might include one or two white persons.

In addition to that would come the question of my salary for editing the magazine and conducting seminars in perhaps two or three of the quarters of the year. Tentatively I should say that I could not afford to accept less than $2400 for this; but I can not make this suggestion final until I find out about my obligations to the Land Grant Colleges.

I am afraid you may not find this letter very satisfactory, but I am trying to be very frank and put the situation before you as it now stands. Before the end of the month and perhaps by the 15th, I can make a more definite proposal. I am deeply obliged for your kind offer.

Very sincerely yours,
W. E. B. Du Bois

Atlanta, Ga., May 2, 1944

Mr. Charles S. Johnson
Fisk University
My dear Mr. Johnson:

I have your letter of April 19 and thank you for it. I have been retired by Atlanta University, as you will see by the enclosed statement. I should be strongly inclined to accept your offer and that of President [Thomas E.] Jones, but before making final decision, there are certain things that I will have to consider: First, any action taken by the Land Grant Colleges; I am presenting the matter befor the conference of presidents. The difficulty that they will encounter is the matter of my salary and that of at least one assistant. I know they have thought of this before, but I do not know how far they will be able to get definite action. I could not carry on the work with the small pension that I shall receive.

The person that I should like to have assist with my work is E. Irene Diggs, who has been my secretary for five years. She is at present studying at the University of Cuba and will probably get her doctorate in Anthropology this summer or next fall. I am wondering if it would be possible to bring her with me to Fisk.

Atlanta University now furnishes $1000 a year toward the expense of the coordinator's office. If the office should be changed to Fisk, this contribution would of course be cut off as the President has never been in favor of it. Would there be any chance of Fisk duplicating this contribution?

Third, you speak of conducting this work "for the coming year." Of course, there is always the question as to how long I shall be able to work, but if my work was reestablished at Fisk and went on satisfactorily under my supervision, I should want to be assured of continuing it as long as I am in good health.

Finally I think I should say that another institution has made me an offer, but it does not include the Land Grant College Project. In any decision that I might have to make between the two institutions, I need hardly say that I would greatly prefer Fisk. At the same time, I must give thought to the other offer, which includes a salary.

While I am getting in contact with the Land Grant Colleges, I would be glad to have you write me frankly about the things I have brought up, and consult with President Jones. I hope to write you something more definite sometime this month. I am deeply appreciative of your attitude.

Very sincerely yours,
W. E. B. Du Bois

Howard University, Washington, D. C.
May 11, 1944

Dear Dr. Du Bois:

I am in receipt of both of your letters, the first containing the copy of the letter from Charles Johnson.

I have talked the matter over at length with President [Mordecai W.] Johnson and said something to Dean [Charles A.] Thompson, who doubtless has written you concerning a seminar in Negro education. President Johnson has suggested that I secure from you certain specific information in regard to several matters. First, if you came to Howard University, what would you expect the University to provide in regard to compensation, secretarial service, office space, etc., and secondly, what would you want to do? By the second point I mean, of course, would you want to undertake any lecture or seminar work or do you plan to continue work with the Land-Grant Colleges?

As soon as I receive specific information from you in regard to these two points, I will be in a position to discuss the question formally with the President, who appears favorably disposed to providing a congenial place for you to work.

Sincerely yours,
E. Franklin Frazier

Atlanta, Ga., May 15, 1944

My dear Dr. Frazier:

Thank you for your letter of May 11. I have had as you know an offer from Fisk. I have received another very pleasing letter from Johnson and also an offer from North Carolina College for Negroes to conduct a seminar and edit a school quarterly. On the whole, I should rather come to Howard, first because it is near my home and will reduce my living expense and it is near New York where I have many contacts; and of course it is near the Congressional Library. I am writing the executive committee of the Land Grant College Presidents to see just what they are planning to do. They are, I know, eager to keep this project going and Clement is determined to separate the project from Atlanta University. He does not mention it in the President's Report, nor the catalog and has said frankly that its future is the matter of the Land Grant College Presidents. There is no one here who could carry or would carry it on. Reid has never been interested and has more than a full program without it.

As set up, the project was carried on as follows: I received no compensation outside of the salary paid by Atlanta University; the University contributed (with the opposition of President Clement) $1,000 to the general fund; the Land Grant Colleges have contributed so far this year $1,500. It probably will before the end of the year amount to $1,700 or $1,800. This makes a general fund of $2,700. This fund I am expending as office expense, including travel and clerical aid; an annual conference and the publication of an annual report. For the future, this fund would have to be increased, so as to cover part-time compensation for myself and one or two good assistants. I should want badly to have Miss Diggs back. She is a first-class worker and understands this work. She might however divide her time between the Land-Grant College project and teaching Spanish or Anthropology. She will probably get her degree in Anthropology in September. She is taking all her examinations and doing her thesis in Spanish which shows her competence in that language. Her thesis is going to be on the life of Ortiz and negotiations for its publication in America have begun.

Secondly, you ought to succeed me as co-ordinator and you ought to have an assistant. I have working with me now temporarily, Hugh Smythe, A. M. in Sociology at Atlanta University and candidate for the doctorate in Anthropology at Northwestern University. He was interrupted by the war, but he has been discharged from the army, although subject to recall. He has a first class mind and is good in execution.

The cost of the conference if held in Washington would be less than at Atlanta University and could be made gradually a significant meeting. The annual publication could be made important. I am enclosing an estimate of the cost of carrying on this project and of its possible division between Howard and the Land Grant Colleges. This is simply tentative and I have not yet got the concurrence of the Land-Grant College executives about centering this project at Howard. I shall be very glad to have you present this to President Johnson and get his reaction. If Howard could, by this step, begin to place itself in the position of central graduate school from which the courses of study in the nineteen Land-Grant Colleges were directed and co-ordinated in the Social Sciences, this would be one of the greatest steps that Negro education could take.

I am so glad to know of your interest.

Very sincerely yours,
W. E. B. Du Bois

In the midst of this excitement, Du Bois received a letter from the person then editing the Crisis *that surely pleased him; he complied with its request.*

New York, N. Y., May 8, 1944

My dear Dr. Du Bois:

First I want to say that I have noted with approval the action of the Board of Trustees on April 28. The first report of the situation seemed incredible, but even if it was a true report, the subsequent action was gratifying to your many disciples throughout the nation.

I do not know whether I ever took the trouble to mention it or not, but when, as a youngster back in St. Paul, Minnesota where I enjoyed the friendship, guidance and inspiration of Lillian Alexander (then Turner), I became a follower of the Du Bois school and nothing, I think, has been more astonishing than that I should find myself thirty years later at 69 Fifth Avenue.

What I really started this letter for was to ask you a great favor. You may recall that we used to have hanging in what passes for our entrance lobby some rather depressing drawings and photographs of lynchings and other unpleasant subjects. I have intended for many years to substitute for these some pictures of eminent Americans of Negro descent and we have made a small beginning with two Karsh photographs, one of Paul Robeson and one of Marian Anderson. I should like very much to have a photograph of yourself which we could frame and hang in this growing gallery. The Anderson and Robeson photographs are fairly large, 11 x 14, but I would be pleased to have a standard 8 x 10 of you.

I hope very much that you will grant me this favor.

Very sincerely yours,

Roy Wilkins

Deep unpleasantness remained, however, for in the latter part of May 1944, Du Bois received a letter on the stationery of the executive offices of the Afro-American Newspapers *in Baltimore.*

Baltimore, Md., May 16, 1944

Dear Sir:

Enclosed please find clipping from our current edition. This is the story I was attempting to get you to comment on via telephone Monday evening. Please let me have your comments via Western union Collect.[1]

Yours truly,

B. M. Phillips

Editor—Baltimore *Afro-American*

1. The story begins on page one and runs over to page twelve of the *Afro-American*, 20 May 1944. It is headlined: "Says Dr. Du Bois would have faced charges." It is credited to "Staff Correspondent" and originated from Detroit. In full, its text reads:

Just after Du Bois received this letter of 16 May, another of a quite different nature was hand-delivered to his office at the university by its president himself.

Atlanta, Ga., May 19, 1944

My dear Dr. Du Bois:

I have just seen the *Afro-American* of Saturday, May 20, and I regret very much the statement which appears on the front page signed by Staff Correspondent, which purports to quote me. The statement as quoted is not only unauthorized but untrue.

Yours very truly,

Rufus E. Clement

Shortly thereafter Du Bois sent a letter to B. M. Phillips of the Afro-American *in Balti-more.*

Atlanta, Ga., June 1, 1944

My dear Mr. Phillips:

On May 16, 1944 you published in the *Afro-American* [issue dated May 20] an article from your staff correspondent in Detroit, quoting certain comments by President Clement on me and the situation at Atlanta University. You called me by

---

Had Dr. W. E. B. Du Bois not accepted automatic retirement from the faculty of Atlanta University, he would have faced charges from President Rufus E. Clement asking for his dismissal, it was learned this week. Dr. Clement, here attending sessions of the AME Zion General Conference, told this reporter that relations between him and Dr. Du Bois had reached the place where it was the case of him or Dr. Du Bois running the university.

When reached by telephone in Atlanta, Monday, Dr. Du Bois said he did not care to comment by wire, but promised to give a statement in writing. As head of the department of social sciences, Dr. Du Bois was the highest paid faculty member. He retires June 30.

President Clement indicated he would have asked the board of trustees to remove Dr. Du Bois because he was "uncooperative, antagonistic and worked against rather than for the university."

He said that Du Bois' attitude was manifest in his classes where he reproved students who asked questions. As a result, after electing his classes the first year, students did not repeat. At present, Dr. Clement indicated, enrollment in classes taught by Dr. Du Bois is very low.

When his attention was called to a column by Ralph Matthews in last week's *Afro* in which he bemoaned the retirement of Du Bois, Dr. Clement said that there would be no feeling on the part of the students that a "great inspiration" had left their midst.

President Clement added that he had not spoken out and had hesitated to make a public issue of the case, but that Dr. Du Bois himself had exposed the matter. As soon as the board of trustees confirmed the retirement last week, reports were circulated that Dr. Du Bois had been retired without notification and without pension.

At that time President Clement stated that in the first year of his retirement Dr. Du Bois will get his full salary; forty percent for the next five years and twenty-five percent for the remainder of his life. Dr. Du Bois returned to Atlanta University ten years ago at the age of sixty-five, which meant that he could not join the college's pension fund system, so a special arrangement was made in his case.

telephone concerning the matter, but it was impossible for me to understand clearly enough to make any intelligible comment.

In the meantime, President Clement had delivered to me May 1, the final letter on my retirement, and on May 19, he brought to this office personally a denial of the truth of your article. On May 25, there was sent to President Clement a letter from nine students of mine, written entirely without my knowledge and on their own initiative, copies of which I understand were forwarded to you.[1] I write to ask: (1) Did you receive a denial of the truth of your article from President Clement? (2) If so, have you published it and may I see a copy? (3) If not, may I have the name and address of your Detroit staff correspondent?

I am enclosing a copy of the President's letter for your publication and of your letter and the letter from the students. If you wish to see the original copies, I am forwarding them to my daughter in Baltimore, 2302 Montebello Terrace and she will let you see them.

Very truly yours,
W. E. B. Du Bois

Du Bois received no answer from B. M. Phillips and no correction was printed in the newspaper. Therefore, on 12 June 1944 Du Bois wrote to Carl Murphy, the newspaper's owner,* stating the facts, indicating that he had received no response to his 1 June letter, and asking for a reply "at your earliest convenience." It came the same day.

Baltimore, Md., June 12, 1944

Dear Dr. Du Bois:

In reply to yours of June 1, I beg to state (1) that we did not receive a report of the denial from President Clement, which of course takes care of two also.

1. The letter to President Clement was dated 25 May 1944; it was signed by nine students at Atlanta University, Morehouse College, Clark College, and Spelman College: Eddye Queen Brown, Butler T. Henderson, L. Juan Burt, Louis S. Peterson, Emmett White, Alma Upton, Nina L. Charlton, Carolyn Y. Taylor, Helen J. Bridges. It expressed their disagreement with Clement's remarks as quoted and summarized in the May 20 *Afro-American*, stating that Du Bois had "never failed to entertain questions at the close of each lecture and never have we experienced rebuff because of questions asked him." Further, they said that the loss of Du Bois would be "keenly felt by the students." The letter closed: "The differences between you and Dr. Du Bois are not our concern, but it is unfair and unjust for you to assume the responsibility for expressing the feelings of those of us who have worked under him and have come to have much affection and respect for him as a teacher and scholar. The Atlanta University System will certainly be poorer because of Dr. Du Bois's retirement. We are not only registering with you our disagreement with these charges against Dr. Du Bois, but, also, our disapproval of an open attack on a professor in the System."

* Carl Murphy (1889–1967) was born in Baltimore and educated at Howard, Harvard, and the University of Jena in Germany. He taught briefly at Howard but his main work was with the *Afro-American* newspaper. From 1918 to 1944 he was its editor and from 1922 until his death was chairman of its board of directors. He was a Spingarn Medalist in 1955, a trustee of Morgan State College, and a member of the board of the NAACP from 1931 to his death.

Our Detroit correspondent was B. M. Phillips to whom your letter was addressed. Mrs. Phillips' notes indicate that the statement made was given her by President Clement and was printed in the *Afro* only in part.

In keeping with its custom in not printing anything about an individual without giving that person a chance to answer in the same story, I had Mrs. Phillips call you on the phone and read Dr. Clement's charges and ask for your comment.

Had you said at that time that there was not a word of truth to it we would have printed your statement side by side of that of Dr. Clement.

I am greatly surprised that he has issued a letter of retraction because we sought no statement from him and the information which he gave Mrs. Phillips was entirely voluntary.

> Very truly yours,
> Carl Murphy

In June 1944 Du Bois corresponded with two (white) members of the board of trustees of Atlanta University; these letters throw additional light on his connection with the university and the circumstances of the severance of that connection. One was addressed to an officer of the Southern Bell Telephone Company in Atlanta, Kendall Weisiger.

> Atlanta, Ga., June 6, 1944

My dear Sir:

In a letter which you wrote to Dr. Louis Wright of New York, you say among other things that I had signed in 1939 an agreement to hold my professorship at Atlanta University five years and then be retired. I am afraid that you do not know the facts of the case, and I am therefore venturing to lay them before you.

In the early history of the various mission schools for Negroes, contracts for teachers were drawn for one year, since most of them planned to serve only temporarily. Despite this, many of them served periods varying from ten to forty years. This was customary at Atlanta University when John Hope came, and he was planning to change it as soon as he had selected a permanent personnel for the new institution.

I think it goes without saying that I would never have left a life position with the expressed unwillingness of my employer to release me, for a one year appointment at Atlanta University. My clear understanding with President Hope was that my appointment was for life. Meantime, he died and I was among the group who early urged upon his successor, President Clement, the adoption by the Board of Trustees of a fixed policy of tenure and retirement for the teachers of Atlanta University. After a year or more of urging he presented the matter to the Trustees, the result and action as printed and distributed was as set down in the enclosed leaflet.

After the Trustees had adopted the resolution concerning rank, President Clement came to me personally and said in these words, "This is as much as I have been able to get from the Trustees, and I trust you will agree to it." As a result, he sent me the letter, a copy of which is enclosed, and I accepted it December 12, 1939. You will note that in this contract, absolutely nothing is said concerning the termination of my period of services at Atlanta University, nor could the age of retirement mentioned above be applied to me in my case, since I was 65 when I returned to the University.

Very sincerely yours,

W. E. B. Du Bois

[Enclosure 1]

ATLANTA UNIVERSITY

RANK

The following principles covering the tenure of faculty and staff members of Atlanta University are approved by the Board of Trustees:

Professors

Initial appointment shall be for one year. Subsequent appointment shall be for a period of five years. Upon re-appointment at the end of the five-year term, professors shall serve continuously until such time as they reach the age of retirement.

[Enclosure 2]

Dear Doctor Du Bois:

At the November meeting of the Atlanta University faculty, I announced that the Board of Trustees had approved the schedule of rank and tenure for Atlanta University faculty members. I am enclosing a copy of the rank and tenure provisions.

I am glad to inform you that, in conforming with the new schedule, you have been appointed Professor of Sociology for the period of five years, beginning July 1, 1939, at a salary of $4,500 per year, to be paid in 12 equal monthly instalments.

Sincerely yours,

Rufus E. Clement

This contract accepted

W. E. B. Du Bois

December 12, 1939

With the second trustee, Trevor Arnett, a lengthy exchange occurred. Trevor Arnett (1870–1955) was born in England and came to the United States as a youth; he was educated at the universities of Minnesota and Chicago. He began his career as an auditor for railroads and then moved into financial management for the University of Chicago, the Rockefeller Foundation, and the General Education Board, and published studies on university money management.

Atlanta, Ga., June 13, 1944

Dear Mr. Arnett:

There has just been called to my attention a statement by the Trustees of Atlanta University dated May 1, 1944.

"At the annual meeting of the Board of Trustees of Atlanta University held in Atlanta, Ga. on April 28, 1944, tribute was paid to the service of Dr. W. E. B. Du

Bois, now over 76 years of age, whose appointment as Professor of Sociology comes to a close on June 30, 1944, at the expiration of a five-year appointment which he accepted in 1939."

The implication here is flatly untrue and I am sorry that it has been set down in this way in the minutes. The agreement which I signed December 12, 1939, was as follows:

"I am glad to inform you that, in conformity with the new schedule, you have been appointed Professor of Sociology for a period of five years, beginning July 1, 1939, at a salary of $4,500 per year, to be paid in 12 monthly instalments.

> Sincerely yours,
> (Signed) Rufus E. Clement

This contract accepted
(Signed) W. E. B. Du Bois
December 12, 1939"

This agreement was simply a preliminary step to permanent appointment signed not only by me but by all professors, and [it] was not intimated in my case that permanent appointment would not follow the five-year appointment. Dr. Clement explained that this was simply a method of transition from the old yearly appointments to permanent tenure. Neither he nor you assumed that the yearly appointment in my case was anything more than an old custom.

Certainly I would not have been so idiotic as to leave a permanent position to accept a position which depended upon either a yearly appointment or even a five year appointment. This was signed not as indicating that my tenure would close at the end of the five-year appointment, but simply as carrying out the following printed provisions with regard to rank, issued by Atlanta University:

Professors
Initial appointment shall be for one year. Subsequent appointment shall be for a period of five years. Upon re-appointment at the end of the five-year term, professors shall serve continuously until such time as they reach the age of retirement.

Nothing was said at that time or any other time (until the April meeting of the Board of Trustees) of the application of the age limit of 65 to me. As I have repeatedly pointed out, I was 65 when I returned to Atlanta University. I came here under clear understanding with John Hope to serve for life or during my ability to work. When the 65 year age limit was adopted, if it did in any way apply to me, why did not the Trustees or the President say so? Why did they wait to discover its retroactive application to me five years after it was adopted?

I am writing to ask that this entry in the minutes of Atlanta University be changed, so as to be in agreement with the truth. I am sure you cannot refuse so reasonable a request. The right of Atlanta University to dismiss me, I am not calling in question. I am denying their right to say that five years ago I agreed to dismissal in 1944.

Very sincerely yours,

W. E. B. Du Bois

Grand Beach, Mich., June 19, 1944

Dear Dr. Du Bois:

I have your letter of June 13, 1944, and am sending it to Atlanta University for the information of the Secretary of the Board of Trustees and to be placed on file.

The paragraph you quote is the first one in the statement dated May 1, 1944. This statement is not a transcript of the minutes of the Board of Trustees of the University but is an historical summary of the principal facts relating to your periods of service in the University and particularly to the actions taken by the Board with reference to the completion of your active service and the considerations which led the Trustees to make the generous retiring allowance for you.

I note your interpretation of a five year appointment provided for in the regulations of the University relating to professional tenure. It does not follow that such an appointment is "simply a preliminary step to permanent appointment" for it is evident that at the expiration of the period the University may either take no further action, in which case the appointment ceases, or it may re-appoint the professor. In the latter case the appointment becomes a permanent one which ends automatically at the prescribed age of retirement.

Since you were past the age of retirement when the regulations governing tenure of appointment were adopted the University had to determine which of the following plans to adopt (1) to let your early appointment which you then had end your period of active service; or (2) renew the appointment for another year; or (3) renew the appointment for a longer period. It adopted plan (3) and gave you a five year appointment ending June 30, 1944. This action of the Board was most exceptional in view of your seventy-one years of age.

Inasmuch as I participated in the framing of the regulations relating to tenure of appointment and fixing the age of retirement at sixty-five years (and also at several other institutions) and strongly believe that retirement should take place at that age without exception, I certainly felt and understood that in your case the said five year appointment should be and was to be the final one. Moreover I did not assume as you indicate in your letter that your previous appointments of one year each meant anything otherwise than for the period specified.

I deeply regret that any difference of opinion has arisen in this matter for I am sure that the Trustees of Atlanta University, in view of your long and distinguished service, wish that the close of your active service in the University might have been on a friendly and harmonious basis.

Yours sincerely,

Trevor Arnett

Atlanta, Ga., June 23, 1944

Dear Mr. Arnett:

Your letter of June 19 increases my surprise at your action and that of the Board of Trustees. You give me to understand that some six years ago the Board took action looking to my retirement in 1944. If this is true, may I have a copy of the minutes of the meeting of the Board covering such action? Moreover, would it be too much for you to explain why this matter was kept secret for six years? It seems to me that under the circumstances a straightforward and courteous thing would have been to notify me immediately, instead of leaving me to infer, as I had every right to assume, that the five-year appointment was but preliminary to permanent appointment during my working years, unless of course my work was not satisfactory. If it was on the other hand, notice of retirement although couched in exactly the same form as the others who received permanent status, would it have been too much to expect that straight-forward and sympathetic officials, knowing what I have tried to do for Atlanta University, would have immediately told me that I would have four years to prepare for retirement. It is to me nothing less than astonishing that this information should have been kept carefully hidden for six years and then suddenly, quite without notice, sprung upon me.

I am enclosing a copy of my communications with the Baltimore *Afro-American* Newspapers. I am doing this, not that I expect from you or Mr. Clement any attempt to right another of many wrongs. It is merely to show that I have not been the one who has brought this scandal into public print and also to show that while Mr. Clement hastened to assure me in a private letter that what was printed was not true, he did not deny the truth of this interview to the editor of the paper which printed it. I have not the slightest doubt but what he said exactly the things that the reporter wrote down. She is a reliable woman of experience and standing and the things that President Clement is reported to have said are exactly the kind of talk which he has spread in Atlanta and elsewhere by word of mouth.

Sincerely yours,
W. E. B. Du Bois

Grand Beach, Mich., July 3, 1944

Dear Doctor Du Bois:

I have your letter of June 23, 1944, in answer to mine of June 19.

In accordance with your request I have made inquiry with regard to the minutes relating to your five-year appointment. I am informed that the record is as follows:

University Executive Committee, November 13, 1939
Approved appointments as to rank and tenure recommended by President Clement listing eleven professors by name for five-year term.

In all these instances in conformity with the rules of tenure the appointment ceases at the close of the term unless the University decides to make a re-appointment; in that event the professor is on permanent tenure until the age of retirement at sixty-five. Under normal conditions the University would not exercise its option to re-appoint or not to re-appoint until sometime during the final year of the five-year term.

As I pointed out in my letter to you of June 19, when you received the five-year appointment you were several years older than the retiring age, therefore the appointment was an exceptional one. It extended your period of active service in the University for the period mentioned with no implication of any further extension. Apparently you did not so understand it, a misunderstanding which I deeply regret to the extent that it has caused you needless anxiety. But even so, inasmuch as you were informed in November, 1943, over seven months before the appointment would terminate, that your appointment would not be extended, and inasmuch as in April, 1944, the University granted you a generous life annuity which provided a sum for the first year beginning July 1, 1944, equivalent to your present annual salary, you would seem to have been given adequate time to make the necessary personal adjustments.

In this communication and in that of June 19, I have endeavored to make clear the reasonableness of the University's position and I do not see that I can do anything more. In the years to come I wish you the greatest joy and satisfaction.

Yours sincerely,
Trevor Arnett

Meanwhile, the opportunity developed for which, without doubt, Du Bois was yearning: the chance to return to the NAACP *in the capacity of research director. With the end of World War II impending and with the need for the Afro-American people—and African-derived peoples of the world—to make themselves heard in organizing the post-war world, who better than Du Bois could be chosen to lead this effort?*

The invitation came from the secretary of the NAACP.

New York, N.Y., May 17, 1944

Dear Dr. Du Bois:

On behalf of the Board of Directors I am happy to transmit to you an invitation voted by the Board at its meeting on May 8 to devote full or part time, whichever is agreeable to you, to the preparation of material to be presented on behalf of the American Negro and of the colored peoples of the world to the Peace Conference or to Peace Conferences, at compensation and under conditions which are mutually agreeable.

Will you be good enough to let me know if you are willing to consider this invitation?

The Board at its meeting in September, 1941, voted to have such a committee. Active functioning was postponed when the Phelps-Stokes Fund announced its plan for a committee, of which you were a member, for its study of Africa, the War, and Peace Aims. After that report had been completed, dealing as it did only with Africa, the Board in April, 1943, requested the committee to proceed with its work. Judge

William H. Hastie was appointed Chairman of the committee and invitations were sent to persons voted by the Board to be asked to serve. I enclose a list of those who accepted membership on the committee.

If you are willing to consider this offer, details regarding compensation, office space, secretarial assistance and the like will be worked out with you.

All the members of the Board and staff join me in the hope that you will accept this invitation.

Ever sincerely,
Walter White

Within a week came another letter, this one from his old friend Arthur B. Spingarn, president of the NAACP.

New York, N.Y., May 23, 1944

Dear Dr. Du Bois:

I assume that you have received the invitation of the Board of Directors of the N.A.A.C.P. to undertake the preparation of the cause of the colored people of the world, to be presented to the Peace Conference.

I want to add my personal hope that you will give this proposal your most serious consideration; not only the future of the colored people, but the peace of the world is at stake and there is no one in America who is as qualified as you to do it. I earnestly hope that you will make a favorable decision.

With cordial regards, I am, as always

Very sincerely yours,
Arthur B. Spingarn

The day after Spingarn wrote the above letter, Du Bois conferred with him and with another NAACP *board member and old friend, the Black surgeon Dr. Louis T. Wright. In result Du Bois sent both men a memorandum.*

Atlanta, Ga., June 1, 1944

Since my talk with you both, May 24, I have given careful and almost uninterrupted thought to what you said. I feel deep gratification at your assurance of confidence in me, particularly at this crisis of my life.

There is a work that I would like to attempt, in leisurely peace and financial security, if it were made possible and would lie within the scope of the offer made me by the N.A.A.C.P.

I would like to direct a bureau or department of research and literature, designed to collect and make available:

    A. Data concerning the various parts of Africa and their governments and culture

    B. Data concerning the various groups in the world, of African descent

    C. Carefully organized and continuous data concerning the American Negro.

As illustrative of these data, I should like to write and collect literature and objects of art.

To do this I should need an office for myself and for a secretary; salaries for both, and an expense account for postage, books and periodicals; and for some travel.

I should not want in any way to have part in the policy-making activities of the N.A.A.C.P., the editing of the *Crisis* or any of the regular literature; except that it might prove advisable to publish some of the data collected as occasional papers, or even as a quarterly review.

I should expect a set budget for regular ordinary expense, to be spent at my discretion, but any extraordinary expenditure for travel or publication I should expect to clear through the secretary and Board of Directors.

I should, of course, be ready on special occasion to represent the Association on request by speech or article.

To undertake this work I should have to turn down offers from Howard, Fisk and the Land-Grant Colleges, which are attractive, but at the same time might so disperse my efforts and strength as to seriously cut short my working years. My financial condition requires that I work and earn as long as I can. All my savings were swept away in 1933 including my life insurance. Since then I have saved a lot and home in Baltimore, worth perhaps $10,000, on which I shall pay off the final mortgage this summer. I have to provide as much as possible for the education of my granddaughter and the support of my widow. If the University pays my pension as it has promised, I shall devote this entirely to my granddaughter's education.

For this reason I think the following budget would be necessary:

My salary $5,000 annually

A secretary $2,500 annually

   (I have in mind Miss Diggs, my helper for six years; A.B., University of Minnesota; A.M., in Sociology, Atlanta University; candidate for the Ph.D. in Anthropology, University of Havana, Cuba, in September, 1944)

Rent of two offices, preferably in some quiet quarter

Monthly budget $100

Publications

I should like to have both of you consider this proposition carefully, and decide how far it looks worthwhile in itself; and how far it will gain the approval of the executive officers and the Board of Directors. Unless these bodies would accept it with substantial unanimity, I seriously doubt if it should be entertained.

W. E. B. Du Bois

Atlanta, Ga., June 23, 1944

Dear Mr. White:

In answer to your letter, I am writing simultaneously to you, Mr. Spingarn and Dr. Wright.

I am trying to make reservations to come North next week so that we could have a conference Wednesday the 28th, Thursday the 29th or Friday the 30th. I will let you know by telegram if I can get reservations, so as to be in time for any or all of these dates; if not the best I could do is July 3, 4 or 5.

I think that before we meet for conference, you and the committee with whom I am to meet, should carefully consider certain fundamental points. You wrote me sometime ago, suggesting that I join a committee on Africa. I did not consent because I was too far away from New York to be of use or to take any responsibility. Then when your letter of May 17 came, the offer seemed to me like the conventional offer of a secretaryship to a committee in order to promote a specific drive. I had almost made up my mind that this was not the kind of work for which I was suited. Such a secretary ought to be a young active promoter, traveling, writing, speaking and organizing; and on the whole this assignment would in the nature of the case be temporary.

Before I wrote you, I called on Mr. Spingarn and he brought the matter up and emphasized the fact that I was wanted for scholarly work in collecting data which perhaps only I could do; and he urged me to accept and to make a specific offer. I then talked with Dr. Wright who put the matter on a still broader basis. He said that I ought to have time to pursue my work with reasonable leisure and financial security and that this was what he had in mind in making this offer.

This of course attracted me, but I still wondered if the Board of Directors and the executive officials of the NAACP were disposed to go as far as this with Mr. Spingarn and Dr. Wright. And for that reason, in order to make my attitude perfectly clear, I wrote letters to these two officials.

You will realize that any decision that I make now will have to be final for the rest of my working days. I have had four other offers of which two are with leading Negro Colleges and in many ways attractive. I have put final decision off in the case of these two institutions, but naturally, I cannot make them wait much longer. I could not afford to turn down these offers and take a temporary job at high pressure which might leave me at the end of a year's work, exhausted mentally and physically and without any prospect of employment.

On the other hand, the offer which I make would fit very well into any scheme for collecting authoritative data concerning the Negroes of Africa and persons of Negro descent elsewhere in the world. Much of this data is already collected; much is in the process of collecting and there would be no lost time in making this body of knowledge full and authoritative. But to do this, I would have to have skilled clerical assistance; I must be situated where I could do my work without undue interruption and be free from financial worries. Finally, I would want to be assured that so long as I could do satisfactory work in this and cognate lines, I could continue to do it.

This then is the situation and I think that members of this committee should be turning it over in their mind before I come for conference. I will write you as soon as I can suggest exact dates.

Very sincerely yours,
W. E. B. Du Bois

Atlanta, Ga., July 5, 1944

Dear Mr. White:

Enclosed you will find my statement of the findings of our conference in New York, June 28, 1944; they are naturally subject to modification in accord with the judgment of the Committee. I am sending carbon copies to Mr. Spingarn and Dr. Wright.

Also, I enclose my bill for travel expenses. May I thank you for courtesies extended.

Very sincerely yours,

W. E. B. Du Bois

[Enclosure 1]

In a conference held at 36 West 44th Street, New York City, June 28, 1944 there were present: Mr. Arthur Spingarn, President of the National Association for the Advancement of Colored People; Dr. Louis Wright, Chairman of the Board; Judge [Charles E.] Toney, Vice-Chairman, Mr. Walter White, Secretary; and myself.

The following matters were unanimously agreed upon:

1. That beginning September 1, 1944, W. E. B. Du Bois, be invited to join the staff of the National Association for the Advancement of Colored People as Director of Special Research.

2. The main work of Mr. Du Bois will be to collect facts and documents, and arrange statements, articles and booklets, concerning the peoples of Africa and their descendants, and concerning other colored races, so as gradually to form a body of knowledge and literature, designed to educate the world in matters of race and cultural relations.

3. His initial work in this direction will be the preparation of material to be presented to the Peace Conference or Conferences after the close of this war in behalf of the peoples of Africa and other colored groups so as to demand for them an assured status of security and progress in the post-war world. In this work he will act as secretary of the committee already appointed by the Board on this subject.

4. That the salary of Mr. Du Bois be $5,000 annually, and that he shall continue in this work as long as his health permits and his services are, in the judgment of the Directors, of value to the Association.

5. That Mr. Du Bois be allowed to appoint Miss Ellen Irene Diggs as Research Assistant, at a salary of $2,500 a year; that the Association furnish him two offices, and a current expense account, not to exceed $100 a month. All other expenses for travel or publication would be left to the decision of the Executive Officers and the Board.

It was agreed that these recommendations be laid before the Board of Directors for action at their next meeting.

[Enclosure 2]
Travel Expenses of W. E. B. Du Bois

Railroad Fare—June 26, 1944
   Atlanta, Ga., to New York, N.Y. $41.39
     July 4, 1944
   New York, N.Y. to Atlanta, Ga.   41.39
                                                 $82.78

Hotel Room (bill enclosed)   19.40
                                                $102.18

Board—8 days at $3.00 per day   24.00
                                       Total $126.18
                                   Received $100.00
                            Balance due $ 26.18

Submitted to:
   Mr. Walter White, Secretary
   N.A.A.C.P.
   69 Fifth Avenue
   New York, New York
July 5, 1944

On 18 July 1944, Du Bois received the following telegram.

Mr. White informs me board at meeting last Friday authorized employment on terms given in your letter with minor modifications about which Mr. White will write you
                                     Arthur B. Spingarn

                      New York, N.Y., July 21, 1944
Dear Dr. Du Bois:

   As Mr. Spingarn wired you on July 18, the Board of Directors unanimously and enthusiastically approved at its meeting on July 14 you re-joining the Association under the terms set forth in your letter of July 5, with the following minor modifications:

   The appointment is to be made on the same terms, with respect to manner and tenure, as other members of the staff are appointed. The Board charges the Executive Secretary with authority to make appointments of regular staff members for the period of the regular calendar year, with regular renewals befitting each case. I, therefore, by virtue of that authority and responsibility, in this letter and with much pleasure make the appointment beginning September 1, 1944, for the balance of the calendar year, which also is the Association's fiscal year. By virtue of the same authority I am writing Miss Diggs regarding her appointment. Copy of my letter to her is enclosed.

We are attempting to find for you offices in this building. In the event that that is impossible for the time being, since most of the leases run from February 1 to January 31, we shall try to find suitable offices in the vicinity.

Now that the formal part of the letter is finished, may I add my personal word of great satisfaction at your re-joining the staff. I am sure that the work you are going to do is going to be of great benefit to all concerned.

Ever sincerely,
Walter White

Several letters reached Du Bois, especially from young Black people, upon their learning of his difficulties with Atlanta University. One such came from a Black private in the Quartermaster Corps; it was undated but Du Bois's reply is dated 7 July 1944.

Somewhere on the east coast

Dear Dr. Du Bois:

We have been getting some pretty bad reports about the university. It seems that nobody sits on the Library steps, nobody walks on the grass, and the professors either have to dye their gray hair or take it some place else.

I guess we are just an unlucky generation all-round. When we get back, I guess we will have to dye our gray hair to keep from embarrassing the professors! For a lot of us youngsters on the campus, no matter what our field, it was something of an ambition to get in on at least one of your classes. There is probably not one of us who could say he's above it, beyond it, or could do without it even though we will probably make the same salary with it or without it! The hope of "going back to school" is getting drab. By then they will probably have cleaned all the books out of the library that don't have any pictures.

Is there anything you can say to us?

With a great deal of respect,
William Albert Robinson

Atlanta, Ga., July 7, 1944

My dear William:[1]

The world is certainly in bad shape, and Atlanta University is not doing as well as one might wish. Nevertheless, there is hope for the future. The advance of human beings is not in a straight and upward line but in a wavering line with depression and altitude. You are growing up in a time of depression, but it is justifiable for you to have faith, for during your life the general trend of progress will be upward.

1. Du Bois would not have used a first name unless he knew the letter writer. In this case, William Albert Robinson was the twenty-one-year-old son of W. A. Robinson, Sr., who was educated at Atlanta University and Columbia University and who was, during World War II, principal of the Laboratory High School connected with Atlanta University.

I hope you will not for a moment think of giving up your formal education, or come to the conclusion that no determined, carefully planned effort is worth while. That would be a great error. Do your job in this war, and then afterwards gird yourself for the great era that is bound to come sooner or later.

With best regards,

Very sincerely yours,
W. E. B. Du Bois

At the final meeting, 16 July, of the 1944 Conference of the NAACP, held in Chicago, Walter White delivered an address; at its close he announced that Du Bois was to return to the NAACP as director of special research on 1 September of that year. This announcement brought Du Bois several congratulatory letters. Two are offered here.

Washington, D.C., July 24, 1944

Dear Dr. Du Bois

It is gratifying to me to read that Walter White announced in Chicago that you will return to some work under the NAACP auspices—to me and to many others who were not happy when you left the Association about twelve years ago.

I am sending a copy of this to Arthur Spingarn, Miss Ovington, and Walter, because it is congratulations to them also.

I remember long ago, nearly thirty-five years ago, when our little group of the "Niagara Movement," at your suggestion, gave the new organization its first membership by going into it as a body. I suppose that I have held, and still do hold, membership in more Branches of it today than does any other member.

Best wishes for all you attempt to do.

Very truly yours,
William Pickens

The second letter was from Arthur Capper (1865–1951), newspaper and radio station owner in Kansas, governor of Kansas from 1915 to 1919, and from 1919 through 1949 a Republican senator who consistently took positions favored by the NAACP.

Washington, D.C., August 9, 1944

Dear Mr. Du Bois:

I was very much interested in the announcement that you are soon to be on the staff of the National Association for Advancement of Colored People, as Director of Special Research. I think the N.A.A.C.P. is to be congratulated. I am sure you can be very helpful to them. You have my very best wishes at all times.

If you happen to be visiting in Washington, drop in and see me.

Cordially yours,
Arthur Capper

At this moment, Du Bois was invited by the Haitian government to be its guest and to participate in various cultural and philosophical conferences. From his summer vacation spot in Litchfield, Maine, Du Bois therefore wrote to Walter White.

August 12, 1944

Dear Mr. White:

I propose to make the trip to Haiti an integral part of my work. The expenses of the trip will be borne by the State Department and the Haitian government.[1] But I would expect my N.A.A.C.P. salary and that of my secretary to begin September 1.

My main work, as I envisage it for the first years, will be:

1. The preparation of the case of Africans and persons of Negro descent for the peace conferences and post-war planning authorities; this will take the form of books, booklets, articles, and leaflets.

2. The organization of these and other colored groups so as to clarify and unify their ideas, plans and demands; a 5th Pan-African Congress would help this; and inter-group communication and visits.

3. Collection of facts concerning colored peoples, in war and peace, and the relation of these facts to democracy and peace in the future.

Some of this work has begun. I am in correspondence with persons in Jamaica, England, and West Africa. Miss Diggs is in close touch with Cubans. The proposal that I visit Haiti was broached last winter with the object of increasing the cultural unity of the Caribbean area and the Negroes of U.S., as well as white friends.

It has developed later than I expected but I hope to have its date pushed forward to Sept. 10 or 15. Meantime Miss Diggs expects to receive her doctorate "in philosophy and letters"[2] before Sept. 1. I should like her to accompany me to Haiti (at the expense of the State Department, but on salary from the N.A.A.C.P.). Work on Latin America, as well as Africa, could thus proceed while I was in Haiti.

On return to the U.S., I shall proceed with writing and correspondence and seek to make our African committee an active functioning body. There is no call for undue rush. No unified international effort involving colonies and quasi colonial groups will be settled until after election. Meantime if Haiti, the B.W.I. and Colored Cuba can be brought into unified effort with Black Africa and Negro U.S.A., and eventually with India, S.E. Asia, and China, we can face the post-war world with a program which must be listened to.

Very sincerely,

W. E. B. Du Bois

1. I shall be guest of the President [Du Bois's note].

2. Univ. of Havana [Du Bois's note].

Port-au-Prince, Haiti, 12 September 1944

My dear Mr. Spingarn:

After endless delay and red-tape I finally got to Haiti and have been very pleasantly received. I gave one lecture in English and am going to give two in French this week.

I have met and talked with Bellegarde, Price-Mars and of course President Lescot and many of his ministers. I had a short meeting with the Philosophical Society. They are expecting Jacques Maritain and want me to stay another week, but I have told them it is impossible. I leave here on the 19th and arrive in New York early on the 22nd. I shall bring a consignment of books and wish you could see some of the painting in their first exhibition. I know you would grab some of them. The young intellectuals here have rallied around me and are eager to cooperate with me on the question of colonies and post war conditions.

Miss Diggs came over from Cuba and has been of invaluable service. The Cooks have been most interesting and send regards. Miss Diggs will have to return to Cuba for her last examinations but hopes to get to New York about the first of October.

My best regards to you and Mrs. Spingarn.

Very sincerely yours,
W. E. B. Du bois

Upon his return from Haiti, Du Bois found awaiting him at the Hotel Theresa in Harlem a special delivery letter.

New York, N.Y., September 22, 1944

Dear Dr. Du Bois:

Welcome home!

The housing shortage—both offices and apartments—is so terribly acute that though we have searched high and low, it has been utterly impossible to rent suitable offices for you and Miss Diggs anywhere in the downtown area. All we were able to locate were two small inside offices whose only light and ventilation were from a single window on an air shaft. These, of course, would have been totally unsuitable for you. I mention it, though, to show you what we were up against.

We will, therefore, for the time being have to accommodate you by stretching our already crowded resources here. I have moved the Publicity Department from the office next to mine, as that is the second largest office the NAACP has. At least we can make you fairly comfortable here until the several real estate agents who are looking for space for you find something.

Cordially,
Walter White

The penultimate words in this volume—though they reflect something other than an accurate grasp of Du Bois's position at this time—go to Roger N. Baldwin (b. 1884), writing from the offices of the American Civil Liberties Union.

New York, N.Y., December 19, 1944

Dear Dr. Du Bois:

I note that you are retiring this year and I cannot refrain from a word of warm commendation on a lifetime of significant service in the cause of democracy. You can look back with more satisfaction than most men on an uncompromising fidelity to the underlying principles of human solidarity.

With warm regards,

Ever sincerely yours,
Roger N. Baldwin

Du Bois was—once again—writing letters on the NAACP *stationery; his response to Baldwin ends this volume.*

New York, N.Y., January 17, 1945

My dear Mr. Baldwin:

Thank you for your note of December 19. I was retired from Atlanta University rather against my will and then as you will see was offered employment here with the NAACP. I am enjoying the new work and shall hope to have the pleasure of seeing you from time to time.

Very sincerely yours,
W. E. B. Du Bois

INDEX

to and *from* indicate letters to and from

Marx, Karl, 76, 102, 149, 209, 253
Massachusetts, University of, 126
Mathews, Loulie Shaw Alber (Mrs.
  Edward R.), 4, 41
  to: 42
Matthews, Ralph, 391 n, 402 n
Maverick, Maury, 220
Maxey, George W., 106
  from: 106
  to: 107
Maxwell, L. B., 130
Mays, Benjamin E., 282, 341, 343
  from: 341–42
May, Stacy, 235–36
Mead, Margaret, 68
  from: 69
Meiklejohn Civil Liberties Institute,
  363
Melanesia, 69
Mellon, R. K., 99
Mencken, Henry L., 68, 311 n
  from: 69
Meridian, Mississippi, teaching in, 8–10
Methodist Federation of Social Service,
  147
Miami University, 372
Michigan Daily, 362–64
Michigan, University of, 344; Inter-Racial
  Association, 362–64
Middleton, Lamar: *The Rape of Africa*
  (1936), 228, 228 n
migration, of Black people, 54, 70, 83 n,
  113, 231
Milbank Fund, 128
Milholland, Inez, 269 n
Miller, Herbert, 33
Miller, Loren, 96 n, 302 n
Millsaps College, 307 n
Milton, Lorimer D., 299
Miner Teachers' College, 280 n
Minnesota, University of, 248, 344, 405,
  411
Minton, Henry, 346
Mississippi, 329; University of, 322
Missouri: racism in higher education,
  262–64; University of, 262, 276
Mitchell, Broadus, 68, 78 n
  from: 70–71
Mitchell, George S., 111, 354 n
Mitchell, John, Jr., 275
Mitchell, Kate L., 322 n
Mitchell, Margaret, 209

Mitchell, William L.
  from: 356–57
  to: 357
Moe, Henry Allen, 56
Montgomery, Isaiah T., 198–99, 199 n
Montgomery, M. Estello, 199 n
Moody, Harold A., 375–82
  to: 378
Moon, Henry Lee, 96 n, 119 n
Moore, Fred R., 45
  to: 45
Moore, Herman E., 220, 220 n
Morehouse College, 282, 341, 360, 394,
  403 n
Morgan, J. P., 99
Morgan, Madeline, 298
  from: 298
  to: 298
Morgan State College, 33, 318, 347, 403 n
Morley, Felix, 336
Morley, John, 338, 338 n
Morris Brown College, 290
Morris, Robert, 213
Mossell, C. W., 281
Mossell, N. F., 346
Moton, Robert R., 63, 102, 215, 236–38
Mound Bayou, Mississippi, 198–200
Mount Holyoke College, 185–86, 186 n,
  234
movie industry, 301–2
Mozambique, 381
Mumford, B., 132 n
Munich crisis, 258
Murphy, Carl, 403, 403 n
  from: 403–4
Murray, Andrew E., 195 n
Murray, F. H. A., 287
Muse, Clarence, 302
Museum of Anthropology (Berlin),
  Africana collection, 228
music, 33–35, 153, 234, 295–97
Muskingum College, 325
Muskogee, Oklahoma, 347
Mussolini, Benito, 95, 147
Muste, A. J., 41 n
Myers, Howard A., 98, 99 n
Myrdal, Gunnar, 176, 190, 191, 191 n
  from: 177

Nation, 202–3, 208, 327
National Association for the Advancement of Colored People (NAACP), 1,